Red Dragons

The story of Welsh Football

Red Dragons

Dragons

The story of Welsh Football

Phil Stead

I Mair, Gruff, Ifan ac Owain

First impression: 2012

© Copyright Phil Stead and Y Lolfa Cyf., 2012

The contents of this book are subject to copyright, and may
not be reproduced by any means, mechanical or electronic,
without the prior, written consent of the publishers.

The publishers wish to acknowledge the support of
Cyngor Llyfrau Cymru

Cover design: Y Lolfa
Cover photograph: Getty Images

Paperback ISBN: 978 184771 468 8
Hardback ISBN: 978 184771 488 6

FSC

Published and printed in Wales
on paper from well maintained forests by
Y Lolfa Cyf., Talybont, Ceredigion SY24 5HE
website www.ylolfa.com
e-mail ylolfa@ylolfa.com
tel 01970 832 304
fax 832 782

Contents

Introduction

THE STORY OF Welsh football is worth telling. For over 135 years, the Welsh game has struggled to keep its head above water in the face of challenges to its existence at every step. At first non-conformist religion tried to stunt its growth and then, when the game found its feet, the best Welsh talent was cherry-picked by rich clubs across the border who guarded their purchases jealously. International politics drove a chasm through the sport in the early 1990s as Welsh teams fought legal battles against their own association for the right to play in England. Even recently, Cardiff and Swansea considered playing under the banner of the English Football Association. UEFA and FIFA have hampered Welsh chances of tournament success and the eternal battle for status with rugby union has been destructive. The foundation of a British Olympic side, coupled with restlessness amongst FIFA's members, threatens the very existence of our team. It's a wonder Welsh football has survived as long as it has.

But it has survived, and decades of struggle and misfortune have been peppered with glorious times. Wales were one of the best teams in the world during the 1930s, and the 1958 side could have won the World Cup had John Charles stayed fit. The Red Dragons reached the quarter-finals of the European Championship in 1976, and more recently, heroic victories over England, Spain, Germany, and Italy will live long in the memory. But football in Wales is not just about the football. It's about *us* – those of us who love the game; the generations who idolised Roose, Allchurch, Giggs and Meredith. Football is one of the few things that binds this tribal country and unifies a diverse nation.

The Welsh supporter is not easy to define. Some watch hardly any live club games at all, preferring instead to take in high-quality English Premier League action on TV with just occasional trips to big international games. Others travel every fortnight with half a dozen fellow committee members to watch their village team hack through the mud. Some are loyal to their Welsh Premier League sides, but most follow established names in the English pyramid; Cardiff, Swansea, Wrexham or Newport. Many more travel across Offa's Dyke for their live football. This diversity does not lend itself to pigeonholing, and when ID cards were mooted by Margaret Thatcher's government in the 1980s, the FAW were in uproar. They knew many Welsh fans did not attend professional club football and would not register for a card. For these grassroots volunteers, the national team provides their only live 'big game' experience. The support for Wales can be apathetic during lean times, but for big games against star-studded opponents, these fans of incompatible football tastes come together in fervent support of the national side.

The national team has played its home games at a number of stadia since its formation. It began at the Racecourse, Wrexham, before parading its stars around Wales in search of big international crowds and the income that remains the lifeblood of the sport. Internationals have been played at Aberdare, Bangor, Llandudno, and Llanelli, as well as the more familiar venues in Wrexham, Cardiff, and Swansea. Wales have played home games at 16 locations, including some on the other side of the border. They played home games against England at Crewe in 1888 and at Shrewsbury in 1890, believing crowds would be larger than in Wales. Almost ninety years later, they sacrificed home advantage again to face Scotland at Liverpool's Anfield, a ground made nominally Welsh on three occasions; once on that desperate night in October 1977, and again in 1998 and '99 when they faced Italy and Denmark.

In a country split by a beautiful but divisive landscape,

football has helped Welsh people come together. At international games, Newport urbanites stand shoulder to shoulder with Anglesey farmers. The national team has broadened the horizons of the thousands who have travelled to far-flung places and in return welcomed diverse visitors to our country. To date, Wales are yet to face only four UEFA member teams: Andorra, Lithuania, Kazakhstan, and Macedonia.

I wrote this book because it needed to be written. We might be waiting forever for the levels of success that sees a hundred similar publications hit the shelves, but for now, at one of the lowest ebbs in our history, the game in Wales needs our support and loyalty. We've been here before, and have always followed periods of failure with eras of success. Welsh football *is* worth fighting for. As the future of our game remains uncertain and our national league struggles, as our clubs face seemingly insurmountable odds in European competition and our national team fights for its very existence, I hope this book helps remind you that Welsh football matters.

Phil Stead
Y Felinheli
October 2012

1

THE FIRST INTERNATIONALS
1876–1889

WHEN RUABON SOLICITOR Llewelyn Kenrick posted a notice in *The Field* journal in 1876, asking for "gentlemen desirous of playing" in the first Welsh international football match – against Scotland – he could have had no idea his appeal would kindle an obsession that would brighten the lives of millions, and occasionally send devoted souls into spells of deep depression. Kenrick had been enthused by a letter suggesting the formation of a Welsh rugby team, and publicly challenged the teams of England, Scotland and Ireland to a game of football under association rules. England were busy that year, and Ireland would only play under the rules of rugby, but the Scots were delighted to accept, with the proviso that the game be played in Glasgow. Despite concerns about financing the trip, Kenrick accepted, and set about finding a team.

Those that answered his call to The Cambrian Football Association were an eclectic bunch who qualified for Wales through "birth or certain duration of residence" – the length of which was left helpfully open. Shrewsbury's John Hawley Edwards had already played for England against Scotland in 1874 and goalkeeper David Thomson was an English Army captain. His brother George was amongst the Welsh forwards, and he was the brother-in-law of the full back,

William Addams Williams Evans, a vicar's son from Usk (and the only south Walian in this side). 'Little' Billy Williams made chimney tops and John 'Dirty Jack' Jones was a coal miner. One of the Welsh forwards, Dr Daniel Grey, was Scottish, but willing to donate £15 towards the purchase of the Welsh Cup, he was naturally guaranteed a place. Kenrick, without a hint of embarrassment, picked himself at right-back and made himself captain. This was perhaps not as self-indulgent as it sounds. He was, according to one writer, "the most brilliant and dashing back in the association."

On hearing of the proposed international for Kenrick's north Walian gentlemen, the south Wales football clubs went berserk. They may indeed have preferred the rugby form of the sport, but they were damned if they would allow north Walians to monopolize the association game. C C Chambers, captain of Swansea and member of South Wales Football Club, wrote to the *Western Mail* on 3 March 1876, protesting that no southern club was even made aware the game was taking place. And so began the game's first north-south spat; a parochial fury had been ignited that remains to this day. "I can only come to the conclusion that there must be some error," wrote Chambers, "and that the team to play Scotland is to be selected from North Wales only. I shall be happy to produce from these parts a team who shall hold their own against any team from North Wales, either at the Association or Rugby Union games, the latter preferred."

There was backup from H W Davies, an official of both the Brecon and the South Wales clubs. "If the South Wales clubs had been consulted I hardly think they would have consented to the trials being held at Wrexham. If South Wales is not fairly represented, this is another possible reason why such a club should not be looked on as representing the bona fide strength of Wales, and I cannot help agreeing with Mr Chambers that the term 'Football Association of Wales' is a misnomer as applied to the team about to play Scotland."

The south Walians had a point. While Kenrick had posted

his notice prominently in English sporting journals, little mention had been made of the game by the Welsh press. Undeterred, the stubborn solicitor ignored south Walian objections and arranged four public trials at the Racecourse in Wrexham. The first was played between the already-established sides of Wrexham and Druids on Saturday, 12 February 1876, and then a team of various applicants from as far away as Dorset faced Oswestry and Shropshire. The trials were beset by absentees with as many as six 'disappointments' (the original term for footballers who withdrew from matches) replaced by local footballers from amongst the crowd. Nonetheless, Kenrick's committee was able to select a team and the proposed international would definitely take place. The Welsh team showed off their new white jerseys for the final practice game on Thursday, 23 March, and Kenrick's hastily formed committee of businessmen had succeeded in arranging the first Welsh international football match.

The foundation of the FAW

Like all the best things in Wales, it began with a lock-in. The first meeting of Kenrick's tentatively named Cambrian Football Association took place on Wednesday, 26 January 1876. For whatever reason, he changed the name and wrote The Football Association of Wales in a new minute book for the second gathering at the Wynnstay Arms, Wrexham, on 2 February 1876. It is this meeting that the FAW considers its foundation.

That first committee met again in another hotel called the Wynnstay, this time a few miles away in Ruabon, to draw up the rules and regulations for the new association. The group that gathered in one of the hotel's private rooms that evening was still deep in conversation when the local constable called. This policeman, aware of the status of those present, politely asked that the conversation be continued elsewhere as it was well past closing time and licensing laws were being broken. Unruffled, one of the group ushered the policeman across the road to the courthouse. Sir Watkin Williams Wynn, Baronet, Member of Parliament for Denbighshire and Justice of the Peace, opened the empty building, pulled on his magistrate's hat and granted the Wynnstay Arms a licence extension. Sir Watkin then returned to the hotel and ordered another round for his extravagantly-moustached companions. Nothing would stop the foundation of the Football Association of Wales that evening and Sir Watkin was awarded the presidency.

And so, after weeks of preparation and fundraising, on 25 March 1876, the Scotland and Wales international football teams travelled together to the West of Scotland Cricket Ground in an omnibus pulled by four grey horses. Large crowds cheered both teams through the west end of Glasgow to Paisley where Wales would face a strong experienced Scotland side in front of 18,000 curious spectators.

Some sources have written that Wales played in a variety of coloured shirts in that first game, but this is not so. The colours listed on the team sheet referred to the players' socks, or maybe even caps, worn as identification in lieu of shirt numbers. A *North Wales Chronicle* report confirms that Scotland took the field "clothed in blue with the national arms embroidered on their jerseys, whilst the Welsh were in white, with the three feathers as their device." Not only were Wales wearing white, but their badge was the three feathers, now synonymous with the Welsh Rugby Union, and only connected to Wales through association with the English Prince of Wales: a royal badge for a royalist association.

Kenrick's Wales were up against it from the start and their naivety was evident early on. The first goal Wales ever conceded came from a charge on keeper Thomson as he prepared to kick the ball from his hands. Wales lost four goals to nil, but the Scots were generous in their praise, eager not to lose a potential opponent at the first hurdle. The Welsh defence was described as "the most brilliant players that Scotland had had to contend against," and it was announced

13

that "better men than Kenrick and Evans had never toed a ball." Even so, Scotland eased to victory despite one of their scorers, James 'Reddie' Lang, having lost an eye earlier that year in a shipyard accident.

The Scots were tough alright, but it wasn't just brute strength which won the day. During their four years of existence, Scotland's players had learnt to control the ball with their feet and some even hinted they were passing it. This was all new to the Welsh, still playing the kick-and-rush game that bore some resemblance to rugby. The Scottish goalkeeper didn't touch the ball throughout the game, but despite Wales' failure to compete, they were cheered from the field by their hosts.

Reports of the post-match dinner are as long as those of the game itself. In those days of Corinthian gentlemen, sport was a chance to demonstrate your chivalry. The back-slapping banquet was key to the occasion and a commemorative medal was presented to each Welsh player. Kenrick praised the Scots, and admitted he had "never seen combined play like it." He then offered up a complaint that would define the national team for more than a century: "Wales were not at full strength," he insisted, bemoaning the fact he had been "disappointed in players at the last moment." Each generation thinks player availability problems belong to their era, but Wales has struggled to field its best eleven since that very first game.

In an era when football is the world's biggest sport, it is natural to look back at this first fixture as a momentous occasion. But organized sport was in its infancy in 1876 and the Welsh press paid scant attention to this historic contest. The *North Wales Chronicle* had mentioned the forthcoming game in passing, between an Eisteddfod notice and the announcement of the inaugural meeting of the Llandudno Fox Club. The *Western Mail* barely acknowledged the existence of "socker" until the FAW took a game south almost twenty years later.

A long history of football

This may have been a new sport, but there had been forms of football played in Wales for centuries. There is a school of thought that the Romans brought ball games to their Welsh forts at Caernarfon and Caerleon. If so, those limited games developed into something far bigger. In the Middle Ages, entire Welsh villages faced each other in lawless games, sometimes using the whole distance between two village squares. Hundreds of men would push, shove and brawl over a ball, the only objective being to cross the designated line or reach the opposition's territory. Games could last for hours. This was mock-war.

George Owen wrote in 1603 of a game called *Cnapan* played on the beaches and coastland of Pembrokeshire. Using a small, hand-sized slippery wooden ball, teams of up to 2,000 on foot or horseback from opposing districts would attempt to carry the ball as far from their home parish as possible before nightfall. Players would hurl or run with the ball in a contest vaguely similar to early pre-association football. Owen believed the game was played by the "ancient Britons" as battle training. There were no rules, and opponents could be beaten with fists and clubs. Rocks and stones were thrown at horsemen in desperate attempts to win the ball.

Cnapan was a violent, savage version of today's sanitized game. It remained popular in Wales until the mid-nineteenth century when football emerged as a playful activity for children, or as an amusement for workmen. Football was popular at Christmas, and there were games played across Wales on Christmas Day and one on Boxing Day at Llanidloes in 1870. The traditional Christmas morning game in Dolgellau drew large crowds, and even inmates at Denbigh Lunatic Asylum were allowed to play as a Christmas treat in 1870.

As the competitive game developed in the public schools of England, it diversified. The playing field became smaller and numbers were restricted to a couple of dozen players. But playing in isolation, different schools developed different rules. You were allowed to kick and hack opponents in Blackheath, while various forms of football had been played without rules at Rugby School long before William Webb-Ellis picked up the ball. Matters became complicated when schoolboys progressed to university and found others playing different versions of the same game. If the sport was to develop, agreed rules would be needed. The Football Association was founded in England in 1863, and running with ball in hand was outlawed. There was some debate over the kicking of opponents, but eventually it was agreed to limit violence to attacks on goalkeepers. The decisions split the schools, and they went their separate ways. Some chose football, while others continued to develop their own sport, which they now called rugby.

Association football was taking shape and the organized game spread to the public schools of the Welsh borders, becoming the preferred form at Wem, Oswestry, and Shrewsbury. When pupils left, they continued playing. Shrewsbury School Old Boys attempted to form a club on arrival at Cambridge University in the early 1840s, which suggests Shrewsbury School was one of football's driving forces. Henry de Winton and John Charles Thring, who are credited with the first attempt at a set of rules in 1848, had both attended Shrewsbury. It is safe to assume that some of the school's former scholars returned to Wales and influenced contemporaries who had attended Welsh establishments such as Ruabon. The oldest existing copy of the laws of the game, written around 1856, remains at Shrewsbury Public School.

Organized competitive football in Wales also sprouted from the public schools. A student of Treborth Academy, Bangor, invited a newspaper editor for a game in 1862. There was a contest between Anglesey Collegiate and Holyhead on 11 March 1864, and a match was held between Deganwy and Llanrwst schools in 1875. A year later, Lampeter's St David's College played Ystrad Meurig Grammar School under association rules. Even in south Wales, where rugby was already dominating, there was a game in 1865: one of the teams involved, Swansea Grammar School, was playing association rules by 1877.

The Chapel versus Football

Football had to fight its way to respectability in non-conformist Wales. While parish churches would gladly host post-sermon kickabouts to boost attendances, the new chapel preachers of the early to mid-nineteenth century saw football as an ungodly pastime, and the press heaved with the worries of concerned fundamentalists. At Bangor in 1801 it was "no unusual thing for a game of football to be indulged in, after the conclusion of divine service, in the churchyard." But a letter to a Bangor newspaper in 1834, just after the non-conformist explosion of the 1820s, complained of football being played on the Sabbath in northern country towns. A letter to the *Wrexham Advertiser* in 1856 criticized Cefn Mawr residents spending time on "useless pursuits" such as football. The game would face an unrelenting attack from the chapel throughout the nineteenth century.

The non-conformist message preached total abstinence from Sunday sport. In 1863, a plain-clothes policeman was sent to Segontium Terrace, Caernarfon, to apprehend children kicking their ball on the Sabbath. "On Sundays, young men speak of nothing but football," complained one newspaper correspondent. The pious Welsh-language newspapers were also full of condemnation for this game which distracted the youth from devout contemplations. One brave reader of the *Wrexham Guardian*, writing in 1890, dared criticize the chapel's malevolence: "Ruthin can hardly boast of a recognized football club, neither is it difficult to assign a reason, for it may be readily found in the baneful influence of non-conformist bigotry, which has done its utmost in Ruthin to undermine the manly British game."

There were complaints about young men of Gresford

playing football on Christmas Day in 1890. "Is this honourable?" asked one letter-writer. "Keep up the honour of your club and avoid playing on that day, having been asked by your superiors not to." Football's connection with alcohol didn't help. By 1891, half the teams registered in Wales used public houses as their base. By 1892, a preacher in Llanrwst complained the game had become "an infection on the country." He was right. Football was a disease that could not be contained, not even by a chapel movement with stringent influence over whole communities. On Easter Monday in that year, several thousand supporters invaded his small town in the Conwy Valley to watch a tournament between 18 local teams, including clubs from Abergele, Bangor and Llandudno. There were 700 fans from Blaenau Ffestiniog alone.

Football was a criminal pastime in nineteenth-century Wales. You could be arrested for playing in Ruthin after an 1855 byelaw which lists the game among such unwholesome pastimes as drunkenness, flying kites, emptying of privies and "exposing person". In 1861, a group of donkey carriage drivers in Rhyl were arrested when they left their vehicles for a kick around. In Penrhyndeudraeth, in 1868, David Jones was fined after his ball caused a shilling's worth of damage to a neighbour's field. Three men were arrested and fined for playing football on a public road near Pontypool in 1871, and in 1890, three boys appeared in court, accused of playing football in a Bangor street.

There were injuries too. In 1891, a Llanrwst player broke his skull during a game against Betws-y-Coed and Trefriw. Twenty-three-year-old Arthur Bartley from Flint, the brother of Welsh international Tom Bartley, died from spinal injuries after a training session collision. In 1880, a Conway player broke his leg against Rhyl only weeks after a team-mate dislocated a shoulder against the same opposition. The local press claimed Rhyl were "rough players".

The earliest football clubs of Wales

The earliest mention of a football club in Wales is in Llanmynech, a parish straddling the border six miles south of Oswestry. The club was formed as an amusement for workers on the new railway in 1850. Frustratingly, the field near Glynvyrnwy House where the club was founded lies in the English half of the village. Nonetheless, this was a football club created for Welsh and English in a cross-border community.

There are reports of football at a fete in Gwersyllt School in 1856 and again in 1857. Football was a common pastime at fetes and fairs throughout the Wrexham area in the 1860s and in Llandudno, in 1865, there is mention of "a cricket ground where winter football has taken the place of the more legitimate summer game." Yet calls in the press of 1876 for a football club in the town suggest it was not yet an established sport.

In recently published research by the late Newtown chairman, Keith Harding, a *Montgomeryshire Express* clipping of 1 July 1879 reports an after-dinner speech in which Evan Morris, President of Wrexham FC, states his club was formed 15 years earlier – in 1864. The claim is strengthened by C W Alcock's *The Football Annual*, published in 1877, making Wrexham the seventh oldest football club in the world, and certainly the oldest in Wales.

A *Wrexham Advertiser* report of March 1866 describes "a match played last Saturday between the Volunteer Fire Brigade and the Football Club, which was won by the former." Another report mentions Wrexham Football and Athletic Club playing in February 1866. There are references to the same club up to 1869, when newspaper reports stop until the 1872 meeting at the Turf Tavern, long considered as Wrexham FC's foundation.

It remains unproven whether Morris's 1864 club is linked to the current Wrexham FC, but research proves five members of the 1869 team were present in 1872. The

1869 club included *W Pritchard (captain)*, *E Cross*, *E Evans* and *G Pritchard*. The current Wrexham club was 'founded' in 1872 at the Turf by F Page, *W H Pritchard*, T Walker, N Humphreys, D Dale, *E Cross*, *E Evans*, and *G Pritchard*. Page was named President of Wrexham FC in 1872, but reports have him presenting an award to the 1869 club. Pritchard and the four others present in both 1869 and 1872 surely point to a continuity that proves Wrexham FC was founded in 1864.

There were clubs in the north-west Welsh-speaking heartlands during the 1870s. In March 1873, *Baner ac Amserau Cymru*, in one of the earliest Welsh-language reports of pêl-droed (the Welsh term for football), mentions that 'clwb Caernarfon' played 'clwb Porthmadoc' in heavy rain. Blue Star played in Swansea as early as 1870.

By 1875, there were teams in Oswestry, and Shrewsbury-based Shropshire Wanderers reached the semi-finals of the English FA Cup with a team which included Welshmen. Although the earliest clubs in Wales were gathered around the north-east border, teams were forming across the country, particularly around major railway stations. Entrants to the first national competition, the Welsh Cup in 1877, prove instructive: Newtown, Druids, Wrexham, Wrexham Civil Service, Newtown Stars, Ruabon, Chirk, Oswestry, Northwich, Foresters, Corwen, Bala, Aberystwyth, 23rd Welsh Fusiliers, Llangollen, Rhosllanerchrugog, Bangor, and Caernarvon. Swansea also entered but withdrew upon discovering it was not a rugby competition.

A team from Rhyl played St Asaph School in 1877 and by 1880, there were about ten teams in Flintshire where there was a reported "mania" for football. There was also some association football in Cardiff with reports of a game between the Science and Arts Club and Mr Shewbrook's Club at Cardiff Arms Park in November 1871. In 1880 Tredegarville Football Club played a 12-a-side match against the Twelve Gentlemen of Cardiff at Sophia Gardens. One of the earliest mentions of girls playing in Wales was at Cardiffian Catholics' Whitsun Fete at Tŷ-Gwyn Farm in 1870.

Clubs sprang up across mid Wales in the 1870s too. A meeting was called to form a club in Newtown in 1873/4, and by 1875 a second team was needed in the town. Llanidloes formed in 1875 and by 1876 there were clubs in the Severn Valley at Kerry, Montgomery and Churchstoke. The game spread through the heart of Wales like wildfire. Before the decade's end there were teams in Aberystwyth, Welshpool, Berriew, and Llandysul.

An hour north of Newtown lay the burgeoning iron and mining community of Ruabon, four-and-a-half miles south of Wrexham. The town grew around the estate of the Williams-Wynn family, of which FAW founder Llewelyn Kenrick was a descendent. His father owned a local ironworks. This unlikely parish plays a critical role in the early history of the game in Wales. Ruabon Grammar School was playing football by 1864 and the town's Plasmadoc club was founded in 1869. There were also two more teams in the village, Ruabon Rovers FC and Ruabon Volunteers. Kenrick persuaded these clubs to merge in 1872 to form Ruabon Druids, a formidable outfit known simply as Druids. By 1904, the club had provided 44 Welsh internationals and won the Welsh Cup eight times. Sadly, they outgrew Ruabon, and over the years combined with various clubs before becoming Cefn Druids following a merger with Cefn Albion in 1992.

The Football Association of Wales may have been formed at the Wynnstay Arms in Wrexham, but the Ruabon hotel of the same name was also used for meetings. Early international trials were held on a nearby pitch and a century later, Ruabon was still producing internationals. Mark Hughes was a product of the same school as Kenrick, in its modern comprehensive form.

Kenrick was the founding father of Welsh football, and he dragged the FAW screaming into the chaotic and lawless world of organized ball games in 1876. While the new association was attacked from the south and north-west, the Ruabon solicitor persevered until dissenting parties complied. He would serve the FAW for more than 20 years before resigning over an expenses disagreement in 1897.

There was an early challenge to Kenrick's mandate from Bangor, who formed the Northern Welsh Football Association, after withdrawing from the Welsh Cup and resigning from the FAW following a physical hiding by Newtown White Stars, so-called because of the large white star sewn onto the left breast of their uncoordinated shirts. In those days the referee was accompanied by two umpires, supplied by the teams, but the match against the White Stars in 1879 was abandoned after a full-scale brawl erupted when the Bangor umpire attacked an unruly opposition player. The Gwynedd team claimed victory on the basis of "fair play" despite being 3–1 down and declined the FAW's offer of a replay before leaving to form the NWFA.

The NWFA even tried to arrange international games, promoting itself as the representatives of all-Wales, but Kenrick's fledgling association had already been recognized by the all-powerful English FA. The Ruabon man was well connected in England due to his time with Shropshire Wanderers, and the NWFA collapsed in 1884, with Bangor and Caernarfon returning to the fold. Kenrick continued to face south Walian opposition to his Wrexham-based committee, and in response the north closed ranks. Awarding the first Welsh Cup to Wrexham, Sir Evan Morris said: "This year we have 22 clubs from all parts of Wales competing for the cup. There are clubs to the extreme points of Bangor and Newtown, and throughout the whole of the intervening country, we cannot mention a place of importance which has not a club who has contested."

Morris's speech pointedly dismissed the south, but the new FAW, seeking legitimacy, held out an olive branch. They sent invitations asking south Wales clubs to attend the first general meeting in Shrewsbury in May 1876 to ratify the new committee. It was the first, but not the last time the Welsh national body gathered in England to make its decisions. Half of the committee places had been allocated to south Walian members, but there was still no enthusiasm despite a further request sent by Kenrick to the *Western Mail* in September and an editorial imploring south Walians to join. But the southerners preferred rugby, and that was that. The first FAW committee was exclusively northern, containing solicitors, clerks, teachers, and businessmen. It was middle-class, certainly, but not populated by upper-class toffs like the associations of England and Scotland.

Football or rugby?

The south stipulated its preference for rugby with the formation of the South Wales Football Union in 1878. Since football split, Wales has been a front-line battleground in the struggle between the codes for supremacy. Football clubs were forced to take sides – would they play *association* or *rugby* football? Some tried to compromise and games were arranged over two legs to incorporate both versions. In 1875, Brecon's Christ Church beat Brecon Town at association football, but lost heavily at rugby in the second leg. Recognising where their strength lay, Brecon FC went on to become a founder member of the Welsh Rugby Union in 1881. Builth, meanwhile, voted to play both codes in 1876 depending on the preference of their opponents. In the first fixture of the season they faced Radnorshire Wanderers under association rules, but when their football burst they switched to rugby for the afternoon.

On the south coast, Swansea Cricket Club formed a winter football team as early as 1872, playing their first game against Neath, before switching to rugby in 1874. Elsewhere, there was confusion as clubs struggled with the split. In Merthyr, the town club played against Mr Lloyd's School according to association rules in 1876. Yet a month later they played rugby against Aberdare. Merthyr decided it preferred rugby.

Sometimes teams weren't sure which code they were playing. The *Wrexham Guardian* reported that "the conduct of the spectators was disgraceful" in an 1879 game between Llanidloes and Newtown, adding that the home side "did not understand perfectly association rules."

Meanwhile the resolutely association-based northern clubs continued diligently despite the chaos in the rest of the country. A combined north Wales team was playing regularly against Sheffield, Birmingham and Stafford, and it was no surprise the area provided the first Welsh internationals.

The first home international: Wales v Scotland, 1877

When Scotland accepted Wales' invitation to play that first game in February 1877, the FAW again attempted to attract the best south Walians. The *Western Mail* published another invitation to prospective trialists. "It is hoped that football players in the southern portion of the Principality will not allow South Wales to be accused of apathy in regard to these national contests," it said.

The return fixture at Wrexham was quite an event. The ground was "enclosed with canvas and a spacious tent provided for the accommodation of ladies only, and gentlemen accompanying them." There was an early policy of admitting women free, though this privilege was questioned by one newspaper which complained about the ladies' language. The town even designated the day a "quasi-general holiday" in honour of the meeting "between the renowned Football Association of Wales and the celebrated one of the land of the thistle."

Match reports again praised the Welsh defence, but were critical of other aspects of the performance: "It was noticeable that the Scotch forwards were not ambitious of doing the work of the back players and this was in contrast to the Welsh team. Had the Cymry forwards played well up in the first half several goals would have been scored in their favour, but they would persist in following the ball up and down the ground."

After Scotland had won by two goals to nil, both teams dined at the Wynnstay Arms, by now the unofficial home of the national team. They toasted the Queen with poor jokes – they "didn't know if she played football," but were sure "she would never play with the constitution." There were other toasts too – to the bishops and clergy, to the Army and Navy, to the press and to the ladies, and also to the guests. There were so many toasts the Scottish team was forced to leave for their train before the glass-chinking was over. Luckily they were still there to hear Welsh full back, William Evans, serenade the diners with an impromptu song about the day's match. Schoolmaster Alexander Jones, who also played, died a year later when accidentally shot by a pupil returning from shooting practice.

The first written confirmation of the full Wales kit came in 1877 – "white jerseys with the arms of Wales worn on the front of each; blue serge knickerbockers and stockings of the club to which each player belonged." The *Western Mail* remained unimpressed with "soccer" however and its report of that first international consisted of two sentences squeezed between an extensive Oxford-Cambridge Boat Race report and results from an American Billiards tournament in London.

The Welsh Cup

The English FA Cup was first contested in 1871/72, but by 1877 Wales had only just played their first international. There was no league, and only friendlies between clubs. It was felt that national team players needed serious competitive fixtures if they were to match England and Scotland. With this in mind, Kenrick proposed the first Welsh Cup competition at the second FAW annual general meeting on 17 August 1877. He had appeared in the English version's semi-final for Shropshire Wanderers. The idea of a nationwide trophy was initially thought ambitious, but clubs previously reluctant to travel were beginning to look further afield for opposition. Earlier that year, a combined Bangor and Caernarfon side had played in Wrexham.

Kenrick's competition was open to clubs from Wales and the border counties of England, considered FAW members. The ambitious Druids had become the first Welsh club to enter the English FA Cup a year earlier, even though they failed to fulfil their first round fixture at Shropshire Wanderers. If Welsh clubs could play for the English trophy, why not allow border clubs to enter the Welsh competition?

Oswestry has always held a peculiar status in Welsh football. Oswestry United (latterly White Stars, and then Oswestry Town) is believed to have been founded as early as 1860, making it one of the first clubs in the world. Though individuals from the club were founder members of the FAW, the town is actually in England. An important market town for the border hill farmers, the Welsh influence on Oswestry was so strong that church services were held in Welsh until 1814. Oswestrians were always considered Welsh for the purposes of national team selection. The Oswestrian goalkeeper, Tom Gough, was capped twice and served as FAW President for 25 years until 1934. Gough is unique in that he also served on the English FA while performing his Welsh duties.

When Peter Corrigan spoke, in *100 Years of Welsh Soccer*, of "a ten-mile stretch of country where soccer first found fertile ground in Wales," he meant the seam of football-playing communities from Wrexham to Chirk via Ruabon. He may just as easily have spoken of a 15-mile stretch, adding five miles south, to include Oswestry in the list of pioneering towns. The town's Welsh claims are maintained today by the presence of The New Saints in the Welsh Premier League. Formed from a controversial merger of Total Network Solutions (originally Llansantffraid, the successful Welsh Cup winning village team) and Oswestry Town in 2003, many supporters still question the club's right to represent Wales in European competition.

The first FAW Challenge Cup competition was played without a trophy. Donations were requested and the names of rich contributors were published weekly on the front page of the *Wrexham Guardian*. By 1879, enough had been raised for a deposit on a trophy from London silversmith, J W Benson, of Old Bond Street. The trophy, still in use today, is the second oldest football trophy in the world, after the Scottish Cup, and features the heraldic arms of Ruabon.

The national competition did not appeal to south Walians at first. English immigrants arriving from the West Country to take advantage of burgeoning opportunities offered by industrialization in the Valleys brought with them a love of rugby, giving the code a head start in the most populous regions of Wales. When news of the FAW Challenge Club was announced in the south Walian *Western Mail*, it drew a haughty response in its letters pages: "Most (if not all) the teams that will compete for such a challenge cup, will, I believe, come from North Wales, where the association rules are played. I do not think that the offering of the 'Association Cup' will create any greater liking for association rules in South Wales."

The scoring system of the early Welsh Cup was quirky. In the third round, Wrexham beat Gwersyllt Foresters by "eight and one disputed to none." Wrexham hosted the first Welsh Cup final at Acton Park, then a country manor house. A patch of grass was allocated and 1,500 fans paid two-and-a-half pence each to watch Wrexham beat Druids by a goal to nil. A photograph of Wrexham shows them in scarlet and black hooped shirts like a Dennis the Menace fan club. Unfortunately, there was no trophy to present, as the FAW's Sir Evan Morris explained when eventually handing the cup over in 1879. "For the first year we were without money, and I do not think we had much ingenuity. We did not possess the cup, so we played for something we were going to have. Now we are very much in the same position as regards money as we were last year, but we have more ingenuity and have obtained the cup without money."

The FAW were still paying for the trophy, and it was a while before the 100 guinea bill was met. There was still £35 outstanding in 1881.

Early tribalism

The first Welsh Cup semi-final in 1878 between Bangor City and Druids at Wrexham demonstrated the fractious relationships between Welsh clubs. The Wrexham team had been attacked with "stones, sticks, and clods" at Plasmadoc, home of the Druids. Wrexham supporters cheered Bangor and jeered the Druids, shocking the Druids captain so greatly he refused the offer of extra-time to settle the drawn game. He said the 'hooting' of his team was a disgrace. When Bangor's captain, Docker, left the changing rooms after the match, he was carried shoulder high by the Wrexham crowd to kick an undefended penalty and 'win' the match amid wild celebrations. The FAW were unsympathetic however and ordered a replay, which saw Druids victorious.

The Welsh Cup final that year was postponed a week as a number of Wrexham and Druids players had been selected to play for Wales in Glasgow on the same day. It seems the players involved preferred to play for their clubs and the international was put in doubt. The Scots were so incensed that the SFA secretary travelled to Wrexham, visiting the homes of Welsh players until he had persuaded enough of them to travel.

Unfortunately, not all who agreed to go were of international standard, and the Welsh were forced to call on the services of a ringer – Thomas Britten, an Englishman who played for Parkgrove Glasgow. The 5,000 Scotland fans were furious as the home side romped to a 9–0 win. The result remains

Wales' worst defeat, but the nation's press defended their team, claiming the home support should have been more understanding – after all, the players had travelled overnight to Glasgow, arriving at 8 a.m. on the morning of the game. The *Glasgow News* however, was unrepentant, calling it "the worst exhibition of football that has ever been played at Hampden Park." The Scots were becoming less indulgent of Welsh efforts at their new sport.

To make amends, Wrexham made extravagant preparations for the visit of the Scots in 1879, announcing that "special arrangements will be made for the occupants of carriages to witness the match without alighting from them." There was also an early example of corporate hospitality in the form of a "well-heated room commanding the best view of the match." Tickets for this area were scarce and expensive.

Matches in those early days rarely kicked off on time. Teams treated the publicized hour more as a guide than a commitment. When Wales welcomed Scotland in 1879, even the referee was late and had to be replaced by a substitute. The 4,000-strong crowd was growing restless when the Scots eventually took to the field, but their warm-up was so impressive that numerous bets were immediately placed on the visitors to win. They did not disappoint with a 3–0 victory.

Then in 1879 came Bangor's decision to leave the FAW and form the NWFA, joined by clubs such as Caernarfon, Conway and Llandudno. Welsh football was squabbling; firstly south against north, then north-west against north-east.

Chaotic in-fighting between clubs continued, and it was this divisive animosity which resulted in the farcical team selected to face England for the first time in 1879. Druids had collapsed after the loss of their pitch and a letter to the press in the weeks before the game hinted at a row between Wrexham and FAW Secretary Kenrick. The letter criticized Kenrick for his refusal to join Wrexham despite appearing in a pre-season match and being offered the captaincy. Instead, he joined Oswestry, and an extraordinary spat was played out in the pages of the regional press.

There were accusations Oswestry had poached players from Druids and counter accusations that Wrexham offered illicit inducements. The ill-feeling led to a boycott of Kenrick's national side and matters came to a head when he amended a rule preventing some of his Oswestry team-mates from competing in the Welsh Cup. Oswestry had admitted that half their side lived outside the town, and were paid travel expenses, much to everyone's distaste in the age of amateurism. Against this background of inter-club animosity, the FAW selection committee for the England match, led by the Oswestry chairman George Bayley, met at a hotel in the town. As many as nine Oswestry players were selected, six of whom were English-born.

Fewer than one hundred people watched Wales' first game against England in the south London snow. Despite playing against ten men for the opening twenty minutes, due to the late arrival of England's William Clegg, Wales, wearing "white jerseys, dark blue knicks and red socks" lost by two goals to one. They would have snatched a draw had William Roberts' late equalizer not been brought back for a Welsh free-kick, awarded by referee Mr S R Bastard.

A few weeks later, Oswestry lost to the unfancied Wrexham side rejected by Kenrick and the Wrexham press were as scathing of the recent international "between England and Oswestry". There were gripes and arguments at other clubs too. Ruthin were expelled from the Welsh Cup after refusing to travel to Ruabon to face Druids, fearing reprisals for an earlier meeting. "The Druids on the 18th of December brought an escort of about two hundred men, who, during the game and afterwards, freely, and openly indulged in threats as to what would happen to the Ruthinites when they visited the coal country."

But by now, club football was booming in Wales, and some

intriguing names featured in the Welsh Cup: Rhyl Skull & Crossbones, Equitable, Dolgelley Idris, Wrexham Grosvenor, Newtown Excelsior and Shrewsbury Castle Blues. This game, designed and played by gentlemen, was being eagerly adopted by working men, and the lack of airs and graces at football startled a conservative press. A match between North Wales and Lancashire caused one reporter to peer aghast through his monocle: "It is perhaps hardly possible for those who have only witnessed a quiet and unenthusiastic London or suburban game to picture themselves the wild excitement and party feeling exhibited by the spectators of a Lancashire, Yorkshire or Welsh football match."

In 1880, Wales' first ever goal against Scotland was scored by William Roberts of Llangollen, who went on to play for Aston Villa. Unfortunately, Roberts' goal was only a consolation as Wales suffered another heavy defeat in Glasgow, losing 5–1. But Welsh football was growing fast. By 1881, there were an estimated 2,000 players in Wales, and the national team had improved enough to beat England at Blackburn. This was a watershed for the sport in Wales, and fittingly the team included Llewelyn Kenrick. The father of Welsh football had retired from playing, but travelled to the game as a supporter. When Jack Powell missed his train, and failed to arrive, Wales were resigned to facing the English with ten men. But after 20 minutes of play, William Owen, one of the Welsh players, was startled by a pitch invader: "We had been playing for some time when I saw what I thought was a spectator breaking into the field and making a violent attack upon Marshall and Rostrom, the English right wing. Upon closer inspection I found it was Llewelyn Kenrick of Ruabon. He was dressed in long tweed trousers with ordinary boots and a smart Oxford shirt."

Wales went on to claim their first victory over England in front of a 4,000 crowd thanks to a second-half goal by Jackie Vaughan of Druids. Making his only appearance for Wales was Ruthin's Uriah Goodwin, who arrived at the game

31

with his kit on underneath his clothes. The match was again refereed by Mr Bastard.

Welsh football was gaining respect, and Kenrick's old club Druids faced Glasgow Rangers at Ruabon. Elsewhere, the game was flourishing, with matches regularly played as far west as Anglesey. In 1883, a 2,000 crowd saw Bangor beat Liverpool 5–0. Clwb Madog (Porthmadog) had travelled to Beaumaris for a game in 1880 and Mountain Rovers (Bangor) and Athletic Club (Caernarfon) competed for a silver trophy in the grounds of Vaynol Park in 1882. There was even a game reported in the south, between Bridgend and St Margaret's, one of the first clubs in Cardiff. Wrexham meanwhile were suffering; the Racecourse's landlord had raised the rent, and they spent two seasons playing at Rhosddu, even changing their name to Wrexham Athletic for a while. The rise didn't affect Wales, who continued to play at the Racecourse.

International football was strengthening, and in 1882 Kenrick attended a conference of all the home nations in Manchester. He returned with news that crossbars and touchlines were now compulsory, that throw-ins would be used to restart play, and that there would be a kick-off from the centre-spot after each goal. Football was becoming more identifiable with the modern game. The English had wanted one-handed throw-ins, but the Scots had won the day on that issue.

The result of Wales' first game against Ireland at the Racecourse in 1882 was reported as a "seven goals and one disputed to one" victory. The *Times* said Wales' disputed effort was scored, but "no goal was allowed on the ground of the ball having been fouled".

After the comfortable win over Ireland, Wales faced England at Wrexham in one of the most thrilling games in the history of competition between the two. England went 2–1 ahead before Bambridge "put his shoulder out" and was unable to continue. (England may have had a man with a damaged shoulder, but Wales had faced Ireland with a player with only one arm. Charles Ketley, the Druids inside-forward, had lost his arm in a childhood accident, but continued to play football seemingly unaffected.) After a barnstorming finish, Wales won by five goals to three and travelled to Glasgow in confidence after two excellent wins. But as usual, the opposition was formidable. A 5–0 score meant that in seven games against the Scots, Wales had conceded thirty-three and scored only twice.

The frosty relationship between Wrexham and Oswestry continued, and four years after the poaching row matters came to a head in an 1883 English FA Cup tie. During a fractious match, Wrexham goalkeeper Jim Trainer allegedly insulted the referee and, after some crowd trouble, his team was expelled from the competition. Trainer had earlier joined Everton but left under a cloud after refusing to play for the reserve team. He went on to win honours with Preston, including two league championships, and although Wales suffered numerous heavy defeats throughout the next decade, match reports regularly claimed Trainer's brilliance had kept the scores respectable. Later in his career, he became famous for wearing an overcoat during a Preston game in heavy rain, which he only removed when opponents Reading were attacking. He died penniless in London in 1915 having abandoned his wife and ten children.

In 1883, Wales suffered a 5–0 defeat to England at the Oval in a game which drew first mention of them wearing red: "England wore white, while their opponents were clad in crimson-and-white, which made each side pleasantly distinguishable." That year Wales again lost to Scotland, and played their first fixture in Belfast, a 1–1 draw at Ballynafeigh Park.

The British International Championship

In 1884, the four associations of Wales, Ireland, Scotland and England formalized their fixtures and created a British

International Championship. But with the onset of a formal competition, Wales' creative selection policy began to face objections. England successfully opposed the inclusion of Oswestry's Ted Shaw, born little more than a mile across the border at Llanforda. Shaw, who is rumoured to have later taken to drink and died in America, had already played for Wales three times, but the age of the 'borrowed' Welshman was at an end. With Shaw out, Wales called on William Owen from Friars' School in Bangor whose brother Elias was already selected as goalkeeper. While William went on to become a patron of the FAW, Elias committed suicide under the strain of his college exams. The Owen brothers were joined in the team by debutant John Jones of Berwyn Rangers. Jones died of shotgun wounds in 1902, aged just 41. England also objected to the selection of Northwich-born Fred Hughes, who had already earned six Welsh caps thanks to his club's affiliation with the FAW. The FAW President at the time was G A Hughes of Northwich Victoria, and the Cheshire club had been early members of the Welsh association. Hughes became the third of that 1884 side to die in unusual circumstances when his body was found in Northwich's River Dane in 1923.

Wales finished third in all but one of the seven British Championships held during the 1880s as Scotland dominated and before England grew stronger. One of Wales' few highlights came in an unexpected one-all draw with England at Blackburn in 1885. Wales were still asking players to notify the FAW of their availability, and officials pored over 80 applications. They chose a team which included ten debutants – three from Wrexham Olympic, a new club formed after Wrexham were banned by the FAW in 1883. In an early example of a problem that would dog Welsh football throughout its history, Bolton Wanderers withdrew three Welsh players at short notice, whilst allowing their man Davenport to play for the English. Following the excellent result against England there were hopes that Wales could achieve similar scores against the other championship sides, but a heavy 1–8 defeat at home to Scotland saw reality set in. The Welsh side at the Racecourse included Harry Hibbott at centre forward despite his previously earning two caps as goalkeeper. An end-of-season 8–2 triumph in Belfast completed an erratic season.

Following objections from the English FA, Wales were dealt a further hammer-blow in 1886 when the international football conference in Liverpool decreed that players could only represent the country of their birth. Promising players such as George Farmer and Johnny Roach from Oswestry suddenly became unavailable. Roach, in particular, had been looking forward to a long career after scoring two goals on his debut in Belfast.

Without the border counties players to call on, Wales desperately needed new talent and at last there were developments in the south. Cardiff Association Football Club was formed at the Blue Ribbon Coffee Tavern to create a unified side from the clubs in the area, such as The Dean's Students at Llandaff and St Margaret's from Roath. However, this was not the club that became the Cardiff City of today. The Bluebirds would not be formed at Riverside Cricket Club for another decade.

At the end of the 1880s, a pattern had established; Wales would generally beat Ireland but lose to Scotland and England. The one exception to the string of victories over the Irish was a bizarre affair in Belfast in 1887. Wales failed to raise a complete team and featured Wrexham defender Robert Roberts in goal and FAW Secretary Alexander Hunter at half-back. In the team photograph, Hunter wears his full Wales kit, his Welsh cap and a "they'll never believe this" grin. Wales lost by four goals to one in Ireland's first international victory. Wales' goal was scored by Henry Sabine, a banker's clerk from Oswestry, who qualified for Wales on the "grounds of partial ancestry" despite both his parents being born in Oswestry. Sabine lived until the ripe age of 90 when he was knocked down by a bus en route to a cricket match in Yorkshire.

Matters returned to normal for Wales against Ireland in 1888, though their 11–0 victory came over an Irish team not considered representative by the *Freeman's Journal*: "Some young gentlemen from Belfast or thereabouts evidently took advantage of the fact that there is no law to prevent them from calling themselves 'Ireland'." The report says the game was not one-sided, but fails to mention that three of the Welsh team, including captain Dr Alfred Davies, left before the final whistle to catch their trains or that Wales scored their eleventh with only eight players. The Welsh team for the 1–5 defeat against England in Crewe included Joe Davies, one four brothers from Druids who would represent Wales towards the end of the century.

The haphazard nature of the Welsh international set-up continued throughout the 1880s. Wrexham's Sam Gillam was a late arrival for the game against Scotland at Wrexham in 1889. Allen Pugh, the goalkeeper of a local village team, Rhostyllen, was asked to step in until he arrived. Pugh kept a clean sheet on his short appearance for Wales until Gillam arrived after 30 minutes and took the field for the rest of the game, which ended without score. It was the first time Wales had avoided defeat against the Scots. The season, and the decade, was completed in style when Ruthin's Richard Jarrett scored a hat-trick on his debut against Ireland in Belfast. Despite the auspicious start, he was dropped for the next game and only featured once more. Disillusioned with the selection process, which he claimed favoured certain clubs, he emigrated to Canada.

The lives of those Welsh international footballers of the nineteenth century seem extraordinary by modern standards, and players' individual stories are often more noteworthy than the matches. John Vaughan from Rhyl made his debut against Ireland in 1885. He retired from the game after various operations failed to save his eyesight, but went on to serve in the Boer War. He was also awarded several medals from the Royal Humane Society after saving numerous swimmers off Rhyl, and was an expert on coastal erosion.

Rating highly in the extraordinary players' category was Wrexham's one-armed half-back, Arthur Lea. This extract from Davies & Garland's essential book *Welsh International Soccer Players* tells his story: "Arthur Lea had only one arm but even with this disadvantage he was an accomplished footballer... He was reputedly the highest paid player in Wales. Lea fulfilled his greatest ambition in 1893 when he captained Wrexham to victory over Chirk in the Welsh Cup final. In the same year he captained Wales against Ireland in Belfast. Shortly afterwards, Lea fell seriously ill and at one point was threatened with the loss of a leg."

At the end of a game against Druids in 1895, the Wrexham players were manhandled by the crowd and Lea retired saying "if that was what football was all about, it was the end for him." He also played cricket for Wrexham, principally as a bowler but also as a useful bat.

The FAW survived the 1880s with Wales at least competing against Ireland, if not the more established Scotland and Engand. While football's first 14 years in Wales had seen conflict, argument, pettiness, and general chaos, the game had taken its first steps. It had grown and strengthened in its northern heartland and in the mid Wales towns, but the FAW knew they would have to become missionaries for the new sport if it was to develop into a truly national game. In order to compete with the best, they would need to select from a wider pool of players, and that meant looking south towards the exploding populations of the coalfields.

2

THE AGE OF THE MISSIONARIES
1890–1899

B Y THE 1890S, the competitive game in Wales was finding its feet and opportunities for expansion were tentatively explored. But if the game was stabilizing in Wales, it was booming in England. The English game was now so strong they had taken to playing Wales and Ireland on the same day, selecting two different teams – and usually winning both games too. Despite the stricter rules, Wales were still selecting players with freedom – if you lived at a Welsh address you were eligible. More than a quarter of all Welsh international players thus far had been born in England.

Domestically, this was the era of the petty protest. Whenever teams lost, they would appeal on the most spurious of grounds – the goals were too big, or too small, a player was unregistered, or had worn his opponents' colours. One team even complained that the supporters were "unkind". Boundaries were being pushed by clubs not entirely sure of the rules. FAW records are full of appeals and even though accusations of petty transgression were rarely upheld, other complaints were taken more seriously. Football in Wales suffered crowd problems as the game grew more quickly than clubs could manage. During a couple of seasons around 1895 there were dozens of reports of crowd disorder. Wrexham were snowballed off the pitch at Oswestry, St George's had to apply for protection when visiting Shrewsbury as "they were liable to be interfered with," and Dolgelley FC were banned from hosting games for six months in 1898 due to "rowdyism". A Welsh Cup game at Oswestry witnessed one of Wales' earliest football chants: "If Newtown is in the way, we shall roll it over them," sang the locals menacingly.

In an experimental attempt to expand the game from its Wrexham axis, the FAW formulated plans to take the 1892 fixture against Ireland to Bangor, on the north-west coast. Football was already hugely popular in the city, with four different Bangor clubs entering a competition in Caernarfon in 1890 – Bangor Town, Bangor North End, Bangor Rangers, and Bangor Rovers. Meanwhile, outside their native country, Welsh communities were creating their own teams. The Manchester Welsh club was formed in 1891, while London Welsh attracted 90 exclusively Welsh members with a remit to "honourably uphold the reputation of Wales in the Metropolis."

At the start of the decade, the more successful northern teams were finding themselves short of competition. Bangor even wondered if their "gaudy kit of red and blue stripes" was putting off prospective opponents. A correspondent to the *Wrexham Guardian* asked "is it not possible to form a league of Welsh clubs alone?" The suggestion was met with some enthusiasm by the newspaper who promised to back any such attempt. But when they spoke about a Welsh League, they meant a northern Welsh League; the fledgling clubs in the south were not yet worthy of consideration. Wrexham declined to join the proposed league as "some of the clubs selected would not draw their supporters". Instead they joined the Combination League in England, formed by clubs from Lancashire and Cheshire. The biggest club in the country was already looking to test itself across the border.

But association football *was* developing in the south and an attempt was made to form the South Wales Association League. In 1891 the *Western Mail* reported: "The League of association clubs was formed last season, with the object of fostering the game in the counties of Glamorgan and Monmouth, and it is to be regretted that the efforts of the pioneers have not met with better success."

Thirteen clubs joined the league but by the end of the season only seven had fulfilled their fixtures, blaming their troubles mainly on the scarcity of pitches. Only Blaina, Hotspur (Caerleon), Cardiff, Maerdy, Mountain Ash, Scotch Albions, and Treharris survived. Again, this Cardiff was the not the forerunner of Cardiff City, the Riverside club that would evolve into the current incarnation was only formed in 1899. There was also another aborted attempt at forming a club further west. Swansea Association Football Club appeared in 1890, though interest soon fizzled out, and another club adopted the name in January 1893. This second Swansea played in front of very few spectators on a patch of waste ground called the Vetch Field, but would survive only until 1899. Swansea would be without a senior team until 1912 when the current Swansea City club was formed.

By 1893, the southern association had expanded and was renamed the South Wales and Monmouthshire Football Association. Clubs such as Hay Town, Llanelli, Builth and Brecon joined Barry, Cwmbach, Fairwater, Cefn Excelsiors, Neath, New Tredegar, Rogerstone, Treharris and Swansea under the association's banner. The creation of a club in Llanelli attracted attention in the pages of the *Western Mail* which reported that "the town of tinplates has blossomed forth with a socker club." It went on to quote the *Llanelly Mercury*: "This game which some folks maintain is a much more scientific game than the Rugby, has never yet been played in the town, nor in the County of Carmarthen, for that matter, and it is this fact which explains perhaps the light-hearted indifference which has been manifested towards it by local footballers."

Ironically, a south Walian ex-rugby player from Ystalyfera named T E Thomas was elected as the FAW's first working president after Sir Watkin Williams Wynn was sacked in 1890, having not given "the support expected". Thomas was to be a major influence on the game in Wales. After taking on the head teacher's role at Chirk School, he helped form the Chirk Football Team in 1876 and nurtured a young talent named Billy Meredith. The school produced more than thirty Welsh internationals and Thomas introduced a junior cup competition for smaller clubs. He was also at the vanguard of attempts to professionalize the Welsh game and halt the drift of players to England. When he died in 1928 the FAW went into mourning: "The loss to Wales is irreparable" they wrote, before describing Thomas, a member of the association since its inception, as "the Father of Welsh Football". Llewelyn Kenrick may have disagreed about that, but T E Thomas was certainly an important figure.

The 1890s was a miserable decade for the national side, hampered by the refusal of English clubs to release Welsh players, particularly for games in Belfast, which required a three-day excursion by ferry and train. In ten seasons, Wales finished bottom of the Championship five times, and only twice shared runners-up position.

The decade opened routinely in 1890 with a 5–2 home win over Ireland at Ambler's Field in Shrewsbury. The border towns were almost considered independent of Wales and England at the time, and the FAW felt the game would attract a larger crowd in Shropshire, but the venue attracted comment from the *Glasgow Herald*: "Although having choice of ground for their ninth annual match with Ireland, the Welsh Association decided to meet their opponents on English ground and Shrewsbury being within easy access of North Wales was the place chosen. The experiment proved a success for while very few spectators can be attracted to an association match in Wales, nearly 5,000 people witnessed the game."

In fact, an estimated 5,000 people had watched Wales play Scotland at Wrexham in 1887. And while this was not the first – or last – time Wales played a home game on English soil, it remains the only time Wales have *won* a home game played in England.

Making his only Welsh appearance was former Gloucester rugby player Oswald Davies, now a teacher in Wrexham. There were complaints from the north-west press about the FAW's north-east selection bias, particularly as Bangor had become the first north-western club to lift the Welsh Cup in 1889.

The FAW selection committee consisted of four representatives, from Oswestry, Shrewsbury, Rhostyllen and Newtown, who looked to appease Bangor's complaints when Oxford's Farrant withdrew with an injury. He was replaced by the Dean of Bangor's son, David Morral Lewis, who went on to become the Rhodesian Chief of Police. A second olive branch was offered when the FAW described the Welsh captain Humphrey Jones, one of the founders of football at Bangor's Friars School, as representing Bangor on the team sheet, even though he had left to play club football in Scotland some three years earlier. Jones was later described by the FAW as Wales' "best centre half in years" and played a significant part in nineteenth-century Welsh football.

Wales were again hit by withdrawals when they faced England at Wrexham in 1890. Preston's Jim Trainer was required for a league match against Accrington Stanley and Bolton Wanderers refused to release Bob Roberts. Trainer's late withdrawal earned Sam Gillam another emergency call-up, and he boarded a special supporters' train from Shrewsbury. The England team also travelled by train, leaving Chester at 2.35 p.m. to arrive at Wrexham station just 15 minutes before the 3.30 p.m. kick-off. Wales wore "jerseys of cardinal and royal blue & also new caps of royal blue surmounted with a gold tassel, and bearing the Welsh association badge worked in red silk (supplied by W Thomas of Hope Street, Wrexham, official designer and supplier to the FAW)." Cardinal was a vivid red, and with a royal blue vertical half, Wales of 1890 dressed like an early version of Barcelona.

Embarrassingly, the England team that faced Wales was one of two that wore the three lions that day. A professional England team was beating Ireland 9–1 in Belfast while Wales were losing 1–3 to a mainly amateur side. According to one writer, who labelled the English "vastly superior" to the Welsh and Irish, "these matches are not to be looked upon as of great importance, but as trials for the more important event, to be played in Glasgow next month".

Wales travelled to Paisley for their final match of the 1890 season with Oswald Davies of Llangollen making his only appearance for his country. Davies was an intriguing character according to the *Wrexham Guardian*: "He comes from a 'knowing' stock, and looks it and possesses a face which is an exact index to his mind, inscrutable, calculating and a far-away look, as though he saw greater triumph in the dim and distant future." Davies's enigmatic gaze failed to foresee a 5–0 hammering from the Scots and only the hapless Irish finished below Wales in the table.

The mysterious Llangollen man was dropped from the 1891 Championship team who began with a heavy 2–7 defeat in Belfast in front of up to 10,000 supporters, then the largest gate ever seen at a match in Ireland. Wales again fielded a weakened side with English clubs reluctant to allow their players to travel. The *Belfast News* commented that "several of the men never took part in an international contest". The Welsh team had left Holyhead at midnight on Thursday and, after a rough crossing, spent the whole of Friday travelling. Several players were still suffering from seasickness when they took the field.

Wales were captained in Belfast by Wrexham goalkeeper Richard Turner, making the first of his two international appearances. A former outfield player, he was denied a cap at half-back by a serious ankle injury so switched to goalkeeper. At the after-match dinner, John Taylor, the FAW Secretary compared Ireland's selection woes to those of his own team – while Ireland were selecting players only from Belfast and County Antrim, Wales "could not look very far outside the county of Denbigh for their men". One Welsh debutant, Shrewsbury Town's Alty Davies had played in his club's first ever game, but became unhinged later in life and ended his days in an asylum.

The Scottish team that visited Wrexham in March 1891 combined playing with a spot of sightseeing. After a tour of Chester on the morning of the game they travelled to Wrexham to view the antiquities at the parish church. The Welsh team arrived separately, with each player travelling by train from his area. Wales again wore cardinal and royal blue halved jerseys.

It had been 15 years since Wales' first game, and while the home international fixtures were welcome, they came with a certain predictability. But after a decade-and-a-half of facing the same three teams, Wales' fans were offered some variety when a self-styled touring 'Canada' team, featuring Canadians, Americans, and British ex-pats, played an unofficial game at Wrexham. In terrible conditions, only 500 spectators were drawn to the novelty of the visiting side after torrential rain led to rumours of a postponement. After taking a surprise lead, the Canadians spent the entire second half defending until the game was abandoned when the tourists walked off in protest at the Welsh equalizer, which had hit the bar and bounced behind. To everybody's astonishment, the referee awarded a goal despite the Welsh team's insistence that the effort be disallowed. Even Welsh fans jeered the referee, but the official was unmoved and the Canadians left the field. For a second fixture in October, the crowd had increased threefold as 1,500 people watched Wales win by two goals to one at the Racecourse.

It was announced that the first game of the 1892 British Championship against Ireland would be held at Bangor. But despite promises from the Gwynedd club, the FAW were dismayed by the lax security which lost the association a large portion of the gate money. The entrance to the makeshift ground at Penrhyn Estate had remained closed until shortly before kick-off, but when a dangerous crush developed, police flung open the gates, allowing the vast majority to enter without payment. The all-powerful quarry owner and 'demon of Gwynedd', Lord Penrhyn, was present in the roped-off crowd of 6,000 that watched Wales concede a late equalizer. "There was not a slovenly badly dressed person there" boasted a letter to the *North Wales Chronicle*, though the writer also made the scarcely believable claim that "there were unmistakable signs that the spectators were not all of them teetotalers".

Prior to the game, the FAW had accepted Irish proposals making it only acceptable to attack the goalkeeper while he was playing the ball. One man who would have been happy with the new rules was Welsh keeper Dr Robert Mills-Roberts, who had managed to play against England five years earlier in plaster and splints to his elbow after suffering broken wrists in a particularly bad incident. Mills-Roberts had decided to retire in 1890 to become the doctor at Penrhyn Slate Quarry but was recalled to the 1892 team that lost 0–2 to England at Wrexham. A few weeks later a snowstorm accompanied Wales' 6–1 defeat by Scotland at Tynecastle in front of fewer than 1,000 frozen supporters, many of whom left long before the end.

A dismal Welsh side lost by six to England in March 1893, and then by eight to Scotland five days later. "Seldom has a team with less claim to the title 'international' been put on the field than that which did duty for Wales on Saturday, and seldom has even Wales suffered a more ignominious defeat," roared the *North Wales Guardian*. It was, they said, "the most miserable exhibition ever made by an association." Wales conceded 18 goals in three matches in 1893, probably the worst year yet for a team which had already seen many poor results in its 16-year history. Wales even conceded four in Belfast, and by the end of the decade, had shipped 114 goals in 32 games. One angry fan blamed the FAW, claiming that "the selection of our international teams to battle against the sister countries is becoming more scandalous and humiliating every year".

In truth, the keen but limited amateurs of the Welsh team could not compete with the hardened, experienced professionals from England and Scotland. Many Welsh players had been tempted by the money available from Lancashire clubs even before professionalism was legalized – four Druids players defected to their opponents Bolton after an FA Cup tie in 1883. Under pressure, the FAW finally allowed professionalism in 1892, but selection was still mainly restricted to players from Denbighshire. The FAW knew they had to do more to encourage the development of the game in the south. It was no easy task amid understandable concerns regarding the safety of the game: between 1890 and 1893 there were a reported 71 deaths, 121 broken legs, 33 broken arms, and 54 broken collar bones on football fields across the United Kingdom.

Mindful of the need for expansion, a missionary international was arranged at Swansea for the visit of Ireland in 1894, but the south Walian *Western Mail* was uninterested. While international rugby matches were given the full treatment, including graphics, comment and double-page tabloid-style spreads, football remained willfully ignored. The FAW complained of "certain newspapers in South Wales who refuse to publish any football news". And they had a point. The *Western Mail* was backing rugby to football's detriment: "In this portion of the principality, the association game is practically unknown. There has in the past been one or two clubs playing the game in the principal South Wales towns, but their efforts, necessarily crude, have attracted no attention until during the last couple of seasons the Cardiff Association Football Club, with a run of successes, compelled some slight attention from the South Wales public."

But along the coast, the *Swansea Evening Express* took a more positive angle. "Westerners are getting a good bit interested in the international match that is to take place on the St Helen's Ground," it said, and supporters were promised "far and away the prettiest match we have ever seen in South Wales." In addition, Trainer would play, "showing us south Walians how to keep goal." Goalposts were transplanted from the Vetch Field, and supporter trains arranged. On match day the *Western Mail* produced a diagram of the pitch, and an explanation of the "differences between rugby and association." To the delight of the northern missionaries, Wales won comfortably by four goals to one, and the match gave the south Walian press a first taste of the national team. "The crowd was a big one and about the best-tempered lot I ever remember seeing on the St Helen's field. There were one or two points in the game they were not quite sure of, but on the whole, any smart bits of play were most enthusiastically appreciated."

However, the choice of venue in "the home of the modern rugby game" raised eyebrows in the English press: "This is carrying the war into the enemy's camp with a vengeance. It will be interesting to ask what will the Welsh Association do when the game is firmly established down South. We rather think that the south Walians will kick against being bossed from Wrexham."

Wrexham had built a new 400-seat stand at the Racecourse in 1892, with the expectation that Welsh Cup finals would continue to be held there. They were sure enough of their status as Wales' premier venue to demand the princely sum of £10 to host the Cup final in 1894. There was uproar when the FAW rejected the terms and chose to play the game on an open field at Ruabon.

On the international stage, there were heavy five-goal defeats to Scotland and England in 1894. Wales badly needed some inspiration and a star player – somebody to inspire a game still struggling in the south. One of the new border-crossing professionals was a tricky right-winger who had signed professional forms for Manchester City after reluctantly leaving Chirk. Billy Meredith made his debut at Belfast on Saturday, 16 March 1895, despite the rough crossing inducing such severe seasickness that the youngster had almost been ruled out. The *Belfast News* poured scorn on Meredith's inclusion: "Even against Wales we are still at a disadvantage, which however arises from no other cause than our own conscientious scruples. The Welshmen have no hesitation in scouring the best of the English clubs, and picking up all their available countrymen who have gone over to professionalism. This practice we have not yet descended to, as we feel it our duty to recognize not only the ability, but the patriotism of the men who remain amongst us, and refuse to yield to the temptation of English gold."

The criticism was harsh. Players were lured from Wales by agents with fat wallets. It was not as if Wales sent them over the border to learn new skills. Ireland's high-minded scruples also failed the test of time and within five years they too were choosing players from English clubs.

After playing out a tough 2–2 draw, the Welsh team left the official dinner in Belfast at 9 p.m. on Saturday evening, travelled overnight, and spent the whole of Sunday travelling to London to face England on Monday, in the only football international ever played at the Queen's Club. To huge surprise after those energy-sapping preparations, Wales gained their first point against England for a decade. Meredith said that he had never seen so many top hats and recalled the imposing effect the opposition had: "The size of the ground was an eye-opener to us and the size of the team we had to meet also made us stare a little. Fine fellows they were, some six feet three in their socks and carrying plenty of weight with the inches."

Despite their imposing stature, only a late equalizer robbed Wales of a famous triumph after Trainer's brilliance looked to have secured victory. After just one win in five years, Wales went unbeaten throughout 1895 – a consequence of the extra development and experience its best players were receiving in England. But this development proved double-edged – Wales' best benefitted from playing in England, but their availability became limited. Not even the selectors knew which Wales would turn up from game to game. When stars like Jim Trainer and Billy Meredith were unavailable, as in the final match that season against Scotland, their places were filled by amateurs from Welsh clubs.

On the day Meredith was debuting in Ireland, the Welsh rugby union team played in front of 20,000 at Cardiff Arms Park. The FAW could only dream of such attendances and conceded that more games were needed in the booming industrial south. But if they hoped their bold move to play the 1896 match against England at Cardiff Arms Park would tempt rugby fans to the association game, the result was a crushing blow.

Wales began the 1896 season with a confidence-boosting six-goal thrashing of Ireland, but were brushed aside 9–1 by England. Cheap trains had brought supporters down from the north, and the Monday game saw a crowd of about 5,000, though nowhere near the 20,000 who witnessed the rugby team's wooden spoon contest with Ireland. The south Wales public watched Wales being outclassed. The side was still being criticized for its reliance on old-fashioned "kick-and-rush" tactics while England opted for a more advanced passing game.

The trips south were proving a success financially with a gate of £147 for the 1894 game at Swansea against Ireland. In Wrexham, the match against the more attractive English opposition could only raise £113. The FAW saw the pound signs and allocated more fixtures for the Arms Park and St Helens. But there was a catch: income from games was greater, but so was the expenditure. An investigation committee was called to examine the "gross extravagance" incurred by the FAW's trips to Cardiff and Swansea in 1896 and 1897. However, the committee continued spending and was still defending its expenses 15 years later when it tried to justify the costs at their annual meeting. The excuses of player fees and hotels didn't wash with outraged club officials, one of whom cried out angrily: "all this talk does not explain the whole amount – they are bluffing us."

One of the great Welsh characters of the period was the heroically-named centre half, Caesar August Llewelyn Jenkyns. Jenkyns was a giant; popular with his own supporters and an easy target for the opposition. He was suspended in 1895 for assaulting two Derby supporters and later that season refused to leave a pitch when sent off during a match for Woolwich Arsenal. His appearance at the heart of Wales' defence certainly amused the *Aberdeen Weekly Journal*: "Jenkyns, the centre half-back of the Welsh team, a player of at least sixteen stones in weight, imparting merriment by his numerous tussles with McColl, Paton and Neil, who are very light. At times the Welshman had the best of the encounters, but he had frequently to make his acquaintance with the turf in a very disagreeable manner."

Caesar Jenkyns scored his only goal for Wales in the thrilling 3–4 defeat to Ireland in Belfast in March 1897. Wales, in "red and white shirts and black knickers", were 3–1 up after an hour in a rough game. Ireland won with three goals in as many minutes while Wales were a man down as Sheffield United's John Jones changed his "nether-garments, which had suffered considerably in the heated contest." The Welsh outside-left Bill Nock later became a noted trumpet player in the Rochdale Philharmonic Orchestra. A 0–4 defeat in Sheffield saw the third and final appearance of

Chirk's Hugh Morris, who died from tuberculosis that year aged 25. The English press remained unimpressed by Welsh efforts. "Wales have not yet shown sufficient proficiency in the dribbling code for their international matches to be very interesting," wrote one reporter.

The FAW faced a difficult year in 1897. Secretary John Taylor was imprisoned for forgery and a power shift began to wrestle control of the game away from the association's founders. Kenrick had been reappointed in Taylor's absence but the clubs were getting stronger, and against his opposition, they demanded a share of profits from Welsh Cup semi-finals and finals. The clubs triumphed and Kenrick resigned 20 years after establishing the game in Wales.

The FAW's missionary policy took Wales to Llandudno in 1898, where they lost by a single goal to Ireland. "The Llandudno ground is a very fair one, somewhat bleak, and not providing very luxurious accommodation," wrote a visiting Wrexham reporter. But the outreach policy was proving expensive and the game was struggling financially. The Welsh team travelled to Motherwell in 1898 by third-class rail, as that was all the FAW could afford. The association was dependent on international income and began to implement strict rules regarding free tickets, threatening that Wrexham would lose international fixtures due to the club's insistence on complimentary passes. It was no surprise then when the FAW gave short shrift to a compensation claim from Tottenham Hotspur over left-half, John Leonard Jones, who was injured against Scotland in 1899. Jones would die years later after falling down a 12-foot stairway at work.

It was in 1898 that the FAW placed an order for 18 new badges, the design of which seems the precursor of the modern association logo with "white ground, green rim, feathers in white, and the red dragon in the centre". The date was also to be included on the badge – 1898–99. It is not known whether these were enamel or cloth badges, but the national team didn't begin using the crest in its current form until 1951.

For the first time in their history, Ireland called on English-based players to face Wales in 1899. Previously, the Irish game had been mainly restricted to Belfast, and their international fixtures were often referred to as "a city playing against a country", but a 13–2 defeat by England had persuaded the Irish that the selection of players in England, and even from the clubs emerging in Leinster, was necessary. Meanwhile five Welsh players, including Billy Meredith, were again refused permission to play by their English clubs, and eight debutants took the field. The *Belfast News* wrote that "this circumstance is unfortunate, but its repetition is likely to be prevented by future legislation". They were referring to a proposal by the FAW granting countries like Wales and Ireland the right to call on players with English and Scottish clubs. Sadly the proposal was defeated in favour of a meaningless recommendation that national associations "use their influence with clubs to ensure to other national associations the services of players in international matches".

Wales lost eight consecutive games between 1897 and 1900 with English clubs still refusing to make their players available. The clubs' attitude caused the FAW to approach their English counterparts, and ask that they "recognize the right of this association to call upon Welsh players who are members of English clubs". The request was to echo around the cavernous corridors of the English headquarters at Lancaster Gate for decades. Five years later, the International Board was again asked to consider the FAW's motion that international teams be given the right to call on players in other countries, but a decade after that, Ireland were still asking that clubs be forced to release players.

It had been a gruelling decade for the team regularly referred to as "gallant little Wales," and there was little more they could do than fight to avoid defeat. They had played 30 games, won three, drawn five and lost 22. Yet still they played on, improving all the time, just not as quickly as England and Scotland. Star players were emerging, and the body of Welsh professionals was expanding. Their first 11 was better than Ireland – that was not in doubt – if only they could get them on the field. It was time those southerners began producing international players.

3

THE CELEBRITY FOOTBALLERS
1900–1915

WHILE WELSH FOOTBALL has struggled to compete at the very highest level, the country has always produced players considered among the best in the world. Ryan Giggs, John Charles, and Gareth Bale spring to mind, but in the first decade of the last century there was no better footballer in the world than Billy Meredith.

Born in 1874, Meredith was a product of Chirk School and the coal-mining area which was home to many eminent players of the time. He was sent to work as a pony driver down the pits by the age of 12 and there was little family support for his football. His father only saw him play once and never understood his son's interest in such a frivolous pastime. His mother went further, banning her children from the game, complaining it ruined their footwear. She chastised Manchester City's scouts when they came calling, as reported in John Harding's biography, *Football Wizard*: "It is all very well for you gentlemen to leave your big cities and come to our villages to steal our boys away. You gentlemen come and put all kinds of ideas into their heads. Tell them they can get more money for play than they can for hard but honest work. If Billy takes my advice he will stick to his work and play football for his own amusement when his work is finished."

Meredith ignored his mother and left for Manchester in 1894. He could have stayed in Wales where he played for Chirk and Wrexham, but professionalism was not a possibility in his native country, where a miner's strike had devastated the workforce. Meredith's career is symbolic of the game's early growing pains in Wales. He was one of the new wave of working-class players taking the sport from the public schoolboys who had introduced it. But Meredith could never forget his roots. It baffled him that people made a living playing games. He wanted to work, and the raging conflict between amateurism and professionalism was epitomized by the bandy-legged wizard with a toothpick in his mouth.

Even after turning professional, Meredith continued to work in Chirk's Black Park mine for a time. His Manchester City debut came at Newcastle, so Meredith worked down the pit on Friday, caught a nine-hour overnight train to the game and returned to Chirk ready for his Sunday night shift. He continued to fight for a footballer's right to take a "proper job" between matches throughout his career.

At his best, Meredith was peerless. The *Athletic News* led the praise: "I don't suppose there is a man playing better football in the three kingdoms. Nature has certainly endowed him with advantages above the common and, lithe of foot, an awkward customer to tackle, slippery as an eel, and a rare buttocker as they say in Cumberland, with shooting powers extraordinary, he is a real gem."

His international career also serves as an allegory for the problems suffered by our national team since its earliest days. As far back as 1895 Manchester City withdrew him from the Wales team to face Scotland, insisting instead he play against Lincoln City in the league. Meredith was furious, and punished Lincoln by scoring five. Wales' star player went on to miss six of the next 18 internationals as the club versus country conflict gathered pace.

Meredith was not short of company in Lancashire. Amongst the other north Walians who travelled east in search of a pro-career was his close friend David 'Di' Jones, from Chirk. Jones went on to captain Manchester City, but tragedy struck the Welsh international left-back in 1902 when he was sent home to recover after suffering a gashed knee in a pre-season friendly. In a critical error, the doctor only stitched the cut and the wound turned septic. Within a week, Di Jones was dead from tetanus. After this incident, Meredith paid close attention to his own minor injuries, applying secret concoctions which he later patented and sold from his sports shop in Manchester.

Meredith's career took a turn for the worse when he was charged with paying Aston Villa's Alex Leake £10 to lose the final match of the 1904–05 season. There are claims he was set-up due to his growing trade unionism and Bolshevism, but Meredith believed there was another motive. "Had I been anyone but a Welshman I would have been better dealt with," he later said. In support of their hero, the FAW prepared a legal challenge to his lengthy suspension. Meredith had been found guilty without trial, based only on the claims of an unidentified Aston Villa supporter and England international Leake. Leake initially claimed the bribe had been a joke until pressed by his FA, who appeared eager to make a scapegoat of the problematic Welshman. Meredith protested his innocence vehemently to no effect. While out of the game, Meredith began proceedings forcing Manchester City to continue paying his wages, citing his previous reliability and claiming promises had been broken.

"In 18 seasons I don't think I was ever badly hurt or had a real illness," he said. "I don't think I have cost £3 in doctor's fees." During the legal battle, Meredith discovered the socialist radicalism that distinguished his later years. While still under suspension he transferred to Manchester United and became a leading light in attempts to reform the game through the creation of a Players Union. Meredith remained a thorn in the authorities' side with disagreements over wages and conditions, culminating in threatened strike action after union membership was banned. He would play professionally for 30 years, and speaking in 1919, claimed to have never missed a game through injury. He was practically ever present at City for seven years, something he put down to his training regime: "I've always realized that to play the game well a man must be fit. I never take intoxicants – I do smoke a pipe, and I train regularly two days a week."

Incredibly, Meredith always played with a toothpick in his mouth, and this, along with his bandy legs, made him a star attraction for the cartoonists of the day, who in turn raised his profile and made him one of the game's biggest characters. There was no television or internet, and if a player had a trait easily caricatured, he was more likely to feature in the news. Meredith's gimmick had its downside however. In a 1908 match against Ireland, a rough challenge sent him flying into the crowd and he swallowed the sharp wooden toothpick.

Whenever Wales has produced a star, the English press has been quick to search for dissatisfaction. They want to hear the player say he would have preferred to have worn the three lions; that a career spent in a weak Welsh team is a career wasted. Things were no different in Meredith's day. The famous English journalist Jimmy Catton reported a discussion with the proud Welshman in 1910, just hours after Wales had lost yet again to England: "As we were wandering about the streets of Cardiff... he revealed a troubled soul, for he muttered 'I wish I had been born in England.' This surprised me. 'What a time I should have had if I had been born an Englishman. I'm sick of being on the losing side. But there, never mind, little Wales will win some day. May I be there at the death.'"

It was natural for a competitive sportsman to reflect on his international qualification, but make no mistake, there was no prouder Welshman than Billy Meredith. No doubt Ryan Giggs, John Charles and others have wondered what their status might have been as an England player, but

Catton's interrogation immediately after a painful defeat gave a skewed impression. At the end of his international career, Wales at last beat England. At first they beat them in a friendly, and a few weeks later, they beat them again at Highbury in the British Championship. Meredith cried unashamedly. These weren't the actions of a man who wished he was English – he had waited almost 30 years for that moment. He played his last game against England, aged almost 46 and then followed the Welsh team for 20 years after his retirement, rarely missing a game, home or away.

On 26 February 1920 before Wales played Scotland, Meredith was presented with a silver centrepiece to commemorate 50 international appearances. Unfortunately, the FAW had included a game against Ireland in 1899 from which Meredith was withdrawn, and there were other games wrongly attributed. In reality, he earned 48 caps in an international career spanning 25 years. Colwyn Bay hosted a testimonial match for him upon his retirement, but it seemed he was better appreciated across the border. His benefit match in Manchester raised £1,400 while two games in his native country managed just £147.

The Welsh wizard died aged 83. More than 39,000 people had flocked to his testimonial, but his funeral in 1958, a couple of months after the Munich air crash, was attended by just 100. There was no minute's applause at Maine Road or Old Trafford and no fans unveiled a tribute banner. Only Chirk FC marked his passing, with black armbands and a lone bugler playing the last post. He was buried in an unmarked grave until the FAW, the Professional Footballers' Association and both Manchester clubs paid for a headstone in 2001.

The influence and fame of players like Meredith helped popularise the game in Wales, which was at last spreading from Denbighshire and the border counties. A Mid Wales League formed in 1900, featuring Brecon, Hay, Builth Wells, Rhayader, Knighton, and Llandrindod Wells. Newtown would also have been founding members, but the team had been decimated when half its players went to fight the Boer War. There is a proud history of the game in Newtown – Newtown White Stars were founded in 1875, and took part in the first ever Welsh Cup tie against Druids in 1877. The White Stars were the first club to receive the competition's trophy in 1879. A few years after another Welsh Cup final appearance in 1881, they merged with Newtown Excelsior to form the current Newtown AFC.

During the 1900s, the SWFA also grew stronger and more confident. They demanded occasional meetings in the south – "at Hereford, Cardiff, or Shrewsbury," and players were at last being produced to help the national cause. Aberdare provided the first Welsh international to come through the south Wales league when captain Bill Jones played for his country during the 1901 season.

Founded in 1893, Aberdare were ideally situated to take advantage of the huge influx of mine workers to the south, and were a force in the Welsh game for 30 years as the industry flourished. At the start of the century, the club began to lobby for the south Walian cause. Convinced that Aberaman's long train journey to Wrexham for the 1903 final was behind the record 0–8 defeat, Aberdare suggested that every year, one Welsh Cup semi should be held in the south. The FAW refused to budge that far, but when Aberdare reached the penultimate stage in 1904, their game against Oswestry was held at Hereford. They won by two goals to nil. Nonetheless, the south Wales clubs were still disadvantaged by a final almost always played at Wrexham. Aberdare lost to Druids in 1904 and to Wrexham themselves at the Racecourse in 1905, with hundreds of fans travelling in special trains from the Valleys. Aberdare may not yet have won the cup, but now south Walians were threatening the dominance of the north. There was also more money in the south. When Cardiff provided record takings for the 1906 game against England with a gate three times the size at Wrexham, the north's dominance of international football suffered a fissure that would never mend.

After the 1900 international season had begun with a sorry 5–2 defeat against Scotland, Wales returned to Commissioner's Field, Llandudno, once more to play against the Irish. The FAW had been pleased with the result of the visit two years earlier, and were rewarded with a crowd of 6,000 for Wales' 2–0 win. There were only 4,000 watching as the match kicked off, but the noise attracted more people from the town as the game progressed. Both teams dined at the town's Royal Hotel after the match, where it may have been discussed that Welsh half-back Billie Harrison had in fact been born in Ireland. Harrison went on to become landlord at the Turf Hotel in Wrexham.

Leigh Richmond Roose

Making his debut at Llandudno was a charismatic goalkeeper named Leigh Richmond Roose, who would go on to steal as many column inches as Billy Meredith. But while Meredith dominated the sports pages, Roose was just as prominent in socialite gossip columns. Regarded as the greatest goalkeeper ever to play for Wales, his off-the-field antics cemented his reputation as football's first playboy. Roose was from Anglesey stock, but born in Holt near Wrexham in 1877, where his father had been posted as minister. One of his teachers was science-fiction author H G Wells who, despite bemoaning the football being played, was expected to referee school matches as part of his duties. During one of these matches the author of *The Time Machine* and *War of the Worlds* suffered a ruptured kidney following an accidental kick from Roose's brother Edward. At least, we assume it was accidental.

Roose first played organized football at UCW Aberystwyth while training to be a doctor. He became the team's goalkeeper, but soon began redefining the role. With no restrictions on handling, Roose found he could carry the ball to the half-way line to launch attacks. Nobody had attempted such a thing before and it was Roose's tactic which caused the FA to restrict a goalkeeper's handling to the penalty area in 1912. He signed with Aberystwyth Town, where he is still judged the greatest player in the club's history. He never forgot the role Aber had played in his development and continued to wear the green and black shirt underneath his Welsh jersey throughout his career. After moving to London, Roose's stock rose as he mesmerised writers across the country. "Everything he does is magical," they wrote. "He is the Prince of goalkeepers."

While in London, Roose became a celebrity. He had discovered a penchant for entertainment at Aberystwyth, where he would play up to the crowd at every opportunity. He would tell jokes, wobble his knees for penalties, and even swing himself up to sit on the crossbar. He was one of the first players to appreciate the opportunities that arose from combining sport with personality. He invented a strange pre-match routine of pacing between the posts which aroused plenty of curiosity, but was in all likelihood simply an attention-seeking device. Off the field, he became a London socialite and spent his time in the most exclusive bars and restaurants. The *Daily Mail* called him "London's most eligible bachelor". When he began a relationship with the music hall artiste Marie Lloyd, his fame transcended the game. Marie and Leigh were the Posh and Becks of their day, and the boy from Holt became one of the most famous men in Edwardian England.

While his appearance off the field was immaculate and fashionable, Roose became famous for playing in a scruffy, unwashed kit, as noted in *The Cricket and Football Field* in 1904: "Roose is one of the cleanest custodians we have, but he apparently is a trifle superstitious about his football garments, for he seldom seems to trouble the charwoman with them. Considerable amusement was created at Stoke on Saturday and again at Liverpool on Monday, when it was noticed that Roose alone failed to turn out in spic and span garments. His pants, we should say, carried about them the marks of many a thrilling contest."

He was rumoured to have had many a thrill in those pants, and it was said to be a "terrifying experience" to spend time in his company. He certainly proved himself unpredictable when he took offence at comments made by a director's guest at a post-match meal in Sunderland. He may well have been upset by a 0–1 defeat, but he probably should not have punched the gentleman in the face.

Roose did not shy from a fight, enlisting for the First World War as one of the first volunteers. His goalkeeping skills were employed to good effect by the Army who made the most of his ability to throw grenades huge distances. After winning the Military Medal for bravery, Roose served with the Medical Corps in Gallipoli, where he was reported missing, presumed dead. However, a chance remark to a family member revealed he died at the Battle of the Somme some time later. The Thiepval war memorial in France still refers to L Rouse, though a campaign led by biographer Spencer Vignes and a group of Welsh football historians has received assurances the mistake will be rectified.

Like Meredith, Roose was a north Wales product who moved on to further his career, and the north was getting left behind in other ways too. The Wrexham press were still smarting from the exclusion of the Racecourse as a venue throughout 1900 when they travelled to Cardiff Arms Park to see Wales' 1–1 draw with England: "Although the Association game is steadily finding favour it cannot as yet be said to have obtained a firm hold in South Wales and many of those who attended at the Cardiff Arms Park enclosure, did so with but a rudimentary idea of the points in the play."

There was external conflict too as English clubs continued to display double standards with regards the international game. Nottingham Forest had refused permission for Grenville Morris to play for Wales at Cardiff, but allowed Spouncer to turn out for the English. Morris had been in superlative form and his presence might have brought about a Welsh victory. Even Roose had been withdrawn as he was required for a cup match by Aberystwyth, who were one of the most successful Welsh clubs of the first years of the twentieth century. If Meredith's career illustrated the plight of the Edwardian footballer, then Aberystwyth's history highlights the problems faced by the new Welsh clubs, struggling with class transition and searching for a natural level amidst the confusion caused by moves towards professionalism.

The rise and fall of Aberystwyth Town

A football club was formed by the gentlemen of Aberystwyth in 1876, though the game had been played by ex-pupils of English public schools even before the arrival of the university. The college formed a team soon after its foundation in 1872 and played fixtures against St David's College, Lampeter, which it usually lost. But the earliest clubs in Wales were often dependent on a single enthusiast to pull the community along – somebody like Llewelyn Kenrick in Ruabon and T E Thomas in Chirk. The driving force in Aberystwyth were three brothers, Arthur, Hugh, and Jack Hughes, the latter another Welsh player who had graduated from Shrewsbury Public School. Recognized as "one of the best forwards in the United Kingdom," Hughes became the first Aberystwyth man to be capped in 1877.

The club's early development offers a significant insight into the social tensions created during football's handover from the gentry to the working class. Reformists had been campaigning for a reduced working week to improve employee morale, and the 'half-holiday movement' won concessions in the 1880s, freeing up Saturday leisure time for the working man. The Aberystwyth team formed and populated by the gentry was now under pressure to include the best of the proletariat. This was beyond the pale for some upper-class members, and the early "gentleman's team" was soon usurped by a more democratic eleven called the

Mechanics, a team filled with factory, steelworks, tannery and railway workers, in addition to just four of the original Aberystwyth toffs. There was a similar shift in Wrexham as the team of insurance clerks made way for manual workers. Meanwhile Chirk FC was formed in 1876 by middle class teachers and dignitaries to provide a pastime for employees of Chirk Castle and Black Park Colliery.

The Mechanics were to disappear after a few seasons, and the club now recognized as Aberystwyth Town was founded in 1884 at the Belle Vue Hotel. The club remained unbeaten in 1890 before all but disbanding, possibly turning to rugby for two years, and then reforming at a public meeting in 1892. Now they were serious about creating a first-class side, and in 1893 re-entered the Welsh Cup for the first time in 11 years. Aberystwyth Town celebrated its anniversary in 1984, but could just as easily have chosen 1876 or 1892 as the year of its foundation.

In 1896 the club took the decision to join the Welsh League, which despite its name was made up only of clubs from the north-east – Brymbo, Chirk, Druids, Newtown, Oswestry, Rhostyllen, Westminster Rovers (of Wrexham) and Welshpool. Aberystwyth even entered the English FA Cup, but were knocked out by Druids in a qualifying round. The travelling proved too much for the Green 'n' Blacks and they withdrew from the league after just one season, citing arduous ten-hour train journeys. While the team was made up of amateurs such travel was simply unsustainable. Many have since discovered that the lack of a decent transport infrastructure remains a major problem for any organized football on a national scale in Wales.

After a couple more seasons of friendlies, a frustrated Aberystwyth joined the Combination League, featuring the likes of Wrexham, Birkenhead and Everton Reserves, for a season in 1899. They were surprised by the professionalism they found. Arriving 20 minutes late by train for one game at Newtown, they were shocked to see the referee waiting to enter the carriage they were about to vacate. He had cancelled the game in their absence. Evidently teams in the English-run Combination League took kick-off times more seriously than the FAW. The first Welsh Cup final was delayed by the late arrival of local gentry and the second started almost half-an-hour late thanks to Wrexham's relaxed approach to the concept of time. The third final was delayed an hour while the teams argued over the choice of umpire.

Despite their relative isolation on the west coast, the loyal Aberystwyth followers made great efforts to watch their team. In 1898, they took 150 fans in a single bus to Aberdare for a Welsh Cup match. When the rain started, they used the vehicle as a grandstand. And in 1900, a train "full of green and black clad supporters" arrived at Oswestry for a semi-final against Caernarfon. They were to witness a great victory, as the addition of a few professionals gained them their only Welsh Cup win. Aberystwyth were so good that during one game against Newtown that season, the Green 'n' Blacks captain felt confident enough to leave the field early in order to attend a local concert. But like so many clubs in Wales, Aberystwyth were to discover they could not afford success. Just a year after their Welsh Cup triumph they were almost extinct, in debt to the tune of £163, as club officials complained that Aberystwyth was "geographically most unfortunately situated".

The historic animosity between the "unfortunately situated" neighbouring towns of the west was still very much apparent. When Bangor were drawn against Llandudno in a Cup semi-final, Caernarfon was chosen as the neutral venue. However, the location was not as neutral as had been hoped. Hundreds of local supporters backed Llandudno, and at one point in a fractious game, a mass brawl developed. The press reported the "utterly ferocious display of feeling given by the Caernarfon crowd," and when Llandudno won 5–1 they were carried shoulder high through a mass of cheering Cofis to the Eagles Hotel.

After Scotland had put 11 goals on Ireland in the first fixture of the 1901 Championship, their March trip to Wrexham was greeted with trepidation, particularly as four Welsh players had withdrawn. The *Athletic News* suggested that the Scottish might be ready for a change of scenery after meeting Wales at the "uneven Racecourse" for the umpteenth time. It was an awful day, with heavy rain making the pitch almost unplayable. Scotland faced a howling gale in the first half which sapped their strength and enthusiasm, and Wales escaped with a 1–1 draw. If the result held out any promise for the rest of the season, it was wiped away by a six-goal defeat against England. Billy Meredith was Welsh player of the tournament which finished with a win in Ireland. Wales still weren't wearing red – a 1901 photograph shows them in quartered shirts of white and green.

The 1902 British Championship was dominated by the tragedy at Glasgow's Ibrox where a wooden stand collapsed after heavy rain, killing 25 and injuring hundreds more. John Davies, the secretary of the FAW was attending a conference in the city at the time, and had accepted an invitation to the game against England. Davies was greatly affected by the experience and a £50 donation was made from FAW funds towards the Ibrox appeal.

The British associations shared common aspirations in Edwardian times, and formed an unofficial brotherhood united by self-regard and a suspicion of developments in the game across Europe. In May 1902, the FAW received a letter forwarded from the English FA. It contained a Dutch proposal to create an International Football Association for Europe. It was to be the first of several invitations the UK associations could only reject for so long. The Europeans were keen to develop the game outside its founding homeland.

In 1910, the FAW politely declined another request to join FIFA. The secretary was asked to reply, "thanking them for the invitation, and to say that the association could not see their way clear to join." It seems the FAW then agreed to the request before FIFA wrote again in 1912, requesting a place on the International Board. Eventually, in 1913, the home nations finally agreed to allocate them a place at football's top table. The sport had already outgrown the United Kingdom.

One of the curiosities of the Welsh game at the turn of the century was the trial matches held at the start of each international season. These games were little more than fundraisers; often pointless affairs with the top players absent. The 1902 game for instance, "by the stupid action of one or two players who ought to have known better was rendered farcical". The games had little bearing on actual selection decisions. Despite a shocking performance, in which he scored two own goals and gave away a penalty, Billy Meredith's brother Sam was selected for the first game of the season against Ireland. Perhaps fortunately for Wales, his team Stoke City refused to release him for duty. Clapton Orient's Roger Evans, earning his only cap, was heavily criticized after a match winning hat-trick from Ireland's Andy Gara embarrassed Wales at the Arms Park, in a game where goalkeeper Bob Evans played with a dislocated knee. Wales put up a much better display against a fully professional England side, though once again, mention was made of the appalling state of the Racecourse pitch. The *Times* reported that "Wales might well have won, as, indeed, they deserved to, for they had distinctly the larger share of the play, but the uneven turf on the Wrexham Racecourse, which is practically in furrows, was all against accurate shooting. The fine play of the home team greatly delighted 10,000 spectators, the biggest crowd ever attracted to an international match in Wales."

Wales suffered a heavy 5–1 defeat in Scotland in March 1902 with Hugh 'H' Morgan-Owen making his debut. Hugh and his brother Morgan Maddox Morgan-Owen, known as MM, were Oxford University players. Such was their commitment to the amateur code they both turned down invitations to play for Wales against Ireland in 1903 because it clashed with the Arthur Dunn Cup final, in which they played for Old Salopians against Old Carthusians. M M Morgan-Owen became a member of Corinthians in London, and as a captain in the Army, was gassed and wounded at Gallipoli in 1915.

It would be almost a year before Wales played again, losing 2–1 to England at Portsmouth at the start of the 1903 Championship, even though they were the better team on the day. Bad luck also cursed the team against Scotland at a muddy Arms Park when Wales again outplayed their opponents only to see a goal disallowed, the Scottish bar skimmed and a rare blunder from M M Morgan-Owen which gifted the Scots the only score. A 0–2 defeat in Belfast in a match suspended due to a violent hailstorm saw Wales finish with a single goal and no points in an unfortunate year. Six of the original 11 had declined to travel to Belfast in an all too familiar tale. It was the first time Ireland won two games in a season.

Wales had turned out in various coloured shirts – green and white, red and blue, and red and white. But a meeting in January 1904 officially decided "the colour of the shirts for the international players be scarlet with the exception of those for the away matches this season." As the only away game was at Scotland, and Wales only ever played three teams, it's difficult to see why there was a need to differentiate. The players were requested to wear white knickers, but there was a review after complaints about the variable lengths of players' pants. The issue of away colours for domestic games was also vexing the FAW – more clubs meant more clashes, so they came up with a solution: "should two clubs have similar colours, the club which is the younger member of the association shall change its colours." The idea, contrived to appease the grand old members, lasted only a few seasons until the current system, forcing away teams to change, was put in place.

When the only home fixture in 1903 was awarded to Cardiff despite the Racecourse attracting a record crowd to the previous season's game against England, 25 Denbighshire clubs sent a letter of protest to the FAW. This was a northern game after all, and they felt betrayed by the FAW's new affection for the big rugby grounds of the south. Such was the agitation in Wrexham that they requested a special general meeting of the FAW, who refused to budge. The Wrexham-based entertainer Walter Roberts amended the words of a popular song to express local feeling:

> Football's a game that we greatly admire
> And we'd go miles to observe it,
> But to be boycotted raises our ire,
> I don't think we deserve it
> Our town has supported the pastime for years,
> Our ground now is second to none,
> But when you get men who have prejudiced minds,
> Fair play and just treatment are gone.
>
> Over the hills and far away
> Outings are nice when there's nothing to pay
> At scenery they'll peep and it's all on the cheap
> Over the hills and far away.

The FAW decision to play at Cardiff was vindicated by the 6,000 crowd and £380 gate. This surpassed that achieved for the same fixture in Wrexham two years earlier, but was some way short of the game against England when the weather was finer. On the field, it was generally agreed this was the finest team ever turned out by Wales, and they were only narrowly defeated by England in Portsmouth. Stars such as Charlie Morris, Billy Meredith, Gren Morris and Bob Atherton were reaching their prime and Wales were showing potential at last. For the first time, Scotland included players from English clubs in their side, such was their respect for this improving Wales team, and they came away from Cardiff with a narrow 1–0 win. But no matter how good the first 11, Wales still suffered the same old problems, and were deprived of six players for their visit to Belfast, where they lost 0–2.

England were first up in 1904 and Wales achieved a creditable draw on a frozen Racecourse in front of 7,000 fans. Richmond Roose was immense, playing on despite fracturing a finger. Wales played a "long passing and hard kicking game which they constantly looked like winning," but ended up drawing 2–2. With Roose out of action, there were calls for former rugby international Dai Davies to feature against Scotland, and he became the first Welshman capped in both rugby and football, though the call came in unusual circumstances. The FAW had originally sent for Blackburn's Bob Evans after Roose withdrew, but received a confusing telegram in response: "Cannot come as reserve goalkeeper ill in bed."

It seemed that Evans was refusing to be called up as a reserve, adding as an afterthought that he was ill in bed. It later transpired the intended message had been that Blackburn's reserve goalkeeper was ill in bed, and therefore Evans could not be released by the Lancashire club.

A fine performance secured Wales their first ever point in Scotland in March 1904, and appropriately, it was Bobby Atherton who scored the Welsh goal. Born in Bethesda, Atherton had moved to Scotland as a child, playing for Hearts and Hibernian in Edinburgh. He became another Welsh international to die during World War I when his submarine was lost in the English Channel. "I suspect he must have been a good player," wrote FAW Secretary Alun Evans in 1987, "because the cost of bringing him into Wales at the turn of the century must have made as big a hole in the Association's finances as it does to fly over Mark Hughes and Ian Rush." Arthur Davies was one of three Davies' in that Welsh side against Scotland. He would go on to become a Wrexham FC director before his body was discovered in the River Dee in 1949.

All areas of Wales were now clamouring to host internationals. Bangor told the FAW they were "prepared to erect stands and make all the necessary arrangements" for the 1904 fixture against Ireland at Bangor Cricket Ground. Every Irish-based player who crossed the sea to Holyhead for the game was seasick, but they seemed to recover well enough, winning by the only goal. Both teams paid a visit to Lord Penrhyn's quarries, and a special blast was arranged for entertainment. However, once again, poor organisation saw the FAW miss out on vital income as Bangor locals used a variety of means to watch for free. There were large numbers on a road overlooking the ground, many sat on the roof of a nearby school, and some even erected viewing platforms in their own backyards. The official crowd was 4,037 and the club incurred a loss of £17 when the accounts were tallied. Unsurprisingly, this proved to be the last full international held in Bangor.

The 1905 All Blacks

It is a common complaint of Welsh football that rugby is perceived as the national game even though football is played and watched by more people. The misconception can be traced to a single rugby match at Cardiff in 1905. While Welsh football had gone through a barren period of only four wins in 44 games, Welsh rugby was providing a hungry public with success. The touring New Zealand rugby side came to Cardiff Arms Park in 1905 after beating the other home countries and 45,000 people turned out to see them. The Welsh crowd sang 'Hen Wlad Fy Nhadau' in response to the New Zealand haka, the first time a national anthem had been sung before a sporting fixture. Wales won 3–0 – the only defeat in New Zealand's 35-match tour, and the game drew such huge attention that it has fused Wales and rugby in the minds of outsiders forever. From that day, rugby and Wales were inseparable in popular culture, to the detriment of football. Rugby had stolen a march that it would tenaciously try to protect. By 1905, the round ball game was popular enough to warrant its own section in the back pages of the *Western Mail*, but still of only equal prominence to those other niche sports, hockey and pedestrianism. Rugby had a firm hold in the hearts of south Walians and took priority in any clash of interests. An important football match between Llanbradach and Treharris in March 1905 had to be postponed because several players had travelled instead to Swansea to watch Wales beat Ireland at rugby.

Elsewhere in Wales, clubs were finding it increasingly difficult to maintain order. It was not an isolated incident when a referee was attacked at Mold in 1905. There were dozens of clashes across the country. Chirk's ground was closed for 14 days and there were problems at Bontnewydd, Bangor, Blaenau Ffestiniog, Rhosllanerchrugog, Ruabon, Ruthin, and Holywell. The FAW insisted on a police presence at matches in Oswestry after a player was attacked by supporters when he was shown a red card. In one infamous incident, a train containing Aberystwyth fans was stoned at Tywyn following a game between the two sides, and reports talk of a running battle at half-time. "During the interval free fights occurred between the rival partisans and matters became rather exciting. Some of the combatants got tangled in the goal net." At Holywell, a referee was locked in his dressing room for two hours while an angry mob was dispersed, and after a game between New Tredegar and Pontlottyn in 1906, only the players' efforts stopped home supporters throwing the referee into the nearby river.

If 1905 was the year rugby became the iconic sport of Wales, at least the Welsh football team was also to demonstrate improvement. After so long in the shadows, Wales would finally emerge to beat the finest exponents of the game. Unfortunately, the doubling of entry fees ensured that fewer than 5,000 were present for the visit of Scotland to

Wrexham. There were also the usual player availability issues – second division Liverpool refused to release Maurice Parry as they pushed for promotion. The first Welsh international to play for Liverpool, "Parry had lengthy and loosely jointed limbs, and his unique methods defied explanation," said one report. Sadly, the Oswestry-born half-back was another Welsh international gassed during the First World War. At the end of his career, he defied bronchitis to coach Liverpool and Barcelona as well as Eintracht Frankfurt and FC Köln.

Wales beat Scotland for the first time after almost 30 years of trying in March 1905, thanks mainly to Roose in goal and "the delightful dribbling and shooting" of the Nottingham Forest star Grenville Morris. Morris started his career at Aberystwyth as a 16-year-old in 1894, scoring 111 goals in 75 games for the club and winning three caps as an Aber player. He moved first to Swindon before becoming Nottingham Forest's record goalscorer. The young forward had been badly injured during the first half against Scotland, and there were doubts he could continue as he limped from the field with Wales a goal up. Asked whether he could continue, Morris replied: "I should think I will if I only have half a leg." Morris inched closer to a historic victory with a goal soon after half-time before Meredith "breasted the ball into the net" for Wales' third. Scotland claimed a late consolation but the result shook the foundations of international football. After so many dark days, the *North Wales Guardian* could be permitted a little hyperbole: "One can quite imagine the feeling of intense gratification and pride which must have swelled the breasts of all true and loyal sons of Cambria."

Wales were a match for anybody, and, after a decade of defeats peppered with occasional wins over Ireland, the landmark event was commemorated at a celebratory post-match dinner. The Welsh FA President, Stanley Edisbury, was presented with a handsome pipe, while captain Horace Blew received a cigarette holder from members of the team.

Encouraged by victory over Scotland, more than 2,000

Welsh fans swarmed across the border to watch their side face England at Anfield in March 1905. Roose was overwhelmed at his appointment as skipper. "To captain one's country is the honour of honours, generating the kind of pride within a man that is difficult to define in words," he told the *Athletic News*. This would be the first time the national side contained not a single player from a Welsh club. Historian Martin Johnes has blamed the reliance on English-based players as one of the reasons the national side has often failed to generate the enthusiasm shown for the nation's rugby team. The travelling supporters in Liverpool saw their team lose 5–1.

Both Roose and Meredith, plus the exciting Gren Morris were all missing from the trip to Belfast, but Wales were already used to muddling through without their best players. They went home with a 2–2 draw. It had been a good season with Wales finishing as outright runners-up – an unprecedented achievement for the tournament's perpetual whipping boys. Beaumaris' Bangor-born Alf Oliver earned his two appearances in 1905, staking a claim to be only the second player – after 'Bob Lee' Roberts in 1890 – from Anglesey to be capped until Tony Roberts played against Ireland in 1993. Since then Wayne Hennessey has also represented the island in the Welsh goal, though he too was actually born on the mainland, in Bangor.

Wales continued their improvement in 1906 with a fine win in Edinburgh to beat Scotland in successive seasons. According to the London *Times*, "the match demonstrated the great improvement that has taken place during the last few years in Welsh Association Football." At last the Welsh were playing as a unit, using teamwork instead of individuality to compete. One of the Welsh scorers was debutant John Love Jones, who died of tuberculosis at the age of 28. The other Welsh scorer was another Chirk School product, Lot Jones. Jones would go on to manage Aberdare when they were elected to the Football League in 1921.

Welsh success drew a record crowd to see England's 1906

visit to Cardiff Arms Park with thousands streaming into the newly-appointed city on excursions from the Valleys. The Lord Mayor of Cardiff allowed schools to finish early on the Monday in order that children could watch the game, though with the bell going at 3.45 p.m. and the match kicking off at 4 p.m. it didn't allow them much time to get to the ground. The game was played before a crowd that grew and grew as the action continued. Thirty minutes before kick-off there had been just 2,000 around the ropes, but by half-time there were between 17,000 and 20,000.

In that same season, the 4–4 draw with Ireland was recorded on camera by film-makers Mitchell and Kenyon, and now exists as the world's oldest surviving footage of a football international. A former player called Ted Robinson was appointed secretary at the Racecourse that year. His involvement with the club would span more than three decades and Wrexham took their 'Robins' nickname in his honour.

The growth of southern football continued unabated. After seven years without a senior side, an amateur club called Swansea Town was formed in 1906 and played at Victoria Park. But in 1912, the current professional Swansea club was formed to meet requests from the expanding Southern League. Swansea children had traditionally played on a patch of land in the town covered in vetch – a type of legume used for feeding cows – and in 1912 the new club leased Vetch Field from the Swansea Gaslight Company. There were huge efforts made to get the pitch ready for the new season and on 7 September 1912, Swansea Town played its first Southern League match against Cardiff City in front of 8,000 spectators.

1907 – Champions at Last

The improving Wales side would better their 1906 second-place finish in the British Championship in 1907 as Billy Meredith returned from his long suspension to inspire the national side to a historic triumph. Wales began the season with a 3–2 win in Belfast, and then a Gren Morris goal at Wrexham saw Scotland defeated for the third time in succession. A photograph of the Racecourse was taken from the balcony of the Turf Tavern which served as changing rooms for the teams. There are no visible stands and the crowd is packed ten-deep around the pitch. In the foreground, ladies and children stroll around the mud of a fenced area, seemingly uninterested in the forthcoming match. A brass band plays on the field as a few pairs of gentlemen walk across the pitch, either advertising their officialdom or simply taking a short cut. Behind one of the goals, half-a-dozen marquees give the scene a carnival atmosphere.

With Wales on the verge of their first British Championship, more than 1,000 Welsh supporters travelled to London for the Monday afternoon game. A draw at Craven Cottage against England would give Wales a share of the trophy but even for such an important fixture, they were without Derby's Charlie Morris and Wrexham's Horace Blew, acclaimed as his club's best pre-war player and a regular for Wales. Blew rejected offers from English clubs throughout his career, becoming a director of his beloved Wrexham. He would later become town mayor and was granted freedom of the borough in 1948.

Playing against a strong wind in the first half, Roose's innovative technique of rushing out to play as a sweeper denied England the goal they had expected in the blustery conditions. When the ball did hit the back of the Welsh net it was disallowed for handball. Lot Jones scored the opening goal, and a second-half defensive display after England equalized earned the draw which made Wales favourites for their first Championship title. A last minute penalty should have given Wales outright victory, but the referee ignored a blatant handball – a decision which would always rankle with Meredith. The Welsh players might have all played for English clubs, but reports show the north of Wales was still recognized as the nation's football heartland. "We do not suppose there will be bonfires on the tops of Snowdon down to the hill of Holyhead, but there will be a quiet sense of satisfaction," predicted the *Athletic News*.

Sadly, there was little opportunity for a big celebration as the title was not secured until England failed to beat Scotland in their final game a few weeks later, but on 26 June 1907, each of the 21 players used in the three games were awarded a gold medal by the FAW at a celebration in Wrexham. Wales' achievement was noticed throughout the game, and the *Times* wondered how powerful the team could become: "If the Welsh association can only develop Cardiff as seems possible, and some of the more populous centres of the south, they might become as dreaded as their rugby brethren in international tourney."

The thousands who followed Wales to games in England during Edwardian times should not be seen as unusual. Fans would regularly travel in large numbers to away games which would now be classed as unimportant. Drawn by attractive rates on special train excursions, an away game was seen as a cheap day out. With little competition for their leisure time, Edwardian supporters made the most of their away days. The 1907 Welsh Amateur Cup final saw 800 Aberystwyth supporters travel to Newtown for a tie against Buckley where reports stated that "The fifty or sixty Buckley supporters made themselves heard by their shouts and musical instruments." The amateur game was now strong enough to provide an international side of its own and in February 1908, Wales played its first amateur international at Edgeley Park, Stockport, losing 1–0 to England.

Wales began 1908 facing Scotland at Dundee as champions. They were missing Meredith who was required by Manchester United for a Cup tie against Fulham. Scotland though were without all their English-based players. Wales were favourites to maintain their superb recent record against their oldest rivals and Lot Jones gave them a half-time lead. But the Scots equalized and Wales succumbed to a goal two minutes from time to lose against Scotland for the first time in four years. Wales were really brought down to earth with a 1–7 home defeat to England in their next game, which saw them use three different goalkeepers. Roose was knocked out by a heavy charge after 15 minutes and defender Charlie Morris took over between the posts in terrible weather conditions. Wales were further depleted when Edwin Hughes of Nottingham Forest left the field "suffering from a cold". Bolton's David Davies was in the crowd, and the English FA agreed he could come on as Roose's replacement at half-time with Wales already four goals down. Roose had been unimpressed by the challenges of the English forwards and during the interval "had an unpleasant conversation with the England selectors, who thought that the speech of the goalkeeper was not such as might be expected from a gentleman."

The Irish FA were unhappy with the choice of Aberdare as the venue for the 1908 fixture, as the trip entailed 20 hours of travelling via Holyhead and Crewe. The FAW were unsympathetic and were rewarded for their faith in the burgeoning south Wales mining community by a 15,000 crowd. Colliers had started work an hour early in order to clock off in time for kick-off, but the large crowd was to be disappointed as only four of the selected Welsh team were released by their clubs, and Wales lost by the only goal.

Ted Robbins arrives

In 1909, FAW Secretary A E V Berkeley resigned amid accusations of "negligence and carelessness in regard to his duties". In an inspirational move, Ted Robbins was appointed in his place, and set about improving the fortunes of the national team. He was to remain at the helm of Welsh football for the next 36 years, making him the FAW's longest serving secretary at a time when the role encompassed all aspects of football management. A fervent Welshman, he would often give passionate speeches to the team, saying "Welsh football begins on the hearth". In his autobiography, Wales captain Walley Barnes called Robbins the "greatest man in Welsh football history" and said he "appealed to the players through their mam and their dad, inspiring them to fight against odds, and beyond normal ability, not as individuals, but as a team for the honour and glory of our little country." Whenever Robbins is mentioned, reference is always made to his charm and his battles with English clubs over the release of players for international duty, and the cheery demeanour that persisted despite his many rejections. A popular amateur comedian, Robbins' lively wit resounds in the stories which surround his life. One reporter believed the Welsh players often felt they were playing for Robbins, "because he himself is almost regarded as the Welsh FA".

Inspired by Robbins, Wales regained their form and beat Scotland on St David's Day 1909 mainly thanks to Roose and Meredith. According to the *Times*, "Roose in the first half kept out many good shots, but the most prominent individual had been Meredith, whose control of the ball in dribbling and accuracy in passing and shooting represented the perfection of forward play." With Scotland to a large extent controlling the game, Meredith was the one man to cause them much anxiety, and Roose continued to provide serious hindrance to the Scottish forwards. The *Western Mail* claimed Roose was "probably the most dazzling goalkeeper the Association game has ever known. Still he is an erratic player and at times has done things that would discredit a member of a third class team." It was a prescient observation that signalled the inexorable decline in Roose's form.

A defeat in Nottingham against England was disappointing and there were more concerns when Roose turned up for the final game at Belfast with his hand heavily bandaged. He set about telling all who would listen that he had broken a couple of fingers, but as Wales kicked off he removed the bandage, wriggled his perfectly healthy digits, and with a wink at the assembled pressmen proceeded with the game.

The Wrexham left-back Horace Blew missed the 3–2 win as his club again refused to release him, even though he was purportedly an amateur.

An incident in Wales' first game of 1910 showed that Roose was becoming distracted and, at 32, his game was deteriorating. With just minutes left of a close game against Scotland in Kilmarnock, a speculative shot flew past the Welsh keeper while he chatted to a spectator with his back to play. Wales lost by a goal to nil. In November, Roose suffered a broken arm while playing for Sunderland against Newcastle. Desperate to play for his country, he rushed himself back into action and struggled badly in the March 1911 match against Scotland. For the first time in his international career, Roose was dropped. He was never to play for his country again, though he did appear for several amateur sides, including Blaenau Ffestiniog after his retirement in 1912.

The defeat to Scotland in the first game of 1910 had been illuminated by another fine performance from Meredith. Wales then lost to England in Cardiff where hundreds of Aberdare supporters arrived to cheer on their former captain Billy 'India Rubber Man' Wedlock, who was playing for the opposition. With Cardiff City soon to turn professional and build a ground of their own, the fixture would be the last international played at a rugby ground in Cardiff until 1989. Ireland visited the Racecourse in April hoping for the win that would give them their first Championship trophy, but were denied by a rampant Welsh team who won 4–1 with Robert Evans scoring a brace.

Evans would become the subject of an eligibility row in 1911, even though he had already worn the red shirt several times. The English FA had been alerted to his Chester birthplace by his club secretary at Sheffield United and the FAW were forced to answer England's claim on the player: "Your letter of the 17th has been laid before a committee of this Association and enquiries have been made as to Evans' birthplace. Of course the certificate of his birth must be counted as conclusive, but up to the present no doubt has existed in the minds of the members of the Council of this Association that Evans had the necessary qualifications to play for Wales. This Association regrets that the English Association should, at this juncture, lay claim to Evan as an English player, being already aware that he had played in ten international matches for Wales. True, you intimated last March that it had been represented to you that Evans did not possess this qualification, but enquiries then made confirmed us in our previous conviction, Evans stating to our President at Cardiff that he had been born in Wales and had stated so on his registration form. Nothing more being said from that time we thought the question had dropped, and accordingly last week selected him to play for us against Ireland. Our astonishment was great to find later that your selection committee had chosen him to play for one of the teams in your trial match. This of course, put us on inquiry, with the result that we find he was born a short distance out of Wales. This shows your contention to be technically correct, but in all other respects we believe he is a Welshman."

Despite the FAW's contention that Evans was Welsh in every respect except place of birth, he jumped ship and played for England four times, including once against Wales.

The Growth of the Miners' Clubs

Between 1906 and 1910, a huge expansion of the game took place in the south, with the number of clubs affiliated to the South Wales FA rising from 74 to 262. English scouts were regularly seen at south Wales' club matches, keen to prise away the cream of local talent. South Wales needed a big club to compete with the English professionals, and one of these potential 'big clubs' was Riverside FC in Cardiff, whose secretary, a club-footed Bristolian called Bartley Wilson, successfully applied to change their name to Cardiff City in 1908.

The English Southern League was looking to expand and, noting the demand for top-class football in south Wales, its officials toured the area at the end of 1909 inviting clubs to turn professional in their second division. But while Ton Pentre, Merthyr Town and Aberdare were pleased to accept the offer, Cardiff City's facilities were deemed below the required standard, and Wilson's application could not be made until the end of the 1909/10 season, when Cardiff City turned professional. The Corporation Refuse Tip at Leckwith had been chosen as Cardiff's new ground, next to the Taff Vale Railway Line, hence the adoption of 'I'll Be There', with its line 'When the coal comes from the Rhondda down the Taff Vale Railway Line, with my little pick 'n' shovel I'll be there,' as the club song. Short of money for development, the club was assisted by Lord Ninian Crichton-Stuart and he officially opened the new Ninian Park in 1910. Earlier in the season, Cardiff City had been forced to play Middlesbrough at the home of Newport Harlequins.

Cardiff's first professional signing was 'the Bala Bang', a Welsh-speaking printer named Jack Evans. Formerly of Wrexham, Evans had been playing for Cwmparc, near Aberdare. Many of the remaining signings were Scotsmen, known to Wilson's new manager Davy McDougall, from Glasgow Rangers. League Champions Aston Villa opened the new ground officially on 1 September 1910. The new status of the Cardiff club changed the way football was perceived in south Wales and the development of Ninian Park would also serve the Welsh national side.

In March 1911, just six months after the stadium's opening, with the primitive ground still without hot water and the grandstand holding 3,000 people tightly packed on wooden benches, Scotland played the first international at the new venue. Debris from the rubbish tip still rose to the surface whenever the pitch was rolled, and Cardiff City players and staff would scour the grass for glass, coal and metal at 6 a.m. each morning before training. Sadly for

Scottish left-half Peter McWilliam, they missed a piece on the morning of the Scotland game, and his knee was gashed so badly he never played again. Meredith also claimed his knees were cut by the rough ground. Life was also uncomfortable for the spectators – in strong winds, fans on the Bob Bank were covered in the ash banked around the ground from the local gasworks. Notwithstanding the conditions, a record 17,000 people turned up to watch the first Ninian Park international, including Lord Ninian Crichton-Stuart. It might have been even more had Cardiff Council not refused an appeal by the FAW for schoolchildren to be given a half-day holiday, asserting that "the committee should not encourage children to go and stand shivering watching others play." Even the *Western Mail* reported the event with something approaching enthusiasm: "All roads led to Ninian Park, Cardiff, and the great boom which has been the marked feature of the soccer code locally this season, mainly through the advent of the Cardiff City club as a professional organisation, was fully exemplified by the large crowds that were making their way towards the spacious enclosure of the Cardiff City club. When the gates opened at 1.30 there were long queues at every one of the many gateways, especially so at the cheap entrance where the queue was four deep and fully a couple of hundred yards long."

During the game, railings collapsed opposite the grandstand and the crowd spilled onto the pitch, stopping play until they calmly returned to the banking. After the match, the Welsh team and officials accepted the Cardiff City Supporters Club's invitation to a 'smoking-concert' at the Royal Hotel, before catching their train at 7.40 p.m. Bolton's Ted Vizard was not among them – he was to be honoured in his home town of Penarth with a celebration to mark his international selection. Vizard received a gold chain and pendant to attach to the watch he had won for good attendance at Cogan School. He went on to become one of the greats of Welsh football, managing Swindon,

QPR and Wolves, where he laid the foundation for Stan Cullis' great side of the 1950s.

After the celebrations, it was too late to deposit the record takings at a bank, and all the money, in silver and coppers, was given to Ted Robbins in a suitcase. Prior to catching the train, Robbins put the bag down on the station platform and went to tend to the players' needs. In a last-minute rush, everybody boarded the carriage. It was only as it was pulling out did Robbins realize the suitcase had been left on the platform. There was nothing for it but to pull the communication chord and hurtle back along the track to where the bag of cash remained.

The 2–2 draw with Scotland in Roose's final appearance meant victory over England a week later would give Wales their second Championship. After holding the English for an hour and with heavy snow, sleet and the wind at their backs, a win and the trophy for Meredith's team was still a possibility. But when England went ahead there was no recovery and the game was lost by three goals to nil. Wales lost four consecutive games after Roose's departure, including all three games of the 1912 season.

The game in the south was now well established and club sides from the industrial areas heavily populated by English migrants were becoming stronger than those in the traditional football heartland of Denbighshire. Cardiff City became the first south Walian side to win the Welsh Cup in 1912 and the *Western Mail* was getting worried: "While it has not come on so fast nor attained the high position that Welsh rugger has, the dribbling game in Wales is steadily on the upgrade, and, with the impetus that is being given in the South, should soon rise and occupy the same proud position in the soccer world as its sister code does in the rugby arena."

Other workers teams who competed in the Southern League included Mardy, Cwm Albion, Treharris, Llanelli, Newport, Swansea, Pontypridd, Mid Rhondda, Ton Pentre and Barry AFC. The latter went on to enjoy a long history as

Barry Town, dominating the League of Wales in the 1990s and enjoying considerable success in Europe, becoming the first Welsh club to win a Champions League tie when they beat FC Shamkir of Azerbaijan in 2000/01. Mid Rhondda, nicknamed the Mushrooms, played at their Tonypandy ground with some success, and in 1919, with ambitions to challenge Cardiff, they signed Jimmy Seed, who went on to play for England despite being gassed during the war. In 1928, with the area in deep economic depression, the club, like many in the area including the once powerful Aberdare side, was forced to disband. But during the 1910s, it was the local derbies that attracted big crowds. Cardiff's largest attendance of that first year was away at Ton Pentre, where 14,000 crammed in to see their local team take on the big city side. Cardiff's biggest home crowd of 1911/12 was an 18,000 attendance at Ninian Park against Pontypridd.

Wales had an opportunity to claim the 1913 Championship when they went into their final game with England at Bristol after a win and draw against Ireland and Scotland. Unfortunately, the waterlogged pitch rendered the game a lottery and Wales succumbed by four goals to three. There were still problems with player availability and Wales had been forced to call upon their 32-year-old trainer George Latham to turn out in Belfast after a three-year absence from the team. It was reported that "poor old George played the full ninety minutes and must have lost pounds in weight." Latham had been a veteran of the Boer War and went on to win a Military Cross during the First World War. He had been a Liverpool squad player, but it was as a coach he really made his mark, becoming a major influence on the Cardiff City successes of the 1920s, and the Welsh national side of the same era. His standing in his home town of Newtown was such that the town's football stadium was named Latham Park in his honour.

With football developing globally, FIFA was finally given a place on the International Football Association Board alongside the home countries in 1913. However, the voting system meant it could not overrule the combined votes of the UK, a system which has helped maintain the UK's position in the game's governance. In the same season, Union Sportive Servannaise received permission to play a friendly against Canton Parish Church. The continent was getting closer – and it would not be long before Wales found new opponents across the sea. Had the war not broken out, it is probable that continental matches would have arrived sooner than 1933, when Wales played in Paris for the first time.

In 1914, with the First World War impending, the FAW took the controversial decision to carry on playing, while other national organisations curtailed their activities. "It would be nothing short of a national disaster if we attempted to interfere with the regular progress of football," wrote FAW President Tom Gough. Competitions however were restricted; the Wales v England Amateur International was cancelled, and the Amateur Cup had to be abandoned due to the number of clubs who had disbanded. At a December 1914 international conference at the offices of the FA in Russell Square, it was decided to recommend that the international matches be abandoned for the season.

In the final tournament before the war, Wales managed a solitary point in Glasgow in a match the *Times* called "the worst match ever played between the two countries," sandwiched between disappointing defeats to Ireland and England. The Championship win of 1907 seemed a long time past and Wales had returned to its dismal form of the early years of the decade. Robbins complained that the English clubs had been "antagonistic" when approached for players, but there were more pressing issues on the horizon. Ireland finally won the trophy for the first time in March 1914, just months before the outbreak of the Great War, which would disrupt football and claim the lives of so many of its participants.

As war raged across Europe, many clubs in Wales

disbanded as players began enlisting. In many instances, entire teams enlisted together. The clubs who remained fought on to fulfill their obligations, but at great financial loss. Many clubs contributed to the war appeal and the FAW donated £200 to the Prince of Wales War Fund. The massive fall in the number of registered professionals saw emergency measures imposed in 1915 when it was agreed to schedule the next FAW election meeting for the first day of August after the war ended, whichever year that may be. Football did continue in Wales throughout the First World War, though on a much reduced scale with many clubs arranging friendlies and small competitions in order to raise funds for the war effort. Footballs were sent out to Welsh players and regiments during those dark days, but the game lost its importance among the horrors being relayed from the trenches of Europe.

4

THREE TITLES
AND AN FA CUP
1919–1929

A S AGREED AT the 1915 meeting following the outbreak of the First World War, the full FAW council gathered once again for an election on the first day of August after the cessation of hostilities. No one could have imagined that day would take four years to arrive. In truth, the FAW did meet during the conflict, notably in 1917, but it would be another two years before the full council came together. The 1919 meeting must have been emotional – it began by listing the football administrators lost in the fighting, including Robert Ellis, chairman of Wrexham, and both the chairman and manager of Llanelli. Tribute was also paid to the players who had fallen. "The Welsh footballer in this great war has upheld our great traditions on the field of battle, as he has done on the field of sport. The records show that among the many honours gained by Welsh footballers are two Victoria Crosses and 17 Distinguished Service Orders." Eight full Welsh internationals are known to have died in the war. Bob Atherton, Bobby Davies, Fred Griffiths, George Griffiths, Bill Jones, Leigh Roose, George Williams and James Williams all perished in action.

One player whose career was curtailed by the hostilities was Walter Otto Davis of Millwall. Born in Mold, Davis had been making a name for himself in London, where his father had become mayor of West Ham. Knee injuries sustained during battle ended his career early, and he died in 1937 when, despite being a strong swimmer, he drowned in Bow Creek. Other Welsh players suffered injuries, including future international Fred Keenor, whose career was threatened by shrapnel in his knee.

A number of players who were unable to resume professional careers after being injured in France were granted special permission to be reinstated as amateurs, and there were many charity games played as the country tried to find its feet. A team of Welsh internationals played a benefit match for the international half-back Jos Jones while Chirk played Manchester United to raise money for a new hospital. During the war, clubs had contributed to a war fund, but when it was discovered that Welsh players were ineligible to benefit from the English scheme, their contributions were refunded.

While Merthyr, Newport and Swansea joined Cardiff in the English Southern League first division in 1919, the Southern League second division was composed entirely of Welsh clubs. These were Aberaman, Abertillery, Barry, Caerphilly, Ebbw Vale, Llanelli, Mid Rhondda, Mardy, Pontypridd, Porth and Ton Pentre. It didn't take long for clubs torn apart by the conflict to recuperate, and in the year after the war 60 clubs entered the Welsh Cup and 62 entered the Amateur Cup.

Ted Robbins travelled around Wales trying to arrange competitive matches and his efforts resulted in the formation of the national leagues. One of the founding members of the Welsh National League (North) was Rhyl FC. Rhyl were founded in 1888, but struggled to maintain a consistent identity like many junior clubs on the north Wales coast. The club reformed, and merged and disbanded while playing in a variety of competitions, including the North Wales Coast League, the Welsh League, the Combination and the Welsh Alliance. After suffering two rejections from the Football League, the club entered the Birmingham and District

League as they searched for a suitable level. After settling in the Cheshire League in 1936, they became one of the most successful Welsh teams in the decade after the Second World War, winning two league titles and the Welsh Cup twice. In the 1990s, the club became one of the strongest participants in the newly-formed League of Wales, and has played in European competition many times.

In an atmosphere of post-war British pride, the FAW joined forces with the English and Scottish associations in refusing to recognize their war enemies, the central powers of Germany, Austria, Hungary and Bulgaria. They even banned clubs from playing teams that still arranged matches against those countries until 1921. The FAW were delighted when the Prince of Wales accepted an invitation to become the Patron of the FAW, and the association adopted the three feathers on their letterheads.

Caught up in the post-war spirit, England agreed to play 'victory' matches against Wales in order to assist the FAW in raising much-needed funds. However the first match, due to be played at Stoke in 1919, was postponed due to a railway strike and rearranged for the week after the teams had been due to meet in the return fixture at Ninian Park. A healthy crowd of 18,000 saw Wales beat England for the first time in 37 years in the friendly international at Cardiff, though the press reports the game "was not one to go into ecstasies about."

English selectors looked upon the match as a trial for the upcoming British Championship and restricted their selection to one player from each club. The visitors struggled to deal with Meredith, who was "easily the best forward on the field," despite now being more than 40 years of age and without a game for months. The winning Welsh side was presented with a souvenir medal, but the match was never given official status, which annoyed Meredith in particular. In the return match at Stoke, England chose a completely different 11 and, with a stronger side, won by two goals to nil.

Wales were grateful for the help in raising funds and the FA was granted permission to represent the FAW at a meeting in Paris on the future of the International Federation. Relations had never been better between the British associations.

Making his international debut in the Cardiff Victory match was a young native of the city named Fred Keenor. Keenor would become an all-time great of Welsh football. While the Cardiff City captain's game was not based on skill, his driving play and inspirational presence emboldened his team-mates, and his commitment to his country was unquestioned. The Roath man loved playing for Wales, and made no secret of his favourite opponents. "I do not mind very much if Scotland or Ireland beat us, but I do love for Wales to slam England," he once said. The famous Evertonian Dixie Dean would confirm Keenor's commitment to the game, complaining that "he would kick his own mother for a couple of bob". Keenor had signed for Cardiff from local parks side Roath Wednesdays in 1912, and had been hit by exploding shrapnel at the Battle of the Somme in World War I. His knee injury was so grave that it was thought he might never play again but thankfully he recovered after six months recuperation in a Dublin hospital, and went on to become one of the leading footballers of the 1920s. According to the *Times* of the day, "Keenor is one of the great centre half-backs of the Century, and without him Cardiff City are only half a side."

You might think domestic football would have been played in a friendlier spirit in the first season after the war, but old hostilities remained. One notorious match between Aberystwyth and Newtown in 1920 developed into a mini riot. According to the *Cambrian News*, "the referee was pelted with pieces of muddy turf, many of which landed on the target while others which went a little stray hit some of the Aberystwyth committee men and policemen escorting the referee off the field. It was a very regrettable affair." There are also reports of teams and officials being hounded out of Aberystwyth after matches. Following one game, the referee was forced to avoid a crowd of hooligans by disguising himself as a vicar and leaving the Central Hotel via a side door. Meanwhile, Llanidloes players were forced to run the gauntlet of a "howling, mud-throwing mob" after their charabanc broke down and they were pursued through the streets only to find hundreds more waiting at their hotel. The FAW threatened to close the Aberystwyth ground.

But Aberystwyth was not the only dangerous place for visiting teams. There was trouble across Wales in the 1920s and police were forced to intervene after Barry supporters threatened Cardiff City reserves in one match. In March 1920, the Llanmynech ground was closed for the remainder of the season due to serious crowd disorder when a referee was attacked, and a game was abandoned due to crowd trouble and a pitch invasion by visiting Rhosymedre fans at Chirk. At the same time Flint were warned about crowd behaviour at home games, while Rhos' ground was closed for a fortnight in 1925 after a referee was "kicked, hit and scratched".

The FAW were so worried about crowd problems that it made special mention of its concerns in its annual report of 1919/20: "It is regrettable that cases of misconduct have been more frequent than previous seasons and undesirable spectators have caused trouble in certain areas." An FAW promise that "such cases will be dealt with firmly on all future occasions" usually meant instructing clubs to put up signs forbidding crowd trouble. They were very big on signs and warning notices.

At the end of the 1919/20 season, the first division of the Southern League moved en bloc to form the new third division of the Football League. While Swansea, Newport and Merthyr stepped into the new division, Cardiff City stole a march on their Welsh rivals and applied directly for admission to the second tier, despite only finishing fourth in the Southern League. Merthyr's application had been successful as there was no competition from rugby in the town and the club could claim support from nearby Aberdare's 50,000 population. It was decided to split the remainder of clubs in the Southern League into English and Welsh sections. Eleven Welsh teams competed for the right to meet their English section winners in a play-off, and though Barry came out on top, it was runners-up Aberdare who were elected to the Football League, along with Charlton. Wrexham became a founder member of Division Three (North) in 1921.

Back on their Feet

The explosion of football in the Cardiff area after the war forced the council to find new pitches for returning servicemen keen to play. There were 64 applications to use 12 available pitches in the city and so public band concerts were curtailed at Roath Park, with the grass given over to football. There was still a shortage of pitches as the 1919/20 season began. Meanwhile, the main Welsh teams were beginning to attract top players as south Wales fed the ever increasing demand for coal in the post-war era, and a large number of footballers from the north-east, Scotland and London transferred to the industrial Welsh clubs where huge populations meant big crowds. Mid Rhondda were particularly well supported, taking 2,000 by train to the 1919 season opener at Aberaman. The *South Wales Football Echo* reported on this surge in interest: "This season's experience has shown that there is room in south Wales for the two codes, but there is surely strong evidence that soccer has now obtained a grip that will enable it to win through."

Amidst football's growing popularity in south Wales, the British Championship recommenced and Wales played their first post-war game in 1920, drawing 2–2 with Ireland. Ivor Jones became Swansea Town's first Welsh international and helped form a four-strong contingent from south Walian clubs for the first time. After gaining an unexpected point in Belfast, the team sailed home via Liverpool on the *Duke of Argyle* steamship. It would be the last time they would face a combined Ireland side, as a new republic would soon be formed. Following requests from the Scots for a midweek date, the Thursday game against Scotland drew a crowd of 16,000 to Ninian Park. Before the match, Cardiff City director Sid Nicholls presented a silver table centrepiece to Billy Meredith, mistakenly believing it to be his 50th cap. After a second draw of the season, Wales went to face England at Highbury, the home of Arsenal, looking for the win that was needed to give them hope of the title.

It was to be a historic day as Wales claimed victory in an official game against their old enemy for the first time since 1882. The win at Highbury had looked unlikely when England took the lead on a wet, muddy pitch in front of 22,000 fans, but the unquenchable spirit of 45-year-old Meredith drove Wales on and goals from Stan Davies and Dick Richards gave them the lead. Meredith knew it would be his last chance to win the title before retiring after an incredible 25 years in the national side, and so did his team. When Rotherham's Welsh full back Harry Millership went off injured before half-time, it seemed "gallant little Wales" would eventually crumble. But not this time; the ten men showed a "grim determination" with the forwards dropping back to cover gaps as the English onslaught continued. When the final whistle blew Wales celebrated a famous victory.

They were now relying on England to beat the Scots in their final match at Hillsborough in Sheffield three weeks later. At half-time, the telegrams reaching Wrexham would have been read despondently as Scotland went in with a 4–2 lead. But during an incredible second half, England scored three goals and Wales were champions. The FAW received letters of congratulation from Scotland and Ireland on their success, and Wales issued a victory medal to each player. These were heady times indeed – football was booming in the south Wales coalfields, and the international side were champions of Britain.

At a meeting of the International Board in 1921, England proposed that all international goalkeepers wear the same colour in order to distinguish them from other players. They bizarrely suggested red, but the board decided on deep yellow to avoid confusion when Wales were playing. Wales began their title defence with a 1–2 defeat in Aberdeen, thanks mainly to the goalkeeping of Ted Peers who kept the score down. Peers had started his career with his hometown club Connah's Quay before joining Wolverhampton Wanderers. He spent a decade either side of the war at Wolves, amassing 12 caps for the national side. But there was no shame in losing to a Scottish side that would win seven of the next ten championships. Wales would take the other three in a barren decade for the English.

Despite the inclusion of Watford's professional boxer, Frank Hoddinott at centre forward, a dull 0–0 draw with a "machine-like" England was played out in Cardiff and Wales returned to Swansea for the first time in 27 years to beat Ireland 2–1. Hopes of a good crowd to fill the much improved Vetch Field for its first international were not helped by the hardships faced by those in south Wales, where the 1921 miners strike sent many into poverty. It is surprising that football still managed to draw the crowds, but for many, the game became an outlet as the economic gloom took hold.

In this climate, the FAW's decision to maintain its lowest entry price at two shillings – twice the cost of attending a club game – drew much criticism. There were also clashes with other fixtures. Newport played Swansea at Uskside the same day, while 30,000 people were at Cardiff's home game against South Shields. In the event, it was hardly surprising that only 11,873 supporters saw Wales' 2–1 win, though there were 14,000 at the Vetch a few days later for the visit of Newport.

So why were club attendances much larger than those for international games? The 1921 strike caused great misery in the coalfields and many clubs allowed free entry for spectators. "The immediate future of football in these isles passes into an inscrutable darkness," wrote the *Western Mail*.

Football in the south was a miner's sport, but despite the hardships, it was an optimistic year for the game. Cardiff City's promotion to the first division caught the public imagination, while Aberdare and Wrexham both gained admission to the English Football League. Around 50,000 fans turned up for Cardiff's first game in Division One and the club's success helped raise enthusiasm for the game throughout Wales. When the famous *Athletic News* visited Aberystwyth to report on ground improvements, they noted the hunger for football in the area, remarking that "Cardiff City seems to have set the heather on fire."

The growth of south Wales football was so rapid that by 1922, concerns were being raised about the unsustainable salaries being paid to the hundreds of professional players. The FAW issued a stark warning: "There can only be one result when fancy salaries are offered to unknown players – Bankruptcy." The season was considered financially disastrous for the FAW, chiefly due to the heavy snowstorm which decimated the gate for the Scotland game. The national team was also suffering by comparison to the huge success of Cardiff City. While 40,000 crammed into Ninian Park for a Wednesday afternoon match against Southampton, fewer than 10,000 saw Wales beat Scotland at the mainly uncovered Wrexham ground the following Saturday. The match went ahead in four inches of snow with conditions "just about as bad as they could be for football."

One of the goals in Wales' 2–1 win over Scotland was scored by Cardiff City's Len Davies, who would win 23 caps. Davies would become notorious for missing the penalty against Birmingham in 1924 which could have won Cardiff the league title in a season when they sacrificed their own hopes to provide players for the national side. He would later become player-manager at Bangor City where he devoted much of his leisure time to rabbit shooting. Another Davies goal earned a point for Wales at Belfast in the final game of 1922 after the team, based in Newcastle, County Down, had been treated to a motor tour of the Silent Valley. Davies had beaten three defenders in a mazy dribble before lobbing the Irish keeper. It was a goal "which only Davies could have scored," said the *Western Mail*. But there was little time for celebration – after sailing overnight, Davies joined Wales' three other Cardiff City players on an early morning train to Edinburgh for a Monday game against Hearts.

The hunger for football throughout the 1920s was not restricted to the big professional clubs and the international team. People watched games at all levels in huge numbers. Around 12,000 spectators turned up at Cardiff Arms Park in March 1922 to watch England Ladies play France in a match refereed by Cardiff City captain Charlie Brittan and 10,000 fans saw a Welsh Schoolboys international against England at the Vetch. Meanwhile, an amateur international drew a crowd of 5,000 to Llandudno in 1924. The exploding population of working class men flooding into the country needed to be entertained, and football was their favourite outlet. Teams were created by businesses keen to occupy their employees in their spare time, and some became respected clubs, competing at a high level. In 1923 the FAW reported with pleasure "the interest large firms are taking in the outdoor life of their employees. Football is being fostered by these firms in no mistakable manner and such is proved by the appearance in the (FAW Trophy) semi-finals of two well-known firms such as Lovell's and Courtaulds." Lovell's Athletic was the works team of a sweet factory in Newport, which achieved notable success during its existence between 1918 and 1969, winning the Welsh League six times and beating Shrewsbury to claim the Welsh Cup in 1948.

By 1922/23, there were six Welsh clubs playing in the Football League: Cardiff, Swansea, Wrexham, Newport, Aberdare and Merthyr. The growth of professional football in Wales helped the national side. "The Welshmen have always laboured under the handicap of being indebted to English clubs for the services of their players," wrote the *Times*, "but that handicap is being reduced as the code grows in the Principality." As envious north Wales clubs gazed upon the successes of their southern counterparts in the early 1920s, they proposed an amalgamation of the South and North Welsh Leagues to create a national competition. But the request was rejected by southern clubs keen to maintain the status quo. Meanwhile, the North Wales Coast FA asked the FAW to lobby the authorities and obtain an exemption from the punitive entertainment tax on admission to football matches. It is not recorded whether the Coast FA cited the absence of entertainment from their games as evidence in their defence.

There was a deeper north-south split across the Irish Sea. After the civil war in Ireland and the resulting division of the country, a meeting was convened by the IFAB (International Board), inviting representatives of the (Northern) Irish FA and the newly-formed Free State Association. IFAB's loyalties were closely tied to their long-standing friends in Belfast, and Free State's application to join the International Board was rejected, despite its immediate acceptance by FIFA. While Wales did consider an invitation for a match against the Irish Free State team, they had already agreed to play (Northern) Ireland and so politely declined, as they would do again in 1927. The Welsh welcome to its republican neighbour was less than warm, and with the best Free State players continuing to play for the existing Ireland team until 1950, there seemed little point in adding a fixture against the south. The Welsh League (southern division) welcomed the chance to send a representative team to Dublin however, and drew 3–3 with the Irish Free State at Bohemians on 9 February 1924, in the first of several annual matches.

Conceding to public pressure in times of hardship, the FAW finally reduced admission prices to a shilling for the visit of England to Ninian Park, and the impoverished crowd saw Ivor Jones equalize for Wales with the last kick of the match. England, as usual, were based at the Esplanade Hotel in Penarth, their favourite choice for Cardiff internationals. Jones was one of five brothers who played football professionally. His brother Bryn was a fellow international and his son Cliff would play with distinction at the 1958 World Cup. The rest of the season was a disappointment to an expectant public hoping Wales would continue to progress after their 1920 triumph. Missing five players, Wales lost 0–2 in Scotland before a team including three Cardiff players lost to Ireland at the Racecourse by three first-half goals. The FAW were not reticent in showing their feelings about the Wrexham game which left Wales rooted to the bottom of the table: "A disastrous defeat by practically a new Irish international side must convince the selectors that a new infusion of blood is required."

Cardiff's sacrifice earns a Triple Crown

Following stinging FAW criticism, the Welsh team for the 1924 season contained three new players. Oldham's six-foot-three goalkeeper Albert Gray took over in goal, while Brighton's John Jenkins came in at full back and Swansea's Willie Davis also made his debut. Davies went on to play for Cardiff in the 1925 FA Cup final, but was missing in 1927 when a bout of pleurisy saw him confined to a sanitarium. Between 1922 and 1929 Cardiff City provided at least two players to the Welsh team for every game, and usually more. Occasionally, the release of players for international duty affected the Bluebirds in their quest for trophies, and never more so than in 1924, when they lost the Football League title by the narrowest of margins.

When Cardiff faced Tottenham Hotspur on 16 February 1924, they were three points clear at the top of Division One with a game in hand over Sunderland. On the same day they allowed four players to appear in the Wales against Scotland fixture at Ninian Park. Cardiff City, without Blair of Scotland, and Keenor, Evans and Davies of Wales, managed just a draw. They would lose the title by a goal average of 0.024 goals – still the closest finish in English football history. If today's goal difference or goals scored rules applied, Cardiff would have won, and if they had not released their international stars, the English Championship would surely have been theirs.

Despite a poor season in 1923, respect for Wales was now high enough that Scotland chose their strongest 11 and still lost 0–2, with Cardiff City's Blair and Keenor captaining their respective sides. According to the *Western Mail* "the fact that a record crowd of well over 25,000 witnessed the match is conclusive evidence of the tremendous grip association football has now on the people of Wales." But recent club games in Cardiff had attracted crowds of between 35,000 and 50,000 and successful club football still appeared a bigger attraction for the fans.

A Welsh team inspired by the "positively brilliant" Keenor and including the amateur debutant Jack Nicholls of Newport County took the spoils in the Championship's next game at Blackburn in what the *Times* called "a triumph for Welsh tenacity" when they came from behind to beat England 2–1. Nicholls was the nephew of legendary rugby player Gwyn, and there were unproven accusations that his surprising selection may have been influenced by his father Syd, a Cardiff City director and FAW Vice-President. Wales sailed to Belfast in March knowing a draw would give them the title while a win would see their first ever triple crown. Despite the Tottenham setback, Cardiff again released their three Welsh players plus Ireland's Farquharson from their own crucial game against Notts County. In Ireland, a Moses Russell penalty was enough to give Wales victory – the first time Wales had won all three games, and doing so with no more than a dozen players throughout. Meanwhile, Cardiff's home defeat probably cost them the championship. Cardiff's decision to sacrifice their own glory for the international cause was recognized at an official dinner following Wales' meeting with Ireland in Cardiff in 1927 when the club was honoured by both associations. "Cardiff City did not measure their ambitions in the game by the trophies to be won," announced Charles Watson of the Irish FA. "It was not so long ago that the City lost the league championship for the sake of Ireland and Wales."

Just 12 months on from their harsh criticisms of the 1923 team, the FAW were gushing in their praise for their new champions and hinted at Cardiff's sacrifice in their report: "Twelve stalwart players have created a record for Wales by winning the International Championship without forfeiting a single point and with only one goal scored against them. Your council wish to thank the players for the splendid services they rendered in all the games, and also the clubs who so readily and kindly released the players often at great sacrifice."

One of the reasons for the Welsh success in 1924 was that Ted Robbins and his committee had been able to select their strongest side for all three matches. But things returned to normal for the opening game of the 1925 Championship when half-a-dozen players withdrew from the trip to Scotland in February. The selection of northern replacements baffled reporters from south Wales. "Perhaps when the Southern councillors arrive in the North the position will be re-considered," they hoped. And it appears their hopes were met. The FAW may have shown gratitude for Cardiff's sacrifices with speeches and proclamations, but their demands on the club did not slacken in 1925. The Bluebirds' Scottish manager, Fred Stewart, was sitting in the manager's office at Ninian Park, preparing for the next club game when an urgent FAW telegraph arrived from Edinburgh: 'Six players ill. Send Keenor and Beadles.' Stewart was furious. He had already lost Len Davies, Willie Davis and Jack Nicholls to the Welsh team, as well as Nelson to the Scots. He composed a letter of complaint: "Whilst recognising the compliment paid to the city team by the selection committee of the Welsh Football Association, one cannot help deploring the paucity of talent which compels the selectors to take so many of the city team to represent the principality." Stewart had some backing in the press. "The WFA have the right to claim as many players as they choose, though we shall be surprised if the present excessive demand may not bring the matter to a head, as by their action the WFA has seriously jeopardised the position of Cardiff City now and in the future."

Nonetheless, Stewart released his players, and a weakened Cardiff City could only draw one-all at home to Notts County while Wales, including five of his team, were being easily beaten 3–1 in Scotland. To make matters worse, Len Davies was carried off injured during the Wales game. One of the Welsh replacements, Harry Beadles, had served on the front line in Gallipoli and Palestine during the war as a 16-year-old, earning a Gold Medal for saving a Serbian officer.

While Wales faced England at the Vetch for the first time in 1925, Cardiff faced Newcastle with a reserve side, missing seven players to internationals as well as the injured Len Davies, but still managed to win 3–0. This was the first time England had agreed to travel to Wales on a Saturday after years of pleading from the FAW. For this weekend fixture, the Welsh team contained nine players from Welsh clubs. With Davies injured, Wales turned to Swansea's Fowler for the game at his home ground and their hero set up Keenor for the Welsh goal in a 1–2 defeat on a waterlogged field. The final fixture against Ireland turned out to be a disastrous day for the FAW, as torrential rain saw a crowd of just 8,000 pay 2s each, double the price of usual admission to the Raceourse. Reliant on the income from international games, the FAW were treading a fine line between maximizing income and alienating fans. Wrexham had beaten off a proposal from a cash-strapped FAW to move the game to Liverpool or

Manchester, arguing successfully that "the sole purpose of the Welsh Football Association is to foster Welsh football, and what encouragement does it give Welsh clubs, if whenever there is a plum, it is taken somewhere else?"

The first Wembley final

The Cardiff club was at the peak of its powers, and became the first Welsh side to reach the FA Cup final in 1925. It seems astonishing now that, just a week before their Wembley appearance, Cardiff City would release three Wales players for a scoreless draw against Ireland to decide the bottom two places in the British Championship. The FAW had offered to rest Cardiff's players ahead of such an important game, but Stewart was unworried, answering that the club's directors "very much appreciate your kindness in offering to release them in view of the Cup Final. We do not however, think the match will give them any harm, and we have pleasure in giving them permission to play." Cardiff's opponents Sheffield United were more careful, and withdrew the Irish captain, Gillespie from the game as he was "suffering with a chill". Cardiff might have considered themselves fortunate to be competing in the FA Cup at all. In 1922, there had been attempts to ban Welsh clubs from entering, but instead a compromise was reached, limiting Welsh entries to 14, with the FA reserving the right to select which teams would enter. When Cardiff City reached the final, there is no doubt they represented the whole country in the mind of Welsh football fans, and they were backed by supporters from across the nation.

Cardiff, the first non-English team to reach the FA Cup final since Queen's Park in 1885, faced Sheffield United with four Welshmen in the side, while Len Davies was unlucky to be left out. "Tomorrow will be the greatest day that sporting Wales has ever known," trumpeted the *Western Mail*, while the *Times* commented on the travelling Welsh support: "It was an invasion such as which had not been witnessed in the

South since the days of primitive warfare a thousand years ago, for not only did 11 blue jerseys come over the border, but all their admirers followed them over too. Thousands of enthusiasts carried leeks with them throughout the day, and, to the uninitiated Sassenach, these looked very formidable indeed."

The *Western Mail* chartered two trains for what it snappily called "the greatest event of footballing history in connection with Wales" and there was support from all over the country. Newtown applied for 700 tickets alone. While 25,000 Cardiff supporters arrived by train, only 10,000 of them had travelled from Cardiff. A specially chartered train from Swansea confirmed the western press' assertion that "Swansea's soccer fraternity are undoubtedly all behind the City today."

Around this time football fans began to sing at games. The influx of working men had seen the creation of male voice choirs in mining towns as chapel congregations joined together to sing for pleasure, and then took their singing to rugby and football games. Swansea supporters regularly sang 'I'm Forever Blowing Bubbles' during the 1921 season, and it is said West Ham took on the song after three FA Cup ties against the Swans in January 1922. Much of the Welsh following at Wembley in 1925 had experienced the singing at club games, and during half-time when the band played 'Hen Wlad Fy Nhadau', the *Times* reported that "the great gathering stood up bare-headed and joined impressively in the singing. It was a thrilling episode emphasising the, to Wales, national character of the event."

Film of that Cup final was to be delivered to Cardiff post-haste by aeroplane. There was a backup plan if the plane was unable to land at Ely Racecourse. "The film will be tied up carefully in a sack and dropped out of the aeroplane attached to a parachute bearing the words 'Official Cup Final Film'. Whoever picks this up and delivers the package to the cinema to which it is addressed will receive a reward and also a free pass to view the screening of the film." Sadly, cinema viewers would see Cardiff lose, but the Bluebirds would return within a couple of years for another attempt at taking the Cup out of England.

Swansea also won promotion to the second division in 1925, and after 5,000 Jacks had travelled to Plymouth for a vital game, a crowd of 25,000 packed into the Vetch for the deciding win over Exeter. Flushed with success, the winners' medals and trophies were proudly displayed in a High Street shop window, only to be stolen in a smash-and-grab raid. Swansea went on to reach the FA Cup semi-final in 1926, losing to Bolton in a disappointing end to the season.

Welsh club football was close to its historic peak, as Cardiff and Swansea enjoyed success, the national team was doing well, and the professional clubs in the Valleys looked set to challenge for a future in the Football League. Industrial depression still affected Wales and clubs were instructed that "fancy wages should be cut down," but against a background of poverty, professionalism increased.

Another report in the London *Times* confirms that rugby had all but capitulated under pressure from the association game: "Oddly enough the association menace is far more pronounced in west Wales than in the area entertained by Cardiff City, who would have had a most unprosperous season but for its players' notable triumph in the FA Cup competition. In Swansea there was such a loss of interest in rugby that a Swansea v Cardiff match that in the old days would have attracted over 20,000 people and engaged at least a quarter of a million in preliminary and retrospective argument for at least a fortnight, passed almost unnoticed. The spectacle of only a sprinkling of silent ghosts on the famous bank is said to have sent a cold shiver down the backs of the few hundred of loyalists in the splendid new grand stand opposite. The crowds of 20,000 are now to be found on the once despised Vetch Field where The Swans perform."

The game may have been growing exponentially, but its popularity was not shared by everybody, including one irate newspaper correspondent who complained about fan behaviour at Cardiff in 1925: "We shall see crowds from all directions making their way to Ninian Park to hoot and brawl like a lot of wild savages. Not only is football the danger; as soon as a match is finished a great number of football supporters make headway for a public house to disgrace themselves and the country they live in."

The game was growing on the continent too, and requests began to arrive from new international sides looking to test themselves against the established British teams. The FAW were invited to Scandinavia to face Sweden, and club sides Gothenburg and Stockholm. A South African invitation for the UK associations to form a touring Great Britain team was turned down and an invitation from the Spanish FA for Wales to play in Spain in 1927 was not entertained, nor again in 1929. The clubs were not so insular, however and in 1923 Swansea began annual tours to Denmark, and Cardiff toured Europe in 1924.

Under threat from football's popularity, and the emergence of rugby league sides in its heartland, rugby union could no longer rest on its laurels and the WRU introduced its own law to make the game more attractive. One reporter called it "a desperate attempt to keep the game of amateur rugby attractive to watch, and so to hold at bay the invasion of those curious allies, Northern Union rugby and professional Association Football. It is regrettable that the rules of a great game should be altered largely on the basis of popularity; but the fact remains that the modern Welsh spectator, if he cannot get an open game of rugby, has shown every sign of turning to an open game of Association."

For the first game of the 1925/26 Championship at home to Scotland, the FAW found themselves short of players once again, and the unruffled Robbins, used to such emergencies, was forced to apprehend the uncapped Jack Lewis as he waited on a Newport platform for a train to Birmingham where he was due to play for Cardiff. When Bolton Wanderers again withdrew Jennings and Vizard, Robbins made a special visit to Burnden Park and after using his persuasive charm, returned with the services of Vizard assured. This was a typical event for the jovial secretary, who spent much of his time persuading clubs to release their players.

His weakened Wales team was further handicapped by the loss of talismanic captain Keenor, who left the field with a dislocated knee after just two minutes. It was no surprise that the game was lost 0–3. In the Welsh goal Bert Gray proved himself a worthy successor to Roose and Peers. "His anticipation was wonderful, and time after time he swooped down on balls which seemed to be beating him… There may be differences of opinion as to who is the best custodian in the game, but there is certainly no question as to who is the greatest Welshman in the position," wrote the *Western Mail*.

Wales, minus six absentees, travelled to Windsor Park, Belfast, where Ireland won comfortably even after the loss of a player to injury. After two such comprehensive defeats it was a shock when Wales went to Crystal Palace's new stadium, Selhurst Park on St David's Day 1926 and beat England by three goals to one, despite the usual late panic to find a team. Plymouth's Jack Pullen had been travelling to London on a social trip with his Welsh international clubmate Moses Russell when the message came through that Wales were a man short. Russell persuaded Monmouthshire-born Pullen to step in and earn his only Welsh cap, alongside debutant Charlie Jones of Nottingham Forest, who was inspirational in the Welsh victory.

The FA Cup comes to Wales

If 1905 was the year rugby became engrained in south Wales' culture, then 1927 was the year football earned its place in the public consciousness. Cardiff City's FA Cup final win against Arsenal on 23 April 1927 was a cause for national celebration – the Bluebirds didn't just win the cup for Cardiff, they won it for Wales. And this was a country that needed some relief as unemployment rose to 23 per cent. The Cardiff support at Wembley came from all over the country. There were 1,700 from Swansea and stations further west who travelled on overnight trains, arriving in the early London morning adorned with the leeks that so bewildered the Londoners. The game was followed in north Wales too – a loudspeaker was erected at the Racecourse where 2,000 Wrexham fans listened to commentary of the final while their team lost to Barrow. Cardiffians travelled on organized train excursions, although some decided to drive. Tragically, a fan from Albany Road was killed when his vehicle collided with a London tram.

The *Western Mail* described the carnival atmosphere created by the travelling support: "All through the Friday night and the early hours of Saturday morning, the streets of London were musical with Welsh hymns and songs. The leek and the daffodil were almost as abundant, worn as favours in the City colours. It was not merely a Cardiff City occasion. It was a Wales occasion."

There was a special flavour to the atmosphere inside the stadium too. The *Swansea Daily Post* was unimpressed by the acoustics of Wembley, but was pleased that the Welsh tradition of public singing was catching on in England. "The community singing also suffers from the distance over which the mass of singers are dispersed. It needs concentration in a more limited area to tell. At long last, English football crowds look like borrowing permanently an old Welsh football custom that was once the unique possession of Wales."

After a tight opening, the game turned on an error by Arsenal's Welsh international goalkeeper Dan Lewis. "I am surely the most disappointed man in the world," the Maerdy man would say. His mistake was enough to let Hughie Ferguson win the Cup for Cardiff. Watching the game was former Prime Minister David Lloyd George who celebrated wildly by waving his hat "with all the uncontrollable ecstasy of a schoolboy". According to one witness he shouted: "Good Old Cardiff. Da Iawn! Ardderchog!"

While Cardiff's success was celebrated on front pages across Wales, the authenticity of the club's success was questioned by the traditional rugby media of the *South Wales Daily Post*: "The interest in and enthusiasm aroused over the victory of Cardiff City are to be justified rationally on the ground that this was the second occasion on which an ostensibly Welsh team had reached the final of one of the great competitions of sport. Otherwise there is a vast deal of make believe about the whole business, for a team of professionals, recruited from all quarters of the Kingdom cannot command the same genuine following as the home bred player, which amateur Rugby alone provides."

There was even an outrageously racist item in the Swansea press mocking Cardiff's win:

PROMINENT CARDIFFIANS' VIEW OF WEMBLEY

Mr Pook Wing Chang: "Velly good! Chinkee mamee plentee glad."

Ibraham Abdullah: "Salam bazaar! Allah Marshallah Inshallah Wallalah: Tried to knife our representative."

Gomez de Gonsalvez: "Carambo! Chili con carne tamales fandango!"

Lazarus Feinmessir Shystersky: "Oy! Vat a pithneth! Fife shillin' I vill advance on der Gup!"

Racial riots in Bute-street prevented further interviews.

There was more racist resentment from rugby supporters too, complaining of the scarcity of Welshmen in the Cardiff side. One correspondent to the *Western Mail* considered the future members of the cosmopolitan Cardiff team: "From South Africa it may import a huge long-limbed Zulu whose arms span halfway between the posts for goal."

Long before Sam Hammam published his uninformed vision of Cardiff City as the team to unite the whole country, the Bluebirds made less conspicuous, but more genuine efforts to garner support in other areas. On the Friday after winning the Cup, Keenor's team received a civic reception at Merthyr where they were beaten in a friendly played in front of 8,000 people at Penydarren Park. Another civic reception was held in Wrexham. They also visited Newtown, the home town of trainer George Latham, where City would play an annual charity game, and the FA Cup trophy was displayed in Aberystwyth when Cardiff played a friendly on Boxing Day 1927.

Following their Cup triumph, City had a scarcely credible schedule of games. They faced Birmingham at St Andrews on Wednesday, Barry in the Welsh Cup on Thursday, Merthyr on Friday and Everton at home on the Saturday. After travelling north on Sunday, they beat Wrexham on Monday and then won the Welsh Cup by beating Rhyl on Thursday. The FAW made an official statement congratulating the team: "We wish to place on record the delight of all lovers of the game in the Principality at our Premier Club bringing to Wales the English Cup for the first time in History." At the request of Cardiff City, the English FA donated £73 from the gate of the Charity Shield match between Cardiff and Corinthians to the FAW Benevolent Fund.

After defeat to Scotland in the 1927 Championship, supporters had to be removed from the roof of the Racecourse grandstand where they had clambered for a view of Wales' exciting 3–3 draw with England, in front of a record 16,000 attendance. With a flu epidemic running through the squad, Wales were still without a full team late on Friday evening before the game, owing to several late withdrawals. The *Western Mail* even questioned whether it was worth continuing with international games after Bolton refused to release Vizard, but allowed Seddon to play for England. Wales included six new caps, including Everton's Tommy Griffiths, who would be facing club-mate Dixie Dean just a week after making his club debut. This was a thrilling game which swung both ways, and evidently the Welsh team made up in enthusiasm any deficiency in technique. Both sides hit the bar as they went in search of the winner. According to the *Times*, "The game was remarkable for the dash and the untiring energy that the Welshmen put into all their play. Taken as individuals they were, perhaps, slightly inferior to their opponents, but their greater quickness in going for the ball neutralised their individual shortcomings to a great extent." England goalscorer Walker was concussed during the game and remained blissfully unaware of the result until Sunday.

Two goals from Sheffield Wednesday's David Rees Williams earned a 2–2 draw with Ireland in Cardiff. Williams was one of four Merthyr men in the Welsh line-up, in addition to Charlie Jones, Dai 'Gethin' Evans and Dai S Nicholas. With such a strong local representation, 24 Merthyr choirboys were taken by the local vicar to see their heroes play. "They idolise Merthyr footballers who have kicked themselves into big league fame," said Rev. E R Davies. Williams, once seen as the successor to Billy Meredith, committed suicide in 1963.

Another Welsh Title Win

Despite recent poor performances, Wales were boosted by the success of Cardiff, and were confident that club performances would be transferred to the national side. Dewi Lewis, a journalist better known as 'Citizen' in the *Western Mail* looked forward to the 1927/28 British Championship campaign ahead of Scotland's visit to the Racecourse: "There is nothing, I think so thrilling as to see a Welsh international side in action. They are wonderful fighters who seem to have an uncanny knack of rising to the big occasion."

The season began against Scotland in October. Finding themselves two down at half-time against a clever Scottish side, the Welsh rallied in front of 15,000 fans, eventually forcing an equalising own goal after Cardiff City's young FA Cup hero Ernie Curtis had got them back into the game on his debut. Curtis would have won many more caps, but a move to Birmingham saw his international career curtailed, and he played just once for his country in five years at the Midlands club, who were loath to release him. After his career ended, Curtis would suffer four years as a Japanese prisoner of war, and survived by teaching his captors to play football with a paper ball in return for food. In later life, the longest surviving member of Cardiff's 1927 Cup-winning side was forced to sell his medals and international caps to make ends meet.

Wales outclassed England in a 2–1 win at Burnley in November 1927, and a victory over Ireland in Belfast in February would ensure only the Scots could reach the same number of points. Both Wales and Ireland were severely weakened due to important fixtures being played in England, and Cardiff City once again sacrificed their own championship hopes by releasing five players despite the club facing Newcastle in a crucial league fixture. Wales were the better side in a tense contest against the Irish, and with the score at 1–1 with ten minutes left, Swansea's Wilf Lewis charged both the goalkeeper and the ball into the net to win the match. Wales may have been assisted by sacred forces; the Welsh outside-left that day was the Rev. Hywel Davies, rector of Denbigh.

But there would be no party for the rector as the spread of Championship fixtures meant Wales had to put the champagne on ice in anticipation of a title success. When Ireland later beat Scotland at Firhill three weeks later, Robbins and his team could celebrate the Championship outright. "The season's results provide a monument to pluck and perseverance from which all those who find football an uphill game can derive encouragement," wrote the FAW. Wales were heralded as "the most workmanlike team in the national tournament," and according to 'Citizen', "the wonderful progress of Association Football in Wales... has been the envy of the rest of the football world."

In 1928 Wales, along with the other United Kingdom

associations, resigned from FIFA in protest at their insistence on expenses payments for players who competed at the Olympics. The UK believed that there was still a place for the amateur game, and that the Olympics should remain untainted by professionalism. The resignation letter included a snide poke at the international association: "The great majority of the associations affiliated with FIFA are of comparatively recent formation, and as a consequence cannot have the knowledge that only experience can bring."

Scotland's Hughie Gallacher put a makeshift Welsh side to the sword in Glasgow with the first of his two Championship hat-tricks that season in a 4–2 win. Keenor had injured his neck and was heavily bound in strapping, with a doctor's ban on heading the ball. "I gave my consent knowing full well that I could not keep my word, but I was in agony throughout," he admitted. Wales lost 2–3 to England at the Vetch and the FAW were again left to bemoan being denied their best players. "After all, national sentiment is stronger than club sentiment," they complained, while reminding clubs "these matches were played before the league existed." The *Western Mail* went as far as to suggest that "there appears to be a kind of conspiracy afoot."

Swansea-born Willie Davis scored both Wales' goals at Ibrox, but Huddersfield refused to release him to appear at the Vetch, despite Cardiff releasing their players. The Bluebirds were battling relegation yet the FAW still called Keenor, Davies and Warren for the international wooden spoon decider. In a disastrous series of events, Keenor was carried off with a burst blood vessel during the 2–2 draw while Cardiff lost 1–4 to relegation rivals Bury and were relegated.

An invitation from Canada was favourably received by the FAW at the end of the 1929 season, and 20 players were selected to make the tour, remaining unbeaten in their 15 games against club and district sides. The party set off by boat, and Keenor said of the journey: "Our first two days at sea were like a nightmare and most of us spent the time in our bunks wishing that the ship would go down." The Welsh party covered 13,000 miles and was regally welcomed wherever they went, though there was disappointment in Regina, where the local Welsh community had hoped to hear at least one of the team speak their native tongue. The football was undemanding, and Len Davies claimed seven out of the eight goals scored when Wales beat Lower Mainland, Victoria. In one nasty incident, out of character with the rest of the tour, Moses Russell was threatened with a gun during a pitch invasion. Russell was famed for his baldness which developed from an early age after a bout of rheumatic fever, and he was a great favourite in the Welsh team. "Wales owes much to this lion-hearted defender, who is worth a great deal to any side," wrote the *Western Mail*. Simon Shakeshaft, the foremost authority on Wales' football kits, believes the tour saw the first use of numbers on the back of Welsh match shirts.

The south Wales public was warned they could lose future international games to other parts ahead of the 1929 match against Scotland. "So disappointing has been the support given to international soccer in Wales that the parents body have seriously considered the advisability of transferring the venue of all home matches to Liverpool," wrote the *Western Mail*. Swansea and Cardiff clubs could attract larger crowds than the national side, in stark contrast to rugby where international attendances dwarfed those of the clubs. "The best rugby club sides in South Wales would cover themselves in clover if they averaged 5,000 per home match," said the newspaper. Wrexham's biggest gate for a Wales international had been 16,840 in 1927, but three years later the club would draw 22,735 for the visit of Bradford.

Thankfully, the threat of playing in Liverpool was never realized as 30,000 people witnessed a masterful display from the talented Scottish front line as Wales went down by four goals to two. Despite the large crowd, this was to be the last international allocated to Cardiff for four years. Wales then suffered a humiliating 0–6 defeat at Stamford Bridge. One writer claimed the Welsh side to be the poorest he had ever seen. He may have changed his mind had he seen them lose 0–7 in Belfast in their next game. However, the match was "sapped of all interest" by withdrawals and described as "an utter farce" by the local press. Bambrick scored six for an Irish team containing eight Irish League players. Making his only appearance in goal for Wales was Dick Finnegan, a gypsy rumoured to have been discovered by Wrexham while performing in a circus.

The final seasons of the 1920s saw the economic depression reflected in the performance of Wales' professional clubs. Cardiff were a long way from the heights of 1927 and Aberdare, Newport and Merthyr were all forced to apply for re-election after finishing at the foot of the third division. Swansea meanwhile had fought relegation from the second. By 1931, south Wales had lost three of its five Football League clubs.

During their final campaign of an exciting decade for the game, the national side conceded seventeen goals in just three games. As the south Wales boom ended, Welsh football was in freefall. It was no wonder Robbins was in a dreadful mood when he wrote the FAW report for 1929–30. This was the "bleakest report for the past quarter century," he warned. "The season just ended has been anything but fortunate for the Association and in no department has there been any real sunshine." Wales sank deeper and deeper into the gloom. Spectators were unable to afford admission and smaller clubs closed down. Robbins wrote that the "International tourney had been severe and unkind." There were, he said, "no laurels to speak of."

5

FROM UNKNOWNS TO CHAMPIONS
1930–1939

A FTER SUCH A difficult time in the latter years of the 1920s, Ted Robbins was pleased to welcome in a new era. The final year of the decade had been one of the worst in the history of Welsh football and the FAW had no choice but to look to the future. "It has been a bleak and troublesome season and such being the case we prefer to draw the curtain on the past and start afresh with the cheery news that we believe the future will be brighter."

Robbins' optimism would be justified after a tough start and it could be argued that the 1930s were the glory years for the Welsh national side, which may be surprising considering the economic hardship facing the country. In 1930, with the community suffering huge job losses, Merthyr Town finally lost their Football League place, disbanding completely in 1934. Wales' capital city club had also hit rock bottom. Cardiff's Cup-winning side was a thing of the past and the club would finish at the foot of the entire league in 1934. Cardiff's fall from grace was such that in 1932, the city's other sports clubs arranged a charity event to provide funding for the Bluebirds. Whereas Cardiff had been such a fruitful source of international players during the previous decade, Les Jones's appearance in Paris in 1933 was the club's only representation for an official game between 1932 and 1944. Just seven years after their FA Cup triumph, Cardiff faced Aldershot in front of 2,660, without a single spectator on Bob Bank. Perversely, Wales seemed to improve without Cardiff's help. Three British titles were won outright between 1932 and 1937. The 1930s record is one of Wales' best, but at the start of the decade it seemed international football had little future in Wales.

The FAW were stunned by a 1930 Football League ruling prohibiting clubs from releasing Welsh players for internationals scheduled the same day as league fixtures. Clubs could not allow Welsh players to play for their country, even if they wanted to. The ruling was intended to force international teams to switch fixtures to midweek afternoons. In previous years, at least Robbins had been able to rely on the top Welsh clubs for players, but with Cardiff in freefall, Swansea became the top Welsh side, despite perpetually struggling in the lower half of Division Two.

The new rule was disastrous for Wales, who relied on the income from international games. The FAW wrote to their English counterparts, claiming their long history "entitles the weakest of the four countries to kinder treatment than that meted out by the Football League." Robbins also made a plaintive appeal on behalf of the other UK associations: "We rightly claim with the others a sporting chance to carry on our legislative duties with the only income at our command – An International Gate." Even the English press criticized the decision: "International matches are one of the few truly sporting events in professional football today and to relegate them to an inferior place is to do much harm to the game. In all the other countries but England they are regarded as of the highest importance and attract wider interest and enthusiasm than the ordinary league games in which players rarely have a local connexion."

The Unknowns

This sorry state led to a depleted Welsh team travelling to Scotland in 1930 as whipping boys, returning famously as 'The Unknowns'. The Wales team at Ibrox contained three amateurs, four players from non-league clubs and nine debutants. Bookmakers were offering Wales a five-goal start. The side deserves naming: Evans (Cardiff City), Dewie (Cardiff Corries), Crompton (Wrexham), Rogers (Wrexham), Keenor (Cardiff City), Ellis (Nunhead), Collins (Llanelli), Neal (Colwyn Bay), Bamford (Wrexham), Robbins (Cardiff City), Thomas (Newport County).

The players came from clubs with a mixed pedigree. Nunhead were an amateur London side; Swansea Town and Cardiff City were rooted to the bottom of the second division while Wrexham and Newport were both in the lower leagues. Wrexham's half-back Billy Rogers would die five years later of tuberculosis, aged thirty. Fred Dewie's Welsh League team Cardiff Corries were formed in 1898, a year before the better known Cardiff City club, and even turned professional for a few seasons in the early 1920s. In 1921 the Corries played a series of friendlies against Barcelona, losing 4–0, 2–1 and 2–1. The club still exists and now plays at Radyr Cricket Club.

From the north, John Neal represented Colwyn Bay. Bay had been formed in 1881 and played in the North Wales Coast League until the 1920s, when they tried their luck in Cheshire and Birmingham Leagues before returning to the Welsh League (North) in 1937. In 1984, the club moved to Llanelian Road, which coincided with their admittance to the North West Counties League in England, gaining promotion to the Northern Premier League first division in 1991. After Bay had spent just one season in the league, the FAW announced its intention to form a national League of Wales, and a disgruntled Colwyn Bay was forced into exile at Northwich and Ellesmere Port while fighting their case in court, returning to Wales in 1995. In the mid Nineties, the club faced Blackpool in the second round of the FA Cup, and they remain in the English system.

Fred Keenor, now in his mid thirties, was the only man of real international experience in the Welsh team, and requested time on his own with the players at least four hours before kick-off. He spent the morning playing music to relax his team-mates before spending half-an-hour on basic tactical instructions. When the time came to face the partisan Glasgow crowd, Keenor offered a pre-match exhortation: "There's eleven of them and eleven of us, and there's only one ball, and it's ours." Wales took a sixth-minute lead and battled bravely to leave Ibrox with a point. Keenor was awesome. He chased down every Scottish attack, and urged his shattered players to fight until the end. The old hero played like a man possessed, and was warned by the referee for swearing at his team-mates. The official received his own volley of Cardiffian expletives which would have cost Wales their captain had the referee been a less patient man. "Keenor was so engrossed in the game and getting everything out of his players that he did not know what he was saying. I did not send him off and to this day I considered it was the best decision I ever made during my time as a referee."

Wales' display was described by the Scottish press as "the pluckiest display in the history of international football," and Robbins wept with pride. Keenor's greatest game saw him presented with an Airedale dog by a Scottish admirer, but it ran away from home just days later.

Almost the whole team was selected for the game against England; they lost 0–4 despite another gutsy performance. Llanelli's Elvet Collins was the only Unknown missing – due to a knee problem.

The Welsh press was despondent over the difficulties securing players. "This year's struggle for the Triple Crown is the most one-sided affair ever conceived," complained Citizen. "The rules governing it are such that England can scarcely fail." To the *Western Mail*, the championship had become "a meaningless sort of thing not worth winning." The FAW were still struggling financially and Robbins claimed the Football League ruling was biting hard. "The public were not encouraged to attend the match with England owing to our depleted side," he complained. In response to the problem, a November 1931 BBC radio broadcast by Harry Ditton proposed the formation of a national Welsh League to ensure the availability of international players. It was no surprise when England won the championship three years in succession after failing to claim an outright win for 17 years.

Wales and Ireland bonded in adversity and games against the Irish were notable for the social activities surrounding the game. Before the 1931 fixture, the Irish team took a trip around Llangollen on a decorated canal barge, and Wales enjoyed motor trips around County Down and a visit to the Giant's Causeway before games in Belfast. On one occasion, the Welsh party witnessed a house fire and helped rescue furniture as the blaze roared. There were other entertainments when the International Board meetings took place in Wales. At Llandudno in June 1937, board members were taken on a tour of Conway, Llanrwst, Blaenau Ffestiniog, Beddgelert, Llanberis and Caernarfon. These excursions weren't uncommon and visiting teams would often visit Snowdonia when internationals were played in Wrexham during the Thirties.

Writing his annual report, Robbins was relieved when an agreement of sorts was reached between the Football League and the International Board in 1931. He was convinced Wales' situation would be eased the following season. "The position is now known – there is no bitterness after the fight – all countries will be able to choose of their best and may the tourney gladden the hearts of those who love the international spirit," he wrote. The compromise meant the Football League would require 21 days notice of intention to select players for any team other than England. But clubs would still only be obliged to release players for England – release of players for other nations was optional. The FAW would also be required to insure the player, and pay his wages for the week of the game. This was no small requirement – the FAW's finances were now so precarious that members stopped travelling to games and meetings. All complimentary tickets were withdrawn and even council members were allocated just one ticket each.

In an attempt to extend sporting participation in the Valleys, Robbins approached the mining companies, asking them to adjust working hours to allow miners to attend games. "There is no area in the British Isles that is affected by industrial depression so much as Wales," he said. "Our football in the main is played in the mining areas – and in these towns and villages gates have fallen to tragic amounts." Half of the men in the Rhondda were unemployed in 1932, and most of them remained so for the remainder of their lives. But there were some encouraging signs of growth for the women's game, though the FAW were still reluctant to give full support. Permission was granted for charity ladies' matches at Swansea and Llanelli with the strict FAW proviso that "No other ladies' matches will be allowed."

Wales faced Scotland at the newly-improved Racecourse in the first game of the 1931/32 tournament with Linfield's Tom Edwards in their line-up. Edwards remains the only Welshman capped while playing for an Irish club. While Robbins had secured the release of some of his English-based players, a promise from the major English clubs to be more understanding proved false. Scotland had bypassed the problem by simply selecting only from their own league and their 3–2 victory was well deserved. Before and after the game, the Scottish team dined in railway carriages at Wrexham station.

The choice of Anfield as home venue for England's 3–1 victory over Wales proved popular with the Welsh press. "A more convenient venue could scarcely be desired for these games. There is ample foundation for this statement considering the vast number of Welshmen that reside in Liverpool." Making his Welsh debut was Ben Ellis from Aberbargoed, who joined Motherwell in 1930 from Northern Irish side Bangor. After earning six caps, he was selected for the Scottish League team to play the Irish League and was a member of the SFA party which toured the USA and Canada in 1939/40. After retirement, Ellis remained at Fir Park as a groundsman and his contribution to the club was recognized by the naming of Ellis Way, close to the Motherwell stadium.

As agreed in the Football League compromise, the 1931/32 Championship ended for Wales in December 1931 with the view that an earlier schedule would relieve pressure on the English clubs' end of season fixtures. Wales lost 4–0 in Belfast after Robbins had called the attitude of English clubs "scandalous" when some who had promised greater co-operation refused even to release reserve players. Throughout the season Robbins found it difficult to fill his team, and 26 players were capped by Wales in just three games. The match in Ireland was notable for the selection of Ted Parris, the first black player to play for Wales. Parris, the son of a West Indian, had been spotted playing for Chepstow by scouts from Bradford Park Avenue. It would be another 45 years before George Berry became the second black player to wear the Welsh shirt.

The Midweek Champions 1932/33

After finishing bottom of the 1931/32 Championship, the Welsh public expected another difficult season. But in October 1932, veteran Fred Keenor, now playing for Crewe Alexandra, was inspirational in his final game as a late replacement, and Wales shocked Scotland with a 5–2 win at Tynescastle. The victory was the first sign that Wales were developing a team that could win the title, though the success was mainly attributable to the FAW's agreement to hold games in midweek to avoid conflict with the clubs. In the Scotland team was Motherwell's Hugh Wales. "The Welsh lads played out of their skins and thoroughly deserved their victory," said Wales. Keenor was glad to finish his international career on a high note after 32 caps, saying: "I shall always be proud of the small part I was able to play in bringing honour to Wales."

Some 25,000 people crammed into the Racecourse for the visit of England in November 1932, making it the largest crowd ever witnessed in north Wales, despite the midweek kick-off. "The Welsh players, cannot as a whole, stand comparison with those who have been chosen to represent England," wrote the *Times*, but the illustrious English team were forced to defend stoutly to come away with a scoreless draw. "I shall never wish to see a better display than Ben Williams gave," said H J Ditton in the *Western Mail*. Williams, who captained Everton and Wales, would return down the mines on retirement from the game in 1938.

There was a scare at Wales' final game in December when Ireland led at half-time, but Wales came back to win 4–1 and secure at least a share of the Championship. Only 8,500 saw Wales' display in Wrexham on a Wednesday afternoon. The title would not be confirmed for almost another four months when Scotland beat England in April 1933. The successful season underlined how effective Wales could be when allowed to select their best players. During those three games, Robbins had used only 15 men, and what a difference a settled team made. Midweek games may not have been as profitable, but they gave Wales a chance. For once, the FAW gave priority to the team, not the accountant, and the results were plain to see.

Broadening Horizons

Robbins struggled to raise a team in the close season for Wales' first game against a European nation. The players chosen earned only £6 per international and were asked to meet their own travel expenses to the south of England from where the Welsh squad would depart to face France. At the Stade Yves-du-Manoir in Colombes, Paris, Wales managed a 1–1 draw with centre half Tommy Griffiths grabbing their goal. Griffiths had taken over Keenor's mantle as general of the side and was sometimes the only north Walian in a team dominated by players from the Valleys. He was an accomplished cellist, and after retirement became landlord of the Turf Hotel, adjoining the Racecourse. Griffiths was not the only musical Welsh international. Liverpool's Maurice Parry was no mean piano player and future Welsh coach Jimmy Murphy of West Brom was a keen organist. The Doncaster centre forward Eddie Perry sang and played the violin.

International success was a much-needed fillip as the game struggled domestically. In May 1933, just six years after winning the FA Cup, Cardiff City beat Swindon to avoid the lottery of re-election to the Football League, though Newport weren't so lucky. Swansea, now the best team in Wales, were joined by newly-promoted Wrexham in Division Two. Chester won the Welsh Cup by beating Wrexham at Sealand Road in 1933, but the FAW were magnanimous about the result. "We have no regrets that the cup went to Chester – or out of Wales – we cannot be parochial – the game is too big for such thoughts." For the next few years, there was no Welsh involvement at all in the biggest domestic match of the season for the FAW. The 1934 Welsh Cup final replay between Tranmere and Bristol City was held in Chester, with the host club writing in the programme that "gallant little Wales is deserving of patronage." The Welsh footballing heartland was under attack – the Welsh Cup was being contested by English clubs, and Robbins feared Wrexham was losing its fight to remain at the centre of the game. The first attempts to move the FAW headquarters to Cardiff began in the mid 1930s though the north Wales councillors fought off the idea.

The title retained 1933/34

It had been four years since Cardiff had hosted an international, and *Western Mail* reporter Harry Ditton pressed Robbins on the matter. "It's no use campaigning for internationals at Cardiff," replied Robbins. "South Walians have proved they are not interested. We may only get 20,000 at Wrexham but they are so keen on the big time stuff up there that we can always double the gate charges and make a far bigger profit than at Cardiff." When Ditton offered unlimited free publicity Robbins relented. Wales' 3–2 win over Scotland at Ninian Park in October 1933 drew a record gate of 40,000, even in midweek. A jubilant Ditton received a letter from Robbins thanking him for "putting international soccer at Cardiff on the map."

After inadvertently boosting Wales by their insistence on midweek fixtures, the English authorities found other ways to hamper Welsh selectors. Tottenham's Eugene O'Callaghan and his team-mate Willie Evans were the subject of an objection by England, who opposed their call-ups because they had been born in Monmouthshire. Robbins had a simple repost to the Spurs Vice-Chairman Mordon Cadman. "Let him try to get a drink in Monmouthshire on a Sunday and he will soon find that he is in Wales," laughed Robbins. He had reason to be glad the FAW fought off English claims. O'Callaghan made the vital pass which led to Wales' opening goal against Scotland in October 1933, though he was knocked unconscious in the process. After a dose of smelling salts, he ran straight into attack, and took a shot which led to Wales' second in the 3–2 win.

A Saturday fixture against Ireland meant a severely weakened Wales were forced to field Tottenham Hotspur's Alf Day, who was yet to appear in a league match. Missed chances in Belfast saw a second-string Wales return disappointed with a draw before the long midweek trip to face England at Newcastle in a winner-takes-all contest for the championship. Wales were able to call on their best players and took a lead into half-time. Young Tommy Mills, spotted by Clapton Orient scouts when playing for a restaurant team, almost failed to reappear for the second half. Overcome with nerves and excitement, he had been violently ill during the interval. A late header saw Wales beat England by two goals to one, as Robbins' side retained the British Championship for the only time.

Wales' winning goal came from Merthyr legend Dai Astley, who recorded 12 goals for Wales in 13 appearances, including nine in successive games. Inside-forward Astley was one of the most famous players in the country, and one reporter praised his "delightful free action, sure in control when dribbling; swerves quickly and shoots hard." There is no doubt he would have played and scored many more had Aston Villa released him for international duty. He would miss 14 of the 27 games Wales played during his eight-year international career. After the war, Astley became a respected coach in Sweden and with Internazionale of Milan.

Despite the Football League ruling and English claims to Monmouthshire, relations between the English and Welsh FAs were generally very good in the years between the wars. In an act of goodwill before the opening fixture of the 1934/35 Championship, Robbins reached an agreement with Tottenham whereby the London club would release Willie Evans if the English sent reserve Willie Hall back to the club. The FA agreed and Hall made his way back to Tottenham. If Wales had any complaints, the problems were with the Football League not the Football Association.

Robbins worked hard to improve relations with individual clubs and was even prompted by Wolverhampton Wanderers to select a young player from Aberaman called Bryn Jones. The FAW enjoyed an excellent relationship with the Black Country side in the 1930s, and Wolves were one of the few big teams who released players to Wales without question. Within a few years, Jones, known as "the brilliant midget", commanded a record £14,000 when he joined Arsenal. The fee caused a sensation at the time of the Great Depression, and a crowd of 33,000 turned up to watch his debut for the Gunners' reserves.

Wales lost for the first time in seven games when they succumbed to a four-goal hammering from England in Cardiff in September 1934. However, Wales were reduced to ten men when Willie Evans – who had already missed a penalty – was carried off unconscious after losing three teeth. The 51,000 crowd had been boosted by huge support from the poverty-stricken Valleys – half the crowd had travelled by train and omnibus from surrounding areas, contributing a record gate of £2,800. Most sport within a 40-mile radius had been postponed as people flocked to see a Wales team containing ten southerners. More women were attending football matches despite the awful conditions at uncovered stadia, and according to one advert in the England match programme, the reason was obvious: "nowadays the housewife has more leisure because she makes good use of electricity in her home." Matches witnessed three pricing levels: adults, schoolchildren and unemployed/ladies. On the evening before the game both teams had been at the New Theatre watching a comedy called *That's a Pretty Thing*.

Wales missed Tommy Griffiths badly in the 3–2 defeat to Scotland, when Dai Astley was joined by childhood pal Idris 'Dai' Hopkins. Brentford's diminutive winger had been born in the same street and shared the same birthday. Wales at least had the satisfaction of beating Ireland in a match refereed by the German, Dr Bauwens.

Watching the Ireland game as guests of Wrexham were miners from Gresford Colliery where a 1934 explosion had killed 266 men. Many of the dead had swapped shifts in order to watch Wrexham face Tranmere the following day. Colliers Park, Wrexham's training ground, now lies on the site of the accident. On the 75th anniversary of the tragedy in 2009, the club paid tribute to the lives lost by delaying their match by 15 minutes – as was traditional when the mine was active. There was further heartbreak at a game in Swansea between Cwm Athletic and South Wales Transport in 1934. South Wales Transport's Edward Cole died after a collision involving the Cwm goalkeeper, Charles Donovan. Donovan was accused of manslaughter, but acquitted on the evidence of a spectator – Trevor Ford, of Merlin Crescent, Swansea. Strangely, the name and address are the same as those of the Welsh international centre forward of the 1950s, though Ford fails to mention the incident in his autobiography.

After the disappointment of the previous tournament, the 1935/36 British Championship started slightly better for Wales with a home draw against Scotland. A crowd of 35,000 cemented Cardiff's claim to usurp Wrexham as the nation's preferred international venue. Wales played their first ever game at Wolverhampton's Molineux against England, and demonstrated their staying power by coming back from a goal down to win 2–1. This was a Wales team demanding to be taken seriously, at least when they played midweek. England's star player Ted Drake had been superbly marshalled by Harry Hanford before injury forced him to leave the field. The *Times* believed the red jersey of Wales turned Hanford into a "great player", though Swansea would argue their captain was already a top-class centre half. The victory over England left Wales needing to beat Ireland to claim their third title in four years, but to the surprise of everybody, Wales lost the game after leading at half-time.

In our cynical modern era, it is curious to look back at the devout loyalty shown to the English crown by the Welsh association. The FAW was a proud British organisation and, at the end of the 1935 season, it urged Welsh clubs to contribute to a fund celebrating King George's silver jubilee. The Welsh season was extended for a week with the proviso that all income should go to charity, with at least 50 per cent going to the King's fund. When George died, the FAW sent a message to King Edward VIII on his succession to the throne: "We humbly assure you of our loyalty and wish you a long and happy reign." Meanwhile, the Welsh Language Youth Movement, Urdd Gobaith Cymru, was refused permission to take a collection at an amateur international at Porthmadog. The FAW also confirmed in 1935 that no women's matches of any kind, including charity matches, would be allowed on Welsh football grounds.

Happy Days Are Here Again

There were signs that the shoots of economic recovery were benefitting football in Wales, and the FAW annual report was unusually positive. "Cardiff City is now beginning to hit the football headlines again. Gates averaging over 20,000 are steaming up." Even though the team was still struggling in Division Three, there were attendances of more than 30,000 against Walsall, Mansfield and Notts County. In the years leading up to the Second World War, Welsh football was seeing the start of a boom period which would not peak until the 1950s.

Wales faced England in October 1936 amid optimistic times with Cardiff City fans singing 'Happy Days Are Here Again'. There was a welcome from the FAW to the new King in the match programme: "God bless him say we Loyal Welshmen." There was also mention of the new President, Lord Davies of Llandinam. Although not a football man, Lord Davies was an influential figure to have onside.

Wales had not won any of the six official internationals played against England in Cardiff. They hadn't even won a competitive game against the English in Wales since 1882, and when they went behind to a Cliff Bastin goal, things looked gloomy. But this was now a team confident in their ability and Seymour 'Stan' Morris scored directly from a corner on his debut to draw Wales level. Grimsby's Pat Glover scored the winner and Ninian Park celebrated wildly. Wales showed their pluck again when two more goals from Glover saw them win at Dundee after Scotland had pulled back from an early Welsh lead. This left the team needing just a draw with Ireland on St Patrick's Day to secure the new King George International Jubilee Trophy, though they knew from the previous season that nothing could be taken from granted. This time Wales made no mistake, winning by four goals to one. The 1936/37 season was only the second time that Wales had defeated all three home nations, but it would be the last when Wales won the Championship outright. "To defeat three fine sides of the sister countries by no fluke has earned Wales the plaudits and congratulations of all the world," wrote Robbins. Wales were awarded an art deco triple crown trophy in the form of a mounted hollow football with an elf-like instrumentalist perched on the top. A report in the London *Times* praised the Welsh heroes: "The Wrexham Racecourse yesterday evening was the scene of a great triumph for Wales. They beat Ireland as decisively as the score of four goals to one suggests and so gained the international championship as well as the Jubilee Trophy, having beaten all three home countries. Ireland fought hard and gallantly, but they could never be compared with their opponents, who, combining thrust, skill, and determination, early showed their mastery and afterwards maintained their grip on the game. Glover, the Grimsby Town centre forward, was in great form, and nothing in the whole match was more attractive than the partnership of Hopkins and Bryn Jones on the right flank."

The Second World War wasn't kind to the reputations of the last Welsh team to win the British Championship. Few achieved the fame their talent deserved as many were stolen away in their prime. Players like Les Jones, Glover, Astley and Hopkins still had years ahead of them. Jack Warner joined Manchester United from Swansea in 1938 but many of his club appearances remain unrecognized having taken place during the war. He too would have won more than his couple of pre-war caps. Arsenal's Bob John was more fortunate as he retired in 1938. John was considered one of Arsenal's greats, playing 421 league games for the Gunners at a time when they won three League Championships and reached three FA Cup finals. Other regulars in that championship-winning Welsh team were journeymen who grew in stature with the dragon on their chest. Albert Gray finished a long career with Chester, while Bert Turner spent most of his career with Charlton. Gray was originally an outfield player who converted after filling in as goalkeeper for his pit team. The Welsh right-half, Jimmy Murphy played for more than 11 years with West Bromwich Albion.

Murphy was a fine player, but will always be remembered for his time as coach with Manchester United. He was given the role at United after meeting Matt Busby during the war. The Manchester United manager would describe his close friend as "my first and most important signing." The man from Ton Pentre took over United while Busby was in hospital after the Munich air crash of 1958, and played a crucial role in rebuilding the team. He had been managing Wales for their home game against Israel when the disaster occurred. Murphy also took control of the Welsh national side from 1956 to 1964 and could be considered its most successful manager. "Five minutes with Mr Murphy provides more pep and purpose than many could put over in a season," said Swansea's Mel Nurse. "The players loved and respected him," agreed John Charles.

While Wales celebrated unprecedented success in the mid 1930s, the importance of the tournament was being questioned by the English press. "Apart from the England v Scotland game," wrote the *Times*, "the Association internationals cannot compare in importance with rugby internationals, but there is a growing interest in them, and in the next few years they may attain a status more in accord with their title." London's attitude may have been influenced by the recent lack of English success. However, England would again claim the trophy in 1938 and the natural order was restored.

Wales began their defence of the Championship in

confident mood and beat Scotland at Ninian Park in October. Every player selected was a south Walian playing with an English club. Their selection attracted a 42,000 crowd which prompted the *Western Mail* to claim: "Cardiff will be the national ground in all future matches." This came despite the stadium's grandstand needing to be completely rebuilt after being destroyed by a fire started by burglars in January 1937.

The *Times'* praise for the Welsh before they faced England in the second game was unintentionally patronising: "Wales have a way of playing above the form shown by their individual players in their club games when it comes to internationals, and this spirit of theirs, and its way of winning matches has done much to stimulate interest in international football. Until recently the attitude of the average English football enthusiast was so far as internationals were concerned 'Scotland first, the rest nowhere.'"

Unfortunately, Wales' spirit was not enough to avoid defeat at Middlesbrough in November 1937, as England won by two goals to one. There were complaints that the match had been held in Teeside to deny Wales the support it could expect in London. The game was also notable for the first appearance of numbered shirts in the British Championship. A disappointing defeat in Belfast due to a late error by Birmingham's Billy Hughes saw the trophy go to England.

While the international sides of the Edwardian era had been crying out for south Wales to provide players to boost a team dominated by Denbighshire, the positions were now reversed. South Wales provided the bulk of the Welsh team. Ten who faced the English in the first game of the 1938/39 season came from south Wales's industrial areas. England was exhorted by the *Times* to be on their guard as "enthusiasm, singing, and those terribly patriotic Welsh colours have a way of conjuring up unexpected victory." The press should also have warned them about Astley who was simply brilliant on the day. A record 55,000 crowd sang English and Welsh songs before the game. With Wales on their way to a 4–2 win, the *Times* reported that "Welsh fervour got the better of the unwritten law in football stands that those who have seats should sit in them." At the final whistle, "hundreds of people vaulted the barriers and dashed across the field to the players." Pathé film footage shows a stadium overflowing with supporters, including several dozen reckless young men perched precariously on the Canton Stand roof.

Defeat to Scotland came next despite the brilliant efforts of the man described as the successor to Tommy Griffiths and Keenor, Everton's Tommy 'TG' Jones from Connah's Quay. There had been successful clubs in Connah's Quay since 1890. One town club had been 1929 Welsh Cup winners, but folded under large debts just six months later. When Jones returned home in 1946, he formed Connah's Quay Juniors, who in turn evolved into the current Connah's Quay Nomads.

Victory for Wales against the Irish ensured a share of the 1938/39 Championship and there were high hopes for the future. "If I had this team together for a fortnight," said Robbins, "we would beat the world." Sadly, the onset of war meant he would never get the opportunity. The programme for the 1939 Welsh Cup final between Cardiff City and South Liverpool, played at Wrexham, contains a chilling warning. "The world is in a very disturbed state and nobody can be sure what will happen…"

6

THE WARTIME YEARS
1939–1949

THE BRITISH CHAMPIONSHIP was cancelled from 1939 until 1946, though Wales did return to France for a 1939 friendly, losing by two goals to one. Even though FAW coffers had been boosted by the large Cardiff crowds of the 1930s, they were still careful with their money. Players travelling to France were reminded in their tour itinerary to bring their own soap and there was good reason why the match shirts were uncomfortable. "As a wartime economy, the international jerseys had been worn and washed over and over again, until they were skintight," explained Walley Barnes in his autobiography, *Captain of Wales*. These players weren't issued with two shirts per game.

Wales played England 15 times to maintain public morale during the war, and there were some great contests. The first charity game in 1939 raised money for the Red Cross, and goalkeeper Roy John captained Wales for his final game before retirement. A converted defender, John was the James Bond of Welsh football: "cool and daring between the sticks, and takes all the risks," claimed one report. There would be no games at John's former club, Swansea, where the Vetch had been requisitioned by the Army for anti-aircraft purposes. Aberystwyth's Park Avenue ground was also commandeered – equipment stores built either side of the grandstand would later become spectator enclosures.

In 1940, Wales made their first visit to Wembley, beating England by a goal to nil. Scotland had already played at the famous stadium during the 1920s and '30s, though Wales were not deemed worthy of the honour. But Wales had been British Champions three times in the previous decade, and a 40,000 crowd vindicated the decision as Wales won by a single goal. Millwall's George Williams marked Stanley Matthews out of the game and inside-left Bryn Jones scored the winner, with England missing a penalty five minutes from time. Debutant Billy Lucas scored the only goal against the English in 1942 – he would go on to manage Swansea and Newport County during the late Sixties and early Seventies. And a 1943 game has entered footballing folklore thanks to the unusual appearance of a future English legend. When Ivor Powell broke his collarbone early in the game Wales were left without a replacement until England suggested one of theirs play for the men in red. Stan Mortensen came on to face his own country.

Large crowds swarmed to wartime games as a beleaguered population looked for relief from the daily grind. And fans began making their own entertainment. Welsh followers had a long-standing custom of taking leeks to games, but England captain Stan Cullis complained when they began throwing them in the English goalmouth during one wartime international at Cardiff. "What can we do about the leeks?" asked Cullis of the referee. "If I was you I'd collect 'em. They make splendid thickening for a stew," advised the official, A E Davies of Aberystwyth.

There was football for the troops too. At the infamous Auschwitz prison camp, the Red Cross provided Wales, Scotland, England and Ireland kits, and soldiers played regular international tournaments in the shadow of the gas chambers. "It kept us sane, it was a bit of normality, but it sounds wrong somehow to say I've got fond memories of playing football, considering what was going on just over the fence," said Welsh goalkeeper Ron Jones of Newport.

The archive of FAW minutes stops in 1939, but recommences in 1946. The first thing the reader saw when opening the cover was a memorial programme for the funeral of Ted Robbins. Robbins' death came at the end of a period when Wales had fought back from near collapse to become British Champions. In a single decade the fortunes of Welsh international football had been dramatically reversed. Operating from a couple of rooms above a gentleman's outfitters in Wrexham's High Street, the charming administrator transformed the association. Mourners at his funeral sang 'Abide with Me' and his coffin was carried by six Welsh internationals, including Billy Meredith. Robbins was mourned by everybody in football, and dozens of clubs and associations from across the UK sent wreaths of condolence in scenes replicated some 65 years later when Wales lost another figurehead. Like Gary Speed, Robbins' biggest asset was his popularity; both men succeeded in securing the loyalty of their players. There is no doubt that Robbins is one of the primary figures in the history of the Welsh game. In 1952, FAW chairman Milwyn Jenkins unveiled a memorial plaque to the driving force of the game between the wars: "The Association was weak and struggling to exist when he became Secretary, but through his efforts the position greatly changed, and when he left us in 1946, Wales was well on the map as a force to be reckoned with." Herbert Powell faced the impossible task of replacing Robbins, and his first assignment was to follow the International Board's recommendation that the UK associations rejoin FIFA.

Wales gave starts in a 1946 Victory International against Ireland to Bill Shortt, Alf Sherwood, Jack Warner, Billy Clarke, Trevor Ford and Billy Morris, who had been shot in the neck in Burma during the war. Even though war had officially ended a year earlier, the game is considered the 17th and final wartime international, most of which had been played against England. Sherwood from Aberaman had played for

Wales schoolboys at football and cricket alongside Trevor Ford, and he would miss only two Wales matches in the next ten years, captaining his country many times. Described by Stanley Matthews as his most difficult opponent, Sherwood was known as the 'King of the Sliding Tacklers', and was also stand-in goalkeeper for Wales and Cardiff City. At the end of his career, during which he gained 41 caps, he spent a few seasons coaching in New York and also managed Barry Town.

Return of the British Championship

In October 1946, Wales faced Scotland in the first British Championship game after a seven-year break and enthusiasm was such that the fixture was made the first all-ticket match at the Racecourse. Before the match, the Scottish team had been relaxing at the Vale of Llangollen, while Wales enjoyed the pleasures of sunny Rhyl. "Time was when we used to meet an hour or so before the kick off, but nowadays the occasion demands more serious preparation," explained secretary Powell in a statement of intent.

It came as no surprise when Wales beat the Scots and one of the goals was scored by Aston Villa's Trevor Ford, who had transferred from Swansea after more than 40 goals in a season. Making his debut for Wales was Ernie 'Alphabet' Jones from Swansea, who had been born in Alice Street in 1920. Remarkably, the Cwmbwrla Street was to produce five Welsh internationals.

Alice Street's curious history began on 30 June 1918, when John Hopkin Roberts was born in one of the terraces that housed the seaport's burgeoning industrial population. Jackie Roberts, as he was known, played for Bolton from 1938 until 1950, finishing his career alongside Jock Stein at Llanelli. He was unfortunate to have played in the same era as the great Bryn Jones, or would surely have made more than just a single Welsh appearance against Belgium at Liege on Wales' European tour of 1949.

Just two years after Roberts was born, Ernie Jones gave his first cry a few doors down from the Roberts' household on 12 November 1920. The two boys grew up together and both joined Bolton in 1937. But unlike his pal, Ernie left soon after the war to join Tottenham and then Southampton. He played four times for Wales in the late 1940s, but perhaps his most notable achievement came as manager of Rhyl when he designed the first floodlights in Welsh football at Belle Vue in 1954. He remained a member of the Inventors Club after his career ended and developed a game called SOTEN (soccer tennis).

Alice Street was quiet for about ten years until its most famous resident arrived just after Christmas 1931. William John Charles, Wales' greatest player, made his name with Leeds United before becoming a legend at Italian giants Juventus. King John earned 38 caps for his country and is acknowledged as the finest player in the world during the 1950s. Of course, John's younger brother was a fine player in his own right. Melvyn Charles was also born in Alice Street in 1935, and despite living in his brother's shadow, was a key member of Wales' 1958 World Cup side. Mel earned 31 caps and played for Swansea, Arsenal and Cardiff before spells at Porthmadog, Port Vale, Oswestry and Haverfordwest.

The final export – so far – of the Alice Street production line was another Mel – Melvyn Tudor George Nurse. Nurse was born in 1937 and played for Swansea, Middlesbrough and Swindon, earning 12 Welsh caps. His most famous hour came in 2001, when as a successful businessman he took on a debt of £801,000 to save Swansea from bankruptcy. Nurse stood at more than six feet tall, and you can only imagine the kickabouts between him and the Charles' brothers in Cwmbwrla Park during the late 1940s.

After beating Scotland in 1946, Wales lost 0–3 to England at Manchester City's Maine Road, before also losing to Ireland. Then in 1947, a number of clubs questioned the FAW about selecting prisoners of war. There were some talented continental footballers in Welsh camps, but the War Office had forbidden foreign captives from playing for British teams. Nor would it allow clubs to play against teams composed of prisoners. There were other, more pressing issues to consider. It was becoming a practice in some parts of Wales for 'mascots' to accompany teams onto the pitch. In some cases the mascot was even tossing the coin for kick-off. The FAW immediately put a stop to the practice.

Arsenal defender Walley Barnes made his full debut against England in the opening game of the 1947/48 Championship. He had originally been considered for the English team, but upon checking his details, the selectors realized he had been born in Brecon. Luckily for Wales, Barnes' father had been stationed in the town when his son was born in 1920. Sportingly, the English FA informed the FAW who immediately chose him for the Welsh team. Barnes had left Wales at the age of four and would not return until his selection 20 years later. When he turned up to the team hotel in Porthcawl, the first person he saw was Stanley Matthews – both teams had booked the same hotel, with the star-studded England team training at Pencoed prior to their easy 3–0 win. Barnes had been given the thankless task of marking Matthews and later admitted: "Stanley ran me dizzy." Barnes went on to captain Wales and became the first Welsh team manager during the 1954 Austria tour. Despite his loose connection with Wales, Barnes came to feel part of the nation: "I have formed a deep attachment for the Welsh people. Unlike many members of the international team I can claim no roots or traditional ties, but Mother Wales has shown no discrimination on that account and I know that I have found a real home with compatriots eager to accept me as one of themselves."

Wales outplayed Scotland and won for the first time at Hampden Park in 1947, with captain Ron Burgess leading his side to a 2–1 victory. Alongside man-of-the-match Barnes in defence, Burgess, from Cwm near Ebbw Vale, was unsurpassable at left-half and also managed to contribute in attack. He was selected for the Great Britain team that played the Rest of Europe at Glasgow in a 1947 FIFA fundraiser, and was later to manage Wales for a game when he deputised for Dave Bowen. Burgess's nephew Clive would become a Welsh international rugby player in the 1970s. Also selected to represent Great Britain in 1947 was Billy Hughes, Birmingham City's Welsh left-back.

Wales followed the Scotland win by denying Ireland the 1947/48 title with victory in front of 33,160 at the Racecourse. The game was originally set for Swansea, but according to the FAW, the "appropriate authorities at Swansea had not found it convenient to meet with the wishes of the council." Three of the Welsh team were lucky to be playing. Cardiff City debutant Billy Baker had spent three years as a Japanese prisoner of war and was reported to have suffered terribly at the hands of his captors. Aubrey Powell had been told he would never play again after fracturing a leg in 1937, and Barnes surprised everyone by recovering from a serious ankle injury.

Before the Ireland game, the Welsh players attened a civic reception in Conwy, and were each presented with a souvenir guidebook of the town. Barnes, captaining his nation for the first time, suggested Wales adopt Arsenal-like tactics in the pre-match meeting. In the manager-free 1940s, the team's trainer and even the team doctor were invited to share their tactical views. On a hard ground at Wrexham, Wales found the ball a problem, so they purposely booted it out of the ground after a few minutes and went on to win 2–0 with the replacement. Wales were denied the Championship only by England's victory against Scotland at Hampden a month later.

The FAW refused another invitation to play in Dublin in 1948, but this came as no surprise from the staunchly royalist association. After Wales' first home game in 1877, the FAW chairman had spoken of his hope that "the good day was coming when the Royal Family would be persuaded that in Wales there was something to be equally attractive with other parts of her majesty's dominion." The royalist connection was cemented when the Prince of Wales, the future King Edward VIII, became the association's patron in the 1920s, and the FAW minute books bulge with gushing deference during the post-war years. They sent "loyal greetings" to Princess Elizabeth when she married Lord Mountbatten in 1947. When George VI died in 1952, they contributed a wreath of red and white flowers. And in 1953 after the death of Queen Mary, FAW Secretary Powell distributed a long list of instructions. He ordered that all Welsh clubs observe a minute's silence, wear black armbands, lower flags to half mast, sing 'Abide with Me' (with an option of 'O fryniau Caersalem ceir gweled') and 'God Save the Queen'.

The relationship was reciprocated in 1952 when the Queen awarded armorial bearings (a form of royal approval) to the association. And in 1954, the FAW congratulated her on her "triumphant Tour of the Commonwealth", and thanked "Almighty God for the safe return home of our Royal Patron." The FAW also sent a telegram of congratulations to the Queen and Duke of Edinburgh on their Silver Wedding anniversary in 1972. To this day, page three of the FAW handbook features a full-page photograph of Queen Elizabeth.

In October 1948, Wales faced Scotland at Ninian Park. The Scots had lost all their fixtures the previous season and a record 59,911 crowd watched a game marred by a controversial decision. Willie Waddell was credited with the Scots' third goal in a 3–1 victory despite Welsh keeper Cyril Sidlow appearing to grab the ball at least 18 inches before it crossed the goal-line. The Northern Irish referee ignored the protests of his linesman and awarded the goal from his position on the half-way line. Wales were annoyed, but as Barnes said "an international pitch is not the place to argue with the ref's decision, so we left it at that." These were times of huge crowds and 70,000 packed Villa Park in Birmingham for the all-ticket international against England, which Wales lost despite having a man advantage from 25 minutes on. The season finished with a straightforward 2–0 win in Belfast, where Barnes had faced a dilemma: "Should a player own up to the referee that he handled the ball with the intention of stopping a goal from being scored? It happened like this... a high cross was aimed at the head of Davie Walsh, the Irish centre forward. I went up to head clear, realized that I couldn't get to the ball, and in a last, despairing effort to get an extra inch of height, threw my arm up to divert the ball from Walsh's head. But for this intervention Walsh would have scored... immediately there was an appeal from the Irish forwards. What did I do? I held my breath and hoped that I'd got away with it."

1948 Olympics

With London's 1948 Olympic Games approaching, a team representing Great Britain was assembled from the best amateurs in the UK, and a number of Welsh players were invited to trials. The FAW wrote to the selectors: "It is true that we hope to see some of our players taking part in the Olympic Games but if it is felt that the other three countries are able to produce the better players then of course your council will be happy to abide by the decision of the selection committee." In the event, Frank Donovan of Pembroke Borough, George Manning of Troedyrhiw, and Doug Smith of Barry were selected. The FAW were grateful to the English FA who agreed to bear most of the considerable costs of the GB team.

The Welsh Amateur team lost to the Indian Olympic side in 1948, with their opponents playing in feet wrapped with bandages. The game raised £735 for the All India Football Federation, who were competing in London. Amateurism was still treated seriously, and the FAW threatened action when they heard clubs were sending wedding gifts to newly-married players. In 1953, Caernarfon were charged with paying players and 16 committee members were banned indefinitely.

Crowd disorder was prevalent throughout Wales in 1948. The FAW were forced to issue warnings about spectator behaviour at Machno, Penmaenmawr, Connah's Quay, Llechid, Nantlle Vale, Shotton, Carmel, Brecon, Aberdovey, and Llanidloes. In almost every case, the referee was attacked or spectators entered the field of play. The FAW also issued a stern warning about bad language. "The good name of the game suffers owing to the delinquency of a small minority," they claimed. Wrexham were threatened with ground closure after repeated incidents of missile throwing and in Blaenau Ffestiniog the referee was knocked down twice and kicked during a pitch invasion. The ground was closed for a month and police were required at all future games in Blaenau.

The 1948/49 international campaign saw Wales lose to Scotland and England before beating Ireland 2–0 with one of the goals coming from Trevor Ford. The Aston Villa striker went on to become one of Welsh football's great characters, scoring 23 goals in just 38 internationals. He was described by John Charles as "absolutely fearless, aggressive and full of energy, which frightened lesser men." Ford was a fiercely outspoken character at a time when clubs treated players as possessions. He was in trouble many times with the authorities, including major rows over under-the-counter transfer payments. After one scandal, Ford was suspended by the Football League for refusing to indict his fellow players, reinstated, and then suspended again. In his autobiography, he accused some clubs of supplying performance-enhancing drugs, but complained that they frowned on his favourite vices: "If you are a smoker then the best thing you can have to steady the nerves is a cigarette. And what about that pint of old and mild? My average is ten cigarettes a day and a pint of shandy when I feel like it – and during the playing season I've never been less than 100 per cent fit."

In 1968, years after his retirement, Ford appeared as a substitute fielder for Glamorgan Cricket Club on the day Garfield Sobers scored his record-breaking six sixes in a single over at St Helen's. The Swansea man was a passionate Welshman and dedicated his autobiography, *I Lead the Attack*, to his two boys, "in the hope they will never forget they are true sons of Wales." Ford enjoyed such a fearsome reputation, that one newspaper claimed he might be banned from international games: "Two of the four countries who play in the home international championship have made it plain that they view with disfavour the selection of a certain player for international championship matches. I understand it is likely that if this player is chosen to play against one of the countries which raised the matter they will ask for him to be withdrawn from the team. If he does not withdraw it will lead to complications."

Ford knew "Scotland and England hated my guts," but was backed fully by FAW Chairman Milwyn Jenkins, who told him to carry on in his usual style. Ford was a traditionalist and was none too impressed with the game played on the continent. His first trip with Wales came in 1949, when he played on an ill-fated tour of Portugal, Belgium and Switzerland.

A foreign tour was a step into the unknown, and the FAW councillors were keen to secure their place on the plane. The travelling party was made up of 15 players and 10 officials, including team attendant C Leyfield, the FAW Secretary, three council members, the doctor, three officers and a press liaison officer.

But the administrators were helpless to prevent the confusion which reigned on that first continental trip. The flight to Belgium was diverted and the FAW were forced to pay import duty on their official gift to the Belgian FA. The choice of opposition meant that Wales, for the first time, would be required to change their colour, creating the nation's first away kit. "Since the costume of all three Continental Countries is Red," said the FAW, "for the purposes of the Tour, Wales will play in Daffodil Shirts with Green Collar and Cuffs, with the Red Dragon on the pocket."

On the pitch, Wales struggled with the continental interpretation of the rules. The opening game in Lisbon turned into a battle, according to Ford. "I was the only player in the side who had not succumbed to the shirt-pulling, ankle-tapping and deliberate tripping of the Portuguese players. The shirt-tugging, body-checking and other fouls, all of which were apparently not seen by the referee, went on, and yet every time I went at the goalkeeper with a perfectly fair shoulder-charge the whistle went for a free kick."

When Wales were denied a penalty after Mal Griffiths was brought down by a rugby tackle, the match degenerated into farce. Griffiths took the free-kick, then picked up the ball and made his protest by diving between the posts for a try.

A bruised and battered Wales team was patched up to face Belgium and Switzerland but lost both games. Only 17,000 watched Wales lose 3–1 in Liege, and the tourists were humiliated 4–0 by the Swiss at Berne's Wankdorf Stadium in a match delayed while Welsh officials complained the match ball was undersized and under-inflated. The Welsh party was lucky to have escaped injury when the team coach was involved in a road accident on their return from a pre-match tour of the Swiss Alps.

With eight of Wales' 15 players injured by the time they came to face Switzerland, the FAW had early warning that continental tours could not be undertaken with a small squad. Making his only appearance for Wales on the tour was 31-year-old full back Jack Roberts, who was under no illusion about the reasons for his selection. "At Bolton I would always go in goal if our keeper was ever injured during the game," he said. "And I think that I was picked for the tour to act as cover for the goalkeeper William Hughes." Years previously, Roberts had been selected to play for Ireland by mistake. The trip proved a worthwhile education in the demands of continental football for the Welsh, but the FAW initially decided not to award international caps for the tour, illustrating that European football was not taken seriously. It was no surprise that Wales would not win on the continent until they travelled to Sweden for the 1958 World Cup.

7

THE
FIRST WORLD CUPS
1949–1959

1950 World Cup

Wales began the 1949/50 Championship knowing that an overall tournament victory would see them heading to Rio with the tournament doubling as a qualifying group for the 1950 World Cup in Brazil. It was the first time UK teams had entered FIFA's competition. "Beat England today, and you'll be well on the road to Rio, with a chance to win the championship of the world," exhorted Newtown solicitor and new FAW chairman Milwyn Jenkins. But the Welsh team to face a formidable England side including Wright, Finney, Milburn, Shackleton and Mortenson, contained seven Division Two players. Despite a brave effort in front of a passionate 60,000 Ninian Park crowd, England won by four goals to one, and Wales' qualification campaign was over before it had even begun. Defeat in Scotland was followed by a tame home draw against Ireland in what was called the "worst game since the war." The match would be the last in which the IFA selected players from the Republic of Ireland, but a crowd of 30,000 for a meaningless dead rubber at the Racecourse demonstrated the hunger for football in the post-war era.

The Home Championship wooden spoon was the sole reward for a 1949/50 season which had started with such hope. Walley Barnes had no answer to the critics. "I suppose it was just one of those seasons when the ball didn't run for us," he admitted. It would fall to an Abertillery teacher to represent Wales at the 1950 World Cup finals. Mervyn 'Sandy' Griffiths was linesman for the opening match, and would officiate at another two World Cups. Griffiths also refereed the famous 1953 'Matthews' Cup final between Blackpool and Bolton Wanderers and, as a linesman, he was involved in major controversy when he denied Hungary's Ferenc Puskas an equalising goal in the 1954 'Miracle of Berne' World Cup final.

Club football in Wales was booming, and Bangor, Merthyr, Llanelli and Barry all applied to join the Football League in 1947. The Welsh Cup was also at its peak and the 1949 final between Swansea and Merthyr Tydfil was played out at Cardiff in front of a record 30,649 spectators. Swansea had just won Division Three (South) but lost 0–2 to the Southern League team formed only four years earlier. The Welsh League flourished in the 1950s and Welsh clubs were able to attract players from across the United Kingdom thanks to growing gate receipts. At Llanelli, games against Barry and Merthyr attracted up to 10,000 fans. One notable player for the Reds was Jock Stein, who would achieve legend status as a player and manager for Scotland. Llanelli had already signed Dougie Wallace from Stein's club, Albion Rovers, and in 1950, Stein himself came south on wages of £12 a week. He was joined by others from Dundee United, Aberdeen and Motherwell. Stein captained Llanelli during their historic FA Cup run which was only ended by Bristol Rovers after a second third-round replay at Ninian Park. Unfortunately, Llanelli's application to join the Football League was rejected ten times between 1922 and 1951. Rejection eventually brought an end to the club's professional era and Stein returned north to sign for Celtic. Llanelli turned professional again in 2005, winning the Welsh Premier title in 2008 and the Welsh Cup in 2011.

Llanelli became embroiled in "the biggest domestic Soccer controversy in the history of Welsh football" in 1958 when the FAW refused it permission to enter the Southern League claiming the club was overstretching itself with an average gate of 'only' 1,200. There was uproar. The whole of west Wales's football came out in support and 35,000 trade unionists and the town's Labour party aligned themselves with the cause. Forty-four clubs called an EGM to issue a vote of no confidence in the association, but there was more anger when that meeting was scheduled for Shrewsbury. "We always pick the Welsh team there, and I do not see why Llanelli should object," said an FAW spokesman. "I have had handed to me the signatures of 16,000 people," said Jenkins. "These people did not bother about Llanelli during the last season." The FAW stuck to its guns and Llanelli remained in the Welsh system.

Belgium became the first continental international side to play in Wales when they came to Ninian Park on a Wednesday afternoon in 1949. "The Welshmen as the home team wear the traditional red shirts and will take on the pseudonym of the Red Devils," wrote Cardiff City chairman Herbert Merrett, asserting Wales' right to use a nickname shared by both teams.

An excited Welsh crowd of 35,000 were eager for a first taste of the exotic passing football they had read so much about, but they were also intrigued by the darker side of the European game. Writing in the match programme, an anonymous Welsh international warned of the difficulties in facing continental teams. "A great deal of pulling, pushing and obstructing which would be condemned by their English counterparts is ignored by these officials who are often incapable of explaining their decisions to the bewildered visitors because of the language difficulty." The Belgians were all amateurs; their goalkeeper Meert was a hairdresser and the right-back was a butcher. Ford scored a hat-trick in Wales' 5–1 victory, something he put down to his early aggression: "The critics said the game was virtually won in the first ten minutes when I went on the rampage in the Belgian penalty area. I stormed around looking menacing, and whenever the Belgian goalkeeper Meert gathered the ball I went for him like a terrier going for the postman. It was perfectly fair intimidation but it broke Meert's nerve."

A nightmare debut for Swansea's John Parry in the Welsh goal gifted Scotland a 3–1 win in the first game of the 1950/51 British Championship, and the hapless keeper never played for Wales again. Arsenal's Ray Daniel made his debut in the next game, a 2–4 defeat by England at Roker Park, Sunderland. Wales were denied a crucial lead by a mysterious offside decision, given against Manchester City winger Roy Clarke, with two English players standing on their own goal-line. Despite a couple of Ford goals, England won the game.

Clarke scored twice as Wales beat Ireland 2–1 in Belfast before facing Portugal at Ninian Park in a Festival of Britain international. As an experiment, it was agreed that substitutes be allowed for players injured before half-time, and a reserve goalkeeper was permitted for the first time. The Portuguese stayed in Porthcawl, and brought with them 90 pints of wine "to cheer us up, win or lose." After Portugal were defeated 2–1, the Swiss were beaten 3–2 at Wrexham with another couple of goals from Ford. The results showed how all international teams faced difficulties when travelling. After losing every game on tour, Wales had beaten each of those opponents comfortably on home soil.

The two victories put Wales in confident mood to face England in the first game of the 1951/52 Championship. Cardiff was bursting with rugby and football fans on 20 October 1951 as the Arms Park side took on South Africa on the same day. There was unusual work for the referee before kick-off when he was forced to call for assistance to clear the pile of leeks left on the centre-spot by Welsh fans. Billy Foulkes, included just a week after moving from third division Chester to Newcastle, had given Wales the lead with his first kick in international football and Wales were the better side throughout. Wales would have won but for Alf Ramsey's late goal-line clearance from a Ford shot. Following the 1–1 draw, Wales confirmed their improvement with a win in Glasgow and the Scots praised "the best Welsh team they had ever seen." Ivor Allchurch scored the Hampden winner with just 90 seconds remaining to put Wales in position for the Championship. "Roy (Clarke) put in a tremendous run down the line and then crossed as I came in to meet the ball. It was the perfect centre and I got my forehead into the right place at the right time to give us a wonderful victory – my first goal for Wales and what a moment to score it!"

Newport-born Clarke became a Manchester City icon, playing 349 games and winning the 1956 FA Cup. His career ended after 22 Welsh caps. Upon retirement, he opened a sports shop in Manchester, becoming the first Adidas merchant in the area. In later years he suffered from Alzheimer's disease and died in March 2006.

Wales faced Ireland in their final game with a chance to win the Championship. Four of Swansea's most famous sons returned to the ground where they began their careers for the first international at the Vetch in almost 25 years. After training with the squad at their Porthcawl base, Allchurch, Ford, Ray Daniel and Roy Paul arrived home to a hero's welcome. Half-back Paul had been one of several players who had been attracted by the promise of great riches in Columbian football, only to return after just one match. Immediately transfer-listed by Swansea, he would go on to an illustrious career with Manchester City, where he captained the side for seven seasons between 1950–57. He is considered one of Welsh football's greatest leaders.

Like his City team-mate Roy Clarke, he too would suffer from Alzheimer's in later life.

Needing a win to ensure a chance at the trophy, Wales comfortably beat Ireland 3–0 on a waterlogged Vetch, but England's 2–1 win at Hampden Park a few weeks later saw the trophy shared despite Wales' better goal difference. Still, it was the first shared title since 1939, and was gratefully celebrated. Magnanimously, the English FA insisted Wales keep the trophy for the full 12 months. In their three games, the Welsh had used just 12 players, greatly influenced by the cultured skills of Ivor Allchurch.

Known simply as "the golden boy", Allchurch played with a grace and style unmatched in his era. Some felt he rarely produced his best for Wales, but he was always identified as one of the main threats alongside John Charles. "Allchurch is one of the few footballing geniuses of the world," said Sandor Barcs, chairman of the Hungarian FA. Matt Busby agreed: "He vies with the greatest of all time, yet he has a modesty that becomes him." After his debut against England in 1950, Allchurch played 27 consecutive games for his country. He was also one of Swansea's most loyal players – in the days of the maximum wage, he saw no reason to leave home for a bigger club, and only tried his luck in Division One with Newcastle after the 1958 World Cup. He continued to play for Welsh league clubs into his fifties and was honoured with an MBE, as well as winning Welsh Sports Personality of the Year in 1962. His record of 68 caps stood for 20 years until overtaken by Joey Jones, and he has been honoured by his hometown club with a statue outside the Liberty Stadium.

In 1951, the FAW marked its 75th anniversary with a game against a combined United Kingdom team at Cardiff. Wales took the match very seriously, determined to beat their illustrious opponents. Two early goals and then a third just after half-time put Wales in command. The UK team rallied but two late goals was not enough to snatch a victory from their hosts. Barnes maintained the UK side "tried as hard as they knew how to win and they fought to the last whistle." After the game, the FAW celebrated with a banquet at the Park Hotel, attended by representatives of the football world, and entertained by the Yvonne Cousin Trio and opera singer Zoe Creswell. Amongst the gifts was a replica of the Ardagh Chalice from the Irish FA, and a bannerette from FIFA.

The match saw Wales adopt a new crest after the FAW were granted armorial bearings to mark the anniversary. The English FA and Queens Park FC were the only other footballing organisations to receive the honour and the FAW was clearly being recognized for its loyalty to the crown. As well as featuring on Wales shirts from 1951 to 2011, the armorial ensign was adopted as the official FAW logo until rebranding in 2011. The Welsh badge was conceived by H Ellis Tomlinson, a Cheshire-born schoolteacher who also designed the arms of Wrexham Borough and Prestatyn. The crest featured the motto 'Gorau Chwarae Cyd Chwarae' – Team Play is the Best Play.

With the 1952 Helsinki Olympics approaching, the FAW announced they would not be sending a team to Finland: "In view of the expenditure involved the Council decided it would be impossible for Wales to participate in the games, and whilst not prepared to bear any financial responsibility itself, expressed its willingness for one Association to send a team representing GB, and for the Association so concerned to make arrangements for the constitution of the selection committee and decide upon the procedure for selecting players."

Despite its protestations, the FAW were flush, and with an overflow of cash, they bought shares. They invested £1,000 in electricity, £2,000 in gas, and £6,000 in the Commonwealth of Australia. They also decided to travel to games by air and authorised refurbishment of their Fairy Road offices. In 1952, two internationals generated £17,000 of FAW's total

£25,000 income. Despite expenses of almost £19,000, the FAW accounts were healthy with a balance of £37,000. In December 1952, they decided to enter the 1954 Jules Rimet Cup "subject to satisfactory set up and concurrence of other three British Associations."

In the first match of the 1952/53 Championship, the best Scottish team since the war visited a Welsh side fast gaining a reputation for teamwork and commitment. Before the Ninian Park match, the crowd were entertained by an archery display. Welsh fans and players alike were taken by surprise at the appearance of goalkeeper Billy Shortt, whose summer regime of "foam baths, dieting and hard training" had seen him shed two stone. After a close-fought game, the Scots won 2–1. Shortt died in 2004 on the same day as Brian Clough.

Although they had made a couple of wartime appearances at the famous London ground, Wales' first visit to Wembley for an official international came in November 1952. "For Wales this appearance on the national stage of Wembley is the culmination of all their dreams," trumpeted the London *Times*. A 96,000 crowd produced record receipts for a British international, and they saw England win 5–2 against a Welsh defence missing Barnes. Allchurch and Charles were outstanding in a 3–2 win in Belfast alongside Harry Griffiths, the future Swansea manager, who was making his only Welsh appearance in a five-man Swansea-born attack. From 1953, FIFA ruled that there should be no team called Ireland. From now on, it would be Republic of Ireland and Northern Ireland. The IFA objected and were permitted to play as Ireland in British Championship.

Despite the problems of the ill-fated 1949 continental tour, Wales took even fewer players to face France and Yugoslavia on a 1953 friendly trip. In a party of 26, there were 13 players and 13 administrators, including seven members of the FAW international committee. Charles was critical of the FAW in his autobiography: "They were good people, but they were totally unaware of their place in the game." It was a disastrous trip. Wales lost 6–1 to France and 5–2 at the Partisan Stadium in Belgrade. The scorelines were enough to cost Shortt his place and he would never again play for Wales.

By the middle of the 1950s fewer crowd problems and a decrease in violence saw the game's popularity grow, encouraging the FAW to crack down on manners and politeness. Two players from RAF Valley were severely reprimanded for making "uncomplimentary remarks to the referee" while Druids United were scolded for swearing in the changing rooms after a game against Llay in 1954. There was gamesmanship too – Llanrwst Town were warned after soaking the ball in water at half-time against Bethesda in 1953. The FAW were dismayed however by the increase in bookings – 66 in all games throughout Wales in 1953/54. At the request of the West Wales FA, the FAW published a Welsh-language translation of the laws of the game in 1953.

1954 World Cup

The 1953/54 Championship again doubled as a World Cup qualifying group, with the top two teams earning a place at the 1954 finals in Switzerland. Wales had been growing in confidence despite their ill-fated continental jaunt, and with stars like Allchurch, Ford and Barnes in their side, there was every chance they could make it, especially with two of the three games at home.

Once again Wales needed a good result against England in their first match. But another 4–1 defeat at Cardiff in October 1953 was a major setback, even though the result flattered the victors. Three goals in three minutes came at the start of the second half after Sherwood had left the field injured. By the time he returned Wales were 4–1 down. Charles's stupendous performance in that game earned him the nickname 'King John'. According to the *Times*, "One man above all stood out in embarrassing England. He was Charles, a giant in stature and performance at centre forward in place of the absent

Ford. Not only did Charles move with a mobility astonishing in one his size, but his speed of thought and intelligent, instinctive linking with Allchurch and Davies on either side of him drew the defence of Johnston, Wright, and Dickinson into the queerest shapes."

Wales could not believe they had lost, and certainly did not deserve to concede four. Even though full back Sherwood would captain Wales to victory over the star-studded English in 1955, it was this game he considered the best Welsh performance of his career. "For 20 minutes we pulverised England," wrote Roy Paul. "Time after time we shoved the ball upfield and Charles would rise as though in a lift, nod it down almost contemptuously, and there would be Allchurch and Davies racing through." What might have been, wondered Paul, "if Trevor Ford had been fit." Community singing was introduced for the game, and the programme included lyrics for the usual Welsh hymns, and popular songs such as 'John Brown's Body', 'Clementine' and 'The Lily of Laguna'.

Despite the English defeat, there was great hope Wales could come away from Scotland with a result to keep them in contention, and an 88th minute Charles goal earned them a 3–3 draw. Wales then needed to beat Ireland at Wrexham and hope Scotland lost at home to England with a six-goal swing. The referee for both Wales' home games was faultless – Charles Faultless of Scotland. But a disappointing day saw Ireland win 2–1 in front of 32,819 at Wrexham. The 1954 World Cup campaign was over. Wales had failed to qualify for a major tournament at the final hurdle for the first time. It would not be the last.

The national team's horizons broadened annually and they returned to the continent to face Austria at the end of the 1953/54 season. Walley Barnes had been appointed team manager for the trip, following the innovative path set by Walter Winterbottom and England, but was unable to prevent a 2–0 loss in front of 60,000 fans in Vienna. Austria captain Ernst Ocwirk described the fixture as "the dirtiest game he'd ever seen". The Austrians weren't familiar with the rough-house play of Tapscott and Ford, and they pointedly vowed to get their revenge at Wrexham a year later.

European fixtures appealed to supporters and games against the top nations started to be held more regularly. Some 43,000 fans finished work early to be at Ninian Park for the 5.30 p.m. midweek kick-off against Yugoslavia in September 1954. Wales were seeking to avenge the defeat in Belgrade and things looked promising when Allchurch gave them the lead. "It was the kind of goal that gave me the greatest pleasure," he recalled. "A left foot shot that smacked into the back of their net." But Yugoslavia had a trick up their sleeve. They brought on a substitute – something all but unheard of at the time – who changed the game with a hat-trick in the final 20 minutes after a dubious penalty turned the game in Yugoslavia's favour. It was Wales' first home defeat to continental opposition. The FAW, suspicious of the new medium of television, had refused the BBC permission to broadcast the game. But they knew they could not isolate themselves from the lucrative overseas game, and in August 1954, agreed to join the Federation of European Football Associations (UEFA). The FAW was officially accepted at a meeting in Vienna on 2 March 1955.

Wales began the 1954/55 British Championship with a 0–1 home defeat to Scotland. A crowd of 58,198 had turned up at Ninian Park to watch a Wales team with a growing reputation. There were four Arsenal players in the side, even though the Gunners had a big game against Portsmouth at Highbury on the same day – Kelsey, Barnes, Bowen and Tapscott all turned out for their country. Charles "stood out like a master among a collection of learners," according to the *Times*. There were an increasing number of people who thought he was wasted at centre half, and Wales did look more threatening when he pushed forward late on. But it was a poor display and the press bemoaned the standard of

British football. "We expect more from international teams and until we get it the rest of the world will go by."

At least the critics were happier with the game against England at Wembley. Charles was moved from centre half to centre forward. With Ford shifted to inside-right and Allchurch at inside-left, this was the most talented front three in British football and Wales' performance warranted a better result. Charles' goal kept his team in front until 20 minutes from time, but a hat-trick from Roy Bentley won the game 3–2 for England despite Charles levelling at two each. Bentley would go on to manage Swansea between 1969 and 1972. Charles maintained his great form with a hat-trick in Belfast to earn a Welsh win practically single-handed. "The amazing John Charles was an absolute tower of strength in the middle of the Welsh attack," wrote the *Western Mail*.

Charles was one of a series of youngsters produced at Swansea in the early 1950s. The Swansea Schools' team dominated Welsh junior football after the war, winning – solely or jointly – the Welsh National Shield 13 times between 1946 and 1960. With a successful home-grown policy, the Swans were able to field an all-Welsh side at Blackburn in 1954, including nine players from the Swansea area. Nine of the team would play for Wales: John King, Mel Charles, Dai Thomas, Ron Burgess, Harry Griffiths, Terry Medwin, Ivor Allchurch, Len Allchurch and Cliff Jones. Fellow international Des Palmer had also been at the club and John Charles served his apprenticeship at his home town side. Swansea Town would provide the backbone of the 1958 World Cup squad.

Debuts were given in Belfast to two players who would suffer in comparison with their more illustrious brothers. Mel Charles and Len Allchurch were fine players in their own rights, but both would admit to spending their entire careers in the shadows of John and Ivor.

Wales had not beaten England for 17 years, and the team that came to Cardiff in 1955 was full of stars. Billy Wright, Tom Finney, Nat Lofthouse and Matthews were expected to continue England's dominance. But there was an unusual optimism in the air. For the first time, all of Wales' key players – Kelsey, Charles, Tapscott, Ford and Allchurch – were available. Wales even prepared tactics. Roy Paul said Wales never usually had any "wild-eyed ideas about plans." When he had asked about his playing role before his debut, he had simply been shown his red jersey. "This is the only plan we need. You are wearing the Welsh shirt. Don't let it down," he was told.

A huge crowd packed Ninian Park, and in these days before managers, Wales were led by captain Sherwood. Ford also claimed it was the first time he heard a pre-match talk with his country. Sherwood chose a man-to-man marking system, and instilled the mantra "chase till you drop" into his team. West Brom's Stuart Williams marked Finney, John Charles had Lofthouse, and Sherwood himself would stick to Matthews like glue. Then they set about the English with venom. After Wales had scored two goals in the space of 40 seconds, a Charles own goal set nerves jangling. "If they think they are going to get away with that, they can think again," muttered Charles as Wales restarted. It looked all over when injury reduced Roy Paul to passenger status, but with goalkeeper Kelsey playing "the game of a lifetime" Wales clung on. "How the Welsh sang that day," remembered Paul. "The Ninian Park crowd has never been more magnificent. Like a vast herbaceous border strewn round the playing pitch with their red flags waving." The team enjoyed the huge celebrations at the Park Hotel, and once again, there were plaudits for John Charles. "Here indeed is the perfect footballer if ever there was one," wrote Dewi Lewis.

Jack Kelsey was picked alongside Charles to represent Wales in the Great Britain side against the Rest of Europe in the FIFA anniversary game in Belfast. He would become a great servant to his country, often winning games for his team with brilliant athletic displays. After an examination late in his career, it transpired he had played for years with a deformed spine. Following retirement, Kelsey managed Arsenal's club shop at Highbury.

Victory over England meant Wales were favourites for the 1955 Championship. But as Charles explained: "We were walking on air after that victory but it must have gone to our heads." His team lost to Scotland and then had a great chance to beat the Irish, only for Roy Paul to miss a penalty with Wales already a goal up. "That penalty miss is the most miserable moment I have ever had in my international career," he said after Ireland's equalizer denied Wales the title. The Championship would be shared between all four teams for the only time in the 100-year history of the competition. Paul, a former Royal Marine, was the uncle of Alan Curtis, Welsh star of the 1970s and '80s.

Mindful of the controversial 1954 game in Vienna, all eyes were on Wrexham in November 1955. The Austrians had finished third in the 1954 World Cup and, with a training regime that included long jump, high jump, hurdling and marathon running, were in good shape when they arrived to face Wales. "We jump higher, run faster and charge heavier than any of the Welsh team. Therefore we are bound to win," they claimed. The visitors were not too impressed with the Wrexham facilities which they described as a "primitive village green." "Did they think we were a third rate team, not worthy of being allowed to play in Cardiff?" they asked. Austria remembered well the tough time they had received in the first meeting, and were determined to avenge their harsh treatment in a game which became known as 'The Battle of Wrexham'. Austria won a brutal game by two goals to one, and Roy Paul sets the post-match scene on the first page of his autobiography *Red Dragon of Wales*: "Our goalkeeper, Jack Kelsey, had scars on both legs. Derek Tapscott, our inside right, had a six inch gash on one knee. In another corner of the dressing room, John Charles, the genial giant from Leeds United, leaned over his brother Melvyn with tears in his eyes. Melvyn lay silent, still dazed by a tackle which had sent him crashing to the ground some twenty minutes earlier."

The Western Mail screamed: "THIS WAS A DISGRACE TO NATIONAL FOOTBALL." "The match degenerated into a game of rugby," said Austrian trainer Herr Moltzer. The Austrian captain blamed Wales. "It was more like a boxing and kicking match than football," he said. "Some players seemed to go almost berserk," wrote the *Western Mail*. At least the Austrians went home with fond memories of the Welsh supporters, who had cheered their play and condemned every foul, whichever side had committed it.

In an increasingly sophisticated sport, it was no longer enough that a captain and his players discuss rudimentary tactics an hour before kick-off. Continental teams were more advanced and Jimmy Murphy was appointed Wales' team manager in 1956. It was only with his appointment that selection decisions were taken away from the committee. The team trainer was appointed on a game-by-game basis, but former boxing trainer Bill Dodman was with the team home and away in his capacity as 'Honorary Masseur'. Roy Paul described Dodman, who was also a Wrexham director, as the team's "guide, philosopher, and friend." If a man was injured, Dodman would patch him up. He had plenty of work to do after the Austrian match.

Wales were inconsistent, and would slip from world-beaters to also-rans between games. Poor finishing in particular let them down, and a draw against Ireland was followed by a 2–2 draw with Scotland in 1956. One FAW councillor claimed to have diagnosed the reasons for inconsistency. "Ford and Allchurch are our problem boys now." The appointment of Murphy saw a change in Welsh preparation for games. He worked players in small combinations to develop partnerships throughout the team and believed in hard training sessions right up to match day. The team found themselves training twice a day before a game, often at Weybridge in Surrey, where they were based when in England.

A series of bad injuries in the 3–1 defeat at Wembley in 1956 prompted calls for the introduction of substitutes to the British game. Wales finished with nine men after Mel Charles had been struck heavily by the ball. When Kelsey was taken off injured, his place was taken by 5ft 7in Alf Sherwood, who played heroically in the Welsh goal for his final international cap. Sherwood had played in 33 consecutive internationals since 1949.

Wales were drawn in a difficult group for the 1958 World Cup, alongside East Germany and Czechoslovakia, one of the best teams in Europe. Murphy agreed to become Wales' full-time permanent manager in March 1957 on one proviso – that he could pick the team. However, he was unable to persuade the committee to allow him to recall Ford – ostracised for his spill-the-beans honesty. But the new manager had his way on most issues. He was an inspirational motivator, often telling players to think about the hard-working miners who had come to watch them play.

The Czechs arrived with an interesting list of demands for their game in Cardiff two months after Murphy's appointment. They wanted ten footballs, reasonably enough, but also a trip to the seaside (specifically not the mountains), 300 stamped postcards, and the opportunity to buy British cigarettes.

Wales were not expecting John Charles to play any part in qualification after his shock transfer to Juventus from Leeds. However, *Western Mail* reporter Dewi Lewis telephoned Turin and managed to speak to Juventus chairman Umberto Agnelli. Lewis claimed that he alone drew out an agreement that saw Charles return for the crucial game against the Czechs. Wales were already missing Ivor Allchurch to injury and Ray Daniel to suspension, but with Charles in the side anything was possible. Welsh preparations were further affected when Tottenham refused to release Hopkins and Medwin until the day before the game, as they were required to play a meaningless end-of-season fixture at Burnley. It was a tough game against the Czechs in front of 50,000 at

Cardiff, but a Roy Vernon goal and a superb performance from Kelsey gave Wales the win and a great start to the group. Ron Stitfall, winning his second and final cap some five years after his first, would become the Welsh team's kitman in the 1990s.

The 16-strong Czech squad at Cardiff confirmed the view of the Welsh press that the FAW's decision to take just 13 or 14 players to Eastern Europe was pure folly. They urged the council to take a larger squad to Leipzig when the Welsh team spent a difficult week behind the Iron Curtain later that month, playing East Germany before flying onto Prague to face the Czechs. Nonetheless, only 12 players flew out to Berlin, alongside ten FAW councillors. There was no financial reason for the FAW to go short on players. Thanks to the huge rise in attendances, it was now considered "a body of influence and wealth." The £3,800 cost of this European trip was practically covered by the single home game against Czechoslovakia which earned £10,000 at the gate before expenses. The FAW now held reserves of more than £50,000, but still scrimped on the playing side. One of the 12 players on the trip, Tapscott, was injured, and Charles would only meet up with the squad in Leipzig. "There were more selectors than players," he told Mario Risoli for his book *When Pelé Broke Our Hearts*. "It was crazy. You've got to put the players first but with Wales it was the selectors first and the players second."

Wales were favourites to beat the amateur East Germans, playing their first competitive match. But the hosts were supported by a crowd of 110,000, all desperate to see the Charles in action. The Welsh had been surprised at their first training session to see the whole East German squad sitting in the stands watching their every move. Their opponents must have learned something, because despite taking the lead, Wales were disappointing and lost 2–1.

With three players injured or ill, Wales had just ten men to face the Czechs in Prague. Even so, the FAW announced it still would not call up replacements. Only after an outraged press corps in Leipzig protested, did they arrange to get Ray Daniel from his holidays in Swansea. Daniel had not played for months due to suspension over illegal payments, and Des Palmer, who was yet to represent his country, also travelled. Daniel was forced to wear new boots, and the pain was so great from the hard leather that he played the last ten minutes in socks. It was no real surprise when the bedraggled and under-prepared Welsh lost 2–0. Things got worse for Daniel – he was chastised by the FAW's church-going secretary Herbert Powell for singing a popular show tune on the bus and was never selected again.

With Czechoslovakia beating the East Germans twice, Wales' qualification attempt was over by the time East Germany came to Cardiff in September. Juventus gave an early indication of the problems Wales would face in future when they refused to release Charles for an admittedly meaningless game. His replacement was Swansea's Des Palmer who took the opportunity by scoring a hat-trick in Wales' 4–1 win. Kelsey was also a late withdrawal and his replacement, the Cardiff newsagent Graham Vearncombe, was out delivering papers when he learned of his call-up.

The introduction of regular competitive games against continental opposition would take its toll on the British Championship. From the day Czechoslovakia visited Cardiff, the glamour of the familiar Brits began to fade, and the 1957/58 Championship seemed dour by comparison.

"England beat nothing," wrote the *Times* of the 0–4 defeat in October 1957. "The worst Welsh side one has seen for years," it claimed. Without Charles, Ford, Tapscott and Allchurch, Wales were swept away in front of a 60,000 crowd singing 'Cwm Rhondda' and 'Sospan Fach' to encourage a repeat of the win at the same venue two years earlier. "Too many of this Welsh side were not of international calibre," cried the *Western Mail*.

While the FAW refused a request for a fundraising match

in aid of the Commonwealth Games in Cardiff in 1958, it did donate 250 guineas. Requests for benefit matches for the Urdd and Undeb Cymru Fydd were also rejected. Entertainment tax was finally abolished and clubs looked forward to the financial boost the decision would bring. With clubs in a healthy shape, the association turned its attention to the issue of football in education.

The FAW had complained about the lack of football in schools four years earlier, and 1957 saw a series of protests across Wales when rugby was introduced as the sole sport in grammar schools across the country. The situation at Fishguard and, in particular, Llandysul, made front page news when the new headmaster effectively banned pupils from playing football outside school. "We boys of Llandysul are unanimous that we want soccer. We have no place for rugby. This district is a soccer stronghold," protested one pupil. The Llandysul headmaster eventually caved in, allowing the boys to play for local clubs when the school had no competitive fixture. But the row was symptomatic of a problem growing throughout Wales since the war.

The importance of education in post-war Wales had seen an increase in the number of young men attending university in England. Rugby was the main game in these colleges and when these students were appointed masters in Welsh grammar schools, they brought their prejudices towards football. Rugby was a more sociable game, they claimed, as it allowed 30 boys to take part, rather than just 22. Most importantly, they supported the game's amateur ethos. There were also complaints from grassroots volunteers that while the Welsh Rugby Union supported youth development, the FAW had little contact with the Welsh Schools Football Association and left junior clubs without backing. The Welsh press joined the attack on the FAW, who, despite their wealth, gave paltry support to the financially crippled WSFA. The WRU donated more than £2,000 annually to its schools association; the FAW gave only £200 to its football equivalent. Education's attitude towards football was still apparent in the late 1960s when Terry Yorath won a Welsh cap as a pupil of Cathays Grammar School, Cardiff. The school displayed framed photographs of rugby players who had received honours, but refused to do the same for a football international.

Out of the blue, news reached the Welsh public in December 1957 that there would be a second chance to qualify for the Sweden World Cup when teams refused to play Israel in the Asian group due to the political situation in the Middle East. First Turkey refused, followed by Indonesia after FIFA rejected their request to face Israel on neutral ground. Egypt also withdrew, allowing Sudan and Israel to progress automatically to the final qualification round, where Sudan then also withdrew. FIFA rules stated no team could qualify for the finals without playing a single game, so it decided to match one of the group runners-up against Israel in a play-off.

When Uruguay and Italy refused to take part in the process, Wales were one of nine names placed in the Jules Rimet trophy for the draw. Belgium were pulled from the cup, but refused the offer as a matter of pride. Wales had no such qualms when their ticket was pulled and they grasped their second chance to reach the finals. Tottenham striker Terry Medwin was adamant however that Wales' place was somehow deserved: "In many ways, we felt that just justice had been done," he said. "We beat the Czechs in Cardiff and crushed East Germany 4–1 there." No one imagined that Wales were using up their quota of World Cup luck for the next 50 years.

Wales were backed for the first leg in Tel Aviv by 90 Welsh servicemen who had chartered two planes from their base in Cyprus to attend the play-off. In a typical example of the amateurism of the time, the Welsh were limited to just physical training before the game when it was discovered they had forgotten to bring a ball. The team were invited to a reception by the British Ambassador who had thoughtfully hung bunches of leeks around the embassy to make them feel at home. The game was won comfortably 2–0 with goals from Allchurch and Cliff Jones.

Wales made heavy work of beating a team "no better than a third division side" in the second leg at Cardiff. A superb performance from goalkeeper Ya'acov Chodorov denied the Welsh time and time again. Constant fouling, especially on Charles and Allchurch, went unpunished, though Wales' golden boy produced a piece of magic late on to break the deadlock. Murphy's team knew they would have to improve quickly for the finals in Sweden, but nonetheless they had made it. Wales were on their way to the World Cup.

The following day, the football world was shaken when an aeroplane carrying Manchester United's young squad crashed on an icy runway at Munich. As the death toll grew, neighbours crowded into the front parlour of a small terraced house in Swansea to listen to the radio. Winifred Morgans made tea as her friends waited for news of her 18-year-old son Kenny, who had made his United debut just six weeks earlier. The family feared the worst when the search was called off without news of Kenny. Miraculously, five hours later, two German reporters walking around the scene spotted Morgans lying under a wheel of the plane. He survived, but was never the same player again, and missed out on selection for Sweden. He finished his career at Swansea and Newport in Division Four. As news of the incident was relayed, John Charles' mother begged her son never to fly again, but he needed to get back to Turin.

1958 World Cup

Wales were given little hope of success in the build-up to the finals, but were encouraged by the draw, which placed them in Group Three with Mexico, Hungary, and hosts Sweden. "We could not have had a better draw if we had arranged it ourselves," beamed Milwyn Jenkins. The optimism was lessened by a doubt over Charles' availability when the Italian

FA looked to block his participation, despite his late release by the sympathetic Juventus board. A second selection controversy arose when the FAW refused Mel Charles and Ivor Allchurch permission to take part in Swansea's summer tour of Germany. In response, Swans manager Ron Burgess threatened to call off the tour if his top players were unavailable, although he later conceded the issue.

Unembarrassed by their previous extravagances, FAW administrators once again took up more seats than the players on the flight to Stockholm. Herbert Powell took his sister for company, while three of the eleven selectors took their wives. An extra five councillors went along for the jolly in an official party that took up 25 seats on the plane. To reduce costs, Wales only took 18 players, four short of the 22 allowed. It was the first time many of the players had met the selectors, and they were astounded at their lack of football knowledge. Several even claimed some selectors failed to recognize squad members.

The players were not kitted out luxuriously for the finals – they were supplied with a blazer and a pair of trousers. They were also loaned a tracksuit which was expected back by the FAW after the tournament. Wales were welcomed on Swedish tarmac with a bouquet of red, white and blue flowers by their Swedish hosts – a mistake exacerbated by the playing of 'God Save the Queen' before each match. *Western Mail* reporter Dewi Lewis told Murphy he expected Charles to arrive in Stockholm the following day. "Well that is good news," said Murphy. The only information coming from Italy was press hearsay. With Italy out, the IFA had arranged a cup competition to fill the empty dates. Generously, given that Charles' appearance would increase attendances, Juve's three opponents sent letters to the IFA asking for Charles' release for Wales.

To the Welsh squad, the World Cup was no big deal – it was merely another competition with the added bonus of a few weeks abroad. "For most of us Sweden was just a nice trip," admitted Colin Webster. Murphy was forced to read the riot act in the tournament build-up when he accused his players of failing to take the competition seriously. Derek Sullivan had forgotten his passport, Cliff Jones had forgotten his training kit, and two others forgot their gym shoes. Embarrassingly, Wales were also forced to borrow training tops from England due to a delay in the arrival of the tracksuits. And after a mix-up over facilities at Finchley FC, they were forced to train in Hyde Park, spending much of the morning hiding from the park warden due to a ban on ball games. It was hardly the best build-up for a World Cup, and Jenkins' promise of a more professional Wales seemed hollow.

During the trip, a group of fringe players took things a little less seriously than the others. Derrick Sullivan, Colin Webster, Colin Baker, Ken Leek and Ken Jones became known as 'The Big Five'. Like naughty schoolboys, they would sneak out to buy beer and disappear into the forest for the afternoon with bottles chinking in a kitbag. Not that alcohol was completely frowned upon – there was beer on the dinner tables – but 'The Big Five' had formed an unofficial social club and spent much of their time hiding from the disapproving glares of the church-going committee. Even Murphy was known to take a few tots of whiskey in the dugout while he watched the games.

The Welsh manager was still in the dark about Charles' availability until three days before Wales' opening game and had prepared for a tournament without his best player. Charles eventually arrived in the early hours, long after his welcome car had driven back to the hotel. As he strolled unannounced into the breakfast room of the hotel in Soltsjobaden, the FAW committee men and their wives began singing 'For He's a Jolly Good Fellow'. But one man who would not have received such a welcome was Arsenal's Derek Tapscott, who insisted his omission had been down to selector Fred Dewey. Tapscott claimed Dewey had promised him a World Cup place if he moved to Cardiff City. The player refused and was left out of the party for Sweden.

It is difficult to overestimate the influence of John Charles on the Welsh team. Standing more than six feet tall and weighing 14 stone, he had no right to be as graceful and skillful as a much smaller man. He could play in defence or attack – many considering him the world's best centre half and centre forward at the same time. He was unquestionably the most valuable player of his generation. We hear so many superlatives about Charles that it is easy to become blasé. "Without doubt he is the most complete player Britain has produced," said Cliff Jones. "If you go anywhere in the world, they know about John. He was the best player I ever played with," said Terry Medwin. Late in his life, Il Buon Gigante – the Gentle Giant – was voted the Italian League's greatest ever foreign import – surpassing the likes of Maradona, Platini and Gullit. During his entire career, even in that cynical Serie A, Charles was never booked let alone sent-off. And that is perhaps his greatest achievement.

Along with his inspirational captain Dave Bowen, Murphy formulated a plan that would play to the strengths of his Welsh side. They would use Arsenal's defensive game – 'parking the bus' in modern parlance. The opposition would be harangued, pressurised and denied the space to play their cultured football. When the team was not in possession, only Charles remained in attack, which left him exposed and vulnerable to brutal treatment. And even he would drop deep.

After winning a warm-up friendly 19–0 against a local side, Wales' first tournament game was against the Hungarians, who had been a dominant force in the previous World Cup. But Hungary had lost several players during the revolution of 1956, and were more vulnerable than their reputation suggested. The Magyars took the lead after just four minutes and spent the rest of the game stopping Charles in any way possible. Journalist Ian Wooldridge, assigned to Wales throughout the tournament, described the Hungarian tactics. "Their fundamental plan was to shackle John Charles by methods either just inside or wildly outside the international laws of soccer," he wrote. The Welsh totem would not be denied however, and climbed above a mass of bodies to head Wales' equalizer. Kelsey, Wales' Player of the Tournament to many, played a blinder in the goal.

Next came Mexico, who had lost 0–3 to Sweden in their opening match. Despite being favourites, Wales were extremely poor on the day and may have been intimidated by the Mexican fans, backed by 15,000 Swedes. By contrast, Wales only had a following of a boat-load of Royal Navy Seaman docked in the area. "Welsh Display was Shocking," screamed the *Western Mail*. These really were times when little was known of opposition. At first Wales, and now Mexico had surprised the pundits. Medwin said: "It was one of the few times in my career when I've felt frightened. About 400 Mexican supporters, all wearing sombreros, created havoc from the sidelines and they were on my side of the pitch. I must admit that I changed wings for 30 minutes to stay clear of them." Wales were criticized for persisting with their defensive game and under-using Charles. After escaping with a fortunate point, they looked with trepidation to their final match against Sweden, who had beaten both Mexico and Hungary.

Sweden's victory over Hungary meant the hosts had already qualified for the quarter-finals. When they faced Wales, they rested five players, much to the fury of the Hungarians, who needed a Swedish win. If Wales thought this would be to their advantage, they were wrong. Sweden's reserves fought like tigers to earn a place in the side. Kelsey, with chewing gum rubbed into his hands for better grip, was again immense, as was the unsung Graham Williams in defence. John Charles spent much of the game in his old centre half position, drawing fierce criticism from the Swedish press. Wales managed the 0–0 draw needed to earn a play-off against the Hungarians, but many felt they could have been more adventurous and avoided the replay which led to Charles missing the quarter-final. "I still think my policy of playing for a draw was the correct one," Murphy said. It is difficult to argue against the manager – Wales had gone four games unbeaten despite their awful history against foreign opposition. The defensive 'funnel' tactic suited them and they became better drilled with each game.

The selectors were left in an awkward position – they had already booked flights home, so certain were they that Wales would be knocked out early. They waved goodbye to a squad that was secretly relieved to see them go, but to everybody's surprise and dismay, they returned the next day having booked another flight from London to Stockholm.

Wales then faced Hungary in the play-off needing their first win of the tournament. A drawn game would see the Hungarians progress on goal difference, so for once Wales abandoned their defensive approach. Only 2,823 spectators watched the biggest game in Welsh history. "The dual was so fierce," said Medwin, "that we hardly noticed the near silence from the terraces." Wales went behind but captain Bowen inspired his team to battle for everything. Charles was the victim of numerous fearsome challenges with little protection from the Russian referee, and spent spells on the sidelines receiving treatment. On his return from one patch-up job, his lobbed pass allowed Allchurch to score a fine goal from distance. A mazy run from Medwin led to Wales' second, and they held out to earn a famous victory despite Burgess being stretchered off after another foul late in the game.

Ian Wooldridge said: "I shall be eternally grateful for the privilege of seeing one of the most dynamic, dramatic and colourful pages in Welsh sporting history carved out in sweat – and in blood – across the green acres of that stadium in Stockholm. The way Wales achieved their 2–1 triumph on this night should absolve them from every other iota of criticism. They were truly magnificent." Charles missed the presence of Trevor Ford. "One thing I know for sure is that had he played I would not have been subject to such a fearsome kicking from the Hungarians. He would have made sure he deflected a lot of the attention." The Welsh press went further. "A Russian referee must not be allowed to officiate where an Iron Curtain team are one of the sides," wrote Lewis in the *Western Mail*. Bowen's tactical switch had surprised the Hungarians, who were magnanimous after defeat: "Wales surprised us with the strength of their attacking and excellent ball play." At last Murphy's Wales had been freed from their shackles to show the world they could play. Next up were the mighty Brazilians.

After the play-off, Wales only had one day off after a 300-mile flight. Meanwhile, in Gothenburg their opponents awaited, nicely rested and settled at the base they used for the whole tournament. With Charles receiving emergency treatment after what one reporter called "the most tremendous battering I have ever seen administered to any soccer player," the whole country crossed fingers that the talisman would be fit to face tournament favourites Brazil. Charles was initially optimistic. "It will take an army to stop me turning out," he said. The Swedish press held little hope for Wales, suggesting a five-goal handicap would be needed to make the tie interesting. The damning forecast seemed justified when news broke that the devastated Charles had failed to recover from his hammering. "I don't think I've ever seen a player experience such bitter disappointment," said Medwin. "John was almost in tears when he finally lost his fight for fitness." Murphy remained defiant, but knew the odds were against his side. "I am not going to say we will beat the Brazilians," he said, "but by gum, we are going to make a mighty effort to do so."

With Tapscottt and Ford absent and Des Palmer injured, Charles had been Wales' only centre forward in Sweden. Ironically, his replacement Colin Webster had already been earmarked for early retirement by the FAW after an incident in a Swedish nightclub which ended with him head-butting a waiter. But the FAW had no choice – there was no alternative to bad-boy Webster.

Charles' absence was critical according to the *Sunday Times'* Brian Glanville: "I still say that if he hadn't been kicked to pieces by the brutal Hungarians in the previous play-off game, Wales could have won because all sorts of very tempting centres were coming across the goal and John wasn't there to head them in." Glanville was being generous. Brazil had many shots, and only fine defensive work from Mel Charles, voted centre half of the tournament, and another wonderful performance from Kelsey kept Wales in the game. In the 73rd minute, a miss-hit Pelé shot struck the underside of Stuart Williams' boot and rolled beyond the Welsh keeper. Brazil were magnanimous in victory, and Bowen's men received an ovation as they left the field. "Wales have won many friends in Brazil with this brave performance," said forward Didi. Pelé still calls it his most important, and luckiest, goal.

Murphy now regretted the defensive tactics which saw the Sweden game drawn. "If we had not played on Tuesday, I've got a feeling Wales would have shocked the soccer world by being in the semi-finals next week," he admitted. What he meant was that Charles would have been available, but Murphy should have no regrets. This was Wales' first experience of a major international tournament, and he had been understandably cautious. Wales had gone out as no-hopers, and returned exceeding all expectations. But there was no reception at the airport, or anywhere else for that matter. The squad drifted back to their clubs and reflected on their World Cup adventure. "I don't think a lot of people in Wales knew the World Cup was on," said Mel Charles, who later described how Pelé's match shirt ended up being worn on the Swansea parks: "When I finished playing professional football I ran a Sunday league pub team in Swansea. We didn't have any money to buy shirts so I brought down all my international shirts that I had collected over the years for the boys to put on – including Pelé's shirt from the World Cup."

In 1958, the growth in international football saw changes to the system that governed the game. FIFA were becoming more influential and their voting power on the IFAB increased. As a result, each British association had a single vote compared to FIFA's four, with any proposal needing six of the eight votes to be carried. The system remains in force today. There were also calls for a combined Great Britain team to replace the individual nations in future World Cups.

In November, Llanelli FC, perhaps frustrated by the FAW's refusal to allow them to join the Southern League, proposed the formation of a Welsh Premier League. The idea was popular among prominent clubs. Abergavenny Thursdays, who were dominating the (South) Welsh League turned down a chance to join the Southern League in the hope the FAW might form a genuinely National League. In the north, the FAW also refused Rhyl permission to join the Cheshire League, while, Lovell's Athletic withdrew from the Southern League to join the Welsh system. But there were concerns about a national Welsh pyramid in Merthyr and Barry where both clubs were keen to retain their English fixtures, believing the Welsh League to be of a lower standard than the English Southern League.

After the novelty of Sweden, it was back to the British Championship for Murphy's heroic side, and Scotland were next up. Both managers for the October 1958 game were employed by Manchester United. Matt Busby was in charge of the Scots while his Old Trafford assistant Murphy managed a Welsh side including Leyton Orient amateur Phil Woosnam from Caersws. Woosnam would soon leave his post as a physics teacher to turn professional with West Ham, and won 17 caps before becoming one of the game's most progressive thinkers. The FAW had even wanted him to head their long-term coaching strategy in 1967, but were dealt a blow when he emigrated to America to coach the

United States national team coach and then become NASL commissioner. A naturalized American citizen, he is a cousin of golfer Ian Woosnam.

Tickets were scarce for the first game in Cardiff after Wales' exploits in Sweden, and players were pestered as they trained at the Guest Keen Sports Ground on Sloper Road near Ninian Park. Wales' erratic form continued, losing 0–3, even with what was described as the best defence in the world. The result was early evidence that Wales could no longer rely on the stalwarts of the World Cup and rebuilding was needed.

In November 1958, Jack Kelsey made history by playing for Wales in the creditable 2–2 draw with England at Villa Park in the afternoon before dashing to London for Arsenal's game against Juventus in the evening. With Phil Woosnam unwell, a police officer was dispatched to the home of Cardiff City's Brian Jenkins to ask him to travel to Birmingham as backup.

Wales had rejected the offer to play the match under floodlights with Milwyn Jenkins arguing that all internationals should be played in daylight. And a proposal from the Football League that all international matches should again be played midweek was turned down by the home associations in 1959. With the FAW reliant on international fixtures to survive, a move away from lucrative Saturday matches would have been disastrous. It was suggested that clubs be given powers to postpone games if their players were called up for their country. Meanwhile the English FA wanted to cancel the British Championship in World Cup qualifying seasons, a move that would have crippled the FAW. Wales were struggling to maintain the status quo, as innovators looked to develop the international game over its traditional calendar based on the British Championship.

Crystal Palace goalkeeper Vic Rouse became the first fourth division player to win an international cap when he replaced the injured Kelsey for the final game of the 1958/59

Championship against Northern Ireland. Rouse conceded four goals as Wales were outplayed. A year after reaching the 1958 World Cup quarter-final, Wales were once again left holding the wooden spoon.

By 1959/60, there was a worrying increase in bad behaviour from players, and to a lesser extent, supporters in Wales. There were 149 bookings, a big increase from the 66 issued in 1953/4, and these increases only grew in following years. By 1962/63 there were 194 yellow cards and 278 by 1963/64. Falling attendances continued to worry the authorities and as the 1950s boom years receded, they looked for answers. Poor facilities were seen as a major factor and clubs strove to make improvements. There was a new terrace and covered stand at Ninian Park, replacing the old ash covered Bob Bank. Wrexham supporters paid for floodlights at the Racecourse and the new lights at Ninian even attracted Cardiff rugby matches as sport cashed in on the novelty of playing at night.

There were no such concerns about attendances at internationals in Cardiff: A record 62,634 saw the 1–1 draw against England in October 1959. Graham Moore became the third youngest British international player when he made his debut, aged 18 years and five months, and his 90th minute goal was enough to earn him the BBC Wales Sports Personality of the Year, one of only nine footballers to earn the award. Incredibly, John Charles is not among them.

Charles made a rare appearance for his country after his Italian move when he turned out at centre half for Wales' second game of the 1959/60 competition, a 1–1 draw at Hampden Park in November 1959. Wales' venerated defence had mounted an impressive rearguard action after losing Mel Hopkins on 13 minutes. "I have never felt so proud to play in a Welsh team as I did today," said captain Stuart Williams. When Wales beat Ireland in the last game of the season, there were signs that a new youthful side was developing that could do well in the 1962 Chile World Cup. Welsh ambitions now looked beyond the British Championship.

8

THE LOST DECADE
1960–1969

S PEAKING AS WELSH manager in the 1980s, Mike England was scathing about the Wales team he captained in the 1960s: "Quite frankly, apart from five or six players, the rest of the team wasn't up to international standard."

It's difficult to know what went so wrong. Wales had good players like Wyn and Ron Davies, Mike England, Cliff Jones, Terry Hennessey, Gary Sprake and Ronnie Rees. It seems that poor results spiralled into apathy and failure. Wales were seen as a 'lost cause' by English clubs who felt under no pressure to release players for fixtures where Wales had no chance of success. Whatever the cause, the Sixties were pretty grim for the national side. At least the clubs in Wales were excited by the introduction of European competition.

At the start of the decade, despite the influence of Jimmy Murphy, the Welsh team was still selected by a committee of 11 FAW councillors, the Welsh Senior Selection Committee. These men had given good service to the junior game, but were inexperienced at the top level. And it showed. One member is said to have provided a glowing scouting report on Ron Stitfall only to be told Stitfall had not played in the game he watched. Another refused to scout players alone. But the association was still all-powerful and flexed its muscles as clubs sought independence. When Cardiff fielded a reserve side against Swansea in 1960, they were ordered to show the Welsh Cup more respect or permission to play in England would be revoked. With Cardiff in Division One, there was pressure on the FAW to increase south Walian representation and move council meetings south. Huge attendances in Cardiff meant Wrexham had not hosted England since 1932 or Scotland since 1946. The north was fighting a losing battle as the power of influence shifted unrelentingly south.

The decade began against new opponents. At long last, Wales faced the Republic of Ireland in Dublin in September 1960. The FAW had repeatedly opposed the FAI's requests to join the British Championship, and it had not gone unnoticed. "We have been especially disappointed at the hostility of the FAW to our association and it is hard to understand," complained the FAI. England had begun fixtures against Eire 14 years earlier, while the FAW consistently refused, displaying strong loyalty to its friends in Belfast. Wales won 3–2 in Dublin with goals from Cliff Jones and Phil Woosnam. It has been said this was Jones' best game for Wales. "He was brilliant," said Terry Medwin. "We had to come from behind and if there was one player you could point to and say 'he's a match winner,' it would have been Cliff in that kind of form." Jones, the son of Welsh international Ivor Jones, was an integral part of Tottenham's double-winning team in 1961, and was considered one of the finest wingers in world football. He was the only Welshmen to feature in the Great Britain side which faced the Rest of Europe in the Stanley Matthews tribute game at Stoke in 1965. Jones won 59 caps for Wales – only Ivor Allchurch had won more at that time. A proud Welsh player, he would say: "When I pull the red shirt over my head I feel ten feet tall."

In the first British Championship of the 1960s, Wales beat a lightweight Scotland for the first time in nine years in the mud and rain of Ninian Park on a foul October day. Seven of the side had won less than ten caps as Murphy looked to rebuild. During the game, the public address announcer appealed for one spectator to return to his ship. That errant sailor would miss a magnificent, battling, long-ball performance which would come to characterize Murphy's young side. It was a performance which would feed optimism growing for success in Chile.

But after five games unbeaten, Welsh confidence was crushed by a 1–5 hammering at Wembley. Stung by the setback, Wales looked to re-establish their credentials when they faced Northern Ireland in April 1961, just a week ahead of their opening World Cup game against Spain. Graham 'Flicka' Williams grabbed two goals on his debut in a 5–1 victory in Belfast watched by Spanish manager Pedro Escartin. "Spain, indeed have tremendous opposition next week in Cardiff," he said, though it was a deceptively weak Northern Irish side.

1962 World Cup

Victory in Belfast created false expectation in the Welsh camp. Murphy presumptuously requested an end-of-season training camp "so that we can go to Chile fully used to each other." Wales were drawn in a group of only two, but to progress they would have to defeat the mighty Spanish over two games and then face Morocco in a play-off. There was great optimism however – Wales were still buoyant after the 1958 World Cup, though the refusal of Juventus to release John Charles for the games against Spain was a blow.

Spain arrived at Rhoose airport in 1961 and were surprised to find themselves sharing a Porthcawl hotel with the Welsh team. They had been banned from training at Ninian Park and were none too impressed with their alternative facilities. "We have never been treated like this before when we have gone abroad," they complained. "There were not even showers for the players when we finished our training." And they were to face a decent Welsh side. Nine of the team were established Division One players, but along with John Charles' expected absence, Cliff Jones, now Wales' best player, also withdrew injured. The crucial moment of the opening leg came when Graham Williams was ruled offside after he had seemingly put Wales ahead with the game in the balance at 1–1, before Spain scored the winner. "We were very disappointed to lose that game," he said, "because even though they had a great side, we felt we were good enough to beat them."

There would be another disallowed goal in the return game at the Santiago Bernabeu a month later where Kelsey gave what Spanish press called "the finest display of goalkeeping ever seen in Madrid." Allchurch's brilliant strike earned Wales a creditable 1–1 scoreline in front of 100,000 Spaniards but with Charles still absent, Wales did well to draw. A single point was not enough however, and they were out.

For the 3–2 friendly defeat against Hungary in May 1961, Red Dragon Travel advertised supporters' trips to Budapest. A three-day excursion by air or a gruelling 12-day coach trip would cost 48 guineas. Continental travel was becoming more common and the FAW were pleased to welcome European dignitaries. The International Board met at the Seabank Hotel in Porthcawl that year and visited Pontypridd, taking afternoon tea at the New Inn.

For the opening game of the 1961/62 Championship, 61,566 people watched Wales face England – an attendance boosted by the inclusion of Charles in the team. There were complaints that due to the huge crowd many could not actually see the game. In the event, Wales could only draw despite a goal from Cliff Jones. It was felt that the selectors had been over-cautious in picking Charles at centre half when he had been playing his club football at centre forward. That dilemma was a bone of contention throughout Charles' career, but for Wales, a conservative approach prevailed. The superstar's return to Italy was delayed by fog, ensuring he missed a Juventus match and making the Italians less willing to release him in future.

Like Charles, Swansea too were delayed by fog as they travelled to Austria on their first European adventure. Despite a poor season the Welsh Cup winners became Wales' first representatives in the European Cup Winners'

Cup when they faced Motor Jena of East Germany over two legs. Unfortunately, East German nationals were banned from entering NATO countries, and Swansea had to find an alternative home venue despite already having sold tickets for the Vetch. After the Republic of Ireland was ruled out, the Swans decided on Vienna, only for UEFA to insist they play in the town of Linz, closer to the German border. Both legs were played in the space of three days, and Swansea unsurprisingly went out.

Not a single Swansea player was selected for Wales' trip to Glasgow in November 1961, where Murphy's team lost 0–2 under floodlights. The town's famous sons included in the side had all moved on: Mel Charles was at Arsenal, Jones at Tottenham, and even the Allchurch brothers had moved to Newcastle and Sheffield United. It would be another 20 years before Swansea's production line of internationals recommenced operations. A former Swan did score all four goals in the victory over Northern Ireland in April 1962. Centre forward Mel Charles was versatile – the only positions he had not played for Wales were goalkeeper and winger, but he preferred centre half. The match had been switched to Cardiff from Swansea due to a smallpox outbreak in Bridgend. "I knocked spots off the Irish," joked Charles.

Making his debut was Birmingham City defender Terry Hennessey, who would later move to Nottingham Forest and then Derby. Brian Clough called him a "world-class defender," and he was John Toshack's most valued international team-mate. "He was a class player who had everything," said Toshack. "He was strong in the tackle, had immense skill and was such a good reader of the game."

International fixtures were increasing and Wales moved from three games a year to six or seven, with glamorous friendlies across the world. Thanks to their showing at the 1958 World Cup, Wales accepted invitations to play in Brazil and Mexico in 1962. Charles' contract came to an end at Juventus and he refused to re-sign unless the club looked more favourably on releasing him for international duty. After securing passage for the tour, Charles arranged an emergency visa and made a dash to Brazil, where he astonished the Welsh party by arriving unannounced at Rio's Maracana Stadium.

Charles' surprise appearance sold another 20,000 tickets for the game against Brazil and more than 100,000 watched a straightforward 3–1 home victory for the World Cup holders. In Sao Paolo, Wales lost by the same scoreline, though it took two late goals from Pelé to see the home side clear. Wales struggled with the altitude in Mexico City for the third game against Mexico and were patronized in the local press after a 1–2 defeat. "It was like a team of teachers playing against hard-working pupils," said *Novedades*.

Playing his last Wales game on the tour was Kelsey, who retired with a haul of 41 caps – a record for a goalkeeper. Following a collision in the Brazil match, it was discovered that he had a deformity of the spine which would have prevented him ever playing football had it been discovered earlier in his career. The chain-smoking Swansea man had been one of Wales's most reliable servants and was considered one of the best goalkeepers of his generation – a claim vindicated by his selection for a Great Britain side in 1955.

Back in Wales, part-time Bangor City surprised Wrexham in the Welsh Cup final and faced Napoli in the Cup Winners' Cup. It would be the greatest moment in the club's history. Eight thousand fans flocked to Farrar Road to see their team beat the Italians 2–0 and become the first Welsh side to win a European match. An away goal from Jimmy McAllister in Napoli meant Bangor were six minutes from overall victory before Pornella scored Napoli's third to take the tie to a replay. Under current rules, Bangor would have progressed on away goals, but instead another late goal in the third game at Highbury saw the Italians through in front of almost 22,000 supporters.

Bangor City hold a special place in Welsh football. Their wide catchment area and relative isolation has formed a unique bond between the city, the club and its supporters. Atlético Madrid visited in 1985 while a year earlier, Bangor appeared at Wembley in a drawn FA Trophy final against Northwich Victoria before losing the replay at Stoke. A great run of form saw the club win three consecutive Welsh Cups between 2008 and 2010 and it was fitting that they left the much-loved, but disintegrating Farrar Road for a new stadium as Welsh Premier League champions at the end of 2011.

Reigning British champions Scotland were huge favourites in the first game of the 1962/63 Championship, but were fortunate to scrape a 3–2 victory at Cardiff. Wales had been bolstered by John Charles, but while his team was being trounced 4–0 by England in their next British Championship game, their talisman was in Italy wondering why he had been dropped. The FAW had cabled their request to Turin on a weekend and when no rely came from the empty Italian office, they assumed Charles was unavailable when a telephone call would have seen him playing at the home of English football. Just 27,000 tickets – the fewest ever – were sold for the game at a Wembley, which was undergoing redevelopment, and 5,000 of those present were Welsh supporters who criticized Murphy for sticking with his defensive tactics. A Cliff Jones hat-trick did inspire a 4–1 April win in Belfast as Wales avoided the wooden spoon with Cardiff's Barrington Gerard Hole making his debut.

Club football in Wales was far more interesting than the international scene during the early 1960s. There was another noteworthy European entrant in 1963, when a tiny club from the north Wales coast appeared in the Cup Winners' Cup. Borough United had formed less than ten years earlier after the amalgamation of Llandudno Junction and Conway Borough, and were very much an amateur side. United's European adventure was funded mainly by bingo events, and

Everton's generous £100 donation helped pay for the club's 31-hour journey to Malta. There was also a big raffle, with the main prize being a bungalow in Llandudno Junction. United became the first Welsh club to reach the second round of the Cup Winners' Cup when they beat Sliema Wanderers at the Racecourse in front of 17,000 curious fans. The north Walians lost the next game to Slovan Bratislava, but their short time in the spotlight ensures them a paragraph in Welsh football history.

1964 Nations Cup

The European Nations Cup had begun in 1958 as the brainchild of the late UEFA secretary Henri Delaunay. None of the home countries entered until the 1962 qualifying games, when Wales and (Northern) Ireland took part, though England and Scotland abstained, unsure of the quality of the tournament. In a knockout competition, Wales were paired against old adversaries Hungary, with memories still fresh from those brutal 1958 encounters.

With John Charles back in England after returning to Leeds United, Wales expected to see a lot more of their star man. But the Elland Road side was no more understanding than the Italians. Don Revie refused him permission to travel to Hungary claiming he was needed for a friendly against former club Juventus. "The presence of Charles is vital to add spice to the game for our fans," Revie told the FAW. Incensed and already unhappy with his new manager's style of play, Charles announced he wanted to return to Italy with Roma, where he had been promised a contract clause guaranteeing international release. But the move came too late for the team that lost in Budapest in typically chaotic circumstances.

Wales' key man Cliff Jones was again a late withdrawal and Terry Medwin flew to Hungary without a visa. Wales were fortunate to escape with just a 3–1 defeat and could then only manage a 1–1 draw in Cardiff, which saw them exit the competition at the first attempt. Like the Spaniards a few years earlier, the Hungarians had been dismayed by FAW arrangements for them to train at Jubilee Park, a patch of public land opposite the Cardiff City stadium.

The best thing about the 1963/64 Championship opener was the half-time trampolining display. Wales were missing half their team due to club commitments and lost 0–4 at home to England in October 1963. It was evident that unless international fixtures were given priority the British Championship had no future. The Welsh shared their Scottish hotel with the touring All Blacks rugby team ahead of their 2–1 defeat to the reigning champions at Hampden. Making his debut as Wales' youngest ever goalkeeper was Gary Sprake, aged just 18 years and 231 days. Sprake, who grew up next-door-but-one to Jack Kelsey's home, earned 30 caps while keeping goal in the successful Leeds team of the Seventies. He has since been ostracized by the Yorkshire club after confirming *Daily Mirror* allegations that Revie had offered bribes to opponents. The controversy, and a famous blunder against Liverpool, has seen Sprake's career and reputation undermined. His off-field reputation as a womaniser, drinker and fighter, however has stood the test of time. One of his victims was to become Wales manager in the 1990s. "Centre forwards like Joe Royle, Andy Lochhead. Alex Dawson and Bobby Gould tried to rough you up. I caught a cross and as I fell Gould kicked me in the privates very hard. He then turned around and called me a f***ing Welsh so-and-so and I lost it and felled him with a sharp left that I think knocked out a few teeth."

Under pressure to save the flailing British Championship, the Football League agreed in 1964 to postpone matches if players were required for international duty. Southampton's Ron Davies also made his Welsh debut in 1964. A fantastic header of the ball, he was Division One's top scorer for two seasons between 1966 and 1968 and labelled the best centre forward in Europe by Matt Busby after bagging four goals for Saints at Old Trafford. Davies suffered hip injuries after his retirement due, he believed, to his constant training. He finished his career with the LA Aztecs in California after being recommended by George Best, and was living in a mobile home in New Mexico when an appeal at Southampton financed a double hip replacement in 2007. "Playing for your country is the biggest thrill you can get," he said. "We were such a small country and it's very hard for us to qualify, but you need a lot of talent and we don't have that many players to pick from."

Sprake would claim Wales' failures in the Sixties could be traced to the FAW. "The international set-up with Wales at this time was amateurish at best but this proved to my advantage as the octogenarian selection committee didn't travel outside of Wales," he said. John Toshack agreed: "The whole set up was a bit of a shambles in those days and some of the players with more fashionable clubs were not too concerned about turning up for the less glamorous games." Toshack's claim that clubs paid players to feign injury was confirmed when Sprake admitted Revie was always happy to cover his £50 international match fee before telephoning the FAW with an invented excuse.

When Jimmy Murphy became unavailable for the match against Northern Ireland at the Vetch in April 1964 after his wife fell ill, Swansea manager Trevor Morris was asked to step in. Swansea had reached the semi-finals of the FA Cup a month earlier, and as a result, Jacks' captain Mike Johnson was selected for Wales. Blackburn's Mike England was chosen to skipper a youthful Welsh side with one eye on the 1966 World Cup campaign. The match should have been a special occasion for Morris on his own patch, but Wales lost 2–3. Ironically, the man who did all the damage was Jimmy McLaughlin, who Morris had just signed for the Swans. Playing his only game for Wales was Roy Evans, who joined Hereford under the management of John Charles. Evans and his Hereford team-mate Brian Purcell were tragically killed in a car crash on their way to a game in 1969.

An historic era ended for Wales in 1964 when Jimmy Murphy resigned after seven years due to club commitments. He had been the first permanent Welsh manager and had certainly made his mark. Looking for a replacement, the FAW welcomed applications from "any Welshman who has the qualifications." After drawing up a shortlist, including Ron Burgess, Tommy Jones, Bill Jones and Jack Kelsey, Wales appointed 1958 World Cup captain Dave Bowen as part-time manager. Bowen had taken Northampton from the fourth to the first division in five seasons and would combine his club and international roles. Initially, he took charge on a match-by-match basis earning £60 per game, but his wage did not cover travel expenses to view Welsh players, and many called for a full-time appointment.

Bowen's first test came against Scotland in October 1964 at Ninian Park in front of 37,000. Two goals from Birmingham's Ken Leek in the final minutes won the game for Wales, though thousands of fans had already left, anticipating defeat. Providing the ammunition to Leek was a new winger, Ronnie Rees of Coventry City. After a career which saw him win 39 caps and become Swansea City's record signing, Rees suffered a stroke in 1995 aged 51 leaving him unable to walk or talk.

The fortunes of Wales' professional clubs were mixed in the early Sixties. Poverty-stricken Newport were forced to beg the local council to buy Somerton Park from them and they also sought a £5,000 grant from the FAW. Meanwhile in 1964, second division Swansea Town beat Liverpool at Anfield to reach the semi-finals of the FA Cup. They faced Preston North End, who they had beaten 5–1 in the league a few months earlier, and 30,000 Jacks travelled in great optimism. But any hopes of emulating Cardiff's 1927 achievement were lost when they succumbed 2–1 despite taking the lead, in front of 68,000 at Villa Park. Cardiff meanwhile reached the European Cup Winners' Cup quarter-finals with a memorable victory over holders Sporting Lisbon.

1966 World Cup

Wales were drawn in Group Seven of the 1966 World Cup along with USSR, Greece, and Denmark. The campaign began in Denmark in 1964, and Red Dragon Travel flew fans from Cardiff to Copenhagen for £29. Those who took up the offer regretted it. Wales turned in one of their poorest performances against the amateur Danes at the Idrætsparken Stadium. The absence of John Charles had taken something from a side only saved from heavy defeat by the brilliance of Sprake and Denmark celebrated a surprise 1–0 victory.

A predictable 2–1 defeat to England in November 1964 didn't help the Welsh cause when it came to retaining fixtures at Wembley. Members of the English FA were already advocating a return to provincial stadia when playing Wales, who hadn't won in England for 28 years.

In December, Wales travelled to Greece for the second World Cup qualifier. The Welsh attack of Ken Leek and Wyn Davies was subjected to brutal treatment in Athens as Wales went down 2–0 and the match degenerated into a 12-man brawl. Local police struggled to withstand two pitch invasions as Greek fans looked to attack the Welsh team and FAW Secretary Powell was furious. "If this is the way football is played abroad, then I do not want to see any more of it," he complained. With a referee admitting he had missed the linesman's flag for Greece's second goal because of the crowds surrounding him, and a Welsh team reduced to self-protection it was no surprise Wales lost. Bowen had started the game with the same defensive tactics employed by his predecessor, and the miserly approach was to define his time as Wales' boss. Debutant Peter Rodrigues, the Cardiff City full back, must have wondered what he had got himself into.

Five months later, Wales gained revenge for the shameful events in Athens with a comprehensive 4–1 win at a boggy Ninian Park in front of just 11,159. The victory came thanks to a masterly performance by Allchurch. "Ivor, Ivor," chanted the crowd, who had had little to shout about in recent games.

Watching was Italian manager Edmondo Sabri. "How any side can play such great football in rain and mud staggers me," he marvelled. A 5–0 demolition of Ireland in Belfast sent Wales to an exhibition match against Italy in Florence with some confidence. But the team wilted in sweltering heat and went down tamely by four goals to one. The Italian press claimed Dave Bowen was too upset to eat after such a disappointing performance.

Bowen's team prepared for their May 1965 visit to Moscow with a public training session in Hyde Park, as they had done ahead of the 1958 World Cup. Meanwhile Secretary Powell was frantically arranging last-minute visas for replacements after Sprake and Rodrigues pulled out. The USSR had beaten Greece to keep the group open and a positive result for Wales would maintain hopes of qualification. However, there were the usual mishaps associated with the national team's arrangements. Firstly, the plane began its take-off without Ivor Allchurch and Bryan Hughes, who were still in the duty free shop. When the flight was finally Russia-bound, Cliff Jones realized he had forgotten his boots. And on arrival, it was discovered the directors' gift to the Russian team had gone missing; somebody had misplaced the 100-pint barrel of beer. How long could Wales continue in such amateurish fashion?

With Sprake unavailable for the fourth successive game, despite playing for Leeds throughout, Tony Millington was called up to face USSR after second-choice goalkeeper Dave Hollins suffered food-poisoning on the day of the game. The brother of an England international John and the uncle of TV presenter Chris, Hollins had been born in Bangor in 1938 when his father Bill was playing for the Gwynedd club and was unaware of his Welsh qualification until selected. Millington, meanwhile, went on to earn 21 caps as cover for Sprake, who only played seven times in over twenty internationals played between the end of 1964 and 1969. Millington's career ended in a car crash in 1975 and, after suffering further health problems, he helped form Wrexham Disabled Supporters' Club.

Wales' 1965 defeat in Moscow was close-run and they almost snatched a draw after pulling a goal back from two down. The Russian news agency *Pravda* was impressed by the team from "a small corner of England," and young Russians were advised to follow the Welsh players' sporting example. Almost 110,000 Soviet fans flocked to see Charles' final appearance in a Wales shirt along with a group of supporters who had made the six-day trip with Red Dragon Travel. The 1–2 Welsh defeat was a sad farewell after just 38 caps, but Charles' move to Italy had robbed him of many more appearances. However, Wales' greatest player has admitted that it wasn't always his club who decided he should miss a game. "I loved playing for Wales but I missed a dozen or more matches because I could not face the travelling. I wasn't injured and the club didn't stop me – it was just me saying no to friendly internationals." Wales needed to look to a future without him.

From nowhere, Wales found some form against England in October 1965 as Fulham coach Ron Burgess took charge while Bowen was required by his club. Embarrassingly, even the Welsh manager could be unavailable due to club commitments. Burgess admitted he had not watched Wales since his retirement from playing, but Gil Reece debuted in a 0–0 draw which many felt Wales could have won. Two years earlier, Reece had been resigned to life as a plumber when he was released by Cardiff. Rescued from the scrapheap by Newport County, his form at Somerton Park had been so good that Sheffield United paid £10,000 for his services. Most worryingly, just 29,000 attended Ninian Park – half the size of recent crowds. The British Championship was suffering from comparison with the continental fixtures.

Encouraged by their performance against England, Wales welcomed USSR in October 1965. The legendary Lev Yashin and his team-mates enjoyed a morning training session in the grounds of Cardiff Castle after an evening spent watching *The Sound of Music* at a city cinema. But the Russians upset Newport County by leaving their match against Notts County and snubbing the half-time reception. Even though qualification hopes were already gone, 34,000 people saw Wales produce a heroic display. The 2–1 victory over the group's undefeated team was tagged "the soccer shock of the season," even though Yashin was missing through illness. "This Welsh side was splendid. How they failed to qualify for the World Cup is beyond me," said USSR chief coach Nikolai Morosov. It seemed Wales could perform brilliantly on occasions, but lacked consistency which was understandable when Northampton Town took first call on the national side's manager.

The mid Sixties saw the rise of modern fan culture and the Wales Supporters' Association was set up in Llanelli. Membership cost five shillings and enabled the purchase of blazer badges and ties. After a series of good results, Bowen was confident before facing Scotland. "Our lads are playing better than they have done for years," he boasted. "Technically, theoretically, and by results we are a first-class side." History has proved that when Wales allow themselves a hint of hubris, they are soon brought back down to earth. They lost 1–4 to the Scots.

The 1966 World Cup campaign was over by the time Wales faced Denmark at the Racecourse in December 1965. A combination of icy roads, expensive tickets and general apathy saw a pitiful 4,616 crowd – the lowest ever for a World Cup game in Wales. A blizzard had confined the Danes to their Llangollen hotel, and the FAW even considered moving the game south. A 4–2 win saw Wales finish runners-up to USSR, but above Denmark and Greece.

Ever inconsistent, Wales were trounced 1–4 by Northern Ireland at Cardiff in April 1966, before another visit to South America. Bowen's team flew to Brazil where they lost all three games to Brazil, Brazil B and Chile.

Where it all began: The Wynnstay Arms, Wrexham.
Photo: Green Lane

Plaque commemorating the foundation of the FAW at The Wynnstay Arms in Wrexham.
Photo: Phil Stead

The Welsh team that played Scotland in 1882.

The Welsh team that faced Ireland in 1887.

The Welsh team pose at the Racecourse before beating Ireland 11–0 in 1888.

Photo: Keith Harding Collection / www.penmon.org

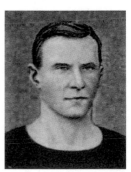

A cigarette card featuring playboy goalkeeper, Leigh Richmond Roose.

Captains Billy Meredith of Wales and Arthur Knight of England toss up before the 1919 victory international which Wales won 2–1.

Photo: © A R Coster / Getty Images

The Welsh team line up at Ninian before facing England in Cardiff in March 1921.

Photo: © Topical Press Agency / Getty Images

David Lloyd George kicks off the 1929 semi-final of the Welsh Amateur Football Cup, between Llanfairfechan and Cardiff Corinthians, at Llanfairfechan.

Photo: © Getty Images

Eugene 'Taffy' Callaghan (left) with Willie Evans, Tottenham Hotspur players who played for Wales against England in Cardiff in September 1934, about to leave Paddington Station. Arsenal's England players, Eddie Hapgood (left) and Ray Bowden look out of the carriage window.

Photo: © Popperfoto / Getty Images

The Welsh team of 1937.

Photo: Ken Davies, Newtown / www.penmon.org

'King' John Charles with his wife Peggy and 15-month-old son Terence in 1955.

Photo: © Popperfoto / Getty Images

Seventeen-year-old Pelé shins the ball past Welsh goalkeeper Jack Kelsey during the World Cup quarter-final between Brazil and Wales in Gothenburg, 1958.

Photo: © STAFF / AFP / Getty Images

Wales manager Dave Bowen (right) with trainer Cyril Lea prior to the Home
International Championship match against England at Wembley Stadium in 1973.
England won 3–0.

Photo: © Bob Thomas / Getty Images

Arfon Griffiths scores the winning goal for Wales against Austria in the European
Championship qualifying match played at the Racecourse in 1975 .

Photo: © Bob Thomas / Getty Images

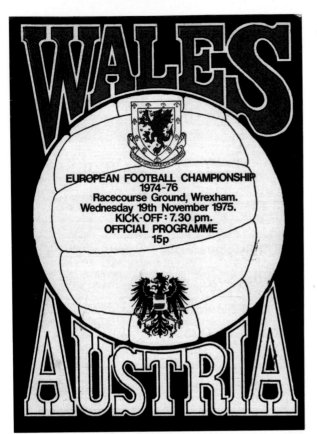

Wales v Austria 1975: Match programme cover designed by Welsh goalkeeper, Brian Lloyd.

Bottles litter the terracing after Wales played Scotland at Anfield in 1977.

Photo: © Getty Images

John Toshack is pictured relaxing in bed holding a poster of Osvaldo Piazza in March 1977.

Photo: © Bob Thomas / Getty Images

European Championship qualifier in Valletta, 1979: Wales did well to beat Malta on a dusty surface.

Photo: © Bob Thomas / Getty Images

Wales manager Mike England (blue jacket, nearest to camera) and captain Brian Flynn (seated, left) watch the agonising final minutes of the European Championship qualifying match against Yugoslavia in the pouring rain at Ninian Park in Cardiff, 1983.

Photo: © Bob Thomas / Getty Images

Mark Hughes scores a spectacular volley for Wales in their 3–0 victory over Spain at the Racecourse in 1985. Many consider this to be Wales' best ever goal.

Photo: © Bob Thomas / Getty Images

Paul Bodin hits the crossbar with a penalty kick which could have sent Wales to the 1994 World Cup finals.

Photo: © Bob Thomas / Getty Images

Cardiff's magnificent Millennium Stadium which opened in 1999, and drew huge crowds in support of Mark Hughes' Wales team.

Photo: Phil Stead

Italian police try to control angry Welsh fans at the end of the Euro 2004 qualifying match at Milan's San Siro in 2003.

Photo: © Mark Thompson / Getty Images

John Toshack returned for a second spell as Wales manager in 2004.

Photo: Phil Stead

Bryn Law interviews his friend Gary Speed at the National Eisteddfod in Wrexham in 2011.

Photo: Tommie Collins

FAW Chief Executive, Jonathan Ford at Llanelli's Parc y Scarlets.

Photo: Phil Stead

Aaron Ramsey who became Wales' youngest permanent captain at the age of 20, in 2011.
Photo: Phil Stead

Gareth Bale is the latest in a long line of world-class Welsh players.
Photo: Phil Stead

A close-up of the FAW badge worn by Wales during the 1920s.

The red shirt worn by Fred Keenor against Scotland in 1927.

Trevor Ford's 'daffodil yellow' badge from Wales' 1949 European summer tour.

The Welsh-made 1980–84 Adidas home shirt.

A rare long sleeve version of the classic Admiral home shirt.

The Welsh Cup.

Photo: Phil Stead

Ivor Allchurch made his last, and record 68th appearance on a dusty field in Santiago as Wales lost 0–2 in the final game of the tour. Bowen had no doubt about Allchurch's worth. "I used to put the names of John Charles and Ivor Allchurch down and start from there," he would say. As Allchurch's international career ended, another's began. Derby County's Alan Durban would earn 27 Welsh caps, before finding success as manager of Shrewsbury, Sunderland, Stoke and Cardiff. A fine tennis player now in his seventies, he has competed in the British Closed Veterans National Grass Court Championships at Wimbledon.

1968 European Championship

The Nations Cup became the European Championship in 1968. The knockout qualification changed to a group format and Wales were placed in the Great Britain group with England, Scotland and Northern Ireland. The aggregate points gained from both the 1966/67 and 1967/68 British Championships would be tallied in the battle for qualification. England's World Cup winning 'Invincibles' started as huge favourites, but Scotland's famous 3–2 win at Wembley in April 1967 put them top of the group at the half-way stage.

Wales' campaign began with a creditable 1–1 draw at home to the Scots in October 1966. They might well have won had the referee spotted Denis Law elbow the ball to score Scotland's late equalizer. When asked if he had handled the ball, Law replied: "Records will show that I scored." But football was unimportant: a day earlier 144 people died when a coal tip collapsed onto a school in Aberfan. A collection at the ground raised £620 and the Welsh and Scottish associations donated 100 guineas each to the relief fund, while the players wore black armbands. A poor season ended with heavy 5–1 defeat at Wembley and a 0–0 draw by a makeshift side in Northern Ireland.

The 1967/68 British Championship was contested by a

spirited but limited group already aware qualification was beyond them. Wales began the season in an all-red kit for the first time, losing to England and Scotland before beating Northern Ireland 2–0 at Wrexham for their only win in six qualification games. There would be no participation in the European Championship this time, and Wales' part-time manager was struggling in the battle for players against the increasingly powerful clubs.

Under current rules, Bowen may have boosted his side with a young defender who would make his mark across the border. In 1967, Emlyn Hughes made his under-23 debut for England. Hughes' father was a rugby league international, born in Llanelli and proud of his roots. But when Hughes made his debut, he had no choice of country as the ruling allowing qualification by parentage wasn't ratified until too late. Hughes was also a business partner of John Toshack, running a sports shop with his Liverpool team-mate in Formby.

With such a weak international status, it was no surprise that club football was the bigger draw in the late Sixties. In May 1968, Cardiff faced Hamburg in the second leg of the European Cup Winners' Cup semi-final at Ninian Park. Around 43,000 packed the ground to see Cardiff denied in the dying moments. A week later, Wales faced West Germany in a friendly at the same stadium in front of just 8,705. The Germans were without their Hamburg players, and the Welsh public showed their apathy for this low profile fixture. A Wyn Davies goal earned a 1–1 draw for a team including Rod Thomas from third division Swindon Town and debutant David Powell of Wrexham in Division Four. "It was a match we should have won," claimed Bowen.

1970 World Cup

The draw for the 1970 World Cup was not kind to Wales. While there were only three teams in Group Three, Italy were reigning European Champions, and East Germany were also strong. The refusal of English clubs to release players for midweek internationals counted heavily against Wales and when the Italians visited in October 1968, they faced a curious looking Welsh side. Cliff Jones was playing his final competitive international at the age of 33. Bowen had struggled to find 11 players and Birmingham defender Colin Green was picked at inside-left while Newcastle's Ollie Burton returned to the team after five years' absence. But despite the unusual make-up of his side, Bowen was defiant. "I refuse to wallow in self-pity," he said. "We've got to square our shoulders and fight like blazes for Wales." His team showed plenty of courage, going down to a single Gigi Riva goal. When the strike, by Italy's all-time record goalscorer, beat fourth division Peterborough United's Tony Millington in the Welsh goal, Bowen knew that qualification for Mexico was unlikely.

Another patched-up side, with only 13 fit players, travelled to Frankfurt in March 1969 to face West Germany in a return friendly. Winning his first cap having scored 19 goals for Cardiff that season was a young John Toshack. Toshack had been a promising rugby outside-half until he fractured a shoulder and committed full time to football. These days, Toshack could have chosen to play for Scotland, as his father was from Dunfermline. "Scotland's gain was to become Wales' loss," he would say. "There's only one country I ever wanted to play for. I feel that no-one should play for anyone other than the country he was born in. I can see it being abused." He would adopt a more liberal attitude when appointed Welsh manager.

Toshack's arrival and Jones' departure symbolized a new era for the Wales side. They came within seconds of victory in Frankfurt with a goal by a reborn Barrie Jones, now at Cardiff and recalled to the Wales side for his first start since 1964. They were denied a famous win when the legendary Gerd Müller saved his team's embarrassment in the final minute by converting a cross which had gone well out of play. "It was never a goal," said Sprake. "It was disgraceful."

Wales were again forced to travel without five of their most experienced players when they lost 1–2 in East Germany in April. A last-minute winning goal in the hail and snow of Dresden inspired a pitch invasion from the 45,000 crowd at the Heinz Stayer Stadium, but the match is better remembered for the administrative chaos that surrounded the deflating result. Journalist Norman Giller tells how Wales left behind a player so that committee members and press could travel to the game: "There were ten blazered officials, manager Dave Bowen, trainer Jack Jones, eight pressmen and ten players. It was the usual old story that some clubs were not releasing their players until the last minute, and it had been arranged for two other players to join the squad the next day, just a few hours before the kick-off. The flight was called and there was the usual panic rush from the duty-free shop to the departure gate. This was in the days before passengers were allocated specific seats, and there was quite a bit of jockeying and jostling as the party filed on to the plane, with players trying to get with mates and officials trying to get as far away from the players as possible. Finally, they were all seated with the exception of one veteran Welsh FA councillor, who was standing in the aisle looking lost. The flight had been overbooked by one. After several minutes the airhostess announced that the last person named on the checking-in list would have to leave the plane and catch the next available flight. She read out the last name. Mr G Reece. This, of course, was Gil Reece, one of the 10 players. 'Would Mr G Reece please leave the aircraft.' A couple of the officials fidgeted uncomfortably in their seats, and the old boy standing in the aisle tried to make himself invisible. Nobody moved. Eventually, with a gesture of disgust and disbelief, Gil got up and walked off the plane. The rest of the players, who had been picked to represent their country in a prestige international, didn't know whether to laugh or cry as the plane took off with nine players. After the flight had been under way for about half an hour, the head of the Welsh FA delegation approached the pressmen, who were gathered at the rear of the plane. They were expecting an explanation, or even perhaps an admission that it had been wrong to leave Gil Reece behind. They leaned forward, notebooks at the ready. 'I feel it only right that I should mention this, boys,' he said. 'I thought one of you might have had the decency to volunteer to stay behind.'"

The North Wales Coast FA contacted the FAW asking them to investigate the scandal, but the FAW remained unrepentant: "A player was not actually left behind at London airport, he took an alternative route." Indeed, Reece travelled alone to Dusseldorf and was detained at the East German border while the rest of the players made their way to Berlin by coach.

Alf Ramsey proposed the abolition of the British Championship in 1969 believing England's time would be better spent facing foreign teams. But a compromise was reached and from that year, all games would be played in a single week in May. There were five players missing from the opening championship game against Scotland at Wrexham. Wales lost 3–5, a result which Toshack blamed on Sprake's end-of-season partying. The problem of player availability was still demeaning the status of the international game and, in trying circumstances, Wales put up a brave fight in a 2–1 defeat at Wembley. Bowen often could not pick a side until the day of a game because he was never sure who would be available. The Welsh players were at least spirited, and the new championship schedule did give them a chance to familiarize themselves with each other, but a 0–0 draw in Belfast saw Wales finish bottom once again.

Ron Davies formed a three-pronged attack with Wyn Davies and Toshack during the campaign which promised much, but he later explained why the tactic rarely succeeded. "Wyn Davies was fantastic in the air," he said, "he was brilliant – so strong and powerful, but he would always head them back across the box – he never stuck them in the net. John Toshack was good in the air too. The problem is we had three of us up front and you need the supply. What's the point of having the three best guns in the West if you don't have any ammunition?" Toshack and the Davies' only played together once more after that season.

As part of Prince Charles' investiture celebrations, Wales lost 0–1 to a strong Rest of the UK side live on television in 1969. The UK team, featuring George Best, Billy Bremner, Bobby Charlton and Archie Gemmell, wore plain white shirts, unadorned with a badge or logo, navy shorts and dark green socks. The match marked the last appearance of Cardiff City winger Barrie Jones, who had been beset by a series of injuries. After recovering from a fractured leg, he fractured it again in training, and then broke his arm after a fall outside his house. Sadly he decided to pack it in at the age of 28. On 17 June 1969, former international Trevor Ford was seriously injured during a Bridgend car crash in which a Swansea woman died.

With Wales needing to win their last two group games, Bowen abandoned his defensive philosophy and opted for all-out attack against the East Germans in the World Cup qualifier at Cardiff. Yet again he was deprived of seven first-choice players including the unlucky Barrie Jones. After the 1–3 defeat, several members of the East German team visited the stricken midfielder at Rhydlafar Hospital.

A few weeks later, Wales were available at 20/1 for the difficult trip to Rome in circumstances which highlighted the impossible task facing Bowen. As midnight approached on the eve of the flight, he still did not have 11 players, and at one stage it looked like Wales would forfeit the game in the manner of a Sunday morning pub team. It was 2 a.m. before Wrexham's Gareth Davies was contacted at York and sent on a sleeper train to London. Meanwhile, a large group of players broke curfew in Rome and went out drinking two nights before the game. Bowen admitted they would have been sent home had he had other options. Terry Yorath recalled his shock at seeing a group of senior players smoking before a training session. The 20-year-old made his debut as Wales' inexperienced side were fed to the lions in front of 76,000 Romans, who relished the 4–1 victory. Yorath had been spotted as a youth by Jack Pickard, the same Leeds scout who discovered John Charles, Sprake, Leighton Phillips, Carl Harris and Byron Stevenson. Defeat meant Wales finished bottom of their group without a single point. It was a fitting way to end a dispiriting decade.

9

THE DRAGON ROARS AGAIN

1970–1979

WELSH INTERNATIONAL FOOTBALL was in a sorry state at the beginning of the 1970s. It was difficult for the national side to be taken seriously when it shared a part-time manager with fourth division Northampton Town. The North Wales Coast FA, often a thorn in the FAW's side, lobbied for a full-time manager in 1970 'to stop the decline' of the international team. But the council defended its manager, blaming difficulties in securing the release of players for its recent poor showing.

At least the FAW was becoming more progressive in other areas. The rule insisting that "Clubs, Officials, Players or Referees are not permitted to associate themselves in any way whatsoever with Ladies' football matches" was finally deleted in 1970. Things were changing at Swansea too. The town was awarded city status, and the club changed its name accordingly.

Meanwhile, Trevor Morris met with the Home Secretary in 1970 to discuss football hooliganism after serious incidents involving Cardiff City fans in 1969 – one idea was to ban skinheads from attending matches. There had also been trouble at two Merthyr games in September with pitch invasions (one including the club president) and an attack on a referee. In 1971, a metal fuel tank cap was thrown at the Northampton goalkeeper in a game at Newport.

The first year of the new decade went pretty well for the national team. Wales went unbeaten throughout 1970 and shared the British Championship with England and Scotland. But problems over player availability remained; Barrie Hole chose travelling to America with Aston Villa over turning out for Wales. Such were the problems before the opening game against England that Dave Bowen held one training session with just six players.

The Welsh goalscorer in a well-earned 1–1 draw was Ryszard Krzywicki, the son of a Polish soldier who had served near Wrexham. (The north Wales wartime Polish community went on to produce more internationals in the shape of Caernarfon's Ray Mielczarek, who earned a cap in 1971 while Eddie Niedzwiecki deputised for Neville Southall during the 1980s.)

The result was promising, but the team needed to prove they were no flash in the pan. The public were also showing more enthusiasm, and the crowd of 40,000 at Ninian Park was a welcome boost. Welsh players were in good shape too. Captain Terry Hennessey was in the best form of his international career and Ron Davies was a real threat in attack. The centre half pairing of Mike England and Sheffield United's David Powell was the best in years and allowed Bowen's team to earn a scoreless draw in Glasgow before gaining a 1–0 win against Northern Ireland. The Northern Irish squad had trained at Afan Lido, with George Best the main attraction to Port Talbot's autograph hunters. This was not Best's first international appearance at a Welsh ground. He had scored for Northern Ireland Youth at Aberystwyth in May 1963, and spent the evening at a reception in the Belle Vue Hotel. He made his full international debut at Swansea a year later. It was no coincidence that Wales' upturn in fortunes coincided with Bowen choosing an unchanged starting 11 for all of the three games.

1972 European Championship

Wales were drawn in Group One of the 1972 European Championship with Czechoslovakia, Romania and Finland. In a league table of European Championship results published before the qualification rounds, Wales were listed 26th out of 30, above only Norway, Finland, Albania and Cyprus. With only group winners progressing to the quarter-finals, qualification would be no easy task.

Wales' defence continued its good work in a dour 0–0 draw against group favourites Romania at Cardiff in November 1970. But the promising central partnership came to an abrupt end when Powell succumbed to injury; he would never again play for Wales. It appears Powell's club-mate Gil Reece still hadn't forgiven the FAW for leaving him at a London airport, and, on discovering he was not selected for the match day squad to face Romania, he walked out of the team's Porthcawl hotel and went to visit his mother in Cardiff. "I've been thinking of doing this before," he admitted. "It's been coming." Chairman of selectors Arthur Barritt was furious. "I think it's disgusting that an international-class player should decide to pack his bag and walk out on the national team," he complained.

In March 1971, Cardiff City played a match that would go down in the club's history. Real Madrid went to Ninian Park a point off the top of La Liga, following successive wins over Atletico Madrid, Barcelona and Athletic Bilbao. City had lost John Toshack to Liverpool, but surprisingly, Real came looking for a draw. When Brian Clark's famous goal broke the deadlock the Spaniards had no reply. Nigel Rees, who supplied the cross, had been released by the FAW from a Wales Youth game at Wrexham that evening. Cardiff lost the second leg 2–0, but victory over mighty Los Merengues at Ninian Park was unforgettable.

Herbert Powell's death in 1971 after a quarter of a century of distinguished FAW service saw Trevor Morris installed as the association's new secretary. Morris had played professionally for Ipswich and Cardiff before the war, where he served in Bomber Command and won the Distinguished Flying Cross. He was awarded an OBE for services to Welsh football in 1976 and died in 2003, aged 82. As the Queen presented Morris with his award, she commented on the difference between footballs and rugby balls. "Ours is the one that really matters," Morris assured her. During his time in international administration, he pushed to change one law that irritated him. In what became an obsession, the former Swansea manager repeatedly proposed that FIFA abolish indirect free-kicks, but his suggestion was never accepted. Morris' first task, accompanied by a group of Welsh MPs, was to lobby Minister of Sport, Eldon Griffiths, to force English clubs to release Welsh players. After a 'full and frank' discussion, Griffiths would only offer to mention the issue to the English authorities. Morris also set up an FAW sub-committee exploring the feasibility of a National League by 1973.

With Dave Powell absent, Cardiff's classy defender Leighton Phillips debuted when Czechoslovakia visited Swansea in April 1971. Phillips would earn 58 caps during a career with Cardiff, Aston Villa, Swansea and Charlton. Also playing was Watford's Caernarfon-born midfielder Tom Walley, who became better known as a youth coach, managing the Welsh under-21s in 1996. Wales looked set for a famous victory after Ron Davies' penalty, but an error by Tony Millington late on gifted the Czechs the first of three quick goals. In four disastrous minutes, Welsh fortunes were transformed.

Reece was forgiven his walk-out and recalled for a miserable 1971 British Championship. Despite the presence of Ron Davies, now considered a world-class forward, Wales remained goalless in the three games. Bowen was unlucky to draw the so-called 'aqua-international' against Scotland at a waterlogged Ninian Park, before another scoreless draw at Wembley. Wyn Davies became the second disgruntled player in six months to walk out when he left the team's London

hotel, upset at his selection as substitute. And finally, Wales'
1–0 defeat in Belfast was considered their worst performance
in years, though it seems some players' minds were elsewhere.
Sprake had booked a flight back to Manchester immediately
after the game and warned reserve keeper Millington he
would feign injury if stoppages meant he would miss the
plane.

After taking just one point from two home games in the
European Championship, Wales needed a win in Finland. The
Welsh party to Helsinki included 15 players and ten FAW staff,
only two of whom were on the selection committee. The large
blazer-wearing party confused the Finns who asked "have
you brought two teams?" Football people across the country
wondered if the FAW would ever learn from past mistakes
but they were seemingly immune to embarrassment. Nine
players had withdrawn and Morris put together a scratch
team which was considered by one commentator as "the
worst bits and pieces side ever." Morale was low as players
struggled at the end of a tough season.

With such an ignominious build-up, it was a surprise when
Toshack scored the only goal in Helsinki – the first time he
had played in a winning Welsh side after 11 appearances.
The part-time Finns complained about Wales' tough tackling,
but it was young Tosh who finished the match covered in
bruises. At 16, Toshack had been Cardiff City's youngest ever
league player when he scored on his debut against Leyton
Orient in November 1965. Aaron Ramsey has since claimed
the record.

The side chosen for the Helsinki trip could hardly be called
representative. The difficulties involved in obtaining player
release had been insurmountable and the reorganization of
maternity hospitals in mid Wales saw more and more Welsh
children born across the border. Against this background,
the qualification criterion was relaxed to allow selection
according to the birthplace of players' parents. Welsh debutant
Malcolm Page hadn't needed the 'parentage' rule however. He

had been born in Radnorshire when bad weather delayed his mother's return to England after visiting an aunt just across the border.

Following Cardiff City's trip to New Zealand a few years earlier, the FAW accepted an invitation for an unofficial Welsh side to visit the rugby-mad country in 1971. With many players unavailable, the tour was deemed to be unrepresentative and several of the team made their only Welsh appearances during the tour, without going on to win a full cap. While the players were granted £2 spending money per day, the provision of suits was deemed an unnecessary expense. After travelling for 20 hours and arriving at 5 a.m., Wales lost 2–1 to Tahiti that same day, thanks mainly to a referee who, Arfon Griffiths claimed, "refused to give the home team offside."

The party then flew to Auckland where they would be based for most of their three-week stay. The British Lions were in New Zealand at the same time, and the Welsh squad would often arrive in cities a few days after the Lions had left. They won six games in New Zealand but lost to Victoria in Sydney just two hours after landing in Australia. "It's hard to believe the schedule we had," said Griffiths, "but we just got on with it." The tour ended with a 2–2 draw against Malaysia.

The parentage rule saw Yorkshireman Trevor Hockey become the first official 'Anglo' to represent Wales when he helped the land of his father beat Finland 3–0 at home in October 1971. This result left Bowen's team needing wins in Czechoslovakia and Romania to qualify. Unfortunately, the Czechoslovakia fixture coincided with the fourth round of the League Cup. It seems peculiar now that the League Cup took priority over the European Championship, but it did. The absence of eight key players meant a debut for exciting 18-year-old Leighton James, whose £350,000 transfer from Burnley to Derby made him Wales' most expensive footballer. Without an experienced attacker, Bowen turned to former Bethesda player Mick Hill of Ipswich. Despite a brave performance, the 0–1 defeat meant qualification was over.

On the homeward trip, Terry Hennessey had to be hidden from airport officials after suffering an unidentified allergic reaction which, if discovered, would have seen him detained in Prague.

Several English clubs refused to release players for the final group game in Bucharest, retaining them instead for their Texaco Cup matches. England, Burton, Hennessey and Durban were unavailable in advance, but another eight would withdraw after selection. Bowen was forced to include Swansea's Herbie Williams, who had not been selected since 1965. Only 12 players flew to Romania while the FAW searched for backup. Five of the team had won less than three caps – Wales would take on Romania with a reserve team. What reporters called the "weakest Welsh side ever," caused Romania no problems. They lost 0–2, leaving them behind their hosts and Czechoslovakia in the table.

In 1972, the Professional Footballers' Association lobbied the authorities to increase international match day fees from £60 to £250. England and Scotland were willing, but the Welsh and Northern Irish FA's complained they could not afford any increase. According to the *Times*, the FAW had lost £60,000 in the past two years – including a £6,000 deficit from the European Championship. Wales were under threat from other forces too. Uruguay, backed by the entire South American continent, pledged to ask FIFA to force the formation of a combined United Kingdom side. But in August 1972, the International Board agreed concessions to ward off the attack on the home nations. There was pressure on Welsh independence from within the UK too. In May 1972 after England had been defeated by West Germany, a motion in Parliament proposed the formation of a combined United Kingdom side. The issue often raises its head when one of the other home nations can call on the talent of a genuinely world-class player – we've seen it with Giggs and Bale recently, but in this instance, it was Northern Ireland's George Best that England coveted. Cledwyn Hughes, MP for Anglesey, took the opportunity to defend his patch: "If Welsh football players were released by the league to play in international matches for Wales, then Wales would be a match for England, West Germany or any other country," he insisted with some justification.

In May 1972, 35,000 watched Wales play England in Cardiff wearing a one-off kit, sponsored for just this one game by AP Sports shop of Clydach. The red shirt had a yellow winged collar with a triangular insert and yellow cuffs. Sadly, the kit was more noteworthy than Wales' performance on a sandy Ninian Park surface. Wales lost 0–3 in what captain Hennessey considered "the poorest display I can remember from a Welsh team." "We were not in the same league," admitted Bowen. A straightforward 1–0 defeat in Glasgow did little to raise spirits and Wales moved their dismal scoreless game against Northern Ireland in Wrexham to a Saturday evening, concerned about a clash with the televised England v Scotland game in the afternoon.

1974 World Cup

Wales were drawn with England and Poland in Group Five of the 1974 World Cup qualifiers. A seeding system had been used for the first time, based on results in previous competitions with Wales seeded in the third of four groups. Despite the unremitting failure of recent years, when Wales had won just twice in five British Championships, Bowen remained in charge with the acceptance that he had been working with an impossible handicap, regularly missing half his team, and operating on a part-time basis.

Before the tournament Wales were given an unusual boost when a Romany gypsy from mid Wales called Mansel Idris Thomas looked into his crystal ball and saw a home win over England. He also had visions of a 0–0 draw at Wembley, but had not yet investigated the matches against Poland. Many poured scorn on the man from Llanwrtyd Wells, but not Wyn Davies. "I would take notice of a real Welsh gypsy – and there are still a few around. You don't have to cross their palm with silver, they seem to possess an uncanny insight into life," he told the *Daily Mirror*. Trevor Morris concurred: "Gypsies warnings and prophecies seem medieval in this scientific age, but I would not dismiss them out of hand."

Despite the 1–0 scoreline, Wales were easily beaten by Alf Ramsey's star-studded England in front of 36,384 fans at Ninian Park in November 1972. "Wales' inability to score goals has now reached the 'sick joke' stage," wrote the *Western Mail* after a sixth game without finding the net. The attacking failures were hard to explain. Alongside the young Toshack, and the dangerous Ron Davies, Bowen could call on Wyn 'the leap' Davies, a former slate-quarryman from Caernarfon, whose heading ability at Newcastle United had Gallowgate End voices praising 'the Mighty Wyn'. He was unlucky to have played in a weak Welsh side, restricting him to just six goals in 34 appearances.

In January 1973, The United Kingdom and Denmark entered the European Common Market and a match was arranged at Wembley to celebrate the occasion. The team included representatives from England, Scotland, Northern Ireland, Republic of Ireland and Denmark, but not a single Welshman was selected by manager Alf Ramsey. Three weeks later Wales travelled to Wembley as whipping boys in England's World Cup qualifying campaign. Bowen considered the 1–1 draw that they achieved to be the happiest night of his career, while Ramsey was frustrated. "They simply came to defend," he complained. In truth, Bowen was utilising a 4–5–1 formation decades ahead of the football world. It was similar to the formation played in the 1958 World Cup when Charles had been the lone attacker in the team Bowen captained. With defence a priority, Wyn Davies was dropped for the Wembley trip and Toshack played as a lone target with wide-men Leighton James and Brian Evans dropping into midfield.

It worked perfectly, though James claimed Sprake had "played against the English on his own" in a world-class performance.

Poland were still on their mid-season break when they came to Ninian Park in March 1973. They were accompanied by a good number of exiled supporters who made up a fair proportion of the 13,000 crowd with Welsh fans still smarting from the poor form of previous seasons. Making his debut was Dave Roberts, a Southampton-born Anglo-Welshman with Welsh-speaking parents from Llangefni. "I have the name, and just for good measure, I know a couple of Welsh swear words," he said. Poland had lost just one of their previous twelve games, but Alf Ramsey had provided Bowen with a full dossier on the visitors and Wales did well to win with goals from James and Hockey. Victory ensured Bowen remained optimistic, and it seemed his new 4–5–1 tactic was paying dividends. "We still have a chance to qualify for the last 16, particularly if we can beat Poland in our last game," he said. "We shall be going for a win, and if we do pull it off, then our fate will rest upon England's results in two matches with Poland."

Before that crucial game in Katowice, Wales had the 1973 British Championship to contest and Bowen was upbeat before the opener against Scotland. "Having achieved outstanding results in our last two games, Wales must have a good chance of doing well in the home series," he claimed. The good form was a blip however and Wales lost all three championship games in May without scoring a goal. Against Scotland "they resembled a local parks team," disappointing a 17,000 crowd at Wrexham. Bowen's team was then easily dispatched 3–0 at Wembley before playing Northern Ireland at Goodison Park due to the civil unrest in Belfast. Fewer than 5,000 saw Wales lose by the only goal. Things were bad and there was conflict within the FAW: a motion to appoint a full-time manager was only narrowly defeated amid concerns over the perilous financial situation.

A Welsh trip abroad would not be complete without an administrative mishap, and the visit to Poland in September 1973 was no exception. This time Trevor Hockey forgot his passport, which was dispatched to London via an obliging guard on the Birmingham to London train. Everything was riding on this game. Victory would practically ensure qualification and finance the appointment of a full-time manager. Wales knew Poland would be tough – they had beaten England 2–0 in Chorzow, but nothing could have prepared Bowen's men for the reception they received from 120,000 hostile fans in Katowice. Several hundred Wales supporters made the gruelling journey to see what Peter Jackson called "the most vile, brutal international I've seen in ten years." "The determination of the Poles to exact revenge had to be experienced to be believed," wrote Michael Boon. An emergency landing and several coach delays were hardly ideal preparation. "I am not saying it was all deliberate," said Sprake, "but sometimes it seemed far too much of a coincidence not to have been staged."

Terry Yorath called the match the hardest of his career. "It seemed at times your physical well being was at risk," he said. Trevor Hockey retaliated and became the first man ever sent off for Wales as Poland scored three times without reply. It was to be Hockey's final game, and also the swansong of Peter Rodrigues, Brian Evans and Wyn Davies. "I was a victim of provocation," protested Hockey. "If we had won there we would have gone into the World Cup finals – we were so close," said Bowen, who knew his job was now seriously under threat.

The Polish manager defended his team, and particularly their rough treatment of John Mahoney: "The Polish players never kicked Mahoney when he did not have the ball," he protested. 'Josh' Mahoney was in his prime, and his Stoke manager Tony Waddington considered him "one of the finest midfielders in world football." He was also admired by the famous Holland manager George Knobel, who said "he plays like a star but he does not act like one." Mahoney, the cousin of Toshack, and son of a professional rugby league player, grew up in the Potteries, and it took an official at his club, Crewe Alexandra to point out he qualified for Wales. After his Welsh awakening, he went on to become the most fervent nationalist in the team, learning the language and playing tapes of Welsh hymns on the way to internationals. "I feel deeply about playing for Wales," said Mahoney. "As a person I care about Welsh causes and the Welsh language."

The FAW turned down a request from Wrexham to send an international team to the Racecourse to celebrate the club's anniversary, but they were more generous to foreign national associations. A replica of a bardic chair was deemed a suitable gift for the Scottish FA's centenary, and FAW President Terry Squire travelled to Istanbul to present the Turkish FA with a miner's lamp on their 50th anniversary.

Bowen went into the 1974 British Championship knowing the manager's job would soon be made full-time, and that the FAW would be interviewing a number of candidates. A good Championship campaign would confirm his position as favourite. Sadly, a nervy performance by Chelsea goalkeeper John Phillips was responsible for a grim 0–2 defeat at home to England in May 1974. The attitude of a muted Cardiff crowd seemed to rub off on the team. Reports spoke of "a pitiful sight of 22 men plus 25,000 fans acting out a game as though it were taking place at a pessimist's conference." There was further misery in a woeful 0–2 defeat at Hampden before Dave Smallman's goal against Northern Ireland at Wrexham gave Wales their first championship win in four years. They hadn't scored in a championship game since 1970, and the relief was palpable.

Another player tug-of-war developed in 1974 when Wales selected Barry Powell, the son of former international Ivor Powell, to play in an under-23 game against England. The matter was complicated when England also called him up for the match. A 10-minute appearance for England Youth had made Powell ineligible for Wales, who claimed England had granted written permission for his selection. England won the day, but never once picked him for the senior side, though he would undoubtedly have won numerous caps for Wales.

In the summer of 1974, Wales offered Bowen the manager's position full-time despite his record of just 11 wins in 57 games. "I knew from the moment I took charge of my first national team, against Scotland in 1964, that the importance of Welsh football demanded a full-time appointment," he said. Bowen went home to Northampton and considered the offer for five days before turning the FAW down. "There were too many gaps to bridge. I just could not accept," he explained. The loyal clubman remained in administrative roles at Northampton until his death in 1995. The Dave Bowen Stand at Sixfields Stadium is named in his honour.

After Bowen's rejection, the FAW promoted from within. Mike Smith was the FAW's backup choice and had been promised the job if Bowen rejected terms. Smith was FAW head of coaching and had managed the Welsh Youth and Amateur sides with great success. There was some reticence in the country – Smith was English after all, and it was unusual to appoint a manager from outside. "None of us can be perfect," joked Leighton James, welcoming the appointment. Smith had not played as a professional, though he had been part of the 1960 Great Britain Olympic squad. However the players who had come through the ranks respected him. Terry Yorath was delighted: "Mike's sheer passion for football was inspirational. He was a great motivator and made you feel as if playing for Wales was the best thing in the world." The Englishman was Wales' first scientific manager – he analysed opponents and thought deeply about each game. The team was even given new kit bags and training gear – Wales had never been better prepared.

The first thing Smith did on his appointment was to drive to Ipswich and invite Cyril Lea to become him as assistant.

Lea was a former Welsh international from Wrexham who had been working as an FAW coach since 1972. His old friend jumped at the chance. "I love the job I do for Wales. I'd pay money myself just for the honour," he would say. Smith would never pick a team without consulting his right-hand man.

Despite Morris's attempts to ward off hooliganism, Wales suffered its first major incident in August 1974, when fans rioted before and after Manchester United's visit to Cardiff in the second division. Cardiff's 'boot boys' had been involved in incidents resulting in 135 arrests at Bristol earlier in the season. Fighting erupted on the Ninian Park terraces when United's 10,000 travelling fans on the Bob Bank began chanting 'Aberfan' and the outnumbered home support responded with fury.

1976 European Championship

Mike Smith selected an experienced squad for the first European Championship qualifying game in a group that included old foes Austria and Hungary, along with Luxembourg. He was made aware of the task he faced when the campaign began in unpromising fashion with a 1–2 defeat despite Wales taking the lead in Vienna. In an attempt to solve the Welsh goal scoring problem, Smith had given Wrexham's 33-year-old Arfon Griffiths his first start. Griffiths responded with a goal, eager to grasp the opportunity of international football so late in his career.

With seven defeats from eight games, it was no surprise a post-war record low of just 8,445 turned up at Ninian Park to witness the start of an unexpected Welsh revival as Wales beat Hungary 2–0. In mitigation, there were other attractions that evening in October 1974. Cardiff RFC were playing Bridgend while thousands stayed home to watch George Foreman fight Muhammad Ali in Zaire's 'Rumble in the Jungle'. Before the match, the Mid Rhondda band played 'Hen Wlad Fy Nhadau' and also 'God Save the Queen', which still sounded before every Welsh international. Goals from Griffiths and Toshack delighted those who were there, and also caught the attention of the press. Gareth Bowen admitted that "the Dave Bowen era was never notable for the attacking panache we always expected in the cloth-capped days of Ted Robbins." He wondered if a "Welsh football revival is under way, master-minded by an Englishman?"

Trevor Morris was forced to plead for support for Luxembourg's visit to the Vetch. There were serious financial problems at Swansea and a council buyout of the stadium probably saved the club from dropping out of the Football League. There were hopes the Swans would move to a newly-built ground in the lower Swansea Valley within the decade, but the move never materialized. Smith prepared for the game by pinning blown-up photographs of the Luxembourg team on the changing rooms walls. "This is no gimmick," he explained. "It's a means of ensuring that every player knows what his opponent looks like." In the event, a crowd of nearly 11,000 saw Mike England win his 44th and final cap. Wales needed a win to top the table and they got it in style with a convincing 5–0 triumph.

Smith's men were in a relatively strong position heading to Budapest. Hungary needed to win all three remaining games; Wales could qualify even if they lost this one, which they surely would. After all, no British team had won in Hungary since 1909. And there would be a debutant in goal. Dai Davies, an Ammanford miner's son, had almost quit football a year earlier, frustrated by limited playing opportunities. One of the game's great characters, Davies' pre-match yoga routines worried his manager. "I'm sure he's going to stick in one of those positions one of these days," he said. In 1978, Davies became the first footballer to be admitted to the Gorsedd – the robed druids at the National Eisteddfod – before becoming a pundit on S4C's Welsh-language football programme, *Sgorio*.

En route to Budapest, there was the typical mishap as

Dave Roberts' bag containing his boots went missing on the flight. Two well-crafted goals from Mahoney and Toshack gave Wales a remarkable 2–1 victory at the Nep Stadium and stunned the football world. Suddenly people were taking notice of Smith's team. "Wonderful, dazzling Wales," proclaimed the *Western Mail*. They had already beaten Hungary and Luxembourg at home, but this was different. This was Hungary's first competitive home defeat since 1959. "To beat Hungary on their own pitch was a memory that will never fade," said Leighton James. "Although I seldom pick out players for individual mention," wrote Smith, "it would be quite wrong of me not to record the part that Terry Yorath played in this win. Tactically he solved the problems that the Hungarians presented and as a captain, he possesses this tremendous competitive instinct that drives on every other player." The players celebrated with champagne and a post-match sing-song. "This is the first time I have been proud to jump on a plane and go home with the senior team," admitted Trevor Morris.

After the win in Hungary, Wales were still buoyant as they visited Luxembourg for the first time on May Day, 1975. Smith was appreciative of the several hundred supporters who had travelled to see the mercurial James inspire a 3–1 win. "The fans came by plane, coach, and car and even by lorry as a couple of British drivers, on their way home from Germany, rerouted themselves through Luxembourg to give us a cheer," said Smith. The awful injury and unavailability problems of a decade earlier suddenly eased as every member of the group wanted to be part of a winning side. One player whose international career ended in Luxembourg was Sprake. He later explained why he had been limited to just 37 caps: "It was expected of you as a Leeds player that you put the club first, it was an unwritten law."

Wales faced Scotland in the 1975 British Championship on the crest of a wave after four successive victories for the first time since 1937. "Not since our participation in the 1958

World Cup have I experienced such a level of excitement and anticipation," wrote FAW President, Terry Squire. An exciting game finished 2–2, and Brian Flynn scored one of two great Welsh goals – an intricate passing move that ended with a one-two between the Port Talbot-born midfielder and Toshack, who had defied Liverpool's request to withdraw from the game. "Even now I get pleasure from it," said Flynn years later. "It was a goal in a million." With a shoe size of just four-and-a-half, Flynn needed specially-made boots and at just five-feet-four tall, any mention of him usually comes with a comment about his height. He was certainly a rare example of a short man at the top of the game, but his place in the side was well justified. People often underestimate Flynn's aggressiveness, but he was tigerish in midfield, though he sometimes featured in attack alongside Toshack for Wales, earning 66 caps.

Wales travelled to Wembley in May 1975 believing they could achieve something memorable. Toshack had ignored doctor's advice and captained the side. With five minutes remaining, Wales were leading 2–1 when they were denied a famous win by David Johnson's equalizing header. Afterwards Smith spoke of the "grief of our players in the dressing room." This disappointment at not winning at Wembley was a measure of the startling progress made since his appointment. Wales then made an unhappy return to Belfast where Smith's bubble finally burst as his side lost for the first time in seven games. Despite the progress being made, Welsh clubs were still resigned to seeing the best talent move on at an early age. For example, there were four Welsh youth players with Leeds United at that time – Glan Letheren, Byron Stevenson, Carl Harris, and Gwyn Thomas. Such was the concern about the seep of young talent across the border that a second national coach, Bobby Brown, was appointed to address the situation.

The 1970s were a time of growing national awareness in Wales, and the WRU, embarrassed by booing crowds, controversially omitted 'God Save the Queen' for games against France in 1974. There had been murmurings of discontent over the anthem for some time. After the Welsh anthem had been played out of 'politeness' at Twickenham in 1968, Plaid Cymru had contacted the FAW to ask that it also be played at football's away games. The FAW had been forced to admit that it had no jurisdiction over the issue. They did request the anthem be played at Wembley in the 1975 British Championship, but the English refused.

This growing independent streak was illustrated in controversial fashion before the visit of Austria in November 1975, billed as the most crucial in the history of Welsh international football. If Wales avoided defeat, they would reach the last eight of the European Championship – probably the greatest achievement in their history. For once, there would be no 'God Save the Queen' before the game and only the Welsh anthem was sung by the 29,000 fans packed into Wrexham's Racecourse. There were diplomatic plans that "The Queen" be played after the match, though it is difficult to imagine anybody took much notice as Wales celebrated a famous win.

Toshack was suspended and Welsh resources were stretched. The Wrexham goalkeeper Brian Lloyd was given his debut, and it was he who designed the cover of the match programme. Lloyd was one of two third division players making their debut, the other being Crystal Palace's Surrey-born Ian 'Twiggy' Evans. Another newcomer was Joey Jones of Liverpool, delighted to be making his debut on the pitch that he and his friend Mickey Thomas had tended as part of their Wrexham Youth team duties.

Welsh preparations were further disrupted when the hourly chimes of the bell in Llangollen's main square disturbed players throughout the night, with several requiring sleeping tablets. A thousand Austrian supporters had travelled to Wrexham and 140 international pressmen were accommodated. "You don't need to build this one up," said Cyril Lea, "it could be the biggest ever night for Welsh football." Gerry Harrison writing in the *Times* was drawn into the emotion of the occasion. "What stood out like Snowdon in the Sahara is the Welsh fire and pride, the family spirit within the team, and the consistency with which good professionals play above themselves and the young and old performers put a new dimension into their game with such relish."

Wales only needed a draw but won 1–0 in front of a sell-out crowd. At the end of the game, the weary Welsh players were trooping into the tunnel when Mike Smith ushered them back to the centre of the field to receive the adulation of the Welsh public. Those minutes of fervent acclaim remain one of the most treasured memories in the history of the national team and afterwards celebrations lasted long into the night as the team drank warm ale and sang along to Max Boyce records.

The performance even drew plaudits from the opposition. "Wales are the greatest fighters I have ever seen or played against," insisted Austrian coach Branko Elsner. Yorath added: "Once a Welshman puts on the red shirt he would virtually lay down his life for his country. I wouldn't swap that kind of spirit for anything." These were patriotic times. Welsh football had found its voice.

The goal that beat Austria was scored by Arfon Griffiths, named Welsh Sports Personality of the Year in 1975. Griffiths had made a 35-minute substitute appearance against Czechoslovakia in 1971, but it had looked like his only Welsh appearance until Smith called him up four years later. Griffiths had played 15 games for Arsenal as a youngster, but big city life hadn't suited him and he returned to Wrexham, remaining with his home town club as player and manager for almost a quarter of a century. During his time at the Racecourse, Wrexham became something of a household name thanks to a series of unlikely cup shocks in England and Europe. "People ask me if I'm resentful about missing out on all those years when I could have been playing for

Wales," he said. "Of course I'm not. After all, 98 per cent of the players in professional football never get the chance to represent their country. So I count myself as an extremely lucky man."

This Austria victory was a key moment for the Welsh team. There was a clear sense of independence among the group, and the squad contained some fiercely patriotic, even nationalistic members. The team's core was proud of their Welshness. Yorath, James, Jones, Griffiths, and in particular Mahoney and Davies all breathed fire for Wales. The next two home games were against England, and naturally 'God Save the Queen' returned pre-match. But the anthem was also played before the uproarious match against Yugoslavia at Cardiff in May 1976. One can only imagine the response it got from the boozy Welsh crowd, and again "the Queen" was pushed post-match for the centenary celebrations against West Germany. The programme noted that players would remain on the pitch while it was played, but it is doubtful this actually happened, as the British anthem was dropped completely against Czechoslovakia in 1977.

In March 1976, 100 years after it was founded in Wrexham, the FAW arranged a centenary match against England. It was played on the Racecourse and ended in a 1–2 defeat in front of 21,000 fans. "I'm proud of the way my weakened team kept on battling it out right to the end," said Smith. The match saw the debut of the famous Welsh Admiral kit with thin yellow and green stripes running down the front of shirt and shorts. The Welsh players were each presented with four plastic tea-coasters to mark the occasion at a dinner held at the Wynnstay Arms in Wrexham on 2 February 1976 where President Terry Squire confirmed the town's place in the history of the Welsh game. "The exact time and location of our foundation has long been a controversial subject," he said. "The Wynnstay Arms in Ruabon for instance, can claim to have been an important venue for it was there that our rules and regulations were drawn up. Shrewsbury can also draw attention to the fact that it was there that the Association first held a general meeting. But we believe that it was here in the Wynnstay Arms, Wrexham, that the actual birth took place."

As the centenary celebrations died down, Smith prepared for the first leg of the European Championship quarter-finals in Zagreb. His plan to frustrate the home side was ruined when Wales conceded after 45 seconds in front of 50,000 passionate supporters. Things looked ominous, but they restricted the Yugoslavs to just one more goal, with Dai Davies pulling off a dramatic late save at the feet of Hadziabdic to keep the tie alive. Yorath, the Welsh captain, was proud of the team's performance. "You can hardly imagine a greater disaster than going down in the first minute of an international abroad against a dangerous side. Yet we rode it. We got our heads down and battled," he said. "We are as good as in the semi-finals," proclaimed Yugoslav manager Ante Mladinić. "Wales produced nothing unexpected. That was the best that Wales can play and it was not good enough. We shall not concede two goals in Cardiff."

Wales would warm up for the second leg with three 1976 British Championship games in eight days. An experimental side went down 1–3 to Scotland at Hampden with Smith resting eight first-team players. Then England returned to Wales six weeks after playing the centenary game in Wrexham and won by a single goal in an awful game in Cardiff. Welsh rugby star Gareth Edwards had issued a call to the supporters before the game: "The international atmosphere at Ninian Park can be flat compared to that at the Arms Park. Many thousands of spectators here today will have been singing their hearts out as we won the Grand Slam this year. If you could sing then, you can sing now." However, there were problems in the crowd as Welsh fans hurled cans and other objects at Ray Clemence in the England goal. There were also growing concerns over the future of the British

Championship itself, and less than 9,000 watched Wales beat Northern Ireland at the Vetch. A disappointed Trevor Morris called for the matches against Northern Ireland to be played at the start of the Championship before both teams were out of the running. But at least Wales had managed a confidence-boosting win ahead of Yugoslavia.

The cash-strapped FAW were keen to maximize interest in the quarter-final, and considered an offer from Wembley Stadium to host the home leg. It was tempting to Morris, who admitted Wales needed money to improve their shaky finances. "The prospect of playing the game at Wembley looks attractive, but to play the game outside Wales would, in my opinion, be selling our birthright and national pride for a piece of gold," he concluded. Future administrators would not follow the same logic. Wrexham had been considered, but with the FAW split on the matter, the casting vote had gone to president Terry Squire, who chose Cardiff.

Wales approached the game in poor form. After four consecutive defeats and a scrappy win against a weak Northern Ireland, confidence was not high among the press. But the players were adamant that they could progress. "They will not have enough heart in front of a packed Ninian Park crowd," predicted Yorath. Toshack was also confident: "We're going to score enough goals to beat the Yugoslavs." Ahead of the game, it was discovered Yugoslavia would receive a £2,000-a-man bonus for reaching the semi-finals. They had other incentives too – UEFA had promised that the semi-finals and final would be held in their country if they progressed. Wales were the last UK team in the competition and for once Smith's team received the media attention that was usually absent when they played. Away goals would be irrelevant – Wales simply needed a two-goal win to force a replay in Milan. It wouldn't be easy – Smith's team had been unable to score two goals in any of their previous seven games and Mladinic was relaxed about his team's chances. "Wales have good runners and play with great effort, but we have superior skills and technique," he said. There was a glimmer of hope – the Yugoslavs would be missing three key players including goalkeeper Olja Petrovic, who had crashed his car en route to join the squad.

Before the game, Yorath declared his faith in the referee. "I don't believe that the Yugoslavs will get away with a lot of the tricks that niggled us in Zagreb – the blocking, the obstruction and shirt tugging." He may have been right had Rudi Glöckner not been incensed by the lack of an East German flag at the ground, and threatened to postpone the game. It was later rumoured that Glöckner spent his summers on the Adriatic coast in Yugoslavia, and implied that his easy familiarity with the Eastern-bloc country may have been responsible for his bias towards Wales' opponents.

There was an electric atmosphere in Cardiff with pockets of supporters running onto the wind-swept, blustery pitch even as the players warmed-up, hugging their heroes and wishing them luck. The game was scarred by a series of pitch invasions and missile-throwing, prompted by a series of outlandish refereeing decisions against the home team. The whole messy, drunken chaos was played out to the sound of Welsh hymns from the crowd, including 'I Bob Un Sydd Ffyddlon'.

The visitors were guilty of provocation and intimidation and the Welsh retaliated. It was ugly, tough, and occasionally vicious as Muzinic and Hadžiabdić clattered Toshack and Flynn time after time without punishment. According to John Burgum, writing in the *Evening Post*, "Glöckner's flagrant abuse of the basic principles of refereeing was an affront to the thousands of dedicated officials never likely to have his satisfaction of appearing in two World Cup tournaments." UEFA's referee assessor for the tie was a Turk, Necdet Çobanli, and he saw nothing untoward in the referee's performance. Yorath was less generous: "He is supposed to be a world-class referee and has had charge of many important games. I don't want to say what I think of him."

Yugoslavia took an early lead with a contested penalty when Malcolm Page was adjudged to have fouled Popivoda as he shaped to shoot after the visitors had taken a free-kick with a moving ball. Wales now needed to score three to force a replay, and on another day, with a different referee, they may have succeeded. Ian Evans equalized before half-time and Wales came out for the second half all guns blazing.

The escalation in crowd trouble began in the 65th minute when the first of two Toshack goals was disallowed. Toilet rolls and bottles rained down, and several fans climbed the barriers only to be restrained by players. The field was peppered with young men carrying cans of bitter, hurtling towards the referee with their flares and long hair flapping behind them. The one supporter who managed to reach the referee wore a pin-stripe jacket and black slacks. Flynn intervened, palms outstretched with a look of complete shock on his face. Glöckner, already incensed by the crowd's 'Sieg Heil' chants, threatened to abandon the game, and play was suspended for six minutes until order was restored.

With four minutes left of a breathless, spiteful encounter, Yorath had the chance to put Wales ahead when Glöckner awarded a penalty. But the Welsh captain fluffed his shot. It was the first penalty he had taken in his career, as the usual taker, Arfon Griffiths had already been substituted. Toshack and James had also taken penalties, but had missed in recent games. Flynn also turned down the offer. "There was nobody else, so I had a go," explained Yorath. "I swear to you my knees were knocking – I was petrified." There were further chances for Flynn and Toshack, and it could have been so different. At the end of a sordid afternoon, Glöckner was given a police escort off the field, and, as the players entered the tunnel, Jerkovic reached up and slapped a Welsh spectator. One supporter from Penylan in Cardiff was later charged with using a corner flag as an offensive weapon. He was freed when Cardiff City director Stan Stennett appeared in his defence. Some commentators claimed that Wales' approach had been too physical, and that their aggression had clouded their ability.

After public condemnation of the shocking scenes at Ninian Park, UEFA's disciplinary committee imposed a two-year suspension on Wales at a meeting in Milan. The committee considered the incidents very serious, claiming a linesman had been struck several times by missiles thrown by Welsh fans. The FAW appealed and Morris travelled to Zurich complaining of unfair treatment: "As this was the first instance of misconduct by Welsh spectators in European football the punishment is particularly harsh. It could well be that our case has suffered from the ugly reputation that British football has built for itself abroad in recent years."

After hearing the appeal, UEFA removed the suspension, imposed a fine of 20,000 Swiss Francs, and ordered that all of Wales' games in the 1980 European Championship be played 200 kilometres from Cardiff. Morris was pleased. "There's no question of us having to go over the border to play in England," he said. "We have measured the distances and Wrexham will definitely be available."

Only 14,000 people watched world champions West Germany visit Ninian Park in October 1976 as part of the continuing FAW centenary celebrations. Morris was downbeat and warned that such disappointing crowds had placed a question mark over Ninian Park's suitability as an international venue. The 2–0 defeat to a classy German team was notable for their mid-game request to use a third substitute, which was only granted after consultation with the Welsh management. Making his Welsh debut was Mickey Thomas from Mochdre on the north Wales coast. "I looked across at the Germans and I was looking straight at the great Sepp Maier. I looked along their line and then saw Franz Beckenbauer and Berti Vogts. I was looking at the World Champions. I thought to myself 'What the heck am I doing here?'" said Thomas. At the conclusion of the game, it was announced that the players would stay on the field while the band played 'God Save the Queen'. Unfortunately, the Queen was unable to attend as FAW Patron, and the teams were presented to the Secretary of State for Wales, John Morris.

In tandem with the Welsh national side, John Neal's Wrexham had been making exciting progress. The Racecourse side had reached the quarter-finals of the FA Cup in 1974 and only just missed promotion from the third division, but were struggling again by 1975. The Robins witnessed their lowest league crowd – 2,654 against Gillingham – before welcoming Djurgardens for the first leg of the European Cup Winners' Cup fixture. Just six months later, almost 20,000 were at the Racecourse to see Wrexham draw with Anderlecht in the last eight of the competition. Wrexham went out, but in recognition of their achievement, Adidas presented the club with a new kit. Unfortunately, it could not be worn in league matches that season as the white trim had not been registered. This was the start of a glorious period for Wrexham, now managed by Arfon Griffiths. They were crowned champions of Division Three in 1978 and reached the quarter-finals of the FA and League Cups.

There was controversy in the Welsh Cup when Cardiff manager Jimmy Andrews called for English teams to be banned from the competition. "If our clubs want to make the cup exclusively Welsh," explained Trevor Morris, "they have to be prepared for the English FA to refuse admission to the FA Cup." Cup finalists Hereford had been intent on applying to represent Wales in Europe had they beaten Cardiff in the 1976 final.

1978 World Cup

Mike Smith had made great progress with the senior side, but the national coaching structure he put in place also seemed to be influencing the game at junior levels. Wales qualified for the UEFA Youth Cup in 1976, coming back from three down over two legs to beat England, with young Crystal Palace striker Ian Walsh scoring the decisive goal. The centre halves in the youth squad were Terry Boyle and Tony Pulis. When the draw was made for the 1978 World Cup qualifiers, Smith was delighted when Wales were joined in a three-team group by Scotland and Czechoslovakia. "The prospect of two Celtic nations clashing in World Cup matches will attract enormous interest," he said.

Don Masson was missing from the Scotland team to face Wales in the opening game at Hampden Park in November 1976, blaming Yorath for causing his injury in a recent club match. Andy Gray was suspended, while Wales could select from a full strength squad. But an unfortunate Ian Evans own goal gave Scotland victory, much to the disappointment of an optimistic Welsh public.

There followed a gap of more than four months before Smith's team would face Czechoslovakia, though his plans were disrupted by the absence of a key player. Smith had built his strategy around John Toshack, only for the Liverpool striker to miss the game with an Achilles injury. His was an unfortunate absence in a tough game against the reigning European champions, unbeaten in 22 matches. He was replaced by an intriguing debutant; PSV's Nick Deacy had been playing in a tournament in Holland with Hereford United when spotted by the Eindhoven team. Deacy scored and Leighton James was named man of the match at Wrexham with two goals in an unexpected 3–0 Welsh victory. "That was not my best game for Wales," he said, "but it was the best display I can remember from a Welsh team." Wales were back in the hunt.

The 1977 British Championship gave Wales a chance to pit their wits against the Scots in a dress rehearsal for the all-important qualifier. They drew 0–0 in a drab game which offered no clues to the drama that would follow when Wales faced the English a few days later.

The controversy began as Wales' team coach approached Wembley with John Mahoney's tapes of male voice choirs playing loudly and the whole squad joining in the singing.

Word then reached the players that England had refused to recognize 'Hen Wlad Fy Nhadau' and would only be playing 'God Save the Queen'. The FA claimed that the "song in question was not a National Anthem as such and playing it alongside 'God Save the Queen' might cause embarrassment, especially to any Royal Personage who might be present."

The snub may have been a response to the FAW's decision to drop 'God Save the Queen' against Czechoslovakia, but it infuriated the Welsh. Mahoney was a committed nationalist who had even learnt the Welsh language, which was rare for a Cardiffian in the Seventies. He and Yorath were furious, and set about organizing a protest. What followed on the Wembley pitch was a watermark in the development of the national side. After the military band had played 'God Save the Queen', the English team broke away to begin the game, but, in a display of defiance, the Welsh players remained in line. Ted Croker and the English officials panicked and tried to usher the Welsh team away as the English crowd booed. But Yorath's side only moved once their point was made. Incensed, the FAW proposed dispensing with all anthems.

After their protest, the fired-up Welshmen set about their opponents, and under pressure, the perm-haired Peter Shilton dragged down Leighton James just before half-time. James rose from the Wembley turf and sent the English keeper the wrong way from the spot. "My legs were trembling like jelly," he remembered. "I was deep in enemy territory with 100,000 fans, 95 per cent of them English, looking and about to score the winner against England. Somehow I managed to keep my cool and score. It was a phenomenal experience and a day I'll never forget." Toshack gave the team some advice after the final whistle. "Don't give away your shirts," he said, "because we'll never ever do what you've done tonight again."

History has not been kind to Leighton James, who has been dogged by controversy ever since he opted to play for his junior side Garden Village of Swansea rather than travel with the Welsh schoolboy team to face England in 1968. His post-football career has included a series of public spats, and he was heavily criticized when admitting, like thousands of other Swansea fans, that he would rather see Barnsley reach the 2008 FA Cup final than Cardiff. The comment resulted in an unofficial single release by Leigh Bailey entitled 'Leighton James Don't Like Us'. Then, as a close friend of the Wales manager John Toshack, he took Robbie Savage to task over his retirement in an embarrassing radio phone-in row. All this has overshadowed the memory of James, who wore the number 14 shirt in honour of his hero Johann Cruyff, as a player of considerable ability. In 1975, the *Times'* Gerry Harrison claimed that amongst the Welsh squad "James is the only player to send a thrill round Europe."

After a disappointing 1–1 draw with Northern Ireland in Belfast saw Wales finish runners-up to Scotland in the British Championship, Kuwait became the first Arab team to play a full international on British soil when they visited Wrexham in September 1977. The return friendly in Kuwait a fortnight later was played in 100 degree heat, and neither side scored over the course of the two games. Dai Davies was missing from the return leg after being denied entry to the Gulf state due to an Israeli stamp in his passport. Even though a loss was made from the two games, the FAW contributed £1,000 to the Queen's Silver Jubilee fund. Despite the row over national anthems, the FAW was evidently still respectful of royalty.

The cover of this book features an image which represents the history of the national team in one single shot. North Walian Joey Jones and the Cardiffian John Toshack stand defiantly on foreign soil in front of a large and intimidating opposition support. The photograph was taken at Anfield in 1977, in what was designated a home World Cup game against Scotland. The FAW had been forced to forego home advantage due to the association's ubiquitous financial problems, and the match itself was decided by a controversial penalty decision which sums up Welsh fortunes.

Ninian Park was originally chosen to host the Scots on October 12 in a winner-takes-all fixture which would decide qualification for the 1978 World Cup. However, new legislation imposed such severe and sudden restrictions that South Glamorgan Council could only provide a safety certificate for 14,050 people. There were similar limitations at Wrexham so Wales were forced to look elsewhere. Wembley was given serious consideration, but after announcing the decision to play at Anfield, Trevor Morris was unrepentant. "There are those who, with patriotic heart on sleeve, or some other impractical motive, argue that to preserve 'home' advantage the game should, at all costs, have been played in Wales. To suggest that a match of this magnitude be played in front of 14,000 spectators is, in my opinion, absurd," he said, claiming it would be "irresponsible" to see "thousands of fans being locked outside." The FAW offered to fund improvements to the Cardiff ground if the council would increase the licence to 25,000, but it was to no avail. Morris was scathing in his criticism of Welsh MPs and the Sports Council of Wales who offered no assistance. But Wales were already on the defensive, and the controversy gave the pre-match impetus to the Scots.

The move to Liverpool failed to avoid the havoc Morris so feared. Tickets were sold to Welsh clubs only until September 16, with the rest then on general sale. There were stories of Scots making daytrips to Wales to buy tickets, and it became apparent the Welsh would be outnumbered in the 51,000 crowd despite Mike Smith's forlorn assertion that "Welsh supporters will make themselves heard in no uncertain fashion, and that Wales will truly be able to claim Anfield as their home ground." Match day brought terror to those wearing red as Liverpool streets swarmed with tartan invaders. Welsh supporters were attacked and robbed of their tickets while many others left at half-time fearing for their safety. Terry Squire was one of a number of FAW members who fell victim to pickpockets outside Anfield, and the players were shocked by the scenes in front of them. Before the game Joey Jones ran onto the field to give his usual clenched fist salute to the Welsh fans on the Spion Kop, only to be greeted with a torrent of abuse from the thousands of visiting supporters who had taken over the home terrace. Jones returned disheartened.

But the game itself was evenly contested and after an hour, Toshack produced a powerful drive which Alan Rough somehow tipped onto his bar. If that had gone in, there was a chance Wales would have earned the victory to send them to Prague needing only to lose by less than three goals. Wales were missing Ian Evans in defence, who had broken his leg in a challenge with Fulham's George Best. His absence was a blow, and David Jones was called into the team just hours before kick-off to replace Dave Roberts who had suffered a groin injury. But it would not be a happy occasion for the Norwich City defender. There were just 11 minutes remaining when Jones challenged Joe Jordan in the box. Both players had their arms raised for leverage and the ball struck Jordan's hand. Despite the Scotsman wearing a long-sleeved dark blue shirt with a white cuff, and Jones's arm being bare in his short-sleeved shirt, the referee awarded an outrageous penalty. "I saw Joe punch it and I told the referee so, but he would have none of it," said Dai Davies.

Jones was even more confused: "I had no idea why he had given a penalty. I thought it was for something that had happened behind me." What really hurt Wales' fans was seeing Jordan kiss his sleeve as he walked away. It was that gesture that sealed his infamy, and he will never be forgiven. The godfather of Yorath's daughter, Gabby Logan, recognizes his position as Wales' bête noir. "I will deny it at the moment of my death, which may be necessary if by some cruel fate the sad event should occur in the presence of somebody from Wales," he said in his autobiography.

Masson sent Davies the wrong way from the spot, and Wales' dreams were again in tatters. Chasing an equalizer,

Smith's team allowed Scotland to break and Kenny Dalglish scored the header that confirmed Wales' exit and broke the hearts of thousands of young boys, including my own. There was something particularly cruel about the game – the realization that life could be unfair – the shame of being outnumbered in a home game – the stark reality that more Scots cared about their football. It was a tough lesson to take, and the memory of it still fires the heart of Welsh football.

Thanks to that Scotland game, the FAW made a record profit of £60,000 in 1977, but one can only guess at the millions that may have been lost by conceding home advantage, and a possible appearance at the World Cup in Argentina. Many of that Scottish team have since claimed the choice of venue won them the game, including Lou Macari: "If the Welsh FA had not moved the game, then history may have been oh, so different." After considering offers from Birmingham and Riyadh in Saudi Arabia, Mike Smith was rewarded with a new three-year contract, with an increase of £4,000 taking his annual salary to £11,000.

A 1–0 defeat in Czechoslovakia saw the Swindon and Derby defender Rod Thomas win his 50th and final cap, before Wales travelled to Dortmund for a December 1977 friendly with the bitter taste of failure still in their mouths. Nonetheless a goal from Anfield victim David Jones raised spirits after a difficult winter. Smith's team did well to earn a 1–1 draw in front of 53,000 fans while the FAW committee enjoyed their trip abroad. Speaking at a pre-match function, Morris took great pleasure in telling the German hosts how the last time he had visited their city he had been piloting an aeroplane full of bombs.

Swansea City had begun the 1977/78 season as favourites for promotion from Division Four, thanks in part to its young Welsh stars, Alan Curtis, Jeremy Charles and Robbie James, who had been nurtured by manager Harry Griffiths. After a disappointing start Griffiths tendered his resignation in October but was reinstated when several candidates turned the job down. He resigned again in February. After suffering three more rejections, the Swansea board eventually found somebody who would take the job. His name was John Toshack and Liverpool waived his £80,000 transfer fee in recognition of the service he had given at Anfield. At the age of 28, Toshack became the league's youngest manager with Griffiths as his assistant. He made an immediate impact and the Swans went on a five-match unbeaten run to secure promotion. Sadly, Griffiths would not see the fruits of his labour and died in the treatment room hours before the penultimate game of the season. Toshack would take his Swansea side through the divisions, culminating at Preston in 1981 with promotion to the first division. "This is Harry's team, not mine," said Toshack. "It's his triumph. He was Swansea City."

With Iran drawn in Scotland's World Cup qualifying group, they saw the Welsh as ideal opponents for a pre-tournament friendly in April 1978. Around 65,000 Iranians watched Cardiff City's Phil Dwyer score in the 1–0 win in Teheran. Wales' 1978 British Championship began with a 1–3 defeat to England in a match illuminated by a wonderful strike from Leeds United's Tony Currie. The game was played at Ninian Park where the on-going improvements necessary to comply with the Safety at Sports Grounds Act limited the attendance to 25,000. The Welsh goal again came from Dwyer, playing as a makeshift centre forward. A draw in Glasgow and victory over Northern Ireland saw Wales finish runners-up in the increasingly marginalized competition.

The Welsh League committee requested discussions regarding a possible national league in May 1978, and the FAW agreed despite remaining unconvinced of the demand for such a proposal. It had been noted by UEFA that Wales and Liechtenstein were the only countries who failed to enter the UEFA Cup. In response, the FAW considered a competition between the country's four professional clubs to provide a representative. The idea was shelved when the

Football League refused to allow their Welsh clubs to take part.

There was further controversy when the FAW scheduled the first leg of the 1978 Welsh Cup final between Bangor City and Wrexham for a Sunday, leading to a torrent of protests from churches, chapels and other organizations. As well as Sunday football, there were more changes in the air. Llanidloes Town were granted permission to display the name Hafren Furnishers on their shirts in August 1978, probably making them the first Welsh team to introduce shirt sponsorship.

1980 European Championship

Wales were drawn in Group Seven of the 1980 European Championship, alongside Malta, Turkey and West Germany. The campaign began with a 7–0 thrashing of the Maltese in October 1978 with Chester centre forward Ian Edwards scoring four goals in little more than half-an-hour. Wales' selection had a pleasing symmetry: Stevenson, Flynn and Harris created a Leeds United right flank with Joey Jones, Mickey Thomas and Les Cartwright, all from Wrexham, on the left. UEFA's ruling that away teams took priority in kit choice saw Wales play in yellow.

In October 1979 Tommy Forse proposed a south Wales office for the FAW and Trevor Morris repeated his opinion that a move to Cardiff would benefit the game in Wales. They would be closer to the media, and closer to the majority of clubs, he argued. The FAW bought 3 Bishops Road, Whitchurch which would now act as their southern base.

The tournament ban on Ninian Park had been reduced, and Cardiff would be available to hold the European Championship game against West Germany in May. Wrexham wanted to remain as hosts however, and to support their claim, they implored local people to buy tickets for the fixture with Turkey. Less than 12,000 were sold but it was enough to give Wrexham the decision. A goal from Nick

Deacy gave Wales the win over the Turks, and set up the West Germany game as the one that could well settle the group.

The Germans arrived at Wrexham in a relatively poor state. After a disappointing World Cup in Argentina they had already drawn with Malta and Turkey. Smith watched Germany in Malta and bumped into the Turkish coach Teufig Birklan while spying on a German training session. Bizarrely, the rivals ended up sharing a hotel in Valletta. Wales sensed their chance to beat the ageing West Germans in front of 30,000 at the Racecourse. Instead, they suffered a frustrating 0–2 defeat. The game – and the £100,000 FAW profit – proved a watershed. For the first time, the bulk of FAW income came from commercial and media interests – no longer were they reliant on gate money alone. Making his international debut was Wolverhampton Wanderers' George Berry, who would become a cult figure to Wales' fans over the years. Ironically, Berry was born in West Germany to a West Indian father, but his mother was from Mountain Ash.

It was back to the British Championship after the visit of the Germans, and a Toshack hat-trick gave Wales a good 3–0 win over Scotland. The Scots had selected four debutants, including Alan Hansen, who was given a torrid time by the Welsh centre forward. "That must go down as my most enjoyable international," said Toshack. "The hat-trick gave me extra satisfaction because I performed it at Ninian Park where I began my career and it enabled us to beat the Scots for the first time in 15 years." Draws against England and Northern Ireland were played out ahead of a tricky trip to Valletta in June 1979.

Wales' biggest worry revolved around the state of the Maltese pitch. The Gzira Stadium was notorious in world football, and Welsh doctor Graham Jones made special preparations for the surface, described as white grit sprinkled on solid rock. Jones bound each foot and each individual toe of every player with elastic bandage. In goal, Dai Davies was padded up like the Michelin Man. Wales did well to win 2–0 on a ground where West Germany had failed to score.

When the Republic of Ireland made their first visit to Wales in September 1979, their hosts would be Swansea City, and chairman Malcolm Struel felt the trip was long overdue. "Match for match this area has for a long time now attracted the biggest gates and so financial considerations alone dictate that we should at least have our share of international football. In addition of course, the supporters in West Wales are entitled to expect that they should not have to 'hoof it' to Wrexham or Cardiff for every home international." Struel would come into conflict with the FAW again in 1983 when he labelled the council "bumbling amateurs". The Leeds United squad of the time included five west Walians: Brian Flynn, Byron Stevenson, Carl Harris, Alan Curtis and Gwyn Thomas. Flynn and Curtis would often visit John Charles in his pub near Elland Road. These were good times for west Wales – Swansea City won promotion at the end of 1979 to join Cardiff and Wrexham in the second tier of English football – the first time Wales had boasted three full members of the Football League. Another west Walian, debutant Ian Walsh from St David's, equalized against the Irish after a Joey Jones own goal had given the visitors a first-half lead. Curtis won the game in front of just 7,000, which did little to support Struel's demands for more internationals in Swansea.

In the summer of 1979 it seemed one of Wales' four league clubs would be awarded a UEFA Cup place. Morris was bullish: "I will go so far as to promise UEFA football for the successful Welsh club within three years." The proposal never reached fruition, and Wales would not be awarded a UEFA Cup place until the formation of the League of Wales more than a decade later.

Wales were humiliated by a 1–5 defeat in Cologne on an October evening that marked the end of the careers of Phil Dwyer and John Toshack. A month after their worst defeat for 26 years, they made a seven-hour journey to Izmir to face

Turkey. Wales needed to win, in the futile hope that West Germany would somehow fail in their final matches at home to the Turks and Malta. Yorath won his 50th cap after missing out in Cologne, but Wales lost 0–1 in a physical contest and all hopes of reaching another tournament disappeared. Byron Stevenson was dismissed and banned from European Championship football for four years after an off-the-ball incident saw a Turkey player stretchered off with a broken jaw. Stevenson would return to earn a total of 15 caps, but died from throat cancer in 2007 aged just 50.

At the end of the year Wales were embarrassed when Smith, their most successful manager in years, was tempted away by Hull City. Trevor Morris was forced to admit Wales could not match the offer from a club in the bottom half of Division Three. Hull had offered a seven-year contract worth £250,000 and the salary advertised for his replacement as Wales manager was just £11,000. Morris appeared disappointed by Smith's resignation and stopped short of praising his efforts: "Mike Smith was our first full-time manager. He did a reasonable job for us." The assessment was miserly. Smith had put pride back into a side in danger of dying through public apathy. Despite the wages on offer, the vacant manager's role attracted plenty of attention and the shortlist of six included Jimmy Armfield and Danny Bergara. Instead, the FAW turned to a former Welsh international captain, now playing in Seattle.

10

WHEN ENGLAND
TOOK OVER WALES
1980–1989

T HE NEW WALES manager, Mike England, had been considered the finest centre half in Europe while playing for Tottenham, but he almost didn't make it. As a junior, he had been selected for a Welsh trial, but was ruled out when his mother spilt hot tea on his foot on the evening of the game. But England was too good not to be given another chance, and the Holywell boy became Wales' youngest permanent captain when he skippered the side against Northern Ireland in 1964; a record only broken by Aaron Ramsey in 2011. After an illustrious career with Blackburn and Tottenham he moved to Cardiff City before joining the 1970s American gold rush and signing for Seattle Sounders.

Despite never managing at club level, England's reputation as captain was enough to get the Wales job. The 38-year-old signed a three-year contract worth a reported £45,000 – around the same amount he would have earned in a year had he stayed in America. England turned down a lucrative contract with the Sounders and even gave up his business interests in the States. "Money has never been the most important thing in my life," he would say, "it's not every day you get the chance to manage your country". Already comfortable financially, England continued to manage a timber company he had founded during his playing days while at the helm of the national team.

His first game would be tough, especially as he was aiming to include fresh young talent. One of the newcomers in that formidable challenge against England in 1980 was Paul Price of Luton. Price's father had returned from visiting relatives in Merthyr with an armful of clippings reporting describing how Wales were struggling with injuries. "You were born in England, but I'm Welsh," Price senior told his son. "Why don't you have a go and see where you get?" Mr Price wrote to Luton Town informing them of his son's eligibility and Paul was called up alongside Cardiff City debutants Keith Pontin and David Giles. England met his new side just three days before they were to face the old enemy, and gave a stirring, patriotic speech before dinner. The squad, more familiar with Smith's analytical approach, were won over immediately. By the time the talk had finished, Dai Davies was close to tears. "Forget dinner," said the Wrexham keeper, "let's get out there and beat England now!"

England also had a message for Welsh supporters – a group that had long been splintered by parochialism. "One thing I would like to see in Welsh football is the end of the North v South rivalry between fans," he said hopefully. This was the peak of inter-club feuding, and it is saddening to revisit the first minutes of that historic game against England and hear Cardiff City fans chanting their club's name at Wrexham. For two decades, Wales' games had been an excuse for the thugs of Cardiff, Swansea and, to a lesser extent, Wrexham to act out their battles on each other's grounds. Inter-club rivalry dominated the atmosphere and it deterred people from supporting their country. This damaging situation was only resolved with the move to the neutral National Stadium in 1989.

The mood in Wrexham on that sunny day in May 1980 was frenetic – supporters had been drinking since lunchtime and the pre-match entertainment from a 150-piece Cleveland marching band rekindled memories of America for Mike England. About five minutes before kick-off, fighting broke out at the Kop End. It ignited an afternoon of spite from the visiting support as their side capitulated. The English had made six changes to the team that had beaten world champions Argentina a few days earlier, but there was little reason for Welsh confidence. Wales hadn't beaten England on Welsh soil for 25 years and it seemed the visitors would win again after taking the lead.

But back came Wales with a scintillating attacking display. "Easy, easy," chanted the Welsh fans as Giles, Mickey Thomas and Leighton James tormented the hapless Larry Lloyd. Wales scored four. Mike England had been one of the few predicting a Welsh win and he emerged beaming from the changing rooms to gloat over the doubting press corps. "I told you so," he grinned. The manager could never have imagined Wales would win so comprehensively, but it was just the tonic needed to win over a team and a nation unsure about the new man.

The English supporters didn't take the defeat well. There were 30 arrests, and an Englishman who threw a brick through the window of a Welsh supporters' coach was fined £175. After Wales' second, supporters in the Yale Stand were pelted with "coins and apple cores" according to the *Wrexham Leader*, whose reporter Dylan Iorwerth was hit by a 10p piece. When the fourth goal ensured humiliation, a mob of English hooligans left the ground for Crispin Lane, throwing a hail of stones which bounced off the Kop roof and hit young Welsh supporters congregated at the front of the terrace. There were also reports of clashes between Wrexham and Cardiff fans and there was more stone-throwing at Wrexham station after the game.

Trevor Morris criticized the disappointing 24,236 attendance, when a capacity crowd had been anticipated. "The lukewarm support for our national side never ceases to amaze me," he complained.

Scotland proved stronger opponents at Hampden a few days later when Ian Walsh was forced off with an injury after 15 minutes. He was replaced by Liverpool's new signing from Chester City – a skinny 18-year-old named Ian Rush. It was a dream come true for the Flint youngster, yet to make his first team debut at Anfield. "Playing for Wales is the ambition that stands out a mile in my life. When I think of the thousands who would give anything to achieve it, I realize how lucky I am," said Rush. England admitted he had only seen Rush play twice but that he had shown enough to earn a call-up. The youngster came close to scoring on his debut, but it wasn't to be. Defeat left Wales needing to beat Northern Ireland in Cardiff to retain any hope of the Championship.

Mike England had taken a course in positive thinking while in America, and this mental training produced a confidence that would become such a feature of his tenure. "It will be nice to sit back in front of the telly on Saturday watching England and Scotland fight it out for the wooden spoon," he said ahead of Wales' final game. "That will be after we have beaten Northern Ireland for the Championship." He was brought crashing down to earth when Wales lost 0–1.

The north-south sniping Mike England had sought to overcome would not go away, and the northerners were in retaliatory mood after Morris had criticized the Wrexham crowd. "Now South should Shut Up," blared a headline in the *Wrexham Leader* after just 12,913 watched the Irish visit Cardiff. The Welsh manager shared the dismay. "I was bitterly disappointed we didn't get a decent-sized crowd and so were my players," he complained. He also criticized rugby supporters for not attending. "I hear a lot of people saying it's the wrong shaped ball, but they are not true sportsmen; they are just fanatical about rugby only, which shows they are very narrow minded." He was becoming embroiled in the traditional disputes blighting the Welsh game.

Domestically, Newport County were the most successful Welsh team of 1980. After years of struggle, they won the

Welsh Cup and gained promotion from the fourth division. "A few years ago," said Trevor Morris, "the outlook at Newport was so black that we were advised to wash our hands of a club heading for certain liquidation. But football is more than facts and figures: it is also about fight and giving heart to a club." The FAW had given them £5,000, but little more than a decade later, the two parties would become embroiled in a legal dispute that would cost the FAW far, far more.

1982 World Cup

The draw for the 1982 World Cup qualifiers saw Wales come out in the toughest group. The trips to Czechoslovakia, USSR, Turkey and Iceland were all difficult but at least there would be two teams qualifying. Wales knew all about the difficulties of playing in Turkey, and Iceland were no whipping boys. Commercially, the draw was a disaster for Morris, who complained "you cannot sell commercial ground advertising packages to Russians, Czechs, Icelanders or Turks."

Wales had started the 1980 Championship with a new manager, and a new kit. A three-year £150,000 Adidas deal included a £20,000 cash bonus, which the FAW decided to pass on to the players if they qualified for the World Cup finals in Spain. The cloth for the new kit, which controversially featured white sleeves, was produced by a Pontypridd company and made up by a Swansea firm. The Welsh-made kit was launched by pupils from Llandaff Cathedral School at Cardiff Castle in April 1980. The Adidas sponsorship money helped fund Mike England's vision for football development in Wales, and Terry Casey was appointed Director of Coaching and Development. Casey, from Llanrwst, had been the only Welshman selected for the British Olympic football squad of 1963–4.

Wales' first qualifier was in Iceland in June 1980. The young Ian Rush was initially left out in favour of Gordon Davies, who just two years earlier, had been a schoolteacher at Dowlais, playing part-time for Merthyr in the Southern

League. Mickey Thomas caused problems when he failed to appear for the squad departure. "We just don't know what has happened to Thomas," admitted the manager. At least Stevenson had returned, his ban only applying to European Championship matches.

Wales went to Reykjavik with only three defenders, and after their 4–0 win Mike England was ecstatic. "I am delighted and more confident than ever that we are heading for the finals in 1982," he announced. His optimism seemed justified when USSR struggled to a 2–1 win at the same venue and even more so when Iceland recorded a shock victory in Turkey. "Everything is going our way but we must clinch it ourselves by winning our matches," said England. It seemed his mental positivity was paying dividends and the Welsh team were believing in themselves.

The squad prepared for the home game against Turkey four months later at the FA's training centre at Lilleshall, where they again worked on a new 3–4–3 formation. Disappointingly, only 11,770 fans turned up at Ninian Park for the second 4–0 win in succession, and questions were asked about the continued use of the stadium. A disillusioned England had expected at least 20,000. Unemployment was rife and the FAW had lowered ticket prices. "This is our way of trying to brighten the lives of people who are out of work," explained Morris. "What more do they want?" asked England. The Welsh manager had even spoken of his wish to play at the National Stadium, but this idea was opposed by an FAW unwilling to share revenue with a rival sport. Trevor Morris put forward the case for the Vetch. "Speaking with impartiality, I regard Swansea as the best footballing area in Wales," he maintained.

After two healthy wins, the manager's confidence was rubbing off on the FAW. "It would be wrong to say that tonight's match is a clincher, but victory would take us to the threshold of a place in the World Cup finals,"

wrote FAW President R Gwynfryn Jones as he welcomed
Czechoslovakia to Ninian Park in November 1980. The
Cardiff public redeemed themselves too. Twenty thousand
attended and they were as surprised as the Czechs with
England's next tactical move.

The 21-year-old Swansea defender Jeremy Charles,
expected to make his debut at centre half, was selected
at centre forward. Charles, the son of Mel and nephew
of John, had almost accepted a place in catering college
before committing to football. At centre half, young
Everton debutant Kevin Ratcliffe replaced the injured Joey
Jones, and Mickey Thomas returned after missing the two
previous games, rebutting those who were questioning his
commitment. "I burn with pride when I pull on the Welsh
jersey and it hurts deeply to think that some people don't
believe that," he insisted.

Czech manager Dr Josef Venglos was relieved that Wales
would be without Leighton James, who had destroyed the
Czechs at Wrexham in 1977. A cool defensive performance
from Leighton Phillips helped Wales preserve a fragile lead
against the more technically-gifted Czechs, though Welsh
goal scorer David Giles needed an X-ray before the game
had finished: "I was listening to the match commentary
at the hospital, but became so nervous in case the Czechs
might score that I asked the nurse to switch off the radio,"
said the Swansea winger. After a third consecutive win,
England was more confident than ever. "If we don't get to
Spain now, it will be our own fault," he insisted.

With a four-month gap until the next qualifier, Wales
arranged a friendly against the Republic of Ireland at Tolka
Park in February 1981. Crystal Palace manager Dario Gradi
incurred England's wrath when he refused to release Steve
Lowell, who was required for a Palace reserve team game.
"I am flabbergasted," protested England. Nonetheless,
Lovell was denied his Welsh debut as Yorath capped Wales'
3–1 victory against a weak Irish side with only his second

goal in 57 appearances. Lovell's Crystal Palace team-mate Terry Boyle scored with a header on his Welsh debut.

England warned his players to 'keep it cool' as they travelled to Turkey in March 1981, remembering they had needed a police escort to reach their changing rooms in Izmir 16 months earlier. Ratcliffe, who had been sent off in a recent club match, was billed by the Turkish press as "a bad man" as they racked up the pre-match tension. In a bid to keep the Turks guessing who would replace the injured Thomas, the innovative Welsh manager refused to announce his side until 30 minutes before kick-off.

Wales won their fourth consecutive qualification game in Ankara with a strike from Carl Harris. Harris had been moved from right wing to partner Walsh in attack, and celebrated with his first goal after 18 appearances. The win came despite brutal treatment from the home defence, and even the Turkish attackers were involved in the rough stuff. Dai Davies claimed later that his refusal to react to provocation had been more important than his crucial late save which preserved the lead. "I had suffered a terrific amount of intimidation. The big fellow played like a battering ram kicking and punching me throughout. I had taken all that and not over-reacted, especially as I had no help from the referee," he protested. That 1–0 win in Turkey was impressive, and the surest hint yet that England's words might not be empty. After winning their first four games, Wales looked to be on their way.

1981 British Championship

International football returned to Swansea for the 1981 British Championship. City had spent more than a million pounds transforming the Vetch in preparation for life in Division One. They had become the first Welsh club to reach the top level of English football for almost 20 years when they secured promotion with victory over Preston at the beginning of May. The visit of Scotland was a proud day for

Welsh captain Dai Davies, who became Wales' most capped goalkeeper, beating Jack Kelsey's record of 41 caps.

Also in the crowd at Swansea that day were 15 members of Ian Walsh's family, all keen to see whether the unsettled Crystal Palace player could maintain his international form and fight off the challenge of the developing Ian Rush. They saw their boy score a brace and there was revenge of sorts for Wales as Joe Jordan was shown a red card for elbowing Boyle in the face. "I was in a daze for the last 15 minutes," said Boyle, "and only came round in the bath when I had to ask what the final score was". His team-mates confirmed a 2–0 scoreline.

After outclassing Scotland, Wales went to Wembley on the back of six straight wins. "We certainly won't be going to Wembley in trepidation," said England. His team's burgeoning reputation was boosted by a 0–0 draw, though the main excitement came from rival fans fighting behind the goals in a 34,000 Wembley crowd.

Wales' fixture against Northern Ireland in May 1981 was cancelled when ten Welsh players refused to travel to Belfast during a period of civil unrest while republicans buried IRA hunger strikers. Sinn Fein had given assurances that visiting sportsmen would be safe but the players were unconvinced. "In the circumstances, we did not have sufficient men left to select a team," said Morris. "The players have every right to decide not to go. They have families and wives to consider." The decision cost Wales £14,000 in compensation and their £50,000 television fee. The Belfast situation raised further questions about the future of the struggling championship. "It is in the melting pot," admitted Morris. "Certain countries – and I cannot blame them – feel that their efforts should now be concentrated on the World Cup and European Championship." There was some criticism from frustrated supporters who knew a Welsh win would have earned Wales their first outright British Championship since 1937.

The first signs that Mike England may have been getting

ahead of himself appeared as Wales returned to World Cup action at the end of May. "If we can beat the Russians at Wrexham, we are virtually ensured of a place in Spain," he said. And with ten qualifying points already amassed and a home match against Iceland to come he was technically right, but it remained a big 'if'. A banner on the Racecourse Kop echoed his optimism: "There's only one England going to Spain... Mike!"

The strong Soviet side included the famous Oleg Blokhin, winner of the 1975 Ballon d'Or. But the Ukranian received precious little respect from a psyched-up Joey Jones. "Jones is still a defender to be feared at any level," wrote the *Times'* Clive White, who also appraised the physicality of the sides. "By comparison to the Russians, Wales were an odd-looking lot, of various, shapes and sizes; in Jones and Flynn you had the long and the short of it." Jones would later remember his battle with Blokhin, whose parents had both been Olympic sprinters. "My mum's a cleaner in the hospital and my dad's a porter, so what chance did I have of catching him?" Jones was being coy. The Russians presented him with a *samovar* as man of the match. On being told it was a Russian tea urn, the Llandudno man had other plans. "I'll fill it with lager tonight," he promised.

After six straight wins and a well-earned draw at Wembley, the expectant 29,366 Wrexham crowd was slightly disappointed when the game finished scoreless. Clive White was bemused that Welsh supporters had anticipated victory. "That Wales held one of the world's outstanding teams to a draw is perhaps the most remarkable of all their many remarkable results this past year," he reasoned. It had taken an outsider to add some realism to a Welsh public carried away by their manager's hype. "Don't worry, we'll still qualify," promised the ever-positive England. With five games played and just three remaining, his team were three points clear of the Czechs who had a game in hand. And Wales' main rivals were up next in a game that could prove crucial.

"We'll be taking our own iron curtain with us," joked Jones as Wales prepared for the key fixture in Czechoslovakia. They may have taken their own curtain, but they arrived without boots for Leighton Phillips after his suitcase went missing en route. Wales needed to draw and then beat lowly Iceland at the Vetch to ensure qualification, but it would be tough as they arrived in Prague without three injured central defenders. They also missed the leadership of Yorath, whose form had dipped following his departure to Vancouver Whitecaps. In the event, a freak own goal by Dai Davies helped consign Wales to a two-goal defeat. The 500 travelling fans watched in horror as a Stevenson header rebounded off the post and was pushed over the line by the unfortunate keeper. It was the first goal Davies had conceded in 457 minutes of World Cup football. A second was added in the second half and Wales knew they would need a point in Russia to be certain of qualification, assuming they beat Iceland at Swansea of course.

Czechoslovakia had needed a late equalizer to take a point from their visit to Reykjavik in September, and Iceland had already beaten Turkey twice. Wales, however, were nervous about the Czech challenge at the top of the group, and it was felt that goal difference would be vital in the final shakedown. And so it was that the build-up to the home tie against Iceland in October 1981 was focused on the six-goal win that was required to pip the Soviets. With the Swans sitting second in Division One, Mike England chose six Swansea players to start, and opted again for only three defenders. Mickey Thomas unwisely appeared in a tabloid newspaper before the match, wearing a chimp mask under the caption 'making monkeys out of the Icelanders'. It was all the inspiration the visitors needed.

England's attacking team took the lead midway through the first half and looked on course to record the victory needed. However, Iceland were proving no pushovers, and all talk of a six-goal win disappeared. A minute before half-time, the 20,000 crowd were plunged into darkness thanks to a fire in the electricity supply box. After 43 minutes, the teams returned to play out the final minute of the half before turning straight around to begin the second. Wales had been in control before the unscheduled break, but with long shadows now covering the pitch, Iceland scored almost immediately. Despite Curtis restoring the lead, Mike England's attacking formation left Wales vulnerable to counterattacks, and a final score of 2–2 effectively ruined qualification hopes. "We can still get to Spain with eleven points," said the optimistic England. The Wales manager refused to blame the floodlight situation but did not shy from attacking the Welsh support. "We were fighting for a World Cup spot, but the crowd didn't really lift the team at all," he complained. "Rival Swansea and Cardiff supporters were more concerned at chanting for their own team. We were expecting rousing encouragement but the support we got was very poor."

England's optimism was turning sour. The comfortable situation in May had turned into a desperate struggle for the points. Terry Yorath never played again after captaining his country a record 43 times, and he believes the FAW had asked England not to pick him due to the expense of flights from Canada. Wales' preparations for the decider in the Soviet Union in November 1981 were hampered by Russian insistence that Wales fly to Latvia before stopping at Moscow en route to Tbilisi for immigration checks. The Welsh hotel was also changed at the last minute without explanation. "It is a disgrace that the Russians are prepared to go to such lengths to make things uncomfortable for us," complained England. The manager had selected his most experienced players in anticipation of a difficult trip, and between them his team could call on almost 400 international appearances. In 2004, the FAW introduced the "golden cap", awarded to players who had made at least 50 appearances, and almost half of the 22 who played in Tbilisi would qualify for the honour. Of the starting 11, only Curtis (35 caps) and Paul Price (25 caps) failed to reach a half-century.

At least there were no hard luck stories this time as one of the most experienced Wales teams in history succumbed to a comprehensive three-goal defeat at the hands of the hugely impressive USSR. Wales had fallen at the final hurdle and slipped to third in the group. As they lingered post-match at the fog-bound Tbilisi airport, Mike England had finally lost his gleaming stateside smile.

The harsh truth is that Wales had several chances to reach Spain in 1982. Of course, they would have qualified if they had beaten Russia at Wrexham, or Iceland at the Vetch, or even taken a point in Tbilisi. But even after they had finished all their games, there was still hope. If the USSR could beat Czechoslovakia in Bratislava in the final group game, Wales would finish second. "They have the ability, but I don't know if they will have the desire," said England. His cynicism was substantiated when the sides shared the points in a game played 'in a friendly spirit'. "I knew it would be a draw," said England, "and our match with Iceland at Swansea will haunt me for the rest of my life". USSR and Czechoslovakia finished on top of the group with the Czechs pipping Wales on goal difference. On reflection, this was Wales' best opportunity to appear at a major tournament, and even now it is difficult to believe they failed.

Disappointed but determined, Mike England flexed his muscles and insisted on a national development structure. Wales announced they would compete in the 1982 European under-21 tournament despite reservations from a financially-strapped FAW. "We haven't entered the under-21 competition before because we simply couldn't afford it, and we can't afford it now," grumbled Morris. An attendance of less than 600 for the visit of Holland under-21s to Wrexham in March 1982 backed up his claim that the FAW would lose £50,000 from the tournament. But they were finding other ways to increase income. In October 1982, they handed out their largest ever fine – £200, and banned a manager from the touchline for four months after five separate disrepute charges. The culprit was future Wales boss John Toshack.

As Mike England looked to rebuild his demoralized side in readiness for the 1984 European Championship, he arranged a friendly with Spain in Valencia in May 1982. A Swansea-inspired Wales produced a fine performance despite an intimidating atmosphere, which saw Mickey Thomas hit by oranges and a beer can thrown from the crowd. After Robbie James equalized with a long-range drive, Wales were denied a famous win when the referee mystifyingly ruled out Gordon Davies' goal.

There were echoes of the Football League bias of the 1930s when Tottenham's Ray Clemence and Glenn Hoddle were cleared to face Wales in the opening game of the 1982 British Championship, even though their club-mate Paul Price was not permitted to represent Wales. After a 0–1 defeat, Mike England dismissed England's World Cup chances, calling them "predictable, unattractive and over-rated". The England manager Ron Greenwood took offence and stormed out of the Ninian Park press conference.

Wales were falling as fast as they had risen under England. Defeat in Scotland meant they had now not tasted victory for eight games. But England promised a new era when the team returned to Wrexham, where they scored three without reply against a Northern Ireland side who were heading to the World Cup in Spain. Keeping a clean sheet on his debut was Llandudno's Neville Southall. The 23-year-old Everton goalkeeper had made his Welsh League debut aged 14 and worked as a hod-carrier while playing for Llandudno Swifts. Southall moved to Bangor City and then Winsford, where he was spotted by Bury at the age of 21. By the mid 1980s Southall was generally accepted as the world's best goalkeeper, winning the 1985 Footballer of the Year award.

During the course of his career, his superlative keeping was often the only thing that saved Wales from a hiding or the key factor in a narrow success. But just 2,315 fans saw his debut at the Racecourse, the lowest post-war attendance for a home Wales international.

A week after Southall's debut, Wales achieved a famous victory when a goal from Rush beat France in Toulouse. The French were considered one of the best sides in the world and the bookie's favourites were playing Wales as final preparation for the World Cup. With Platini, Battiston, Tresor, Bossis and Tigana, the French were formidable opponents, and in front of a hostile 35,000 crowd Wales were expected to crumble. Rush dropped deeper and deeper as Wales went on the back foot while the confident French searched for the opening goal. Chris Marustik offered the Liverpool youngster some advice "If you come any deeper Rushy," shouted the Swansea man, "you'll be playing behind Dai". Rush moved back up front and when the French failed to break Wales' resolve, Mike England's team grew in confidence. With 15 minutes left, Flynn set off down the right and produced the perfect cross for Rush to slot home the winner. Leighton James had a further effort cleared off the line, and the Welsh celebrated a famous victory. "Why the hell are we not going to Spain when we can play like that?" asked Peter Nicholas. "I'm pushed to recall a better Wales performance," wrote Rush, "to a man we were superb". There could be no better encouragement for Mike England ahead of the next major challenge.

1984 European Championship

It is a black and cruel pastime of Welsh fans to recount the various qualification disasters or choose the campaign beset by the most misfortune. But there is no real competition. The events that led to Wales' failure to qualify for France '84 are astounding. Drawn in Group Four with Yugoslavia, Bulgaria and Norway, Wales faced a difficult task, particularly as only one team progressed. But nobody could have predicted the pain that Mike England's team would suffer.

After another summer spent watching a World Cup on television, the Welsh team was keen to regroup and press on with a good Euro '84 campaign. Mike England's three-year contract was coming to an end and he was desperate to prove his worth. Under his tenure, Wales had played 19, won nine, drawn four and lost six. Yet the failures of 1982 raised doubts about his future. Those doubts were eased when Wales began the 1984 qualifiers with a 1–0 win over Norway. But there was little sign of the excitement to come, and just 4,340 watched Rush score the only goal at Swansea.

By the time Wales travelled to Titograd just before Christmas 1982, there was a new man in charge of the FAW. Trevor Morris had retired in September after almost 40 years and was replaced by Alun Evans. Evans had been secretary of the Universities Athletics Union before taking over as head of the Welsh game. The Yugoslavs had surprisingly lost to Norway and Wales were in confident mood. England purposely selected another experienced Welsh side, with more than 300 caps between them. Wales were 4–2 down on a mud bath of a pitch when Joey Jones scored his only international goal and Robbie James grabbed a late equalizer before almost gaining a memorable win when he hit the bar in the final minute. Nonetheless, a 4–4 draw was gratefully accepted and the tournament had started well.

Rush's goal in a 1–2 British Championship defeat at Wembley in February 1983 meant he had scored in five consecutive internationals. But a record low of 24,000 on an icy night at the home of English football signalled the death knell for the Championship, and Mike England maintained the game was useful merely as preparation for the 'big game' against Bulgaria in April. "It was like Bambi on ice," he complained. Alun Evans admitted that FAW finances were parlous, particularly after pitiful crowds for the games against Northern Ireland and Norway. Less than 5,000 fans had gone to the Vetch for the European Championship fixture, and with the future British Championship in grave doubt, Evans was despondent. "It would be tragic if such a great and historic event were to disappear from the calendar," he complained.

Mike England's 'big game' came soon enough as Bulgaria made their first trip to Wales in April 1983. Things were tough for Eastern European footballers, and attacker Ivan Petrov was fined £30 for shoplifting a pair of trousers in Chester. He was banned by the embarrassed Bulgarian FA and by the time Wales travelled to Sofia in November, he was working as a docker. Keen to maximize income, the FAW introduced a marketing ploy for the Bulgarians' visit to the Racecourse. The free match programme included vouchers encouraging fans to order tickets for the forthcoming "game of the century" friendly against Brazil. A crowd of 9,000 pleased Evans. "I think the gate will guarantee more international fixtures at Wrexham," he said, acknowledging that the Racecourse was "a much superior stadium" to Ninian Park.

Lacking confidence after a disappointing start to the group, the Bulgars set out to defend in numbers. Mike England ignored the claims of Joey Jones, winning his 50th cap, and handed the captain's armband to Peter Nicholas. The 23-year-old described the honour as "the biggest thrill of my life". A poor match was won with a goal from Jeremy Charles, who had replaced the exhausted Rush, with dad Mel and uncle John watching on.

The final two games of the British Championship were scheduled for the week after the FA Cup final in May, and there was a hearty welcome reserved for young midfielder Alan Davies as the team prepared to face Scotland. The 21-year-old entered the Welsh dining room to applause following his fine display for Manchester United against Brighton in the FA Cup final the previous evening. Neil Slatter became the youngest debutant for a decade at the age of 18, but endured a difficult afternoon against Gordon Strachan as a pitiful performance saw Wales lose 0–2 in front of a spiteful Cardiff crowd. "I was very disturbed by the reaction of some of our supporters, obviously Cardiff City fans, towards Jeremy Charles," complained an irate England. "They crucified him every time he touched the ball, just because he's a Swansea City player. To be honest, the players and I would rather the internationals be played at Wrexham where there is none of the bickering you get in South Wales." Alan Davies was rested for the Scotland game after his FA Cup heroics but made his debut in Belfast. Gordon Davies scored his first goal in eight games in another awful British Championship runaround which left Welsh supporters wondering what the best team in the world would do to their side. The paucity of the 1–0 win did little to suggest that Wales could match the oncoming Brazilians.

The Brazil friendly was a major coup for Alun Evans. When West Germany pulled out of a game against the South Americans on their European tour, they contacted Wales. Despite the requirement of a £50,000 guarantee, Evans felt this was too good an opportunity to miss and arranged the game for June 1983 at Ninian Park. It was a glorious day, and the Cardiff ground was full to the brim, with many English football followers making the short trip to watch a rare visit by the Brazilians. The makeshift Welsh side was missing nine first-choice internationals, but Mike England had a plan. "I'm going to surprise them by playing my three goalkeepers," he joked. "I think we will have two balls on the pitch," added captain Joey Jones, "because we won't get a kick of the one they're using". Wales did get a kick, in fact they got plenty, and after Brian Flynn headed his team into a deserved half-time lead, it took an injury to Charles to gift Brazil a controversial equalizer. With the Welshman lying prone near the touchline, the home defence hesitated, allowing Isodoro to claim a scarcely warranted goal. "We didn't get the win we deserved," said England while the Brazil manager Carlos Alberto Parreira felt it was a fair result. "Wales fought as if they were in the final of the World Cup," admitted the Brazilian. The game was a huge financial success producing a record £200,000 income, leading the FAW to seriously consider designating Ninian Park as a national stadium only weeks after Mike England's complaints and Evans' praise for Wrexham.

Boosted by the Brazil result, Wales maintained their lead at the top of European Championship qualifying Group Four with a 0–0 draw in Oslo in September 1983. They should have beaten Norway after a gritty display, but a free-kick from Robbie James was turned against the post in the final action of the game. It was the second 90th minute effort that James had seen rebound off the woodwork during the campaign – had either strike gone in Wales would have qualified.

With a crucial game against Bulgaria on the horizon, a friendly was arranged against Romania at the Racecourse. In the event, Romania turned out to be poor opponents and Wales easily won 5–0 in front of little more than 4,000 spectators – an attendance which disappointed Mike England. He worked hard to promote international football in the north, personally touring schools along the coast to sell tickets for forthcoming games. On the same evening that Wales trounced Romania, Norway lost 2–1 in Yugoslavia. Wales needed just two points from their remaining games against Bulgaria and Yugoslavia to guarantee qualification. Mike England was no longer making bold predictions, but things looked good.

Despite being bottom of the group, Bulgaria could still qualify if they beat Wales and Yugoslavia, and there was controversy when the Welsh arrived in Sofia in November 1983. England claimed the training ground was "like a gipsy site". After threatening to call in UEFA over the offensive remark, Bulgarian officials backed down. They admitted that poor facilities were provided in retaliation for the treatment they had received in April, when the FAW had refused them permission to train on the Racecourse. "This is what began the war," explained a Bulgarian official. "Our coaches insisted Wales should not be offered the best facilities." There was further disruption when England's team woke to a blanket of snow on the morning of the game, and there were doubts the match would go ahead.

For their own part, if Wales could avoid defeat, they would set up a deciding clash against Yugoslavia, but after conceding early in the second half, they were unable to get the point needed to remove Bulgaria from the equation. England was angry about the treatment received by the Welsh team. Rush in particular was given brutal attention. "That was the most savage treatment I have ever had to take," he complained. "Even when I went to get the ball for a throw-in, one of the substitutes spat at me in the face as I bent down." The result was disappointing, but there was still a good chance to progress. A home win over the Yugoslavs in the final game would see Wales qualify. The FAW knew the game was make-or-break, and looked to their neighbours for assistance. Evans wrote to the English authorities requesting postponement of club games involving Welsh players. His appeal was rejected.

The match was promoted as a showdown, though in hindsight the crowd of 25,000 seems disappointing. Nevertheless, there was an exciting atmosphere at Ninian Park that December evening in 1983, and Wales set about their opponents with gusto. The Welsh midfield took charge, and Wales went ahead in the second half through a Robbie James goal. Then, with just nine minutes remaining, came the all too familiar disaster. Welsh defenders failed to close down Baždarević as he latched on to a loose ball, and his low drive beat Southall through a crowd of players. It was a cruel blow. Despite a determined effort, Wales were unable to find a winner. "If we had played badly you could have accepted what happened, but we dominated the game," said England.

But even after such disappointment, Wales could still book a place in France if the Bulgaria and Yugoslavia game in Split went their way.

Bulgaria needed to win by two goals to progress; Yugoslavia needed any win to claim top spot. A draw or a 1–0 win for Bulgaria would see Wales qualify. Thousands of Welsh fans tuned into radio reports though it seemed unlikely Bulgaria would do Wales any favours against a strong Yugoslav team. But with 90 minutes on the clock and the score at 2–2, it appeared that Wales would be through on goal difference. But as they waited for the final whistle, nervous Welsh fans heard the play that broke their hearts. A Radanovic header won the game for Yugoslavia in the 92nd minute. Wales had come within a minute of qualification. "I have never felt so disappointed," admitted England. "We were 40 seconds away from qualification. There is no more to say."

Wales would lose £80,000-a-year in television fees if the British Championship was discontinued, and Alun Evans was in fighting mood ahead of a meeting to discuss alternative arrangements. "There will be some hard-nosed talking and if they don't come round I may have to escalate things by taking some action," he warned. But there was no going back. After almost a century, the British Championship was dead, and the FAW's primary source of income disappeared at a stroke. The first victim of the championship's demise was the under-21 side. They played their final game in Newport in December 1983, and every one of the side who beat Yugoslavia that night went on to win full international honours. It would be six-and-a-half years before the under-21 side would return.

The final British Championship was played in 1984. In its 100-year history, Wales had won seven titles outright. The loss of the competition left the FAW with a huge hole in their budget, and if the draw for the 1986 World Cup had not been so kind, Wales may have been forced to revert to a part-time manager. The Red Dragons went to Hampden

Park for the last time in the competition with Mike England showing little Celtic fraternity. "Scotland have done the dirty on us by getting together with England to end the British Championship," he told the *Western Mail*. "All our players are very upset by the snub and are determined to prove that we are not an inferior footballing country." His claims of parity were not helped by a 2–1 defeat that left Wales winless at Hampden for 33 years.

At 20 years old and with a smattering of matches for Manchester United, a young man from Ruabon was called into the Welsh side to face England in May. Mark Hughes scored on his debut to give Wales victory in their last British Championship match against their neighbours. Forming a promising partnership with Rush, Hughes took to international football like a duck to water. Joey Jones was more than impressed by the debutant: "His upper-body strength was incredible. He gave the English defenders a torrid time and it was no surprise when he scored." "England always think they are superior to us," he added, "I'm glad we did it here at Wrexham because we always get a good crowd and all the lads like playing here." But in the final home international match, just 7,845 turned out to watch Wales draw with Northern Ireland, who secured the title. In truth, the British Championship was doomed as soon as international tournaments had relegated home internationals to little more than glorified friendlies.

As the FAW contemplated a huge loss of income, a friendly against Norway in June 1984 provided an ideal opportunity to blood three new players – Swansea's Colin Pascoe, Birmingham's Tony Rees and Wimbledon's Glyn Hodges. Born in Streatham, Hodges had almost been lost to Wales when he was persuaded not to play for Wales Youth in case it affected his chances of playing for England. One player who did not take the field in Norway was Gordon Davies, as he was a victim of a bizarre incident when disembarking from the aeroplane at Trondheim airport.

After being bumped by two fellow passengers, Davies had slipped on the gangway and twisted his ankle. He was sent home as new skipper Ratcliffe and goalkeeper Southall flew 10,000 miles from Everton's tour of Thailand to join the party. A lethargic performance saw Wales lose for the first time against Norway.

From Trondheim, England's team flew on to Tel Aviv where a friendly against Israel offered a chance to Andy Holden, playing his first season in the Football League with Chester City in Division Four. Holden's uncle was Ron Hewitt, who starred in Wales' 1958 World Cup side before injuries restricted the man from Flint, and he failed to win another cap. The game in Tel Aviv was played in suffocating heat and Mike England was pleased with a 0–0 draw. Welsh supporters would become used to these tepid friendlies, which offered interesting travel opportunities for adventurous supporters, but were of little benefit to the squad.

Since Alun Evans' arrival the FAW had been seeking respect and parity for Wales in Europe. In 1984, the FAW began lobbying UEFA to recognize the (South) Welsh League as the country's national league, but Simon Barnes, writing in the *Times*, poured scorn on the idea: "As Wrexham, standing 87th in the Football League, continue their heroics in the European Cup Winners' Cup, for which they qualified by being finalists in the Welsh Cup, the Football Association of Wales is aiming to set up further monstrous European mismatches. It has acknowledged the Welsh League, national division as the national championship of Wales, and is lobbying the European football union (UEFA) for a place for the winners in the European Cup. The best football clubs in Wales do not play in the Welsh League, however. Swansea, Cardiff and Newport continue their struggles in the Football League. In fact, the Welsh League does not even contain the best Welsh non-league clubs. Bangor, last season's losing FA Trophy finalists, play in the Northern Premier League. If UEFA accepts the Welsh case, we are faced with such awesome possibilities as Port Talbot Athletic v Liverpool, Ton Pentre v Juventus, or Brecon Corinthians v Real Madrid."

1986 World Cup

Still licking their wounds from their 1984 European Championship failings, Wales were drawn in a group of four alongside Spain, Scotland and Iceland for the 1986 World Cup qualifiers. Only one team would qualify automatically for Mexico and this needed to be Wales. "Failure to qualify could bankrupt the FAW by the end of 1986," warned FAW President Selwyn Jenkins.

A June fixture in Reykjavík was hardly the ideal start to the campaign, and Mike England was missing half a team, including Rush, while Iceland's players were at the end of their domestic season. And there was no warm welcome for Wales. A banner reading 'Go Home Monkey Thomas' left no-one doubting that the hosts had not forgotten Thomas's unfortunate comments three years earlier. A party of just 30 Welsh fans endured a pitiful performance as their team were beaten 0–1. Tony Knapp, the Iceland manager was euphoric: "passion is what we had and the Welsh did not." "It was absolutely disgraceful," raged England, "There were players out there who just didn't want to play tonight. It was an utter embarrassment." Karl Woodward in the *Western Mail* feared it had been "one of the most disastrous results in the history of Welsh football," bearing in mind the financial implications of failure. The Welsh now needed to beat Spain, and that was surely too much to ask.

After the Iceland defeat, and the end of the British Championship, Evans reiterated the fears of Jenkins and Woodward. The FAW was projecting a £100,000 loss for the season, and Evans warned: "If we don't qualify we will be in an overdraft situation and would not be able to fulfil our obligation to FIFA and UEFA." And so it was that Mike England took his team to Seville with another thinly veiled threat ringing in his ears. "If we lose in Spain, our chances of qualifying will be slim, and then people would be bound to ask whether we could afford a full-time manager," Evans had warned. England admitted that pressure was growing. His team did at least put up a fight in Seville, but they were outclassed by the home side, conceding twice in the last ten minutes after Hughes' effort had been disallowed. "Having a fit Ian Rush would have made all the difference," insisted England.

With Rush missing, Wales had failed to score in their four previous games, and when Alan Curtis pulled out on the day of Iceland's visit in November 1984, England's plans were in disarray. Fortunately, Rush was back to lighten his mood after a two-month lay-off due to a cartilage operation. Wales were still expected to win, but it took a second-half goal from Hughes to claim a 2–1 victory. Meanwhile, Scotland beat Spain 3–1 to keep the group alive. "It's always been our aim to split Spain and Scotland," claimed England, "and then beat the winners of the Oceanic group to get to Mexico."

Wales, with Robbie James at centre half, drew 1–1 in a friendly against Norway at Wrexham in preparation for the trip to Scotland a month later. Wales had failed to win in Scotland since 1951, and there was no reason to think the record was about to be broken. After three games, Scotland sat on top of Group Seven, and Wales knew that only a victory would put them back in contention. Before the game, Tommy Docherty upset Wales by claiming that apart from four players, the Welsh team was mediocre. Jock Stein was also boastful. "We have more quality players than Wales," he claimed. But England remained confident. The omens were good – no-one had pulled out, and that was a rarity. "We've got one of the best keepers in the country in Neville Southall, the quickest defender in Kevin Ratcliffe, and two of the best forwards in the world," he said. German-born David Phillips was given a man-marking job on Graeme Souness, and performed his task well. Mike England had scouted Phillips at Plymouth, keeping his interest secret from the English, but he needn't have worried. Phillips had already turned down the FA, and wanted to play for the land of his father, who had been born in Caerphilly. But the key factor that night was the partnership of Hughes and Rush – it seemed that every time they played together Wales went unbeaten and one or the other had scored.

Match preparation was not ideal. Wales were unable to find a hotel in Glasgow due to the World Curling Championships and stayed 40 miles from Hampden Park. But Joey Jones at centre half led a battling, heroic Welsh display, summed up when Ian Rush ran 70 yards from his own half to the corner flag for a no-hope ball and won a throw-in for his team. This was typical of Rush – while it's easy to point to his goal-scoring record, he also worked hard defending from the front.

The match was fierce and Wales' fighting spirit was called upon literally. After Rush had put Wales ahead with a wonderful strike, Souness caught Peter Nicholas with a wild lunge, and then stamped on the stricken midfielder. This prompted a fistfight which saw Robbie James, Ratcliffe and of course Joey Jones pile into the Scot. It was an incident which showed Wales were no pushovers, and Souness publically apologized after the game, though Nicholas was in no mood to accept. "I'm a hard player myself, but I don't set out to do the things he has been doing all his career," he told the *Western Mail*. Refusing to bow to intimidation, Wales held out for a famous victory over the team that had left the British Championship to seek better opponents. The win saw Wales rejoin the race to Mexico and only goal difference now separated the three sides at the head of the table. The result also saved the FAW from financial disaster and ensured large gates for the remaining home games against Spain and Scotland. Evans claimed the win had pulled Wales from the brink of bankruptcy.

Wales remained unbeaten in seven games at Wrexham and it had become the players' favourite venue. "We all enjoy playing at the Racecourse. No disrespect to Cardiff but the atmosphere is better here than at Ninian Park," said skipper Ratcliffe. Ian Walsh agreed when he later recalled games at the Racecourse. "We used to travel up from our hotel in Llangollen and there were fans lining the streets cheering and waving," he said. "We felt we'd won the Cup before a ball had been kicked. The Raceourse's atmosphere was very special. The players absolutely loved it."

Joey Jones was suspended for the visit of Spain in April 1985, but still joined the squad at Wrexham to inspire his team-mates. And he must have had some effect as the Welsh team set about the Spanish at a furious pace. Making his debut was Pat Van den Hauwe, who almost played for Belgium under-21s before it was realized he had renounced citizenship to avoid national service. The decision made him fair game for any of the British sides, and influenced by Everton team-mates Southall and Ratcliffe, he opted for Wales, becoming known to everybody in the camp as 'Dai'. "Bobby Robson came in with a late offer to join the England squad, but I had already made my mind about Wales," said van den Hauwe, adding "when I'm with the squad, I feel 100 per cent Welsh". The 3–0 victory over Spain became one of Welsh football's most famous nights, and it was capped by Mark Hughes' volley towards the heaving Wrexham Kop, still ranked by many as the greatest goal ever scored in a Welsh shirt.

After the extraordinary victory over Spain, the FAW were under pressure to also play the crucial Scottish fixture at Wrexham, where Wales were now unbeaten in eight. Despite the Racecourse being the players' choice, the FAW were desperate for a big gate to provide a war chest against an uncertain future. Evans dismissed rumours that the game could be played at the national rugby ground as "pure conjecture," even though the Welsh Rugby Union President had been a guest at the Spanish fixture.

But Evans shocked everybody by announcing the match would be played at the Arms Park after a meeting in Birmingham came out in favour of the move. "The feelings of the players were considered but the overriding factor was obviously finance," Evans admitted. "It is estimated we can make an extra £250,000 which is equivalent to what we could expect for reaching the World Cup finals." However, even though the WRU had agreed in principle to staging the match, they changed their mind following the Heysel disaster. "It is our view that the kind of confrontation which we saw in Brussels has absolutely no place in the sporting world," said WRU secretary Ray Williams. England and Evans accused the rugby authorities of over-reacting. "Hooliganism is not a Welsh disease," insisted Evans. Without the availability of the rugby stadium, the FAW chose the 40,000 capacity Ninian Park over Wrexham's 28,000.

Alun Evans turned down invites to tour Korea and America due to player commitments, but accepted a friendly from Norway which Wales lost 2–4, with Manchester United youngster Clayton Blackmore making his debut after just two club appearances. Then in September came another qualification decider against the Scots. "I am the manager of the luckiest international team in the world," Jock Stein had written in 1978. He was talking about the fantastic support his country could generate, but to Welsh minds, his words were prophetic.

The situation was clear. A win for Wales guaranteed at least a play-off place against the Oceanic Group winners. If Wales won, Spain would need to beat Iceland at home by one more goal than Wales managed against the Scots to top the group and progress automatically. A draw would take the Scots through on goal difference. The best Wales team in modern times faced the Scots as favourites, but in an all-too-common atmosphere of economic despair, Mike England was aware of the boost qualification could give the country. "We haven't been enjoying the best of times in Wales," he said, "qualifying for the finals of the World Cup would be a great lift for everyone."

There were concerns about the arrival of 12,000 official travelling Scots fans in Cardiff, with police announcing that another 3,000 away fans had tickets for the Bob Bank amongst the Welsh supporters. In fact the Scots were rammed into the open Grange End and also filled both enclosures. But the presence of almost 1,000 police ensured there were only two arrests during the whole game. The 39,000 fans behaved impeccably in front of the watching Justice Popplewell, who was conducting an enquiry into hooliganism. It was a furious contest on the field, spiced by comments from Willie Miller about Wales' rough-house tactics. Determined to set right the injustice of 1977, and determined not to fail at the last hurdle again, Wales took a lead through Hughes and never looked like losing. Mike England's team were on top, and Scotland didn't have a hope.

Then it happened. As Scotland pressed, David Phillips moved in to block a shot and the ball was smashed into his arm from a metre away. Wales were to suffer another unjust penalty decision against Scotland that would rob them of World Cup qualification again. Cooper's penalty crept past Southall's outstretched hand and gave the Scots the point they needed, but scarcely deserved. Would they have got the draw at the Racecourse? Had the FAW sold out success for the sake of money again? "What made our World Cup exit so heartbreaking," said England, "was that we have a maturing young side I'm sure would have surprised a lot of people in Mexico." He slammed the penalty decision. "It cost us a place in the finals and was a terrible blow for Welsh football," he told the *Western Mail*. "The ball was two yards away from David Phillips and the ball was blasted at him." Cardiff City discovered that the penalty spot had disappeared overnight, dug out by a Scottish invader. The net where Cooper scored was also taken.

The Welsh fans' misery was put into perspective when Scottish manager Jock Stein suffered a fatal heart attack at the game. Stein had become annoyed with a photographer working near the dugout, and when the decisive penalty was awarded, he jumped up and collapsed. He was pronounced dead in the ambulance outside Ninian Park and thousands of Scots held a sombre wake for their legendary leader.

Once again Wales had failed to qualify for a major tournament, but there was still hope. If Iceland could hold Spain to a draw in Seville a fortnight later, Wales would enter the play-offs. Hopes were raised when Iceland took the lead, but the Spanish recovered to win 2–1, and Wales lost out on goal difference. At least the £200,000 net profit from the Spain and Scotland games would keep the FAW alive until the next World Cup, though it was scant consolation for a nation of disappointed supporters. The FAW were split over Mike England's future in the wake of the defeat, and some members wanted to return to a part-time arrangement, though the manager received the backing of Wales' top players.

In November 1985, the FAW moved its headquarters from Wrexham to Cardiff, buying a 16-room building in Westgate Street for £175,000. While members had been lobbying for the return to a part-time manager to save money, it appeared that funding was available for administrative offices.

Wales had also lost 0–3 to Hungary at Ninian Park in front of only 3,500 just before the move, and the players were pleased to get away with a trip to play Saudi Arabia in February 1986. The game in Dhahran saw debuts for Malcolm Allen, David Williams and Mark Aizlewood. After a varied career, Aizlewood became a coach and then technical director of the Welsh Football Trust. As a Newport man who had learnt Welsh, he was named Welsh Learner of the Year in 1996, while Allen became a familiar face on S4C's *Sgorio*. Making his 51st and final appearance was Mickey Thomas. One of the game's most controversial figures, Thomas was jailed for 18 months in 1993 for counterfeiting £10 and £20 notes, which he passed on to Wrexham's trainees. A year earlier at the age of 37, Thomas had scored one of the FA Cup's most memorable goals as he helped Wrexham defeat Arsenal 2–1.

Meanwhile, things had begun to go wrong for Toshack at Swansea City. In 1982, the Vetch Field board had budgeted for crowds of 18,500 in their second season at the top level, but poor results saw the average figure fall to 13,000. Improved player contracts and installments on transfers saw the club struggle financially despite Liverpool chairman John Smith writing off a £300,000 debt. Successive relegations followed and Toshack was sacked in March 1984 with the Swans close to bankruptcy. Crowds fell to 3,000 and on Friday, 20 December 1985, it was reported Swansea City FC had been wound up. The situation seemed irreversible, but the Swans refused to die, and permission was granted for them to play their Boxing Day fixture at Ninian Park as options to revive the club were investigated. A collection at Cardiff saw home supporters contribute to a fund to save their rivals. Another £60,000 came after a public appeal and Ron Atkinson's Manchester United played a friendly, raising a further £45,000. The man credited with saving Swansea City during tough negotiations with the High Court was Doug Sharpe, who would become club chairman. In July 1986, the winding-up order was lifted. Swansea had survived.

With the British Championship a thing of the past, Alun Evans looked elsewhere for regular income and arranged friendlies against the Republic of Ireland and Uruguay as well as a couple of games in Canada. He also accepted an invitation to become the first British national side to travel to Saudi Arabia in February 1986. He was surprised to be handed a case containing £20,000 cash by the Saudis, and strapped it to his body while the game was played to the sound of oriental music booming from the tannoy. "It was like playing a match in an Indian restaurant," he told the *Western Mail*. A classy goal from Neil Slatter helped Wales to a 2–1 victory. The next friendly came against the Republic of Ireland in Dublin in March 1986. Joey Jones had announced his international retirement a month earlier, but answered the call to help Mike England's depleted squad. He captained the side to a 1–0 win, making his 69th appearance and breaking the Welsh record. The victory was soured by a serious injury to Southall, caused by a bumpy pitch which had worried both managers. Jones had insisted his reappearance in Dublin was a one-off but returned to face Uruguay when Pat Van den Hauwe raised doubts about his commitment by withdrawing from the squad. Van den Hauwe had missed three of the five Wales games since making his debut and England was skeptical about the converted Welshman. "He looked pretty fit walking off after helping Everton beat Ipswich on Saturday, but apparently picked up a groin injury," he said.

Joey Jones was presented with a silver salver to mark his appearance record before the friendly against Uruguay in April 1986 where Mark Hughes took a battering in a scoreless friendly in front of 11,000 on a muddy Racecourse before leaving the country for Barcelona. Evans bemoaned the financial loss made on the game after paying out £30,000 to the visitors, and Wales headed to Canada in May in a bid to boost the coffers. The Canadians had qualified for the Mexico World Cup, and beat a second-string Welsh side 2–0 on a terrible pitch in Toronto with debuts handed to former Welsh Schools rugby international Andy Dibble and to Mark Bowen, who would go on to become assistant manager to Mark Hughes for Wales. Dean Saunders earned his first full caps as England looked to rebuild. A week later, Wales won 3–0 on an indoor pitch at Vancouver as just 9,000 supporters watched in a 59,000 capacity stadium. Malcolm Allen, one of the proudest Welsh players, scored his first goal. "It was an odd feeling," he would write in his Welsh-language autobiography. "It was as if the whole world stopped to take a breath, and it was like I was in shock."

1988 European Championship

After six friendly matches, Wales were glad to return to competitive football in the European Championship, where they had been drawn in Group Six alongside Czechoslovakia, Denmark and Finland. Hughes was serving the first of a two-game suspension following his dismissal from Wales' under-21s at Newport three years earlier when Wales travelled to Helsinki in September 1986 for the group opener. Southall was replaced by debutant Martin Thomas in a squad stretched by injuries. It was a tough baptism for the Newcastle keeper and Thomas was partly to blame for the Finnish opener. Full back Slatter was the unlikely hero as he rescued Wales with a goal after coming on as a second-half substitute. Mike England had hoped for a win to open the campaign, but at least Wales had avoided defeat.

Swansea City's Ivor Pursey succeeded Selwyn Jenkins as FAW President and welcomed the Soviets to the Vetch for a friendly between the two opening qualification games against Finland. Mike England was missing ten players, but van den Hauwe was welcomed back after a six-month lay-off with a blood disorder. Southall had been a major doubt after a bout of food poisoning just hours before the game, but the big keeper took a walk along Porthcawl seafront where the Welsh team were staying and declared himself fit. The presence of Ian Rush attracted a large posse of Italian journalists and also the Juventus chairman, keen to cast an eye over their new signing, who was due to move to Turin in the summer. A 0–0 draw meant that Wales had gone nine games unbeaten in fixtures in which their star players Rush and Hughes had played together.

Wales beat Finland 4–0 at Wrexham in the return European Championship fixture on April Fool's Day 1987 wearing a new kit supplied by Hummell. With Hughes suspended, England's choice to replace him was Port Vale's Andy Jones, who had scored 46 goals in less than two seasons since signing from Rhyl. Rush was forced to admit he had never seen his new strike partner play, but Jones rewarded his manager's faith with a goal. The result meant Wales were ten games unbeaten at the Racecourse, including seven wins. The players again lobbied for all home games to be played in Wrexham.

On the day after Wales beat Finland, Welsh football mourned the death of one of its great characters. Trevor 'Wild Dog' Hockey was a five-foot-six Yorkshireman whose Abertillery-born father had gone north to play rugby league. Hockey had been the first 'Anglo' to represent Wales when he debuted in 1971. "When I pull on that red shirt, I feel as Welsh as anyone in that team," he once said. It was reported Hockey had been a singer with Roy Wood's band The Move in his younger days, and even made some records. There are even claims he once played a gig at Birmingham City Hall on the evening before an international.

The top Welsh club of 1987 was Merthyr Tydfil, who enjoyed great cup success. After the original Merthyr Town FC had been disbanded during the 1930s, a new club sprang up in 1945 and won the Southern League five times between 1947 and 1954. Despite this success, they were never voted into the Football League, and they disbanded in 2010 amid financial troubles. During their 65-year existence, Merthyr Tydfil FC won the Welsh Cup three times, including 1987, leading them to face the Italians of Atalanta in the European Cup Winners' Cup. Merthyr won the first leg at Penydarren Park before losing in Italy. After they were liquidated in 2010, the original Merthyr Town club was reformed under the auspices of a supporters' trust.

Mark Hughes was back for the vital European Championship game against Czechoslovakia at Wrexham at the end of April. Wales were relieved to escape with a draw against strong opponents thanks to a late Rush goal.

England's team had been outplayed and were fortunate to earn a point on a pitch softened by 50,000 gallons of water provided by the local fire service which left pools of water on the pitch. But Wales survived and the result, grabbed against the run of play, demonstrated the value of Hughes and Rush. Even when their team was outplayed, there was always a chance the attackers could pull something out of the bag, and with Southall in goal, Wales could compete with the best.

A draw between Czechoslovakia and Denmark meant Wales were nicely placed if they could beat Denmark at home in September 1987. When it came to match day, Ninian Park had never seen anything like it. Six thousand face-painted, horn-wearing Danes followed their exciting young side to Cardiff and mixed freely with home supporters in a manner unimaginable for club games at Cardiff. The Welsh supporters were taken aback by their audacity, but the atmosphere was friendly and it was a great night. But there was yet more pressure on Mike England as rumours of discontent amongst the FAW surfaced. "If there comes a time when the Welsh FA think someone can do a better job than me, that's their decision," he told the *Western Mail*. Portsmouth's Barry Horne replaced Robbie James to earn his first cap. Horne had earned a first-class degree in chemistry from the University of Liverpool. He went on to claim 59 caps and captain his country.

It was a typical battling, physical Welsh performance, though the Danes felt David Phillips and Robbie James should have been dismissed by referee Siegfried Kirschen, who had been the linesman struck by a stone during the 1976 disorder when Wales played Yugoslavia. Hughes' first international goal for two years saw Wales through, and once again the door to qualification was open, offering Mike England a reprieve from the over-expectant FAW. While Wales were beating Denmark 1–0 in front of 20,000 fans at Cardiff, the Finns pulled off a shock result when they beat

Czechoslovakia 3–0 in Helsinki. The result meant that a draw in Denmark and anything but a heavy defeat in Prague would see Wales through.

The build-up to the Denmark away game was overshadowed by fitness doubts over Southall, now considered the best goalkeeper in the world. "Neville's presence could be the difference between us winning and losing and qualifying or not qualifying," admitted England. In the event, Southall was replaced by Chelsea's Eddie Niedzwiecki, who made his first Welsh start against the brilliant Danes. There were strong words before the game in Copenhagen when the Danish manager requested a change of referee, while striker Preben Elkjaer warned that the Danes were prepared for the "over aggressive" Welsh. Things became more heated when the 800 travelling supporters were incensed by the playing of 'God Save the Queen' rather than 'Hen Wlad Fy Nhadau'. Hughes and Rush were well-shackled but it took a controversial goal to win the game for the home side. "We were not beaten by Denmark," fumed England. "We were beaten by the referee. The player was four yards offside before Elkjaer scored." With Wales losing for the first time with Hughes and Rush playing together, they went to Prague in November 1987 needing to beat the Czechs on their own ground. The hosts were already out of contention, and nobody was sure how they would approach the game.

John Toshack gave the first example of the outspokenness that would become all too familiar to Welsh fans when he called on Mike England to resign if Wales did not win. "I think it's all too cosy," said Toshack. "They are a nice happy family that needs shaking up." Rush was furious: "The remarks are insulting and the man is out of order." "We don't need these kind of comments before a vitally important match," agreed England. The old selection problems flared up again when the Football League postponed games involving English players but refused to do the same for the Welsh. And so came the inevitable injuries, which saw Wales leave for Prague after a training session with only ten players. Immediately after the game, Mark Hughes would fly to Munich to play for Bayern against Borussia Mönchengladbach that same evening.

Despite their injury worries, Wales threw everything at their hosts in an attacking, fearless display. With 75 per cent possession and some good chances, it looked possible they could claim the needed win. Wales missed four clear opportunities inside 30 minutes and Ivan Hasek cleared a shot off the line as Wales dominated in front of a disinterested 6,443 crowd. But Rush, playing despite an ankle injury, was having no luck in front of goal, and the Czechs took their only two chances against the run of play. The champagne that had been left on ice in their chartered aeroplane remained unopened. Once again Wales had failed at the final hurdle, and this time it would cost Mike England his job.

"In some ways I was a victim of my own success," he would say. "We had some great results against some very good teams but at the end of the day we did not qualify." Mike England went back to north Wales where he became the manager of a nursing home. Brian Clough was the FAW's first choice to replace him, and the Nottingham Forest man was enthusiastic: "I can't promise to give the team talk in Welsh but from now on I shall be taking my holidays in Porthcawl – and I've bought a complete set of Harry Secombe albums." But he was left fuming when Forest refused him permission to take the role.

David Williams was appointed caretaker as the FAW searched for a new boss, still hoping that Forest would change their mind about Clough. Making his debut in a friendly against Yugoslavia at Swansea was Croydon-born Gareth Hall, who had originally intended to travel to South America with the England under-20s that day. A late invitation to play a full international for Wales proved too tempting, and he left Heathrow for Swansea, along with the in-bound Ian Rush, to make his debut for Wales in the 1–2 defeat.

The FAW then drew criticism from Ian Rush after appointing Swansea manager Terry Yorath for just three games in the hope that Clough would still be able to take up the role. "It's obvious he's not going to come so why wait?" asked Rush. "Something must be sorted out, it's no good having different managerial teams all the time. It's so unsettling," he told Karl Woodward on the eve of the April 1988 friendly in Stockholm. For Yorath's first match, his defensive options were limited and the back four that faced Sweden were all midfielders. Phillips, Blackmore, Aizlewood and Jackett were the rearguard of a team that was unsurprisingly beaten 4–1. "Our second-half performance was dismal," admitted Yorath, who had asked the team to play a more considered style, with Hughes switched to a new role in midfield behind Rush and Saunders. On the same evening, HTV incurred the wrath of Alun Evans over their decision to broadcast the Hungary v England friendly in Wales.

Rush captained his country for the first time on a hard and dusty surface in Malta in June 1988 in the second of Yorath's three-match trial and came away with a well-earned 3–2 victory. "I was never one of those players who pulls out of the international squad claiming injury but is always fit for his club's next league match the following Saturday," wrote Rush. "To be selected for Wales was always a great source of pride to me, and to be made captain thrilled me to bits."

Four days later, Wales moved on to Brescia via Milan where a mix-up delayed the 30-strong party by several hours. The home side were booed off the field after Rush's goal gave Wales a shock win that would ensure Yorath's permanent appointment. The Welsh captain relished the victory as he had struggled for form since his move to

Juventus. On leaving his team-mates at Turin, they had each raised five fingers to show how many goals Italy would score against his Welsh side. Rush discussed the game in his autobiography. "I felt I had a lot of things to prove to a lot of people in the game against Italy," he said. "I was as wound up before the game as I ever have been. After Terry had said his piece in the dressing-room, I took to my feet to offer words of encouragement. I didn't refer to me and Italy or the send-off I had received from Juventus players, I simply spoke of the pride we had in being Welsh; that no one expected us to win because no one rated us as a team or individual players. 'Let's go out and show them,' I urged my teammates. 'Let's do something today so that when we're old and have grandkids, we'll have something we're proud to tell them'." On the final whistle, Rush turned to shake the hand of the nearest Italian, Giannini, who sulkily brushed it away: "Wait till you play against Roma next season, see what I'll do to you" he threatened.

11

A NATIONAL STADIUM FOR A NATIONAL TEAM

1990–1999

1990 World Cup

Hopes for a successful World Cup were dampened from the start when Yorath saw that his Wales team would need to top a group containing West Germany, Holland and Finland. It was a serious challenge for the new manager, who had passed his trial period, though at least he could develop a squad with little expectation in his opening campaign. But he would need to do the job alongside his club duties at Swansea with the FAW agreeing to pay a third of his club wages as compensation.

The first game away against the Dutch would be a huge test. Swansea's Alan Knill debuted for a side missing Ratcliffe and van den Hauwe, and was asked to mark Marco van Basten. Knill was outstanding in one of the bravest Wales performances in recent times, and an extraordinary display from Southall saw Wales edge to within minutes of a famous result before a brilliant 82nd minute Ruud Gullit header finally beat the Evertonian.

Yorath had hoped to call in Mark Stein to face the Finns

at Swansea in October 1988, until it was discovered a 20-minute substitute's appearance for England Youth ruled the QPR man out of selection. Ratcliffe made a welcome return after 10 months' absence with a hernia injury to captain the side. It proved an embarrassing evening for Wales. Dean Saunders missed a late penalty after scoring one earlier in the game, and the 2–2 draw effectively ruled them out of Italia '90 at a very early stage. It was then back to Israel for another lucrative friendly in February 1989. Two mistakes from new keeper Andy Dibble left Wales needing a late volley from substitute Malcolm Allen to salvage a 3–3 draw in Tel Aviv.

February 1989 saw the demise of one of Wales' few professional outfits. Newport County had never been a big club and the years before the arrival of Len Ashurst in 1979 had been a perpetual struggle. But with his appointment things began to look up. There was a promotion to Division Three and Newport even spent money. There was £20,000 lavished on the playing surface and £45,000 on Mark Kendall.

Then in 1981, County took their place in the spotlight. After two-leg wins over Crusaders and then Haugar in the European Cup Winners' Cup, they returned with an incredible draw from the quarter-final first leg at East German side Carl Zeiss Jena. The second leg at Somerton Park in front of 18,000 was a travesty. Newport did everything but score. They went out by a single goal, but it was the proudest moment for the club, whose team included future internationals Nigel Vaughan, John Aldridge, and Steve Lowndes. Newport topped the third division when they beat Cardiff in 1983, and they drew with Everton in the FA Cup. But even during this period of success, finances were bad, and the club relied on council handouts to avoid court. The FAW attracted criticism when they refused a request for £100,000 assistance, but then they had already saved the club once in the 1970s.

After missing out on promotion, Newport went into decline. There were losses of £185,000 in 1985, and in 1987 they were relegated. The following year they lost their place in the league amidst deepening financial trouble, and on 27 February 1989, Newport County went out of business with debts of £330,000.

Newport had needed a sugar daddy, and American investor Jerry Sherman arrived on the scene in 1986. Hailing from Newport in Washington, Sherman claimed he had been attracted to the club by its name. He was brash and elusive, with the shifty-eyed evasiveness of a potion seller at a wild west show. He made promises he couldn't keep, and as Newport County went out of business, Sherman became the target of local anger.

He had announced his arrival in Newport, Gwent, by telling the *South Wales Argus* he would be buying the board out for £750,000, thus causing celebrations throughout south-east Wales. The takeover never materialised. In 1987, Newport went into administration and Somerton Park was sold to Newport Council to save the club.

In October 1988, the club faced a winding-up petition over a £132,000 bill, yet the players were still staying in top hotels before games. It was finally confirmed in November 1988 that Sherman was indeed the new chairman. During the next few months Sherman continually promised ever more extravagant amounts of investment which failed to appear. Even when the club was wound up at the end of February, he asked for two days grace due to a banking slip-up. During Sherman's six months as chairman, Newport's debts had increased from £132,000 to £330,000. The Newport manager, former Welsh international John Mahoney, lost everything after remortgaging his house to help the club buy a player. What really happened? Did Sherman embezzle that £200,000, or was he telling the truth when he says those debts were there when he arrived? Tellingly, Sherman was convicted of a million dollar fraud involving a Washington ice-hockey team in 2007. Whatever the truth, Newport County were wound up and the resulting auction of their history produced some of the most heartbreaking scenes witnessed in any place where people love their local club.

Out of the ashes rose a phoenix club, Newport AFC. When the supporters met to establish a new side, County were still actually in existence, were in training, and had been accepted into the Vauxhall Opel League. In the event, County never played another game. They were expelled from the league with Sherman still asking for two days' grace. Newport AFC have since reclaimed the old name and Newport County is back, looking for a return to the Football League.

The friendly against Sweden at the Racecourse in April 1989 had already been arranged when the Hillsborough tragedy occurred. The FAW donated all gate receipts to the Liverpool relief fund. It was a magnanimous gesture from the association, who had been unable to afford caps for their non-league representative side a month earlier. Yorath had witnessed terrible scenes during the fire at Bradford's Valley Parade, and the minute's silence must have been especially poignant for the Welsh manager. Derby's exciting young striker, Dean Saunders began the game on the right flank in a sign of things to come. Yorath would always struggle to accommodate Saunders, Hughes and Rush together, and the solution was to play Saunders wide, or Hughes in midfield. The 0–2 defeat was Wales' first in 11 internationals at Wrexham.

In May 1989, the FAW announced that the forthcoming international against West Germany would be played at the National Stadium, the home of Welsh rugby. It would be the first time an international in Britain would be watched by an all-seated crowd, and the reaction to the stadium was hugely positive. "If it was possible I think we should play all our games here," said Yorath. Mark Hughes was in agreement: "Seeing the packed spectators in the biggest stadium in Wales gave our spirits a real lift."

The West Germany game was played a week after

Everton had played in the FA Cup final, and Pat Van den Hauwe failed to appear. A frustrated Yorath left a message with Everton, warning that the full back would never play for Wales again. A passionate Welsh performance restored some pride and gave glimpses of a better future, but the 0–0 draw was no help to the qualification effort. Had Wales been awarded a penalty for Buchwald's handball then things might have been different. But at least the game was a huge financial success for the stricken FAW and the £250,000 raised allowed the resurrection of the under-21 team.

There were other pressing concerns in 1989. Thatcher's government was keen to introduce the Football Spectators' Bill in the wake of disasters at Heysel and Hillsborough. A key element of the legislation was the introduction of ID cards for every supporter. While this would damage club attendances, it would be fatal for Wales. Supporters with addresses in England, or the thousands who had not registered to watch a professional club, would be barred from attending international games unless they applied for a card. Thankfully, huge opposition ensured the scheme was never implemented.

Defeat in Finland in September 1989 ended Wales' hopes of qualification for Italia '90. John Charles accused Yorath's team of lacking passion after a dreadful display in Helsinki and the manager's evening was worsened by bookings for Rush and Hughes, ruling both out of Holland's forthcoming visit to Cardiff.

Iwan Roberts of Norwich gained his first cap against the Netherlands, while an unknown youngster named Gary Speed was drafted into the squad from Leeds. Wales were outplayed and the Dutch coasted to a 2–1 victory in front of 3,000 travelling fans, who made up a third of the poor crowd at Wrexham. "They were too good for us," admitted Yorath.

Tommy Forse replaced Ivor Pursey as President of the FAW in 1989, and his first job was to devise a plan enabling

Wales to play home matches at an all-seater stadium, as required by FIFA for the 1994 World Cup qualifiers in three years' time.

Wales then faced a series of tough away games and lost each one. At least they gave the West Germans an almighty scare when a goal from Allen put his team in front in Köln in November 1989, and Southall saved a penalty. But Yorath's team could once again take heart from the performance against West Germany, if not the 1–2 result, which left them bottom of their group. Southall then saved another penalty when Wales faced the Republic of Ireland in a friendly at a packed Lansdowne Road in March 1990. The Irish were celebrating qualification to the World Cup but struggled against a competitive Welsh side until Bernie Slavin broke the deadlock late on.

Incredibly, Southall saved a third consecutive penalty when Yorath took an inexperienced side to Stockholm in April. But two goals from Saunders weren't enough and Wales lost 4–2. The Welsh football supporter was now being assisted by an information service called CLUBCALL. For just 38p a minute, fans could hear news, interviews and match coverage. The Sweden game was broadcast live, and as it was an off-peak evening game, rates were reduced. At just 25p per minute, you could listen to the whole game for £22.50. Nobody did.

By now, Wales were regularly being used as a warm-up for foreign teams wanting to sample the European-style game before major tournaments. Costa Rica came to Wales for the first time in 1990 – they would be facing Scotland and Sweden in Italy. Yorath was unconvinced of the Costa Ricans' ability: "If I was having a bet, I don't know whether I would be certain about them winning the World Cup," he mused. Saunders' goal won a dour game, notable only for the debuts of Singapore-born Eric Young, Paul Bodin, and Gary Speed. Nonetheless it was a win – something Wales had not experienced for ten games and almost two years since

Yorath's permanent appointment. Fewer than 6,000 fans were there to see it.

The returning under-21s faced Poland at Merthyr's Penydarren Park for a first game in six years. It had been a long time, and the senior side had suffered as a result. It was probably no coincidence that the return of the under-21s coincided with the return to form of the senior team over the next few years. And as Welsh finances gradually improved, Yorath insisted that somebody was needed to oversee the development of the game in Wales. Former Australia manager Jimmy Shoulder was appointed to take on the task.

In a September 1990 friendly in Copenhagen, Mark Hughes was tried in a new withdrawn attacking role as Wales also experimented with a sweeper system. A low-key warm-up against Denmark was lost by a single goal though the performance gave optimism for the coming campaign.

1992 European Championship

For the 1992 European Championship qualifiers, Wales were drawn alongside Luxembourg, Belgium and the newly-unified German side, who went in as strong favourites. For the first fixture, against Belgium in October 1990, Peter Nicholas was used to shackle Belgian playmaker Enzo Scifo as Wales needed to get their campaign off to a flier. The talented Belgium side had suffered three consecutive defeats, though Yorath's team had now not won in eight competitive fixtures. It proved to be a rare night of celebration as Wales put on a sparkling performance to defeat the Belgians 3–1. Wearing their new all-red Umbro kit, Wales attacked the Belgians at pace, with Saunders shining. Rush scored his first goal in eight internationals and the relief was plain to see. The watching German manager Bertie Vogts was impressed: "It will be extremely hard for us to win in Wales next May," he forecast.

Despite a relatively low 12,000 crowd, the FAW signed an agreement with the WRU to secure the National Stadium for their games. The stadium allowed for large crowds at the centre of Wales' largest population while negating the inter-club rivalries which blighted the 1980s. There were objections that £50,000 would be lost to rugby for each game, but Alun Evans insisted that football would profit in the long term.

Yorath knew that victory over Belgium would mean little if Wales failed to beat Luxembourg away, but the minnows could not be underestimated, having only narrowly lost to West Germany. When Blackmore was sent off after 12 minutes, Welsh hearts sank, but a heroic display after Rush had given Wales the lead saw the ten men through. Yorath's team had begun the campaign in the best possible way.

In February 1991, the country's first 'B' international was held at the Vetch Field where Jason Perry and Gavin Maguire marked Peter Beardsley and Steve Bull. Wales lost to England by a single goal in front of 4,618 fans, though the experiment was deemed worthwhile as fringe players gained international experience. The following evening Wales welcomed the Republic of Ireland to Wrexham for a friendly. The game went ahead at a frozen Racecourse, even though contingency plans had been made to switch to the heated pitch at Goodison Park. Neither manager wanted the match played on the snowy surface, but they were overruled by referee Fred McKnight. A large Irish following, which put the home supporters to shame, saw their team win 3–0, with Yorath substituting Eric Young at half-time, remarking that he had been playing like "Bambi on ice". Little attention was paid to this freak game in the snow as Wales looked ahead to Belgium in March.

"If we can come home with a point and remain group leaders, we will go into the match against Germany at Cardiff Arms Park full of confidence," said Yorath. There was a scare on the flight as turbulence caused a large food trolley to overturn, missing Rush's leg by inches. "I don't know why I pulled my leg from the aisle at that moment," he told the *Western Mail*. "A split second later and it would have been smashed by the trolley." More than 1,600 supporters followed Wales to Belgium where the hosts needed to win after defeat in Cardiff. Yorath's disciplined side was happy to leave with the required point to keep them top of the group on their manager's 41st birthday.

Yorath arranged two friendlies in May against Iceland and Poland in preparation for Germany. He left his assistant Peter Shreeves in charge for the 1–0 win over the Icelanders, while he travelled to watch Germany beat Belgium in Hannover. The south Wales public shared Yorath's apathy about the game, and only 3,656 turned up to Ninian Park. Yorath missed very little action, but one incident would prove significant. When Wales won a penalty in the first half, Saunders declined to take it, passing the opportunity instead to Paul Bodin, who finished high to the keeper's right. From that time onwards, Bodin was appointed penalty taker. He would attempt exactly the same spot-kick at home to Romania in 1993.

Yorath also took a full Welsh team, including Rush, Hughes, Southall, Ratcliffe and Saunders, to Craven Cottage where Wales beat a Fulham XI, including Glenn Hoddle, 4–1. The testimonial for Gordon Davies drew 3,800 just a day before Wales flew to Poland for another friendly. In the Wales squad was Cypriot-born Jeremy Goss, who had already represented England Schoolboys. Goss had actually spent four years in school at Crickhowell as a child but qualified for any of the home nations as the Cypriot-born holder of a British passport. Wales' game against Poland was played at Radom and a pleasing performance saw Rush win his 50th cap in a 0–0 draw.

Less than a week later, Wales welcomed the world champions. The newly-combined might of East and West Germany arrived in Cardiff as the re-unified Germany. The West Germans were unbeaten in 16 games, and were now able to call on the best East Germans to boost their squad. Vogts claimed a draw would suit his team. Yorath meanwhile, still insecure over his own future, knew he needed to win. "I wonder if my position depends on us beating Germany. If so, that is stupid," he said.

The Welsh were now well established at the rugby ground and Yorath was delighted. "I think our players have taken to the National Stadium like ducks to water. The players now think of the National Stadium as their home ground, they like playing here and the atmosphere is absolutely tremendous," he said. In answer to Vogts' criticism of Wales' robust style, he said: "If the Germans stopped diving about all the time it would be a lot better for everybody."

There was the usual pre-match injury scare as Rush looked doubtful, but there was no way he would miss this one. In front of a capacity 37,500 crowd, Wales matched the Germans in a tentative first half. Oxford's Andy Melville was marking Rudi Völler while Bristol City's Mark Aizlewood shackled Jurgen Klinsmann. An injury to Lothar Matthäus, the German captain, saw him replaced at half-time, and when Thomas Berthold was sent off for an assault on Ratcliffe on the hour, Wales took the initiative. A beautiful long pass from Bodin sent Rush racing away from his marker Buchwald. When he struck the ball firmly past Illgner in the German goal, the National Stadium erupted. Two world-class saves from Southall denied Klinsmann and saw Wales through an extremely tense final ten minutes. "There is a lot of football to be played in the group and we are still a long way from Sweden," warned Yorath. Vogts insisted "the Welsh team were very lucky". Three points clear at the top of the group after their 1–0 win, Yorath knew that victory in Nuremburg would seal a place in Sweden. Even if Wales failed to win, there would be other opportunities provided they beat Luxembourg and Germany dropped points elsewhere. They had given themselves the best possible chance.

One effect of the Germany win was the appointment of Yorath as full-time manager three weeks later. He claims the FAW admitted privately their hand had been forced by public pressure. But if the association was not fully convinced about their manager, the squad was happy. At that time, the players met up for the weekend before a midweek international, and Yorath allowed them to socialise in a relaxed atmosphere. There was a night out on Saturday and golf on Sunday and Monday afternoons, with more free time on those evenings. The players certainly enjoyed the camp, and it created a bond which was evident on the field.

All of Welsh football was given a boost by that victory over Germany, and there was a carnival atmosphere at a friendly against Brazil in September 1991. Wales had pushed on with their development of the National Stadium as a venue, and the match was played under floodlights made possible by a £400,000 grant from the Football Trust. A Cardiff-based samba band (which included the author) was invited to welcome the Brazilians in front of 25,000 spectators and they kept a pulsating beat throughout the game, which seemed only to inspire the visitors. Yorath even remarked that he wanted to "put another ball on the pitch to give his side a go." A mistake from Taffarel allowed Saunders to score for Wales in a much improved second-half performance, and Wales had further chances to extend their lead with Southall rarely tested in his record-breaking 53rd appearance as a Welsh goalkeeper. Straight after beating Germany, Wales had beaten Brazil. Something exciting was happening.

Nerves grew as the big match approached, and Wales travelled with an army of 4,000 to Nuremburg for the crucial qualifier in October 1991. The eve of the game saw the famous March of the Leeks, when hundreds of Welsh supporters paraded through the city waving the national vegetable and singing 'Men of Harlech'. But the team looked fragile without Phillips, Blackmore, Aizlewood, Nicholas and Hodges. Ryan Giggs' late appearance as a 17 years and 321-day-old substitute would break John Charles' long-standing record as the youngest Welsh international. Before the game, along with Mark Pembridge, Giggs had been designated as the man to choose videos for the team bus, and he was sent to 'Welsh Breakers Video Rental' in Aberkenfig where the shop owner had agreed to sponsor the team with free rentals. For the young winger his first cap was a dream come true. He had stood proudly for 'God Save the Queen' and scored against Wales as captain of England Schools, but it was Wales he had always wanted to represent, and Giggs had no English qualifications.

It was not a good night for Wales to be under-strength as the Germans gave a masterful display which put the Welsh upstarts in their place. Despite heavy pressure, Southall broke Dai Davies' Wales record for shutouts by keeping the Germans out for the first 33 minutes, extending his record to 434 minutes since conceding a goal. Making his seventh appearance at right-back was Portsmouth's Gavin Maguire, who had only played one league game all season. Hammersmith-born Maguire was also qualified for England or Eire. "I was ribbed by other players who said things like, 'You weren't good enough for England so you had to play for Wales'," he remembered. "My mother is from Wales and it was Wales I wanted to play for as a boy, never England." The Germans targeted him, and after Wales conceded a soft goal from a short corner, it was his dreadful back-pass to the head of Möller which settled the tie. Maguire was replaced at half-time by Gary Speed, but things got worse for Yorath's side after the full back's substitution. Saunders received a red card on 50 minutes, and Germany went on to win 4–1. "We just did not function," admitted Yorath, "and they were a different class to us playing some of the best football I have seen for a long time." Maguire never appeared for Wales again, blaming Yorath for playing him out of position. He retired from football at the age of 26 to run a hairdressing business in Somerset.

Wales needed to beat Luxembourg to put pressure on the Germans who had two games remaining. There had been calls for Yorath to give a first start to Giggs, but wary of exposing the youngster too early, the Welsh manager waited for an hour before throwing him on. In a tight game the young winger made an immediate impact, but it was Yorath's second substitute, Paul Bodin, who had the biggest effect. His 81st minute penalty won the game, though Wales' failure to increase their goal difference meant Germany would have an easier task in their penultimate game in Brussels. "The Germans only need a draw," admitted Yorath, "but I don't think we could have done any more than we have done in the group." The game had seen Peter Nicholas become the most capped Welshman, earning his 73rd cap to overtake Joey Jones' record. The Newport man had been an uncompromising midfielder and served his country with great loyalty. In a sad, but predictable denouement, Germany beat Belgium and progressed to Euro '92 at Wales' expense by a single point.

In a momentous year for the domestic game, 1992 finally saw the foundation of the League of Wales. FAW Secretary Alun Evans announced the formation of the league on 30 September 1991, insisting that it was vitally important in the face of attempts by "third world countries, backed by some Europeans, to create one British entry at international level." Eight clubs announced that they wished to remain in the English system – Merthyr, Barry, Newport, Caernarfon, Bangor, Rhyl, Colwyn Bay, and Newtown. Due to their recent investment in players, Merthyr were permitted to remain in the Conference and were given five years grace to achieve Football League status. Then in May 1992 UEFA confirmed that Welsh clubs would be allowed into the UEFA and European Cups from 1993/94. Vindicated, Evans lashed out at his detractors. "This proves them wrong," he said jubilantly. "They didn't think we could do it." In return, UEFA stipulated that English-pyramid clubs would no longer be accepted as Wales' European representatives even if they won the Welsh Cup. It was a difficult, divisive time for the game in Wales, and some rifts have yet to heal even after two decades have passed.

A friendly was arranged for February 1992 against the Republic of Ireland at the Royal Dublin Society Showground, the home of Shamrock Rovers. Mark Pembridge's goal inflicted a rare defeat for Jack Charlton's Ireland. Southall was magnificent as he marshalled a defence which included debutant Kit Symons. Giggs was missing from the line-up however, and some years later, Yorath told the *Western Mail* how Alex Ferguson had blocked his appearance. "I knew Alex didn't want Ryan playing friendlies," said Yorath. "We used to go through the motions of picking him, but we knew there was no chance of him playing. We all met up in Slough before flying over to Dublin and I stayed up until midnight waiting for Ryan. He never turned up so I rang Alex at home. When he came on he was his usual gruff self. I said: 'Where's Ryan?' He replied: 'You should have had a note saying he's injured and not coming.' I told him I hadn't received any note and that we were the Welsh national team and were owed some respect. United had sent a note but it went to Dublin instead of Slough."

In that same month, Welsh supporters were given the news that Swansea midfielder Alan Davies had committed suicide in his car two years after earning his 13th cap in Dublin. Just 30 years old, Davies had struggled with injuries and depression as his career looked to be ending with a second child on the way. He had spent the evening before his death watching videos of his career with Manchester United. The following morning, he dropped his daughter at school before driving to a beauty spot on the Gower Peninsula where he ended his own life. Born and bred in Manchester, Davies had qualified for Wales through his father, who came from Corwen.

1994 World Cup

There was optimism in the air when Wales were drawn in Group Four of the 1994 World Cup qualifiers alongside Belgium, Romania, Cyprus, the Faroe Islands and RCS, the Representatives of the Czech and Slovak Republics. The two countries previously forming Czechoslovakia had separated too late to be offered individual places in the World Cup, and a combined team was the solution. Two teams would qualify from the group and Wales were serious contenders.

Wales were severely under strength for a friendly against Austria in front of 53,000 fans in Vienna, but managed a creditable 1–1 draw thanks to an equalizing goal from debutant Chris Coleman. The game served as a handy warm-up, but gave no hint of what would follow at the game in Romania a few weeks later. Yorath admits he struggled with the transition from club boss to international manager. It had been easy controlling impressionistic lower league squads at Swansea and Bradford, but there were stars in the Welsh ranks, and a few of them had enjoyed testing their manager.

Yorath took a gamble for the game in Bucharest and dispensed with the sweeper system which had served Wales so well. It was to prove disastrous. Wales were made to look like amateurs in a 5–1 defeat by the thrilling Romanians, inspired by Gheorge Hagi. "I believe the Romanians would have beaten most sides in the world with their performance that night," said Yorath. It was the worst result of his reign, but his mood was lightened when he received a note from his son Daniel – "Don't worry Dad – we'll show them," it read. Daniel would not live to see his father recover from the defeat to inspire the Welsh team. In May 1992, during a kickabout in his garden, Daniel Yorath collapsed and died in his father's arms. The youngster had suffered from hypertrophic cardiomyopathy, a rare heart condition. Yorath was devastated at the loss of his 'best friend'. "I've never been able to get over Daniel's death," he wrote, "and I never will."

As Yorath grieved, Peter Shreeves took charge for the trip

to Utrecht to face Holland in a May friendly. Wales, in black armbands, conceded four. They had now leaked ten goals in three games, despite reverting to their trusted sweeper system, with Speed at left-back after Yorath had selected his team by phone during a number of emotional calls to his assistant. The game was held on Malcolm Allen's wedding day and Huddersfield's young centre forward Iwan Roberts missed out to attend the ceremony.

More summer friendlies came as Wales entered a three-way tournament in Japan called the Kirin Cup in June. Yorath did not travel and Shreeves again took charge against the Japanese and a star-studded Argentinian side. Blackmore was tried in the sweeper role, and it almost worked, with Wales restricting the Argentinians until a couple of minutes from the end, when Gabriel Batistuta beat Southall. Wales then beat Japan with ten men after Roberts was dismissed despite Japanese protests that his foul did not warrant a red card. After heavy defeats against Romania and Holland, the performances restored some confidence ahead of the next round of qualifiers.

Happily for Wales, the tiny Faroe Islands offered no resistance in the first qualifying match, and a first international hat-trick for Rush put him level with Trevor Ford and Ivor Allchurch on 23 goals. Alex Ferguson expressed his displeasure that Giggs had been allowed to face the press ahead of the Faroe Islands' game, and it was little surprise when the youngster was withdrawn from the squad that travelled to Limassol to face Cyprus a month later on what Rush claimed was the worst pitch he had ever played on. The Cypriot coach was well-versed in Welsh tactics – he had earned his badges on an FAW coaching course run by Terry Casey. Wales were lucky to win thanks to Hughes' goal in front of almost 2,000 travelling supporters.

Fortified by two victories, and boosted by Romania's failure to beat RCS at home, Wales looked to close the gap when they visited Belgium, who had won all four group games so far. Belgium comfortably won 2–0 at Anderlecht's Stadium, with Wales failing to muster a single attempt on goal. Everton's Kevin Sheedy then scored for the Republic of Ireland in their 2–1 friendly win over Wales at Tolka Park in February 1993. Sheedy had been born in Builth Wells but chose to represent the country of his Irish father.

Belgium had surprised many with their storming start to the campaign, winning all six games by the time they visited Cardiff in March. But Wales were encouraged again by RCS's failure to beat Cyprus. Yorath had given a surprise recall to 32-year-old Kevin Ratcliffe who was playing for Cardiff in the fourth division. "In many ways that Belgium match was the finest game I ever played for Wales," said Ratcliffe. "I felt I'd justified Terry's faith in me." For the first time, Wales used the new FIFA ruling allowing them to insist on a player's release. They called up Bristol City's Aizlewood, who would miss his club's relegation battle against Grimsby. "We had to do it," insisted Yorath. "It's OK for clubs to say players are important to them, but the World Cup is important to us."

Giggs had been named PFA Young Player of the Year for a second successive season in 1993, but had still made just five substitute appearances for his country. But Shreeves had a new plan. Giggs would take all corners and set-pieces, and from kick-off, Wales would pass to him at every opportunity. He would then simply run through the opposition. The youngster repaid Shreeves' confidence by scoring from a superb free-kick, and Rush finally broke Allchurch's record with his 24th international goal to give Wales a fine 2–0 win over the group leaders. Wales were now unbeaten in six at Cardiff Arms Park, lying just a point behind second-placed Romania.

With Aizlewood and Eric Young suspended, the FAW walked straight into a row with Portsmouth when they insisted on the release of Kit Symons ahead of the next game in Ostrava against RCS. Pompey manager Jim Smith was furious: "The FAW have let everyone down as far as I'm concerned – the fans, Kit Symons, Portsmouth Football Club, and football in general." "Everybody knows the FIFA rules," was Evans' response. But FIFA apparently did not. Portsmouth claimed Yorath had given verbal assurances that Symons would not be called, so FIFA overturned its own guidelines on appeal. Preparations were further disrupted when Gary Speed was punched in the face in an Epping Forest restaurant while dining with members of the squad. Dean Saunders jumped to his defence and was taken in for questioning after the fracas spilled into the restaurant car park. Preparation had been poor for such an important fixture, and to make matters worse the team were allocated a noisy hotel in sweltering heat. There were also problems on the terraces. A Swansea flag was torn down by Cardiff fans, but it was not only the Welsh supporters who were fighting amongst themselves. Czechs and Slovaks booed each other's anthem. Under the circumstances, Wales returned from Ostrava with a good 1–1 draw after Hughes became the first Welshman to score in six visits to the Czech Republic.

On seeing the success of Jack Charlton's predominantly Anglo-Irish Republic of Ireland team, the FAW began a concerted effort to find players with dual Welsh qualification. Yorath was reluctant but resigned to the situation. "I do not want to see the day when the national side is full of people who are only partially Welsh," he admitted. He was denied one of his promising young players when Sheffield United goalkeeper Mel Rees died of cancer aged just 26 in May 1993. He had been a Wales understudy to Southall.

After dispatching the Faroe Islands 3–0 away with Hughes winning his 50th cap, Yorath knew that wins from the home games against RCS, Cyprus and Romania would get them to USA '94. The first of those fixtures arrived in September 1993 when Wales welcomed the RCS. By now, the team had captured the public's imagination and 37,558 fans all but filled the National Stadium. When Wales went a goal down, the crowd could have turned on their team, but instead noise levels rose a few notches as the home support roared "Terry Yorath's red and white army" back into the game. The match ended 2–2 with Wales going close on several more occasions. "I am not dejected about the result at all," insisted Yorath, knowing two home wins would still be enough.

The women's game in Wales was taking shape. The inaugural Welsh Cup was won by Pilkington (Rhyl) who beat Inter Cardiff at the National Stadium in 1992. In September 1993, Wales' women played their first UEFA Championship match against Switzerland at Cwmbrân, having already played their first international against Iceland earlier in the year. The League of Wales was also making progress. On 18 August 1993, Cwmbrân became the first team to represent Wales in the European Cup when they faced Cork City. It was an exciting time for domestic football, and the possibilities seemed limitless. "Who will be the champions of the League of Wales in the year 2003?" asked LoW secretary, John Deakin, "Cardiff City or Wrexham?"

Surprisingly, October 1993 was the first time that a Cyprus team had visited Wales and they would be no pushovers, having already taken a point from RCS. There were still four teams contending the two places available at USA '94, and Wales were fourth behind Belgium, Romania and RCS. A win was vital, though Yorath now looked on the Arms Park as a fortress. "If this game was played elsewhere, we would be back to the days of three or four thousand," he said. Cyprus went down to ten men after 50 minutes when Costas Costa, who had warned he would "give Giggs a whack," was sent off. He was followed soon after by Christofi. Things remained tense for Wales until an inevitable 70th minute goal by Saunders before Rush made it two. Crucially, bookings for Aizelwood and Hughes meant that neither would feature in the winner-takes-all Romania game to be played on 17 November 1993.

This would be the biggest game in a generation. Football was buzzing again, with a vibrant fanzine movement, and the sport had made inroads into popular culture. The dark days of the 1980s had been left behind, and everybody wanted to be part of Welsh success with long queues forming outside the FAW office in Westgate Street the morning after Wales beat Cyprus. The rush for tickets left regular supporters claiming they'd missed out but Welsh fans simply weren't organized – they had never before faced such competition for tickets.

The build-up to Romania was the most intense in living memory. The *South Wales Echo* ran a 30-day countdown to 17 November, and the BBC ran an iconic promotional series featuring Saunders, Hughes and Rush's golf-swing celebration to the tune of Andy Williams' 'Can't Take my Eyes off of You'. The tune caught the imagination and could still be heard at international matches years later. Qualification was so close that many fans began planning a trip to the States for the summer of 1994. Yorath issued a battlecry: "I don't want there to be a violent atmosphere, but I just want them to get behind us and be a bit more hostile to the opposing team than normal." The FAW stood to gain £5 million from qualification. It would also mean they could maintain a full-time manager. The players too, wanted revenge. "When we played in Bucharest 18 months ago, Hagi spat in my face," said Rush. As the last British team with hopes of qualification, the game generated huge interest. Good luck messages were received from George Best, Prime Minister John Major and even Princess Diana.

Wales were still fourth, but within two points of group leaders Belgium on 14 points. Romania came next on 13 with RCS and Wales on 12. The ramifications were spelled out in the match programme: "Belgium need one point from their home game with RCS. Romania need one point here in Cardiff. If RCS win in Brussels they will steal Belgium's place. If Wales win tonight, then they can qualify, but if RCS win by one goal, then Wales must win by two clear goals. However if the RCS win by two or more goals then Wales will only have to beat the Romanians. Of course if RCS don't win, then Wales have only to win."

The visitors started fluently with Hagi pulling the strings. It was no surprise when he scored; though it certainly was a surprise that Southall let his speculative shot slip inside the post. Yorath blamed himself for the goal, as he had forgotten to warn Bodin that Hagi would always come inside onto his left foot. It was probably Southall's first mistake of the tournament. But Wales fought back, roared on by the capacity crowd, and when Saunders equalized, Romania began to wilt. "Their morale collapsed, and I could see from their body language that they didn't want to know," remembered Giggs. The momentum had shifted – if only Wales could get that winner. They pressed – and in the 63rd minute Speed was felled in the area. This was it. This was the moment Wales would be repaid for those awful decisions that had robbed them against the Scots. This time it would be different.

Bodin's left-footed shot was hard and fast, but, with the goalkeeper floundering, it hit the bar. It had been struck with such force that the ball did not land until it was 25 yards away from goal. The Welsh fans raised their hands in disbelief. And then, in the 83rd minute, with Wales pushing on, Romania scored again and it was over. "If the penalty had gone in, we would have run out 2–1 or 3–1 winners because they had folded," said captain Barry Horne. Bodin would never play for Wales again. "What I've always wondered is what would have happened had I stayed on my feet?" pondered Speed. "Would I have scored? Would that have taken us to the World Cup finals?"

With the final whistle blown, the National Stadium dissolved into sorrow, and in one final act of frustration, a pair of brothers from Wrexham fired a marine flare across the arena at 240-miles-an-hour. It struck John Hill of Merthyr, who was watching the game with his son in Row 25 of Block D. He died on the spot despite desperate efforts to save his life. It was the lowest moment in the history of Welsh football and Terry Yorath sat alone in a stadium stairwell and cried. Flights back to Romania were delayed as police searched for the killers, with rumours suggesting an attack by away supporters. The brothers were sentenced to three years in jail after admitting manslaughter. They claimed they thought the rocket was a hand-held flare.

The game marked a watershed. From the moment the whistle blew, the side was in disarray. Ryan Giggs was booked for speeding as he drove home in a daze. Managers were sacked and appointed, and the players dissolved into self-pity. "It was the most painful match of my career," admitted Speed. "I was devastated by it, and it affected me for a long time afterwards." *Observer Sport Monthly* judged Bodin's miss as the 46th most heartbreaking moment in sporting history. From the brink of the World Cup, Wales entered a period of rebuilding, uncertainty, and chaos. When Yorath left his role following a dispute over a new contract, Wales were ranked 27th in the world. "I've had a couple of offers, but the one I wanted has not come," he said sadly. The one he wanted was from Wales.

On Christmas Eve 1993, Yorath received the letter informing him that his contract would not be renewed. He had asked for an increase on his salary. When he lowered his request to fit the FAW's budget, he was told to reapply for the job. A decision on the manager still hadn't been made when FAW President Elfed Ellis died while returning from a trip to Finland. When a decision was finally made after a month of inactivity, Alun Evans explained the FAW position on Yorath: "We don't look on him as a failure; simply that he was unable to take us the extra step forward." Yorath's right-hand man Shreeves was also out. One man who didn't agree with the decision was Ryan Giggs. "It was after their sacking that I started to feel disillusioned about playing for Wales and I didn't really enjoy international football," he wrote.

The man the FAW believed would take them forward was John Toshack, by now manager of Real Sociedad. After

Toshack declared his interest in the Wales role via a *Western Mail* interview with Karl Woodward, Alun Evans contacted the Cardiff man in Spain. After securing agreement with his club, Toshack was appointed as part-time Wales manager. It was not a unanimously popular appointment, with many questioning the suitability of a man already working full-time on the continent.

Toshack's first test came in a friendly against Norway at Ninian Park in March 1994. The profits of the match were donated to the family of John Hill. It was a magnanimous gesture, but a horrible night for the FAW and its new manager. It was the first time the Welsh public had the chance to show their frustration since Romania, and there was still anger at the treatment of Yorath. Toshack swung into town unaware of the resentment towards his appointment. Local heroes Jason Perry and Nathan Blake were selected for their debuts to appease the Cardiff crowd, but the ruse didn't work as chants of "We want Terry back" rang around the stadium throughout the game.

Toshack's first press conference drew unprecedented interest, and the new manager was faced with some awkward questions in the foyer of the Marriott Hotel, not least whether it was true he was earning more than the amount which had been requested by Yorath. Toshack preferred to talk tactics. "I do have some fresh thoughts regarding our playing style which will require some players to take on a different role," he said. He was talking about his "sistema Toshack" which may have worked well in Spain, but was literally a foreign concept to the Welsh players. The system allowed for only one attacker, meaning Rush would play a deep role behind Hughes. Southall turned out for the second half wearing Steve Williams' Cardiff City jersey after the referee asked him to change from his usual black shirt because it clashed with his own. But even Southall could not prevent a comprehensive defeat as an abject display brought howls of protest.

Toshack was unrepentant. "If we don't qualify, we'll fail

doing things the way I want us to," he said. "I cannot allow the frustration of the fans to influence me." Two days later, less than a week after his first game, Toshack offered to quit. And by 16 March 1994 he was gone. Toshack claimed he was unaware that Yorath was still on the shortlist for the job when he was approached by the FAW – according to Toshack he was told only Bobby Robson and Terry Venables were in the running. After just 48 days in charge, Toshack walked out, citing the "dirty war" of Welsh football politics. "I want to wash my hands of the whole affair," he said, "Wales can forget about me." "The association is at a low ebb," conceded Alun Evans, hurt by criticism over his part in the fiasco.

Yorath saw his chance and made it clear he was prepared to drop a claim of unfair dismissal if he could be reinstated. But he was to be disappointed. The FAW acted quickly and an emergency meeting at Caersws decided Yorath would not be considered. Instead Mike Smith was promoted from assistant to fill the role he had left 14 years earlier. "I thought they were going to put me in charge as caretaker for one game, but they said that was no good to them," explained Smith. "These offers don't come along very often so you have to take them. I have been in charge of 207 internationals, 100 of them at senior level, and if I did not think I could do the job I would not have taken it." "It was unfortunate that John Toshack decided to resign, but life must go on," said FAW senior international committee chairman John Evans. "Welsh football in particular must go on, and we are looking to Mike to maintain our progress." In his autobiography, Yorath was adamant that his dismissal was due to the FAW resenting his public popularity.

1996 European Championship

Mike Smith suffered eight withdrawals from the despondent squad that welcomed Sweden to Wrexham for his first friendly game in charge, but at least Southall was present to equal Peter Nicholas' appearance record. "Nev is quite simply the greatest goalkeeper I have ever seen," said Ian Rush. Southall was unable to prevent a 0–2 defeat, but the performance restored some semblance of pride after a shambolic period in which Wales lost three games under three different managers. Gone were the sweeper and "sistema Toshack" systems, as Smith returned to a familiar 4–4–2. Wales then won a friendly versus Estonia in Tallinn by two goals to one.

Wales were drawn in Group Seven of Euro '96 alongside Bulgaria and Germany. The group's other trips to war-torn Georgia, Moldova and Albania would provide a logistical challenge, and when Smith visited Tbilisi to watch a friendly between Georgia and Malta, he was asked to check his gun in at hotel reception. The European game was changing. Boundaries were being redrawn and new teams were entering the international fray, increasing the number of countries to challenge Wales and threatening its historical place at the head table of the International Board.

The campaign kicked off against Albania in September 1994. The Albanian side was a total mystery and when they came to the National Stadium, the match programme was unable to include its usual feature on the visitors. The editor simply had no information and the squad list published was two years out of date. UEFA had even had to demand assurances from the Albanian FA that its players would not abscond during the trip. Rush captained his country to an unimpressive 2–0 win, but when Wales faced two new countries – Moldova and Georgia – in their first games, nobody knew what to expect. What they did not anticipate was two humiliating defeats. Ryan Giggs missed all three games in perhaps the most disappointing series of results in Welsh football history.

Smith made his first serious error when he declined to invoke FIFA's five-day rule and allowed his players to turn out for their clubs ahead of the trip to Moldova. A depleted Welsh squad was forced to call on Barry Horne, who had not played for his club all season. It was Moldova's first home competitive international and a passionate crowd watched them beat Wales 3–2. The *Western Mail* called it a night of shame. Horne would remember the trip a few years later: "We were told not to risk walking the streets after dark. Apparently the place is full of armed bandits."

Smith insisted Wales had played well despite the defeat, but he was all too aware of the mounting pressure. "Nothing less than a victory will do," he said ahead of the trip to Tbilisi a month later. Travelling to Georgia was a logistical challenge and the FAW were hit with a hefty insurance bill to cover visiting a classified war zone. "We'll have problems in Georgia like we had in Moldova," warned Southall, even though Georgia had already narrowly lost to Moldova and Bulgaria. And he was right. Wales were ripped apart by the quick, technical play of their skillfull opponents. The 5–0 defeat was Wales' worst in more than half a century, but Smith was not happy with the public outcry after such a shocking start. "I don't need this type of aggravation," he blasted as the Welsh fans looked back fondly to the Yorath era. "The world of football has been turned upside down," wrote Brian Fear, FAW President. "The break-up of the Soviet Union and Yugoslavia has unleashed scores of top quality players who had rarely touched the heights of international football because of the lack of opportunity for selection." Smith spoke of his "disappointment, embarrassment, frustration and shame."

In such trying times, Wales faced World Cup semi-finalists Bulgaria just before Christmas 1995 with one of the most experienced teams ever to take the field. There were 434 Welsh caps on the pitch, and four players with more than half a century of appearances each. There was also a controversial debutant, as notorious hard-man Vinnie Jones became the first beneficiary of a new rule allowing qualification by nationality of grandparent. Jones, a cockney, took his Welshness to heart after finding a Welsh grandfather.

He was already a close friend of Wimbledon clubmate John Hartson, and learnt the national anthem with enthusiasm. He even had a dragon tattooed above his heart, though this was not his first attempt to find an adoptive country. He had travelled to Dublin in 1992, in an attempt to find records of an Irish grandmother. His debut was nearly denied when, along with Mark Hughes, he forgot to bring his passport to the game, a requirement of all international players. Fortunately a compromise was reached when photographs were taken with the match referee in order to verify their identities for the authorities. Jones' debut ended in an ignominious 0–3 defeat.

Wales faced Bulgaria again in March 1995, and again conceded three on a Sofia pitch which needed 200 soldiers to clear away the snow before the game could begin. Southall was again supreme, but the spirited Welsh side, including debutants John Hartson and John Cornforth, managed only one goal in return. "We'd gone from being hard to beat and well organized under Terry Yorath to a demoralized rabble," admitted Giggs. "We were going out onto the pitch and not expecting to win." A month later, the FAW appointed David Collins as Secretary-General to replace Alun Evans.

Wales had now lost four consecutive games under Smith and things wouldn't get any easier with an away game against the Germans in April. Wales arrived for a pre-match training session in Dusseldorf to find the stadium locked. When entry was eventually gained, they found themselves sharing the pitch with two lorries, four tractors and 20 ground staff engaged in a resurfacing operation. The setback did not affect Wales unduly however, and they managed to gain a creditable draw after Saunders gave them an early lead.

In a controversial move, Wales played their home under-21 game against Georgia at Cardiff Arms Park, the ground of Cardiff RFC, adjoining the National Stadium. Vinnie Jones was then sent off for stamping after half-an-hour of an embarrassing 0–1 home defeat by Georgia in the senior international – a result which left Wales bottom, below Moldova and Albania. Just 16 months after his appointment, Mike Smith was supervising a coaching course in Cardiff when news came from an FAW meeting in Welshpool that his contract had been terminated. "Mike took it like a gentleman, though obviously he's disappointed," said Alun Evans. There was a feeling that Smith had lacked the necessary charisma. He was well enough liked, but it was felt he lacked the personality to inspire the more famous names. The FAW wanted a high-profile manager to take over and Howard Kendall, Lawrie McMenemy, Gordon Strachan and Ron Atkinson were all discussed, as was Welsh under-21s manager, Brian Flynn. What Wales really needed was stability, something absent since the dismissal of Yorath.

Typically, the FAW made a completely unexpected choice by appointing the charismatic Bobby Gould. Gould had been working in the media, presenting a phone-in show on Sky before being offered the position. "I had a dream and that was to become the manager of Wales," he said. "It has now been fulfilled." One of the first things he did was travel to Manchester for a meeting with Alex Ferguson. The one item on the agenda was Giggs' availability, and Gould returned confident he could call on the superstar's services. Unfortunately, Gould then penned a newspaper article on the issue, infuriating Ferguson.

Only 6,721 fans felt inspired enough by the new manager to turn out to watch the stuttering 1–0 win over Moldova in September 1995, with Speed scoring Wales' 600th goal. Maybe Wales would have won more comfortably had Gould been successful in his efforts to tempt Channel Islands-born Matthew Le Tissier to play. Gould did select another Anglo-player with Reading's Adie Williams playing full back. "You wouldn't think by listening to me I was Welsh," Williams told the *Sunday Mercury*, "but my dad comes from Bala, is a fluent Welsh speaker and is very proud of his country."

There were 20,000 more at the Arms Park to welcome the

Germans a month later, and a spirited Welsh performance looked to have earned a draw until a disastrous Andy Melville own goal in the 75th minute. Wales equalized when Thomas Helmer also put the ball into his own net, but Klinsmann scored a late winner. It hadn't been a bad start for the new manager, and he had a chance to push on with an away tie in impoverished Albania. Fog and mechanical problems delayed Wales' departure from Stansted, and after suffering further delays on arrival, they reached the Qemal Stafa Stadium too late to train. In a sign of things to come, Mark Hughes had withdrawn after hearing he would not be starting, and Rush was controversially dropped. Gould gave first caps to Gareth Taylor, John Robinson and Robbie Savage but was grateful for a 1–1 draw in Wales' final match on a shocking pitch, which saw them finish bottom of the group. "Everybody gave their best," said Gould. "Although I wanted to win, because I'm a winner, it's a sound result." Gould had certainly raised morale, which was at rock bottom by the final days of Smith's reign.

The FAW accepted a friendly against Italy at short notice in January 1996, and Wales were badly depleted when they went to Terni in stormy conditions. Hughes was back in, though Gould offered no gushing welcome: "I haven't spoken to Mark and he'll find out that he's in the squad when he reads his name on Teletext." It was a comfortable victory for the Italians as Welsh football saw the last performance of Ian Rush, with David Phillips also retiring after 62 caps. Gould caused further controversy by substituting Wales' record goalscorer after an hour, replacing him with the young Gareth Taylor with Wales three goals down. Rush deserved better, and remonstrated with the manager as he left the field. In his Wales career, Rush had scored a record 28 goals from 73 appearances.

After selection against Italy, Hughes was again left out as Wales, with five new caps lost 0–2 in Switzerland in April 1996. Furious at being dropped for the friendly, he telephoned

Gould and demanded an explanation. "I'm Welsh and I adore playing for Wales," said the Chelsea player.

The national side has suffered many embarrassing defeats, but perhaps the worst occurred at Brisbane Road in May 1996, when Leyton Orient beat Gould's team 2–1. The manager disappeared on the final whistle leaving Neville Southall to explain how a Welsh team, including Giggs, had lost to a team 89th in the League. "We're quite happy, although it might not look that way," said Southall. "Orient were fired up, but so would I be if I were playing against Ryan Giggs. It wouldn't have mattered if we'd lost 10–1." Nonetheless, the defeat earned Gould some embarrassing headlines.

1998 World Cup

If hopes had been high for Euro '96, the Welsh public approached the 1998 World Cup campaign without optimism. The draw for France '98 pitted Wales in the competition's toughest group against Belgium, Turkey, the Netherlands and San Marino, with only one team sure to qualify. The runners-up would enter a play-off with the league positions decided not on goal difference, but on results between opponents with identical points. Wales would have to finish ahead of Belgium and also an improving Turkey side. It was accepted from the start that the Netherlands would win the group.

Wales began with a trip to tiny San Marino without the honeymooning Speed. The part-timers were brushed aside as Hughes scored his first two international goals for three years in a 5–0 win. Wales went one better with a 6–0 win over the minnows in Cardiff in August 1996. Gould had urged Welsh fans to sing 'We'll Keep a Welcome in the Hillsides' ahead of the match, but thankfully the plea was ignored. The opening games had gone to plan and restored a modicum of respectability, but they had not gone without difficulties. "They set out to maim us," claimed Saunders. "We're lucky no-one got seriously hurt."

The Welsh supporters looked forward to Gould's first

big test against Holland and 34,560 were at the National Stadium to watch a game which was central to any hope of progression. The FAW had moved to attract more supporters by playing home games on a Saturday and cancelling all domestic football. But once again it was only Southall's heroics that prevented embarrassment as the Dutch cruised to a 3–1 victory. Some claimed it was the keeper's finest hour, though in a career filled with superlatives, that was a big claim. There was even admiring applause for Ronald de Boer's third goal for the Dutch, who had given a masterclass to their hosts. The return fixture in Eindhoven a month later was approached with trepidation. And rightly so.

The FAW had announced major investment in football development in Wales in November 1996, and Welsh youngsters were at least offering some hope for the future. The evening before the senior side faced Holland, the Welsh under-21 squad travelled to Breda and achieved the country's greatest result at that level by beating the Dutch 1–0. It was a stunning performance and Gould was said to have shed a tear of pride.

But he was hardly optimistic ahead of the senior team's visit to Eindhoven. "I'm always honest and I have to say the training hasn't exactly flowed," he admitted. "In fact, the way we've trained so far we don't stand a chance." Already missing Hughes, Giggs, and Horne, Wales' task seemed hopeless. It was a strange decision then when Gould made Vinnie Jones his captain, and the method behind it was even stranger. The manager announced that a secret ballot amongst players would decide the skipper. After counting the votes, Gould announced that it was Jones who had been elected. The result came as a huge surprise to everyone and later consultations found nobody who had voted for the midfielder. "The players of Wales do not know how to apply the Wimbledon spirit," said Gould, justifying the decision.

The gamble failed spectacularly as Wales suffered their worst competitive defeat in a 7–1 thrashing. "In the 15 years that I have been working as a coach or a manager I have not been educated to the level I should have been," complained Gould. He had no answer to those calling for his head. Wales were now fighting for second place, but at least goal difference was not being counted. "We're at rock bottom," said Gould. "No matter how much money anyone earns it doesn't compensate for the feeling in our dressing room." In a stark illustration of how far the national team had fallen, the star of the 1958 World Cup squad, John Charles, presented a deflated Giggs with the BBC Wales Sports Personality of the Year award.

Gould's behaviour was becoming more erratic, and while training for the forthcoming match against Turkey in 1996, he attempted a stunt intended to galvanize his side after the demoralizing defeat to the Dutch. He knew that John Hartson had been resentful after being hauled off the pitch in Eindhoven, and decided to have it out with the young forward. Hartson describes the incident in his autobiography: "He had turned to face me, right in front of the other players. Then he said, 'Right John, you and me, let's have a fight'. I was only twenty-one and here I was being challenged to a fight by a middle-aged bloke, who also happened to be my boss. We came together, me and my boss, and in truth I just grabbed hold of him for two minutes. I didn't throw a punch or aim a kick. Maybe he sensed it could have become too heated because he suddenly said, 'Right that's enough'. He wasn't hurt, although there were some scratches on his face and his hair was all over the place, but it was all so undignified."

Gould's behaviour and the lack of success, ensured players were becoming less willing to make themselves available. Giggs was forced to defend himself after featuring in just 17 of Wales' 37 games since his debut. "Playing for Wales is the biggest honour of all for me," he said. "There is no bigger thrill for me than playing at Cardiff Arms Park – it's as exciting as playing in any FA Cup final. When I was young, Alex Ferguson might have said that he wanted to rest me from Wales' games – but that doesn't happen now." Gould was grateful for small mercies after Wales' 0–0 home draw with Turkey in December 1996. "Although we were disappointed not to have won, we were at least heading in the right direction by not falling apart as we did against the Dutch," he said. It was a measure of how far Wales had fallen that he was pleased just to avoid defeat at home against Turkey. An inspired performance from Mark Crossley in the Welsh goal earned another scoreless draw against a dominant Republic of Ireland in front of just 7,000 at Cardiff in February 1997.

If Giggs was claiming his club manager was becoming more relaxed about releasing him for Wales, then an incident before the March qualifier against Belgium set that progress back significantly. Welsh preparations were disrupted when Gould received a furious call from Ferguson after Giggs had been disturbed by intruders at the team's Stakis Hotel in Newport. Then, while training in Cwmbrân, the winger was mobbed by fans, mainly schoolgirls. Ferguson was not impressed.

Belgium had lost 0–3 to the Netherlands, and Gould knew a win was essential, even to stand an outside chance of grabbing second spot. The game was played in a strange atmosphere at a one-sided National Stadium where demolition work had already begun in readiness for the new Millennium Stadium. Only 15,000 fans were there to see Wales lose again, despite a goal from Speed, selected as sweeper by Gould. The FAW faced a tough decision about future home games as FIFA and UEFA were insisting matches be played at all-seater stadia. With only 10,000 seats at Ninian Park, options were limited. The National Stadium move had been a huge success. Not only had the stadium witnessed some great performances, but the tribalism which cursed international games for so long had been eroded. The atmosphere was always good, whatever the size of the crowd, and it gave Wales a neutral home away from the small-mindedness of club venues. Wins over Belgium, West Germany and Brazil at the National

Stadium will live long in the memory, but there will always be an association with tragedy after the death of John Hill.

The 1–2 defeat to Belgium ended all hopes of qualification. It was a sordid period for the team, with Blake refusing to play after accusing Gould of making racist remarks during training. Southall, despite seeing his hopes of appearing in the latter stages of a tournament disappear, refused to blame his boss.

"I would love to be able to say that Bobby was shit," he told the *Independent*, "or the players are too old and the youngsters coming in are rubbish. But it's not the case. There are no simple excuses. We are talking about years of incompetence. Sacking Bobby Gould would be the easy option. I don't think you should dismiss someone now because of the inability of Welsh football for the past 10 years. We have a fundamental flaw in our game and it's called bureaucracy. Once we sort that side of it we might have a chance."

Barry Horne's decision to retire as captain was symbolic of Gould's era as he set about regenerating a team that had failed again. "I'm not saying it's all over for the older generation, but this is a chance for the youngsters to stake their claim," he said as Wales travelled to Kilmarnock in May 1997 to face the Scots for the first time since 1985. West Ham's barrel-chested striker John Hartson was the great new hope and it was his goal that lifted spirits in a 1–0 victory. Paul Jones, a former farm-worker, was introduced to replace Andrew Marriott, for his debut in goal.

There was a new competition for Welsh clubs in 1997. Frustrated by the absence of the biggest teams from the Welsh Cup, the BBC helped finance the FAW Invitation Cup – later to become the FAW Premier Cup. It would feature clubs from the Welsh and English pyramids, and was greatly appreciated as a source of income by the semi-professional outfits. Of the biggest clubs, only Wrexham treated the competition seriously and they appeared in all but three finals as Cardiff and Swansea almost always played reserve sides. Sadly the BBC withdrew its sponsorship in 2008 and the competition was discontinued, leaving a hole in the finances of smaller clubs.

Gould's contract was due to expire in December but the FAW offered the controversial manager another two years, leaving many fans in despair. It was argued Gould did much unseen work with development squads, but Wales had slipped to 90th in the world from 27th under Yorath. The bewildered fans were not looking forward to a formidable test in Istanbul where the home side still held hopes of qualification. The August 1997 fixture became one of the most bizarre games in a turbulent period for the national team. An incredible 4–6 defeat to Turkey included one of Wales' best ever goals, as Savage struck a spectacular 25-yard volley. Gould's team had been leading 4–3 after an hour, but a formation which included Giggs at wing back and Speed at sweeper was never going to offer much security. Southall was substituted at half-time, and would never play for his country again after winning a record 92 caps. New skipper Speed criticized the referee: "He was unbelievable. Admittedly, we were all over the place early on when we went 2–0 behind, but in our minds we were undone by some ludicrous decisions." 'TURKS 6 BERKS 4' screamed the *Daily Mirror*.

Gould believed he had unearthed a gem in the shape of John Oster. "I'm not being disrespectful to the people of Wales, but for some reason it is a country that breeds very small footballers. So I'm having a video put together of players like Johnny Giles, Billy Bremner, Ossie Ardiles and Diego Maradona – all small, but top class. I think Oster could be put in that category eventually," said Gould, who also called up Barry Town's Gary Lloyd to face Belgium. "I was told Bobby Gould wanted to talk to me, but I thought it was no more than a joke," said Lloyd, who sat out the game on the bench. Despite his poor reputation as national manager, there are many in Welsh football who respected the work Gould did in other areas of the game; he was certainly a big supporter of the national league.

Wales knew that defeat to Belgium would see them consigned to becoming lowest seeds in the next qualifying draw, and the lowest point in their history. At 3–0 down, and in danger of more humiliation, stand-in captain Giggs transformed the game with a passionate second-half display that saw Wales pull back to 3–2. His selection as skipper embarrassed Giggs, who knew he had missed too many games for his country, and felt it was an undeserved honour intended to encourage future attendance. But the ruse failed as Giggs was again missing from a weak Welsh side which lost 0–3 in Brazil in November.

In February 1998, Welsh football was mourning the death of Robbie James, who died on the pitch while playing for Llanelli against Porthcawl at the age of 40. James earned 47 caps for his country and made 782 professional club appearances in a career which started at Swansea 25 years earlier.

A friendly at Ninian Park against World Cup-bound Jamaica in March 1998 was billed as yet another fresh start, and saw the debut of Craig Bellamy. The 18-year-old came on as a substitute for Gareth Taylor, to become Wales' third youngest international after Giggs and John Charles. The match was a fantastic occasion with 10,000 Jamaicans creating an atmosphere more suited to a West Indies cricket match. There was even a delayed kick-off as supporters without tickets were turned away, and the whole 90 minutes was played out against a cacophony of bells, drums and whistles, despite the paucity of action in a 0–0 draw.

Gould raised eyebrows again when he selected Wolves reserve Ryan Green, who became Wales' youngest ever player at 17 years and 226 days in the 3–0 defeat of Malta. There were some who felt it was merely a public relations exercise for Gould, who wanted his name in the record books. "It was a typical Gould stunt," said Giggs. Green made one more appearance for Wales but never fulfilled his early promise. "Perhaps I was involved in too much nightclubbing when I was younger," he said, "maybe my attitude wasn't right." After victory in Malta, he sat for seven hours with his team-mates as they waited for repairs on their plane from Valletta.

The team moved straight on to Tunisia and gave a shocking display that the *Daily Mail* termed "a mixture of indifference and incompetence". Morale was low and the squad revolted over the state of their accommodation, forcing a move to a seaside resort. "What we were offered was not acceptable and we decided to move," said Gould. "People try you. But I have been travelling with teams since the early Sixties and I told the hotel manager that what they were offering was not acceptable for international football." Gould's young side offered little resistance to a Tunisian team looking for a test ahead of their World Cup game against England. Their coach Kasperczak was not impressed: "I regret the fact that our match against Wales turned out easier than we expected. The Welsh should have provided a good rehearsal for facing England – but they turned out far worse than we had hoped." The shameful 0–4 defeat brought things to a head for Gould, and Speed decided to let him know what he thought. The captain launched into a passionate criticism of his manager, attacking his training methods, tactics and general management style. "The game shouldn't have happened, it was too much in terms of the season and energy levels," said Graham Williams, Gould's assistant. "The Tunisians messed us around something terrible, putting the kick-off time back and putting it forward again. They didn't even give us balls to train with. Everything was getting to people, someone had to say something and Gary did. He was like a volcano, he was disappointed about the result and he just exploded. It was a game too far."

Pressure increased on Gould from an unlikely source. During a concert at Cardiff Castle in 1998, Blackwood rockers the Manic Street Preachers performed a version of their song 'Everything Must Go' with the lyrics changed to 'Bobby Gould Must Go'. Wales had won five of 19 games under Gould, against Malta, Moldova, Scotland and twice against San Marino. He was turning Welsh football into a laughing stock, and despite his genial nature, the public gave up on the man they felt was treating his position too lightly.

But instead of keeping a low profile, Gould made headlines again in September when he humiliated the young midfielder Robbie Savage with the world watching. Savage was hauled before the public and forced to apologize after a television appearance in which he jokingly tossed aside a replica Italy shirt printed with the name of Paolo Maldini. "Players have a duty to put up on the field and shut up off it," said Gould, "otherwise this game which is loved by millions will be in very serious trouble." Yet again, the Welsh team was in the news for spurious reasons. The FAW was forced into issuing a statement: "During the interview, Savage was seen to be both disrespectful to his team-mates and highly derogatory to the great Italian defender Paolo Maldini by throwing away his shirt. This morning team manager Bobby Gould asked the player to leave the team hotel and he has been informed that he has been removed from the team to play Italy this evening at Anfield, Liverpool. A decision will be taken later as to whether Savage will be offered the chance to rejoin the squad. The other members of the squad and members of the backroom staff offer their sincere apologies to Paolo Maldini for this disrespectful act." Savage was eventually reinstated after a players' revolt, but only to the substitute's bench. Gould's over-reaction drew bemused criticism from the football world. Martin O'Neill, Savage's manager at Leicester City, demanded an explanation. By then, Gould had already sacked and reinstated Speed after the ferocity of his captain's reaction. The national side was in chaos.

2000 European Championship

Still reeling from public criticism over the decision to offer Gould a new contract, the FAW came under further criticism when they announced the home qualifying games against Italy and Denmark would be played at Anfield, with Belarus and Switzerland kept at Cardiff. Had the FAW not learned the lesson from 1977 when home advantage was effectively conceded for the sake of financial considerations? Gould had asked his players to vote on their preferred venues for the Italy and Denmark games and the squad voted for Ninian Park, where Cardiff City had agreed to raise capacity to 18,000. The FAW felt unable to meet their request – they depended on income from internationals for their existence, and without the National Stadium, Welsh grounds simply failed to offer enough seats to meet demand. It was another humiliating admission of the association's poverty.

The pressure on Gould became unbearable as Wales lost 0–2 to Italy in September 1998. When the Italians scored their second in front of 23,160 at Anfield, the chant of 'We Want Bobby Out' echoed around the stadium. One banner showed Gould hanging from a gallows. In his defence, this was one of Wales' best displays under his management, with Andy Johnson excelling on his debut. But a home defeat put Wales on the back foot from the start. "The Swiss manager was here tonight and he will have gone away with something to think about," claimed Gould. "We can be very, very dangerous. The situation with the supporters is down to ignorance. The performance didn't justify what these people were saying." When he returned home in the early hours he was furious to read a headline on the BBC teletext service calling Wales 'lacklustre'. He later admitted that he had "got a BBC executive out of bed" to complain, and the headline was changed. "I found the whole incident humiliating," said former captain Barry Horne. Vinnie Jones went further. "Look at the way he has dealt with the talents of Robbie Savage and John Hartson, never mind the rest. It's an absolute disgrace.

These are Wales' young hopes for the future and Gould has embarrassed them publicly. It would not surprise me if they did not play for him again," he told the *Daily Mail*.

Calls for Gould's resignation were at their peak when Wales travelled to Copenhagen in October 1998. 'Wanted' posters sprang up in Swansea and Cardiff bearing the legend 'Gould Must Go!' FAW President J O Hughes added to the pressure by admitting "the next two games are critical to Bobby Gould's career." The income from television and gate money at Anfield had at least left the FAW some freedom to make a decision unrestricted by financial implications. But no decision was necessary as Wales recorded a stunning win with a late goal by substitute Bellamy despite a massive shot count in favour of the Danes. "The team had been written off and so had I before that night in Copenhagen," Gould told the *Daily Mirror*. "No one gave us a prayer. Everyone seemed to be writing my obituary. But we pulled off a win and then beat Belarus at Ninian Park. Suddenly, I was a football manager again instead of someone people had written off as dead meat."

The decision from UEFA to create double-header matches on a Saturday and Wednesday caused much consternation to the FAW. Injured players were certain to miss both games, and if a knock was picked up in the first fixture, there was little chance of recovery for the second. It was a small issue, yet it was another way football was penalizing smaller countries with limited squads. After Wales returned from Denmark, Gould continued his erratic methodology, and took his squad to visit a prison in Gwent, claiming he wanted them to experience the tougher side of life. The plan almost backfired when Gould, Blake and Saunders were accidentally locked up. After the stunning success in Denmark, Ninian Park was buzzing for the visit of Belarus. In the opinion of many this was the last Wales game played in the traditional atmosphere of a tight, floodlit ground, jam-packed to the rafters with loyal supporters. There was not a massive crowd, but they roared Wales to a 3–2 win in a game for the true fan to enjoy. Playing midfield for Wales was Charlton's Rhodesian-born John Robinson, who would be voted Welsh Player of the Year in 2002. "Even though there were only 12,000 inside the ground, the atmosphere was phenomenal," he said, "those fans made so much noise you would honestly have thought 70,000 were in there."

Wales had suddenly found form and travelled to Switzerland in confidence, though Giggs was forced to defend himself again after withdrawing with a hamstring injury – it had been seven-and-a-half years since his debut, and he was yet to appear in a friendly. "The criticism hurts," said Giggs. "I'm a proud Welshman, I've never said anything else but that. It hurts because all my family are Welsh and they read the sort of criticism and it hurts them too. It has never been the case that United frown on me playing friendlies for Wales." One man who could not be accused of lacking commitment was Nottingham Forest's Andy Johnson, who cut short his honeymoon to join the squad in Bologna for the Italy fixture. "It is a real choker for me, but the wedding was arranged way before I even knew I would become an international footballer. I could hardly cancel it, could I? It's a shame for Caroline, but she understands how important playing for Wales is to me."

A victory in Switzerland would take Wales clear of the teams chasing Italy, and they were favourites, even without Giggs. Due to other injuries, Gould called up Pembrokeshire-born Mark Delaney who had been playing for Carmarthen Town a year earlier, before signing for Aston Villa via Cardiff City. The news came as such a shock to Delaney that he hadn't even got a passport. Wales would also benefit from a trimmed down Hartson, told to lose weight by Gould after his last appearance against Tunisia nine months earlier. He arrived at camp 10lbs lighter. It had been a tough time for Big John, who had been fined £20,000 and suspended by West Ham for kicking team-mate Eyal Berkovic in the head during a training session. He had also been given a six-month conditional discharge after admitting criminal damage to a plant-box in Swansea city centre. There was further controversy for Wales when Nathan Blake was charged with threatening and abusive behaviour after a night out in Newport with his team-mates ahead of the fixture.

There was yet more trouble for Gould when goalkeeper Paul Jones slipped a disc during the Zurich warm-up. Wales were denied the opportunity of changing their team by UEFA officials, and instead of immediately calling on substitute Mark Crossley, Gould allowed Jones to play. The injured keeper conceded a goal in the first four minutes, came off after less than half-an-hour, and went home in a wheelchair. Despite pushing hard for an equalizer, Wales were denied by the post and had a goal disallowed before Stephane Chapuisat scored his second, putting the game out of reach. Gould believed his team had struggled to cope with the 'favourites' tag. "They didn't react well to it and maybe Welsh teams are like that. They prefer it if they are written off and have their backs to the wall," he told the *Daily Mirror*. A furious Mark Hughes reacted to the defeat by throwing his shirt on the floor. But Italy had been held by Belarus in Ancona, and there was still plenty to play for when Wales travelled to Bologna in June 1999.

There was brave talk ahead of the fixture, but in truth some good results had only papered over the cracks and prolonged Gould's departure. In a bitterly disappointing performance, Wales failed to register a single shot on target in the 0–4 defeat. Only an acrobatic performance by Jones had limited the rampant Italians to four goals in the Dall'Ara Stadium. Rumours surfaced that the players had selected the team, leaving Gould in an untenable position after his 13th defeat in 24 games. And the travelling Welsh fans were at least given something to celebrate when news broke of his resignation. "I felt I could no longer lift the players," he admitted. "The next game is vital and if Wales are to qualify then it needs somebody else to take over. I believe it's in the best interests of Welsh football if I depart at this time. It's not about me anymore." "Mentally, all the lads punched the air in delight," claimed Giggs. In a final gesture, the departing manager recommended that his position be given to Southall and Hughes, and the FAW agreed.

The response to Gould's departure was unsympathetic. Blake told the *Daily Mirror* his former boss "just didn't cut it". He refuted suggestions that Gould had been unsuccessful because he wasn't Welsh. "At the end of the day, managers are judged on results whether they are English, Welsh, from Pakistan or China," said Blake. "It only matters how their teams do on the pitch. Wales didn't go forward in his four years in charge. In fact, if anything, we went backwards." "I never rated him," added Giggs.

After the great atmosphere at Cardiff for the Belarus fixture, the Welsh players lobbied to have the forthcoming Denmark game moved from Liverpool to Cardiff, and the FAW accepted their request. Gary Speed explained the decision to the *Sunday Mirror*: "Anfield has a wonderful playing surface and is a great stadium, but it's not Wales. We wanted so much to play in Cardiff. No disrespect to Liverpool, but I'd rather play at Colwyn Bay or Newtown, because that's Welsh soil." Unfortunately, UEFA refused to change venue, with the Danes understandably keen to face the same 'neutralised' conditions as Italy. Speed said: "I'm not really surprised by the decision but it just makes us all doubly determined to win the match when it is played in Liverpool, and make sure it's Wales who qualify."

Despite Denmark's laughable claim that they needed more tickets than Cardiff could provide, the game at Anfield was played out in front of just 10,000 fans. Another heroic display by Jones failed to prevent Wales' 0–2 defeat after a battling performance. Wales were unfortunate that two goals were conceded in the final six minutes. "I'm proud of my players and I'm proud to be Welsh," said joint-caretaker manager Neville Southall. The defeat meant Wales needed to beat Belarus away in September and win at home against Switzerland in their final game a month later to stand any chance of qualifying.

Southall did not disguise his ambition to become permanent manager. "If they talk about having to throw a hat into the ring I will throw in a Stetson," he told the *Daily Mail*. "I believe the players have shown more commitment, character and bravery than for a long time." After a seven-week search, interviews were give to Terry Venables, Kevin Ratcliffe and Roy Hodgson, along with Southall and Hughes, though Hodgson ruled himself out after taking a position at Grasshoppers of Zurich. This left Venables as the prime candidate before his demands proved unreasonable. "In our discussions with Terry he indicated that he wanted the job and we took him at his word," said FAW Secretary-General David Collins. "Unfortunately his terms were not acceptable to the councillors. The package would have been too expensive and he is no longer part of our plans." The search took a bizarre turn, when the Manic Street Preachers offered £30,000 to the FAW if they appointed Venables. Collins refused to rule out the move. "If we wish to appoint Mr Venables and someone is genuine about giving money, we will talk with them."

The FAW's eventual decision to appoint Mark Hughes on a temporary basis was not popular. It seemed they were simply buying time when stability was needed. "We have a chance of finishing second in our group if we win our last two Euro 2000 matches and Mark will have the opportunity to prove his credentials to take the job on a full-time basis," said Collins. Hughes immediately made changes ahead of the trip to Belarus, calling in Eric Harrison from Manchester United as his assistant. Jimmy Shoulder, in control of the under-21 side, insisted both squads train together to promote unity, which was Hughes' key message in his first sessions. "Mark doesn't say a lot but what he does say makes sense," said Speed. "If he says something then you listen and that's a good quality to have. Whatever happens in these next two games, I'd like to see Mark get the job permanently."

If there was unity amongst the players, there was none between supporters and the FAW after fans were left off the team's flight to Belarus at Stansted airport when the plane was deemed too heavy. Playing kit, food and mineral water was jettisoned, but the aircraft was still overweight and the FAW had to ask 14 fans to stay behind, offering them a night in a hotel and a later flight. Airport police were forced to intervene as angry supporters confronted officials. One fan, Gwilym Boore, was named as 'Sports Personality of the Week' in the *Mail on Sunday*. "The fans have put more effort into following their country around the world than the players did in Italy and Switzerland, and this is our reward," he complained. As recompense, the fans were offered free tickets to Wales' next game in Wrexham.

When those supporters did arrive in Belarus, they watched Wales come back from a goal down to win 2–1 thanks to Giggs' late goal. The result took Hughes' team to within two points of the play-off place, but Italy's defeat at home to Denmark a few days later dashed any remaining hopes of qualification. With only pride to play for, Hughes was swiftly reminded of the task ahead when Switzerland won comfortably by two goals to nil at the Racecourse to complete a disappointing, disjointed campaign for Wales. Making his debut against Switzerland was Mark Delaney, the six-foot-one defender rejected by Manchester United as too small aged 13.

Hughes was given the manager's job and a four-and-a-half year contract after an FAW meeting in Llangollen on 16 December 1999. "I think everybody has got a little fed-up with waiting and wondering what exactly the situation was," he said following his appointment. "Now it has been confirmed I am obviously delighted and am able to get on with the job." The first 18 months however would be part-time as he fulfilled his obligations to his club, Southampton.

There was promising news for the new manager when Alex

Ferguson announced there were no injuries to Manchester United players ahead of Sparky's first test as a bona fide manager – a friendly in Qatar in February 2000. Hughes knew Giggs' availability would be key to any possible success, and he was fully expecting his star player to join the squad after discussing the matter with Giggs at a boxing match in Manchester. "He is as keen as anyone for us to have a good World Cup campaign," said Hughes. "Ryan knows that the game in Qatar is important to us because it is a big part of our preparations." Hughes was to be disappointed when the winger missed his 18th friendly in succession. "Mark has to accept that Ryan is injured," Mark Aizlewood told the *Mirror*. "He's got no other option – although everyone knows what the truth of the matter probably is. The patience of the Welsh public is being tested with regard to Ryan and it's probably wearing a bit thin." Aizlewood was right – a *Mirror* poll showed that 87 per cent of the Welsh public believed Giggs should never be selected again. Hughes even joked he would step in himself to fill a place in the squad, before confirming that his playing days for Wales were over.

Wales, wearing a new kit by Lotto, won the friendly by the only goal. But it was the only time that the white shirt with a large green dragon on the front was worn before being consigned to the pile of obscure 'third kits' produced only for commercial reasons. John Robinson's goal gave Wales the win with an experimental 5–2–2–1 formation which was criticized for its defensive approach. Hughes however, was unbowed: "Playing with only one striker is not a defensive tactic."

12

THE FINAL
TRAGEDY
2000–2011

2002 World Cup

Wales approached the new millennium with uncertainty. The
FAW had taken a gamble on a respected former player with
no management experience and nobody was quite sure how
things would turn out. Mark Hughes was lucky in that he
followed Gould into the manager's chair. The Welsh support
would have accepted anybody. Financial concerns were still
on Secretary-General David Collins' mind when the draw
was made for the 2002 World Cup qualification groups to
reach the finals in Japan. Collins took one look at the names
Belarus, Poland, Ukraine and Armenia and labelled it 'the
group of debt'. At least Norway was closer – but not much.

Excitingly, the FAW announced a 30-term agreement had
been signed with the WRU and Wales would play home games
at the new Millennium Stadium, starting with a friendly
against Finland on 29 March 2000. It would be a landmark
appearance for Giggs, who had missed all 18 friendlies since
his 1991 debut. Hughes was also boosted by a record 65,614
sell-out crowd, with tickets just £5 for the occasion. It was
to be the first of several huge crowds at the ground, making
Wales the best supported team in Europe. The performance
did not match the occasion however and Wales lost 2–1.

The stadium's capacity was increased after the Finland sell-out and 71,495 took advantage of the cheap tickets to watch Brazil in May 2000. For the first time, FAW marketing was hailed as enlightened, though British Telecom was completely unprepared and Cardiff's telephone lines jammed as fans scrambled for tickets. For once, Giggs had a genuine injury after catching his studs in the turf during training and, ironically, missed a match he would have relished. Without him, Wales struggled even though Hughes had had the pitch narrowed, allowed the grass to grow long, and had the stadium roof closed. Brazil coasted politely to a 3–0 win, as did Portugal in a friendly at Cháves a month later. The Portuguese were due to face England in the 2000 European Championships and saw Wales as the ideal preparation. Welsh legend Leighton James was critical of the fixture. "Are we trying to help Portugal against England?" he asked. "It's about time we put the nationalistic flag to rest and gave our support to the other home countries."

Hughes looked to ease the pressure on his players. "Sometimes our expectations are a bit high," he told the *Independent*. "We had a good spell under Terry Yorath, but it was a slightly false impression. Any game we won would take the form of Ian Rush getting a goal on a breakaway at one end and Neville Southall making 10 saves at the other." He set about transforming the set-up, which he considered unprofessional. Players were issued with daily itineraries, and the squad wore blazers rather than tracksuits.

Preparations for his first competitive test against Belarus in September were disrupted when John Hartson flew from the Welsh camp to Scotland to sign for Glasgow Rangers. When the deal fell through, he pulled out of the Wales squad claiming he was not in the right frame of mind. Wales were already two goals down in Minsk when Bellamy was sent off, and Hughes came back disappointed after a 1–2 defeat.

After their poor start, it was essential Wales beat Norway in the second qualifier at Millennium Stadium in front of 53,360 fans in October 2000. "We have to put things right," said Giggs, "the opening game in the group was highly embarrassing – it just wasn't acceptable." Despite a spectacular header from Blake to open the scoring against the Norwegians, a late equalizer disappointed the home support. Former manager Toshack was highly critical: "Is it too much to ask Ryan Giggs to get down the wing more than five or six times in a game, the way he does for Manchester United? The fans have a right to expect a little better from their national team. I wondered if the players really realized just what huge stakes they were playing for." It was the first of several criticisms Toshack aimed at Hughes' team. "It hurt me deeply," admitted Giggs. "I couldn't believe what was said about me and the rest of the lads."

Wales travelled to Poland a few days later hoping for improvement. A 0–0 draw in Warsaw in difficult conditions showed that Hughes was beginning to instill a sense of organisation and discipline into the team. There was controversy during the game, with Wales subjected to constant cheerleading from the stadium announcer amid billowing smoke bombs. The intimidating environment would have seen capitulation in previous years, and Speed reacted pointedly when asked if Toshack's criticism had motivated the team. "Those comments were made by people we have no respect for anyway," he said. Toshack's words had clearly upset the squad, and they would come back to haunt him.

During the previous winter, Mark Hughes had taken the squad for warm weather training in La Manga, Spain. His request to return in February 2001 in lieu of a friendly was turned down by the FAW finance committee but overruled by the full council. For once, football won over money, and the FAW were backing their manager. But Hughes suffered a blow in January 2001, when defender Chris Coleman broke his leg in a car crash, ensuring he would miss the rest of the season. It was the 125th anniversary of the FAW, and in

February, Hughes unveiled a plaque commemorating the association's foundation at the Wynnstay Arms in Wrexham. An anniversary dinner was held in Cardiff in May, and the event was attended by the presidents of FIFA and UEFA. Sepp Blatter brought an engraved carriage clock as a gift.

Hughes had appointed former team-mate Mark Bowen as assistant manager and both he and David Collins were horrified by the conditions they found on a fact-finding trip to Yerevan where Wales would face Armenia in March 2001. The pair viewed five different training pitches, but Bowen was unimpressed. "One was just a heap of mud with straw thrown over it. Another had glass all over it. And the others just weren't good enough." "It's going to be one of our most difficult and costly assignments," added the ever frugal Collins. Dean Saunders became Wales' most-capped outfield player, making his 74th appearance in a disappointing 2–2 draw with Hartson scoring a brace. A nine-hour overnight flight back to Cardiff was hardly ideal preparation ahead of the vital match against Ukraine four days later.

Hartson gave Wales the lead at the Millennium Stadium, but Hughes' team then sat back and watched as Ukraine played all the football. The inevitable equalizer was not long coming, and the draw left Wales six points behind second placed Belarus. Qualification was hanging by a thread as Wales lost a lead for the third time in four games. The team was better organized, but it would take a lot longer to instill a sense of belief in players accustomed to defeat. Dai Davies was critical of the stadium atmosphere. "I think the games should be taken to somewhere like Wrexham where the fans know football," he told the *Daily Mail*. There were concerned glances too at the results of Jimmy Shoulder's under-21 side, which had gone 19 matches without a win. Shoulder had suffered disciplinary problems with his young squad, and sent four players home from Armenia for breaking curfew.

Poland came to Cardiff in June 2001 as group leaders and were 1/6 favourites to win in front of a 48,000 crowd. The

Poles justified the bookies' tag with a 2–1 victory as Wales again failed to hold on to a lead after Blake scored. It was the fifth game Wales had failed to win at their new home, and Hughes was growing despondent. "It looks as if our chance has gone," he admitted as the team travelled to Ukraine for the second match of the double header. Once again, travel plans did not run smoothly and Hartson was refused a visa due to the state of his documents. "My passport was in a bit of a mess," he admitted. "I've had it for eight-and-a-half years and it's been all over with me. I keep it in a drawer in my kitchen and some water had dripped through onto it and some of the pages were stuck together." The FAW were forced to send an official to the Ukrainian Embassy to resolve the issue.

A strike from Mark Pembridge gave Wales a draw in Kiev and the team emerged with pride from a typically hostile atmosphere, with Pembrokeshire-born midfielder Simon Davies – nephew of Ian Walsh – making the team. "We have come away three times now in four games in eastern Europe with draws," said a satisfied Hughes. "They have been very difficult matches and in the past maybe Wales's sides would not have been able to do that. I honestly think it was the best Welsh performance ever because to come to a place like the Ukraine and get a result is a tremendous achievement." There was an extraordinary incident after the game when a member of the Ukrainian FA followed the Welsh party to the airport. He insisted that security X-rays showed that the Welsh were taking home more balls than they had brought after borrowing some for training. "This is very sad," said the official. "The machine shows there are too many balls. This will probably be taken from my wages now."

There were conflicting views about Wales' recent results. While many rightly pointed out Wales had won none of their seven qualifying games, others noted more optimistically, that five had been drawn. If nothing else, Wales were becoming difficult to beat – at least the unpredictability of the Gould era was gone. A 0–0 home draw with Armenia in front of just 18,000 summed up the situation: Wales were organized, but they were hardly exciting. Hughes' side were disciplined, but needed some attacking flair. The manager was well aware of the situation. "We are at the point where it becomes a question of winning rather than the avoidance of defeat," he said before the match. Unfortunately, his team's conservative style did little to back up his words.

Wales then played more positively in Oslo in September 2001, although they blew another lead and lost 3–2 after Giggs was sent off for the first time in his career. Wales had now gone 12 games since their last win under Hughes, and the vultures were circling. Some of the most critical former players upset Robbie Savage. "Neville Southall would not have saved that shot and Mark Aizlewood would not have scored with it," he said. "As far as I am concerned, people in the Welsh TV game are not fit to lace Sparky's boots." Hughes' record was also defended by Collins: "Mark's position is not an issue. We will discuss terms with him when his playing contract ends this season."

Belarus arrived in Cardiff in October 2001 looking for the win that would ensure second place and a play-off against Germany or England. Poland had won the group, and yet Wales, fifth out of six, could look back and think qualification had not been beyond them. They had achieved a point in Poland and were unbeaten against runners-up Ukraine. Belarus were beaten at the Millennium Stadium by a Hartson goal to give Wales their only win of the campaign, but the performance showed little to suggest that Hughes' team was about to embark on a run of unprecedented success.

The FAW received a surprise request from Argentina in February. The South Americans were due to face England in the Japan World Cup and wanted to play under a closed roof to replicate conditions in the Far East. Unable to turn down such attractive opposition, the FAW swung into action and arranged the game at short notice. They were rewarded with

62,500 ticket sales for the first of three friendly fixtures against formidable opposition. Wales earned a 1–1 draw and plenty of praise from the Argentinians. The team was improving, there were huge crowds at the Millennium Stadium, and the feel good factor being generated was worrying the rugby community. "What's really at stake is the future of Welsh rugby and its very status as our national sport," said Simon Thomas, the *South Wales Echo*'s chief rugby writer. "Right now, that status is looking shakier than it has at any time in living memory. Waiting in the wings to assume the mantle is Welsh soccer."

Central defender Danny Gabbidon was given his debut for the scoreless friendly against the Czech Republic at Cardiff in March 2002, and gave an excellent display in a decimated Wales side that was still hard to beat even without its stars. Cardiff City manager Bobby Gould had plucked Gabbidon from the obscurity of West Brom Reserves, and it seemed the defender would play international football for the next decade. The Welsh team were growing in confidence, and when Robert Earnshaw scored on his debut to beat Germany in a May friendly, they proved they could win matches too. "It is the biggest victory of my managerial career," claimed Hughes, who had been released from his playing contract at Blackburn and offered the Welsh manager's job full-time. Late in the game, the 37,000-strong Welsh crowd gave a warm reception to a Chris Coleman cameo appearance as he failed to recover from the accident that effectively ended his career. The mascot for the game was Luke James, son of former international Robbie.

2004 European Championship

The win over Germany offered hope for the coming campaign. Wales faced Italy, Finland, Yugoslavia and Azerbaijan in the 2004 European Championship qualifiers. The group contained the typical make-up: one world-class team, another with a very good pedigree, some tricky Scandinavian opposition and an awkward Eastern European side that Wales, perhaps unrealistically, were expected to beat. From the outset it was assumed Italy would run away with the group, and while Wales were improving, there was certainly no anticipation of the spectacular campaign to come.

With the first game in Finland in mind, Hughes arranged a fixture against Croatia in August 2002, and came away with yet another draw after a Paul Jones blunder 11 minutes from time. The Welsh goal – a solo effort from Simon Davies, was one of the best in recent memory, and gave some indication of the fine form he would show throughout the campaign. And Wales would need him after John Robinson retired from international football following the death of his father. Another new addition to the midfield was 19-year-old David Vaughan, who chose to play for Wales after rejecting an England under-19 call-up.

It looked like Wales would be without Bellamy when they travelled to Helsinki in September for the group opener. The Newcastle attacker was returning from injury and advised not to travel, but even after ignoring the advice, Bellamy was let down by an airline connection and the FAW were forced to make the unheard of decision to charter a private jet to fly him to Helsinki. It was a worthwhile expense. Bellamy came off the bench after an hour and helped Wales to an unexpected 2–0 away win. "It was a troubled campaign for me," he explained. "I had a lot of grief from Newcastle and every international was an argument between Newcastle and Wales and I was caught in the middle." One-and-a-half thousand Welsh supporters made the trip, and the result got the campaign off to a flying start.

Hughes was offered a new contract on the back of Wales' excellent form. But with Mark Bowen unavailable due to club commitments, Hughes turned to the recently retired Coleman for help with coaching duties. "I would love to have been involved with the Wales squad as I am Welsh through and through and it is heartbreaking after I have put two-and-a-half years of hard work into it," said Bowen, after his club manager Steve Bruce suggested he should quit Wales. Coleman went on to sit alongside Jimmy Shoulder in the dugout for Wales' under-21 defeat against Italy. The youngsters had not won in 26 matches, but the seniors were hoping to show the Italians that Welsh football was on the rise when they welcomed them to Cardiff on 16 October 2002.

"We'll convert Wales to football," promised Hughes as the Azzurri arrived in a rainy Cardiff. Italy were in disarray after several injuries, and manager Giovanni Trappatoni was under pressure following a home draw with Yugoslavia. The Italians trained at Jenner Park in Barry as warm-up for a game that had caught the public's imagination. Tickets had been on sale for weeks, but in the wake of victory in Finland, the 70,000 capacity sold out within days with tickets fetching ten times their face value on the black market. In the build-up to the fixture, Giggs became increasing annoyed when constantly asked whether he would have preferred to play for England. Recent rule changes mean his Manchester schooling would now see him eligible for England selection, but he insisted that he would still have chosen Wales. "The fact is that I would rather go through my career without qualifying for a major championship than play for a country in which I wasn't born or one that had nothing to do with my parents," he told the press.

Pre-match entertainment was provided at the Millennium Stadium by the Manic Street Preachers while Bryn Terfel sang 'Hen Wlad fy Nhadau' at the start of a special night for Welsh football. John Charles made an emotional appearance on the pitch and there was electric anticipation in the Cardiff evening air. Wales got off to the perfect start when Davies, voted Welsh Player of the Year, scored from a narrow angle. Italy levelled with a deflected equalizer, but with 20 minutes left Bellamy rounded Gianluigi Buffon in the visitors' goal to send the Welsh fans into raptures. Wales had experienced isolated glory before, but this was different. The 2–1 win wasn't carved out of battling spirit and stout defending; this was a Welsh team matching one of the game's aristocrats with sophisticated, skillful football.

"In Finland, Wales played OK, but last night they played out of their skins," admitted Trappatoni. "A team would take Wales lightly at their peril." "It was a massive, unbelievable, massive night for Welsh football," said Bellamy, "but these games are why we play football for a living." The *Western Mail* called it a "Night of Ecstasy", and the victory was lauded as one of Wales' greatest sporting moments. "The players should be proud of their display. I'm not going to single anyone out, they were all magnificent," said Hughes. "The emotions at the end were incredible, the stadium atmosphere was amazing."

There was another great moment, if a little less trumpeted, when Wales' under-21s won in Azerbaijan to give Shoulder his first victory since 1997. The senior squad knew the result against Italy would count for nothing if they let things slip when they played Azerbaijan themselves a month later. The Baku trip offered regular Welsh travellers the chance to visit a new country, and a group of more than 200 raised money to take gifts and donations for their hosts. Inspired by trips to three Azeri orphanages, Welsh fans created an official charity to raise money for other places they visited. "Wales have played a lot of Eastern European countries over the past few years," said Neil Dymock, the editor of Welsh fanzine *The Dragon Has Landed*. "One of the striking things is the poverty and lack of resources in some of these countries. But it's always been a privilege to visit such hospitable places and be welcomed so warmly." Since its foundation, the Gôl charity has raised thousands of pounds for good causes across Europe.

There were difficulties securing release of players for the Azerbaijan trip in November 2002, with Hughes infuriating

Premiership managers by imposing FIFA's four-day rule. Birmingham were particularly aggrieved at the loss of Savage, and threatened to sue. Alex Ferguson also made barely concealed threats, but for the first time, he was powerless to prevent Giggs joining the squad. "In the long run I don't think this will help Wales," the Manchester United boss forecast darkly. But a late FIFA U-turn left Wales without backing, and they were forced to concede to the clubs once again. After much wrangling, Hughes was given just 48 hours preparation as the match was being played on a day designated for non-competitive internationals. Predictably, Savage was injured when playing for Birmingham and Bellamy was withdrawn by Newcastle manager Bobby Robson, who claimed his player could not face more than one game a week. Under such trying circumstances, Wales did well to win with goals from Speed and Hartson. "We have a really strong team," said Hughes, "maybe the strongest ever." Wales were in unchartered territory – five points clear of Italy after three games. Qualification was now theirs to lose.

With a crucial game against Serbia and Montenegro on the horizon, a friendly was arranged against opponents of a similar style. Wales were content with a 2–2 draw against Bosnia in Cardiff – a record ninth consecutive game without defeat. There was controversy when Senegal were award FIFA's Most Improved Nation award, even though Wales had climbed 52 places in a year, unmatched by any other country. Still, the Welsh team won the BBC Wales Team of the Year award and Hughes became BBC Wales Sports Personality of the Year. International football was enjoying an unprecedented high profile in Wales.

With support at an all-time high, the March qualifier against Azerbaijan sold out within days. Azerbaijan had drawn in Podgorica against Serbia and Montenegro, placing Wales in a strong position. "I honestly believe that this game is the biggest one in Welsh history," said Savage, "and I believe that we deserve to be called the best team in Wales' history but I don't think it will mean anything unless we reach the finals next summer." There was the familiar pre-match disruption. This time West Brom's Jason Koumas failed to appear at the squad meet-up. "One of my best mates died in a car crash early on Monday," he said. "I just don't feel mentally right to play for Wales at the moment." Bellamy too was in the headlines following an incident at a Cardiff city centre nightclub. But it was he who inspired Wales as they brushed aside the Azeris 4–0 to maintain their 100 per cent record.

Wales had been scheduled to face Serbia and Montenegro a few days after the Azerbaijan victory and who knows what might have happened had the team been allowed to play. Unfortunately, civil unrest in the Balkans saw the game postponed until August. Wales were unbeaten in ten – and had already surpassed the best run of form ever shown by a Welsh side when they drew against Bosnia. A year earlier, the same group had been close to setting the record for the worst ever run.

The FAW announced a friendly in San Jose against the United States and Koumas was keen to be selected. "I let them know what was happening last time but I desperately want to play for Wales, particularly with the way things are going at the moment," he said. It was the dream trip for supporters, but it clashed with Cardiff City's appearance in the Division Two play-off final at the Millennium Stadium and many were forced to make a difficult choice. Those that travelled saw a depleted Welsh side lose 0–2 in an end-of-season game that meant little. Giggs has even suggested the defeat may have started a change in Welsh fortunes and has questioned the decision to play the match.

The game that did mean something, against Serbia and Montenegro, would now be held in August 2003, on a date reserved for international friendlies. The date meant Wales were once again unable to secure the release period awarded for full internationals, and were again forced to travel after just 48 hours preparation. Welsh fans were surprised to see the home side play with little enthusiasm, and by the second half Wales were in control against a team recently thrashed 3–0 by Finland. Despite cries to go for the jugular and claim the win that was there for the taking, Wales kept their containing shape with only Blake in attack. They looked to be settling for a draw, but with 17 minutes remaining, the hosts earned a corner which saw Wales concede. Despite the setback, Hughes could have got his point when Earnshaw rounded the keeper, but could only watch as his goal-bound shot was cleared off the line. Wales laid siege to the home goal in the final minutes, but in the opinion of many, Hughes' negativity had cost his team.

The Welsh manager was hurt by the criticism. These were the same tactics he had used all along, and he claimed the Welsh media and public were being unfair. After all, the Italians would fail to win on the same ground a short time later. But this result was the first setback of the campaign and the FAW were forced to complain about racist chanting during the under-21 and senior matches in Belgrade. The defeat in Serbia meant Wales now needed at least a draw in Milan to prevent Italy overtaking them at the head of the group. Around 8,000 supporters travelled to northern Italy in early September 2003 for what was to become one of the most notorious occasions in Welsh football history.

Wales started well enough and held out for an hour before Filippo Inzaghi scored the first of an 11-minute hat-trick. The game ended in a dispiriting 4–0 defeat, but there were greater concerns at the San Siro, where Italy's hardcore Ultras had been allowed to take up position directly above the Welsh supporters. The travelling contingent was subjected to a hail of missiles and abuse throughout the game, with little or no protection from local police. When some Welsh supporters took matters into their own hands there were ugly scenes as the Italian security staff tried to control Welsh protestors with an enthusiasm lacking when it came to policing their own.

After successive defeats in the most difficult games of the group, Wales faced Finland at home in front of 73,411. This should have been a winnable game, but it was played in the knowledge that a point would give Hughes' team a play-off place. A depleted Wales took the lead, but lost the initiative and were lucky to come away with a draw after Koumas was dismissed. Mikael Forssell's late equalizer was no more than the Finns deserved in a tense, nervous game. At the final whistle the players didn't know whether to celebrate reaching the play-offs or be disappointed at missing out on Wales' best opportunity to win a group for years. Disappointment was heightened when they heard Italy had been held to a draw in Belgrade. Victory against Finland would have put Wales a point clear with just October's home game against Serbia and Montenegro to play.

The final game in Cardiff was a disappointing affair, with Pembridge and Melville rested to avoid picking up yellow cards that would have seen them suspended for the play-offs. It was still possible, if unlikely, for Wales to top the group. If they won and Italy failed to beat Azerbaijan, Wales would qualify automatically. The game was level at 1–1 until a late flurry of goals saw the visitors leave the Millennium Stadium with a 3–2 win in front of 72,500. "Stumbling over the finishing line in the group isn't what we wanted, but people have to remember how well we have done to get to this stage," said Hughes. "We were the fourth-seeded team so to finish above Serbia and Montenegro and Finland is a magnificent achievement."

Hughes was right, but it was hard to escape the feeling Wales had blown their chance. That game in Serbia had been key: if only Wales had pushed on for the win. Even after that defeat, could they have held out for victory against Finland had they played more positively? The momentum had gone and Wales would need to pick themselves up against play-off opponents Russia. "I think it's a good draw," said Hughes. "We avoided a couple of big names and it's positive in that we have the second leg at home."

Wales approached the game after five matches without a win. The Russians would be faced in hope rather than expectation, and also without Bellamy. "Everyone knew I had tendonitis and after the Serbia game that was it. I knew I wouldn't make the play-off games with Russia. I watched them from home because I was in a leg brace," he explained. Around 1,800 supporters made the long journey to Moscow in November to see Wales put in a disciplined and unyielding performance to gain a 0–0 draw. Robbie Savage raised his arms in celebration at the final whistle. The draw was well-earned, especially as it came without Bellamy, Davies and Pembridge. And Koumas played the game of his life. "I was very pleased with the performance," said Hughes. "It's been a great night for Welsh football."

However, all was not as he might have hoped. Giggs was suspended for the opening games of the next tournament when retrospective video evidence found him guilty of elbowing Vadim Evseev. The Russian's gamesmanship came moments after Giggs suffered what he called "one of the worst tackles I have ever had to contend with in my career." Wales had survived severe intimidation on and off the pitch – hundreds of local hooligans attacked the Welsh support at a Moscow hotel, and bottles and flares were thrown onto the field during the game. Nevertheless, the result sparked scenes of celebration amongst the Welsh following who sang 'Hey Jude' long into the frozen Moscow night. But the job was not finished and the tie was finely balanced for the second leg in Cardiff four days later. "We're obviously delighted, but it is only half way," said Hughes. "We've had false dawns before. We don't want any more glorious failures." The Welsh knew that physical recovery would be the key – and so did the Russians.

As they faced another winner-takes-all fixture, Wales were unsurprisingly lacklustre after the long journey home with such little time to recover. The Russians however looked full of energy, and took to their task with zeal. Wales seemed tentative; Russia looked threatening, especially on the break. It was no surprise when the away team took an early lead through Evseev, Giggs' bête-noire. But then Giggs hit the post, and Speed and Hartson both missed good chances to equalize. The second half was disappointing and a familiar gloom fell over Cardiff. Once again, the national side had been thwarted at the final hurdle. "That's the lowest I've felt in a Welsh shirt," Giggs admitted. As the Russians celebrated, U2's 'I Still Haven't Found What I'm Looking For' played out from the stadium speakers. In the programme, Alun Evans had written an article on drug abuse in football, but he would have had no idea of the storm about to erupt. Spartak Moscow captain Yegor Titov had failed a drugs' test after the first leg, testing positive for Bromantan – a stimulant previously used by Russian athletes. Titov then went on to play 59 minutes of the second leg. The FAW appealed to UEFA and the Court of Arbitration for Sport to overturn Russia's victory, but both appeals were rejected. UEFA spokesman Rob Faulkner explained: "UEFA felt there was failure to provide evidence the player himself was under the influence of any prohibited substance during the second-leg match."

Wales were not allowed to introduce witnesses or cross-examine the Russian evidence. Hughes was furious. "Nothing will convince me that we did not have a justifiable case," he complained. "I know that there are people who say that it would have been a back-door qualification. Frankly I do not understand the merits of that argument. But I will say that even the smallest advantage can turn a game. Any player who has performance enhancing drugs in his blood is going to be able to create that advantage for his team."

The country's football community retreated into an all too familiar depression, and just before Christmas in 2003, they were further saddened to hear of the death of 61-year-old Gil Reece, who had been suffering from a long-term illness which resulted in the loss of a leg in 2000. "It's terribly upsetting when former players have health problems in later life because you always remember them as such fit guys," said his former manager Mike Smith.

Once again, Wales needed to rebuild, and Hughes' team was experienced, but ageing. The 4–0 victory against Scotland in February 2004 saw Earnshaw score Wales' first hat-trick since 1992. After he also netted the winner in Hungary a fortnight later, the Zambian-born striker had scored seven in 11 appearances and looked set to become Wales' record scorer with a long career ahead of him. 'Earnie' had lived in Africa until he was nine, but moved to Wales with his mother when his father died. He initially turned down the chance to play for Wales Youth, holding out for Zambia, but logistics forced his hand. "It was just so much easier because to play for Zambia there would have been complications with things like work permits," he explained. "I have never regretted the decision for a moment. I love playing for Wales." Making his debut in the 2–1 win at Hungary's Ferenc Puskas Stadium in March was Ben Thatcher. Thatcher became the first person to play for Wales after representing another country at under-21 level. Thanks to new rules, the Swindon-born defender was able to switch allegiance because of his Welsh grandmother.

Hughes had two years left on his contract, but was downbeat about the future: "I haven't done what I set out to do, which is to qualify for the finals of a major championship. It's up to others to make the decision on my future." There were hints that he had become disillusioned despite the friendly wins against Scotland and Hungary when he complained that "the number of withdrawals before the two games was greater than I was entitled to expect."

A few days after a scoreless May friendly in Norway, Wales made their first visit to Wrexham for almost five years, and a Paul Parry goal saw a poor Canada side beaten 1–0 in front of 10,805. Then it was on to Latvia in August where preparations for the approaching World Cup campaign continued with a 2–0 win. The run of results put Wales in good mood ahead of a qualifying group which included England, Poland, Austria, Northern Ireland, and their first opponents Azerbaijan. Bellamy was optimistic. "The Wales squad is the most together football group I've ever been involved with," he said. "I have so much respect for everyone there; the coaches, the manager. Mark Hughes is exceptional, so much common sense, his eye for detail." Shoulder had left his position as under-21 coach to work in Singapore, and was replaced by a combination of Glyn Hodges, Blackmore and Speed when available.

2006 World Cup

Wales had gone five games unbeaten since their play-off heartbreak, and entered the first match of the Germany 2006 World Cup qualifying campaign with some confidence. They had been pitted against England and Poland, as they were for the 1974 World Cup qualifiers, and also Northern Ireland, Austria, and Azerbaijan. The first game in Baku in September 2004 was disappointing, and Hughes admitted his creaking team, with an average age above 30, was lucky to escape with a draw despite taking the lead through Speed. Azerbaijan were much improved however, and looked likely to take points from other sides.

Next up came Northern Ireland, widely expected to be beaten at the Millennium Stadium, but a bizarre sequence of events led to one of the strangest Welsh games in living memory. Another huge crowd of 63,500 watched Europe's best-supported team, but the game was decided by a sequence of controversial incidents. Things began badly on eight minutes with an awful challenge on Savage by Michael Hughes. Savage leapt up in anger but was knocked back down by Hughes' swinging arm. To everybody's astonishment the Welsh player was sent off along with his attacker. Northern Ireland grabbed a two-goal lead, but David Healy was then sent off for his second yellow card while celebrating a goal. With the Irish down to nine men, Wales scored twice to equalize but the result was a bitter disappointment; Wales had needed to win.

There was a feeling that Hughes was struggling to motivate himself and his team, and the announcement that he was leaving to take over Blackburn Rovers came as no great shock. It was a surprise however that Hughes would remain in charge for Wales' next two games, but John Hartson didn't feel it would affect the side's preparations: "I don't think the prospect of the manager going will make any difference. He won't need much of a team-talk for this game anyway – we've waited twenty years for it."

The game that all of Wales had waited for would take place in October 2004. The first game against England for two decades was played at Old Trafford while Wembley was being rebuilt and around 6,500 Wales fans made the journey amidst arguments about ticket allocations. It emerged that FAW committee men were getting 50 tickets each, and sponsors and hospitality customers also did well. While the match was played in a fantastic atmosphere, there were complaints that Wales hadn't competed after conceding early. Nonetheless, there was only one goal in it until David Beckham's stunning late strike made the game comfortable for the English.

Gary Speed shed tears as he retired from international football after skippering the side for a record 44th time in the 2–3 home defeat to Poland. It was a fine performance from the Poles who scored three excellent goals, but it was a sad farewell for Speed, and also for his manager. Wales had been put to the sword in Hughes' final game, and many felt he should have gone earlier to give a new man the chance to make his mark before qualification was out of reach. Hughes' side had now failed to win in 10 competitive matches. But his supporters argued that 15 defeats in 42 games was a decent record. "My legacy is for others to judge," Hughes told the *Western Mail*. "But I would like to think I have restored respectability to Welsh football."

Three people were interviewed for the manager's job after Gerard Houllier pulled out before the decision was made: John Toshack, Dean Saunders, and Frenchman Phillipe Troussier. Toshack had been one of the most vocal critics of Hughes' Wales leading up to his departure, and there was no doubt he would have difficulties in winning over the squad he had so vehemently attacked. "I think most people know who I don't want to see get the job," said Savage, before naming Speed as the players' choice. "It would be a disgrace if Gary had to apply for the job – it should be offered to him. But it's not just me who thinks that, everybody in that squad wants Gary," Savage claimed. Giggs, in his autobiography, described how the players would hurl abuse at the television whenever Toshack appeared as a pundit during Hughes' reign.

Gary Speed retired from playing just seven caps short of Neville Southall's record 92 Welsh appearances. "The caps record has never been something that has made me want to keep going," he told the *Western Mail*. "That would be disrespectful to everyone who has played for Wales and certainly Neville Southall." Andy Melville joined Speed in retirement in October while Andy Johnson and Mark Pembridge finished their international careers soon after.

The public enthusiastically welcomed Toshack following his appointment in November 2004. The feeling was that Hughes' ageing side needed shaking up, and Toshack's long contract seemed a clear sign he was going to build a new Wales. However, nobody could have anticipated the extent of the rebuilding during his second spell in charge, assisted by the experienced Roy Evans of Liverpool and Salva Iriarte, a Basque who had worked with the manager at Real Sociedad. The former Cardiff, Liverpool and Swansea striker began his reign with a pleasing 2–0 win over Hungary from a depleted

Welsh team which had seen five players pull out less than 24 hours from kick-off.

Another player to benefit from UEFA's grandparents ruling was Sam Ricketts, who, as a teenager, chose football over equestrianism. His father Derek was the 1978 world showjumping champion and his uncle the former champion jockey John Francombe. In March 2005, the FAW announced it would move out of the Westgate Street offices after almost 20 years, and had approved the purchase of a new building in Ocean Way, partially funded with grants from UEFA and FIFA. It was a far cry from Ted Robbins' old office above the clothes shop in Wrexham High Street.

As Wales prepared to face Austria in their next World Cup qualifier, it emerged that Savage had retired from international football aged just 30. "I felt it was important to ring him personally and tell him he wasn't going to be in the squad," said Toshack. "When I told him, he said: 'That's OK, I'm retiring anyway.' And the line went dead." Giggs was the only other option as captain, and Toshack had agreed privately that he would only play the winger for half a game or omit him completely from friendlies.

"There's been a lot of them who have retired at the same time, it's not normal," complained the manager after Savage had become the seventh player to call it a day in a matter of months. But Toshack refused to accept the suggestion that the retirements were connected to his appointment. Instead, he criticized a situation that had seen an entire team grow old. He believed Hughes should have introduced younger players after the play-off defeat in Moscow, and was also critical of the social culture the previous regime had developed, which allowed players to spend a night out on weekends before training. Toshack immediately put an end to 'Super Sundays' as they had become known, but not everybody was against him. Savage's replacement Carl Robinson defended the new man vigorously.

If Wales were to have any hope of qualification, they had

to win both their upcoming games against Austria, played within a week. They lost both. Toshack's first competitive match ended 0–2 at the Millennium Stadium with Giggs earning his 50th cap in front of a still-impressive 47,760 crowd. When Wales lost 1–0 in Vienna, they had gone two years and twelve games without a win in serious competition. A horrendous mistake from Danny Coyne had cost Wales the point but Toshack backed his keeper. "I can assure you the team for the next game will be Danny Coyne and 10 others," he insisted.

Toshack had five long months before facing Slovenia in an August 2005 friendly. Giggs withdrew again and later admitted what everybody had suspected – that it had often been his choice to sit out Wales games. "I wanted to play for my country as often as possible, but I thought the medical care we got with Wales was never as good as it was with United. Not just that, but the preparation, the training, and the pitches used – everything really – was never top class which it should have been. I decided that if I wasn't 100 per cent fit, I wouldn't risk joining up with Wales," he said. Wales played Slovenia at the newly-built 20,500 capacity Morfa Stadium in Swansea. In addition to seven retirements, eight others joined Giggs and pulled out of the game. It was an early sign that Toshack's regime would not be popular. Sadly, the Morfa baptism was not successful, and among the disappointing 11,000 attendance, groups of Cardiff and Swansea fans hurled abuse at each other in a throwback to the bad old days. A scoreless draw did little to enthuse the Swansea public, watching the first international in their city for 17 years. They saw Wales wearing a strange black, red and white kit, supposedly a tribute to John Charles, a year after his death.

Wales welcomed England to Cardiff in October 2005 full of hope but little expectation. In an indication of how Toshack's new broom had swept away the old guard, Hartson admitted he hadn't recognized some of the players at training. During his first year, Toshack introduced plenty of fresh blood, giving debuts to the likes of Ricketts, Richard Duffy, David Partridge, Steve Roberts, Gavin Williams, Danny Collins, Craig Davies, Andrew Crofts, David Cotterrill and Joe Ledley.

There was pre-match talk of a thrashing for Toshack's raw recruits, but Wales fought bravely and almost earned a draw. England needed Paul Robinson to pull off an incredible save to deny Hartson; a save the keeper considers the best of his career. A goal from Joe Cole earned the points for an England team that included the young Bayern Munich player Owen Hargreaves, who could just as easily have been wearing red. Born in Canada to a Welsh mother, Hargreaves was developed by the FAW youth system and had played for Wales under-18s. Reports suggested Hargreaves had committed himself to Wales before England came calling. "I was always an England supporter," he argued afterwards, "so pulling on an England shirt was a dream come true."

Wales went to Warsaw a few days later and failed to score for the fifth consecutive game in a 1–0 defeat against Poland. Having been suspended for the England fixture, Ben Thatcher claimed to be unfit for Poland. "I feel Ben may have been thinking that there is a Manchester derby coming up that he would like to play in and that the Poland game is not really important so he feels he can miss it," suggested Toshack. When Thatcher played for his club days later, his Welsh future seemed over. "I'm not in the habit of going cap in hand and pleading and begging players to play for their country, or even shake their hands after games to thank them for turning up," said Toshack. "We used to say thank you to the manager for picking us."

Southall was the next former player to take a swipe at Toshack when he criticized his training methods, accusing him of taking Wales back 25 years. Unmoved, Toshack took a youthful side to Belfast and won 3–2. The result surprised people as Northern Ireland had recently beaten England.

Toshack's boosted young squad then defeated Azerbaijan in Cardiff, finishing off the campaign on a positive note with a 2–0 win. The games had been dead rubbers with no bearing on the outcome of the group, but these were rare victories for Wales after 14 competitive games without a win. "It hasn't been a positive or successful campaign for us, because from the beginning we got off on the wrong foot and had to make too many changes," Toshack admitted, before taking another swipe at his predecessor. "Four games into the campaign was not an ideal time for the shake-up."

Cyprus invited Wales to Limassol in November 2005. The game was not popular with Everton manager David Moyes. "Wales have a meaningless friendly at this stage of the season," he raged. "What is the point of that? Simon Davies has an injury and will not be going on that trip." Toshack, as usual, was unmoved. "I was brought up many years ago at Liverpool never to pay too much attention to what the Everton manager had to say," he responded. Other influential figures agreed with Moyes however. A meeting was hosted by Northern Ireland on their 125th anniversary to examine the possibility of reintroducing the British Championship. Interest had been stirred after the popularity of the World Cup games involving themselves, Wales and England.

One person keen to make the Cyprus trip was Cardiff City's Paul Parry, even though he was uncomfortable about the travelling. "I've never liked flying – I didn't start flying until I was 17 and, if there are other means of getting to places, I will take those," he explained. Wales gave one of their poorest performances in a 0–1 defeat. It could have been much worse had it not been for an impressive debut by Lewis Price in the Welsh goal. "We must make sure that we never turn in a performance like that again," said new captain Danny Gabbidon. "That was the worst international performance I have seen and, to be honest, I feel a bit embarrassed," admitted Toshack.

But he persevered with his rebuilding. Lewin Nyatanga became the youngest player to represent Wales when he featured against Paraguay aged 17 years and 195 days. The South Americans had qualified for the World Cup in Germany, so Wales' 0–0 draw on St David's Day 2006 was a decent result. But a 12,000 attendance created a funereal atmosphere at the Millennium Stadium, and people began to wonder whether the ground was suitable for games unlikely to attract large crowds. A curious fixture against Trinidad and Tobago in Austria allowed Toshack to give a first cap to the young Southampton full back Gareth Bale, who took Nyatanga's record at just 16 years and 315 days. Wales completed the 2–1 win with seven under-21 players on the pitch. Born in Cardiff, Bale had travelled to Southampton's academy in Bath during his youth. "It is an honour to play for Wales," he said. "I could have played for England because my grandmother is English. She never tried to put any pressure on me though. Nobody ever got in touch with me personally from England, only through my agent. But I wanted to play for Wales." After a fantastic season for Tottenham in 2010/11, Bale was named PFA Player of the Year.

There was another gap for Toshack to fill when John Hartson retired for 'personal reasons' after 11 years, 51 caps and 14 goals in March 2006. Two months later, Toshack returned to the Basque Country, where he had made his name managing Real Sociedad, as Wales played an unofficial friendly against Euskadi. Giggs, playing his first away friendly, scored the only goal in Bilbao. Koumas was the only notable absentee from the squad that gave a tepid performance in an uninspiring 0–0 draw with Bulgaria at Swansea in August 2006 ahead of the first European Championship fixture a month later. The match was notable for Toshack's use of five different captains. Giggs, Delaney, Bellamy, Gabbidon and Robinson all took the armband. Toshack was relieved when Hartson made himself available again after reconsidering his retirement.

2008 European Championship

During these difficult times, Welsh supporters looked for other straws to clutch, and when the draw in Montreux for the 2008 European Championship pitted Wales against Germany, the Czech Republic, Republic of Ireland, Slovakia, San Marino and Cyprus, they were delighted. "It's going to be like a two-year stag party," said Dylan Llewellyn from Pwllheli. "All the destinations are reachable by budget flights." No longer was success a priority, if indeed it ever had been. Pundits looked forward to the campaign with little enthusiasm. "It hurts to admit it but I cannot see any way on earth that John Toshack's side can upset the odds and finish in the top two of their group – whoever they draw," predicted Neville Southall.

Wales suffered a cruel start to the competition when they lost to the Czech Republic in Teplice in September 2006. The first Czech goal was offside while the second in the 89th minute came from a free-kick taken with a moving ball. "At the end of the day we were beaten by two bad refereeing decisions," said Toshack. It was a harsh result as Wales had looked to have gained a point with an 86th minute equalizer. But Toshack's team had no time to lick their wounds. The FAW had been tempted by a big fee to face Brazil at White Hart Lane and the side lost 0–2 in front of 22,000 fans just days after the disheartening defeat in Teplice. Thousands more fans were left complaining having failed to gain entry until half-time. It was another brave, but unrewarded performance from Wales with Gabbidon outstanding.

Toshack suffered his most serious setback yet when Wales were hammered 1–5 by Slovakia, the worst home result for almost a century. Goalkeeper Paul Jones earned his 50th cap despite beginning his international career at the age of 30. This wasn't his finest moment, and he was ill-advised to shave the number 50 into his hair, but he had been a stalwart in difficult times. Bale, meanwhile, became the youngest player to score for the national team. In truth, it wasn't the worst performance Wales had ever given – not even under this manager, but the press was remorseless. "I've managed in six different countries, yet never before in 30 years of football have I seen such an over-the-top and sensationalist reaction to one result," said Toshack.

In 2006, the British Olympic Association announced it would be entering a Great Britain team at the 2012 London Olympics. The FAW opposed the move from the start and refused to have any part in the scheme, fearing for the future of Welsh football. There were many countries who would seize any opportunity to claim the United Kingdom should only take one place in international tournaments. The Scottish FA stood strong alongside the FAW in their protests, but the row would rumble on and divide opinion for the next six years.

Toshack desperately needed a good result against Cyprus in October 2006, and he got one with a 3–1 home win. "We certainly haven't given up on qualifying," he insisted. Koumas was back in the fold and scored against the side he could have represented. He also scored twice as Wales hammered Lichtenstein in Wrexham a month later, and was impressive in a 0–0 draw against Northern Ireland in Belfast. He was starting to produce performances his talent had always promised.

Wales faced the Republic of Ireland in their next qualifier at Croke Park in decent form. It would be Ireland's first football fixture at the famous Gaelic Athletic Association venue and thousands of Wales' supporters crossed the Irish Sea to take their place amongst an emotional 72,500 crowd. The Irish had not been in good form, and this looked like a chance for Wales to put themselves in the reckoning for one of the two qualifying places at the head of the group. But it was a desperately poor performance, and Wales lost 1–0 with Giggs especially disappointing. Members of the squad admitted morale was rock bottom. "It didn't happen for us and we're gutted – we know it's going to be difficult to qualify now," admitted Bellamy. The team was glad of another quick qualifying game as San Marino were comfortably beaten 3–0 at the Millennium Stadium.

Wales returned to Wrexham to face New Zealand in May 2007 with two new players with historical ties to the team. Goalkeeper Wayne Hennessey was a cousin of 1960s stalwart Terry, while Daniel Nardiello's father Donato had earned a couple of caps in the Seventies. Nardiello had looked unlikely to follow his dad at one time. "Maybe his father has had a word with him," suggested Toshack. "He did once say he did not want to play for Wales, but it has been almost a year now since he changed his mind." Wales equalized twice to gain a 2–2 draw against a second string side.

At the end of May 2007, Ryan Giggs announced his retirement. His antipathy towards the current Welsh manager was well documented, and maybe he would have continued to help the developing young side under a more empathic regime. While the Welsh public in general offered Giggs their grateful thanks, there were many who felt he had served his country with little of the loyalty he had shown his club. He had missed 20 competitive games for Wales, and had not played in any of the 18 friendlies between his 1991 debut and the opening of the Millennium Stadium in 2007. He went on to play just ten of the 42 friendlies arranged during his career, and none of those were played outside the UK (apart from the unofficial game in Bilbao). He played in just 64 of a possible 116 games, but as he left the Millennium Stadium pitch a minute before time in his final game, a scoreless draw against the Czech Republic, most of those present rose to their feet while many more watching at home toasted a Welsh great. Others watched in silence and regret.

Wales faced an uncertain future without the crowd-pulling Giggs, and the FAW went to great lengths to help Toshack fill his squad. Wolves' striker Freddy Eastwood believed himself to be of Welsh descent, but it took a visit to the National Library to find proof. Eastwood made his debut against Bulgaria in a friendly in Burgas and scored the winning goal. It was just the boost Toshack needed ahead of the visit of Germany a week later. Admittedly against generally low-quality opposition, Toshack's side had only lost just once in eight games when the Germans came to Cardiff in September 2007. FAW Secretary Collins was extremely disappointed with the 27,889 attendance for a game expected to sell-out when the fixtures were announced. If Wales couldn't fill the stadium for games against the top seeds, an alternative venue was needed. Wales had a new coach as Dean Saunders replaced Iriarte as Toshack's assistant, but he was unable to inspire the team and Wales succumbed to an abject 0–2 defeat. "Usually when we come to Wales we do not win, but this time we fully deserved the victory," said Germany manager Joachim Löw. One man who wasn't impressed was Savage: "There's more chance of me flying to the moon blindfolded than there is of you taking Wales to the South African World Cup," he told Toshack via a newspaper column.

Following Giggs' departure, Bellamy took on the role of central figure in the squad. The strong-minded arrowhead was deemed critical to any chance of success. After missing the Germany defeat, Bellamy was available when Wales travelled to Slovakia for the second part of the week's double header and the Welsh captain was outstanding as his team romped to a 5–2 win. Toshack was impressed: "You normally have 22 players battling away out there, pretty evenly matched. This game saw 21 players, and one who was just unbelievable, it was a scintillating performance. I cannot recall the last time I saw such an individual performance from a player that had so much influence on the outcome of the result."

Unfortunately, Bellamy was unable to have such an influence on Wales' next performance. One of the lowest points in Toshack's tenure came in October 2007 when Wales were beaten 3–1 in Cyprus. "The players will say they do care and it's rubbish to say they don't. But did it look like they cared? It didn't look like it to me," he raged. "Things went on out in Cyprus that made me wonder what we had been doing for two-and-a-half years. After what I saw this evening I'm obviously doing something wrong." He went even further: "We are in another five-star hotel here looking over the beach. It seems a case of 'lads, now if the waves are a bit too noisy for you during the night just ring down and we'll get you moved to the front!' We have a private chef who comes with us, they travel well wherever they go, they have doctors, physios, masseurs, a kit man moving skips about everywhere and sometimes I think some of these players take it for granted."

It seemed every time Toshack's team pulled out a decent result, such as the win in Slovakia, they fell back a step in the next game. When they travelled to San Marino, they met a travelling support that was in no mood to celebrate the 2–1 win against part-time opponents. Toshack's harsh words about modern players had rung true with the fans, and they vented their feelings. Bellamy seemed shocked by the abuse, and confronted a fan after the game. "I have been involved with Wales for several years now and that was the worst atmosphere I have played in," he said. "The Welsh crowd were vicious. We could hear them from very early in the game and maybe it affected the players." Toshack disagreed. "When people have travelled all that way to support the team and paid out a lot of money, they are entitled to shout whatever they want." Things were far from hunky-dory in the camp.

Bellamy was unavailable for the visit of the Republic of Ireland in November 2007, with Toshack calling for a 2–0 win to lift Wales above their opponents and maintain a chance of finishing third in the group. He wasn't to get it, and a 2–2 draw did neither side any favours despite a pair of goals from the outstanding Koumas. There was no doubt

Koumas was now a player who could prove the difference, but he had missed the fixtures against Cyprus and San Marino, and struggled to dispel the feeling that he was a player who could have contributed more. "I'm sick to death of hearing that I am not committed," he complained.

Once again Toshack would be without half-a-dozen first-choice players when Wales travelled to Frankfurt in November 2007, but people were starting to wonder why he had such trouble in attracting a full squad. He had been forced to field six under-21s in the game against Ireland and it was almost easier to select a squad from the players who made themselves unavailable. Was he desperately unlucky or was he starting to realize the cost of his lack of diplomacy? He had criticized the players publically and individually on several occasions, and now those players were turning their backs on him.

But Toshack's team would have become the first Welsh side to win four successive away games had it not been for the debacle in Cyprus, and even the manager was surprised by the strong performance which gained a 0–0 draw in Frankfurt. There were suspicions ahead of the game that Germany did not want to win, preferring the route offered by second place in the group. But this was a battling performance by a young Welsh side that allowed Toshack to hold his head up at the end of a tough campaign. Soon after taking over Wales, he had claimed he would judge himself in November 2007, and when the time came, he seemed satisfied with his efforts. "We've had eight performances out of 12 we can be pleased with," he said, "so that's a 66 per cent pass." He would also have been quietly enthused by the emerging group of players in Flynn's under-21 side, who attracted plenty of attention when they beat France at Ninian Park, having lost only three times in 14 games.

Some time at the start of 2007, Flynn had travelled to Edgeley Park, Stockport, to watch the young Welsh goalkeeper Wayne Hennessey, and noticed that the team-sheet featured somebody called Williams. He made enquiries at the club and discovered that centre half Ashley Williams did have Welsh connections, but these were on his mother's side – the Williams name had been coincidence. Meanwhile, the Welsh public was growing ever more confused by Toshack's side, which seemed to lack morale and lose badly on occasions, while also proving capable of pulling off unexpected victories. Three consecutive wins in friendlies against Norway, Luxembourg and Iceland offered promise for the forthcoming World Cup campaign.

Craig Bellamy earned his 50th cap in the 1–0 friendly win over Iceland in Reykjavik in May 2008. He had become Wales' most exciting talent. Electric pace and an unquenchable desire to win had seen him appointed captain, and he developed an interest in history as he matured, with his arm sporting a tattoo of another Welsh icon. "I'm massive on Owain Glyndŵr," he said. "He's the biggest Welsh hero we have ever had. I've done my Welsh history and he is my hero because of what he stood for. I'm Welsh and I wanted to know where we are in the world."

Welsh football's profile was helped by Cardiff City's appearance in the 2008 FA Cup final when they lost narrowly to Portsmouth. It had been an exciting cup run for the Championship side who narrowly failed to gain promotion a number of times in the first decade of the century. The Bluebirds lost to Blackpool in the 2010 play-off final, and also to Liverpool in the 2011 Carling Cup final. Their near-neighbours Swansea would not be so nervous on their big occasion at Wembley and beat Reading in a dramatic play-off final in 2011 to take their place amongst football's elite.

True to form, after three positive results, Wales lost consecutive friendlies to Holland and Georgia. Georgia were welcomed to the Liberty Stadium at a time of strife for the visitors. The former Soviet republic had become a war zone and the closure of the British Embassy in Tbilisi meant the game had looked unlikely to be played at one point. Earnshaw was recalled after becoming the latest player alienated by Toshack when he was excluded in the previous two games. "I had a long look at it and maybe feel I've been harshly treated because I'm one of the senior players in the Wales set-up," he complained. "There are lots of people in that set-up not playing, and I'm the one who is not in the squad – it's very strange."

Games in the north were now rare, but there was a reminder of the area's rich heritage when the under-21s played Romania at Wrexham in August 2008. The Racecourse was being officially recognized by the Guinness Book of Records as the oldest continually used international ground in the world, having been part of the Welsh fabric for more than 130 years. Questions were still being asked about the suitability of the Millennium Stadium for the South Africa 2010 qualification matches, but the Racecourse was not discussed as an option. The new stadia at Swansea and Cardiff were now a more attractive choice for fans and players.

2010 World Cup

Wales were again drawn with top seeds Germany, as well as Russia, Finland, Liechtenstein and Azerbaijan, in Group Four in the 2010 World Cup qualifiers. Toshack wasn't displeased and it seemed Wales had a chance of playing for second spot. "We are playing Germany again but better the devil you know," he said. The bookmakers' odds seemed more realistic – Wales were 20/1 outsiders to qualify automatically.

Azerbaijan arrived at the Millennium Stadium as the first opponents in the campaign guaranteed to see Toshack emerge as hero or failure according to his own criteria. There was controversy before the match when Coventry's manager, former international Chris Coleman was asked about the likelihood of Freddy Eastwood being fit for Wales' opening game. "I don't care about the Azerbaijan game to be honest," he was quoted as saying. "I couldn't care less.

We need Freddy fit for us for Doncaster Rovers, we signed him for a reason. I don't care about Wales."

A disappointing 17,000 crowd gave more ammunition to those wanting to halt fixtures at the Millennium Stadium, and the faltering 1–0 victory failed to excite ahead of a key fixture in the campaign, Russia in Moscow. Koumas had missed a penalty against Azerbaijan and Toshack admitted he was unsure of the player's intentions. "When we get to the boarding gate, they'll announce, 'Gate No. 26, flight boarding for Moscow' and I'll have a look around. We'll know then whether Jason's coming or not." Predictably, Koumas did not appear at Gate 26, or any other gate. One player who would no longer be available was Paul Parry, who retired at 28 after being left on the bench. "I felt like a spare part when I turned up for Wales," he said. "When two under-21 internationals [Sam Vokes and Ched Evans] go on before you against countries like Azerbaijan you don't have to be told where you stand in the pecking order." Parry had been assured he would start in Moscow, but the Cardiff winger could not be assuaged.

The September 2008 game in Moscow typified the ill-fortune that littered Toshack's reign. Two key players had withdrawn, possibly due to management issues, but an inexperienced side had looked in good shape for most of a difficult game. Bale even had the chance to put Wales ahead from the penalty spot during the first half, but saw his shot palmed around the post. The miss affected him badly, and triggered a poor run of form for club and country. Despite the disappointment, Toshack's young team rallied in front of 113 travelling fans and seemed destined to leave with a point until Pavel Pogrebnyak's late winner. To illustrate the paucity of Toshack's options, Wrexham's Steve Evans became the first non-league player to feature for Wales since the 1930s when he came on as a late substitute. The Welsh performance promised much but failed to deliver, like so many under Toshack.

Only 12,500 turned up for the qualifying fixture at home to Lichtenstein in October and their voices echoed round the huge Millennium Stadium. It did little to help the players as they huffed to a 2–0 win on a terrible pitch. Carl Robinson came off the bench to earn his 50th cap in an uninspiring performance ahead of the daunting visit to Borussia days later. "If we are to qualify, we must come to places like Russia or Germany and take something from the game," admitted Toshack. After the late disappointment in Moscow, Wales needed to repeat the performance of the previous campaign when they had shut-out the Germans, who were so confident of qualification that they were already making reconnaissance trips to South Africa. Despite a brave defensive effort in the rain of Mönchengladbach, Wales went down to a stunning second-half goal by Piotr Trochowski. "It seems to be the same old story," complained Bellamy. "We're doing well but that final little bit; we just seem to be falling short."

The day before the senior side's defeat to Germany, Flynn's under-21s had been involved in the biggest game in their history. Despite winning their qualifying group for the 2009 European Championship, the UEFA system forced Wales into a play-off against England. Led by precocious Cardiff midfielder Aaron Ramsey, the under-21s gained many plaudits in a narrow defeat to the older and stronger English. With Toshack blooding youngsters in his side, and such impressive form from the intermediate squads, Wales' future seemed bright.

But defeat in Germany saw Wales' qualification hopes drifting away, and calls for Toshack's head were increasing. While fans held unrealistic expectations given the quality of the players available, many claimed the manager's personality was driving players away. Others pointed to the stunning progress being made by the under-21s, and gave Toshack some credit for their performances and early introduction to senior football. The best of them, 17-year-old Aaron Ramsey, was rewarded for a series of match-winning under-21 performances with selection for a friendly against Denmark in Brøndby in November 2008. "Aaron has been outstanding whenever I have seen him," said Bellamy. "I cannot recall as much fuss about a young Wales player maybe since Ryan Giggs." Bellamy repeated his feat of ten years earlier by scoring the only goal in an encouraging performance from a team with an average age of just 21.

A curious low-key February friendly against Poland in Portugal was played out in front of just 487 spectators. An inexperienced Welsh side competed well but lost by the only goal. The game was notable for an incident which saw Bellamy again remonstrating with a Welsh supporter during a post-match pitch-side interview. "Maybe it was because of a few drinks," said Bellamy. "I have shown my commitment to Wales by turning up for these sorts of games, but it is me that always seems to get picked on for stick. Maybe it is because I have never played for a Welsh club, I really don't know, but I never seem to get the level of respect that others do."

It seemed to be becoming more and more difficult to persuade players to travel to away friendlies, as Premiership football had grown so powerful that its seniority was now unquestionable. In March 2009 the FAW announced an agreement had been reached to revive the Home Internationals Tournament featuring all four United Kingdom teams. Initially intended to take place on a home and away basis, the tournament was eventually abridged and would go ahead without England, with all games taking place at the new Arriva Stadium in Dublin.

"Any hopes of qualification will evaporate for the side beaten this afternoon," wrote Toshack before facing Finland at the Millennium Stadium in March 2009. Wales were booed off the pitch after losing 0–2 to the ageing Finnish team with much of the fans' frustration aimed at the decision to play with a lone striker. Toshack was unrepentant. "I played with a team [Real Madrid] 20 years ago that broke records with one up front," he insisted. Bellamy was despondent and offered a typically honest assessment. "Where we go from here, God knows," he said.

Expectations were low when Wales faced Germany at the Millennium Stadium in April 2009. Bellamy admitted he no longer enjoyed playing at the half-empty rugby ground. "At the moment, our opposition must think how nice it is playing against us. It's a nice stadium, nice city, there's no atmosphere and so they aren't put under any pressure." Despite a 0–2 defeat Toshack's young side put up a good fight without Bellamy, and earned a standing ovation from the 26,000 crowd. Toshack's team had failed to qualify, but the hardcore Welsh support could see potential.

After picking one of the youngest Wales squads in history for a friendly win against Estonia in May 2009, Toshack took the opportunity to criticize his most senior players for the defeat against Finland. "Prior to the Finland game, we hadn't seen Koumas, Davies and Fletcher for six months. In their absence, youngsters came in for us and did well against teams seeded higher than us in the FIFA ratings. So maybe going back to the older players against Finland was bad team selection on my part." He took the chance to give new caps to Andy King, Simon Church and Joe Allen as the FAW welcomed another new venue at Llanelli's Parc y Scarlets. The new stadium would prove popular with the association, who agreed to host a series of Welsh Cup finals at the rugby ground.

After the dispiriting defeat to Finland, and the promising but fruitless loss to Germany, it was typical of Toshack's inconsistent young side that they then went to Azerbaijan in June 2009 and won the game with a goal from Wolves midfielder David Edwards. Toshack had selected Wales' youngest ever side for a competitive game, with an average age of just over 21, and the usually gruff Cardiffian was delighted. "That was one of the best performances during my time as manager," he beamed. The delighted away support in Baku included 26 Welsh fans who arrived in Azerbaijan after a marathon drive through Europe, which raised more than £15,000 for the Gôl charity.

Discussions about the future of the national side were put to one side during the summer of 2009, when Welsh football was shaken by the news that John Hartson was suffering from cancer. The disease had spread from Hartson's testicles to his lungs and brain. "I had two brain operations and was in intensive care. I got pneumonia and I apparently stopped breathing at one stage," he told the *Guardian*. After 67 chemotherapy sessions, the former bulldozing centre forward lost five stone. However, the strength of the former Welsh talisman stood him in good stead, and he was able to survive brain and lung operations to fight off the deadly disease.

Wales returned to the scene of the 1982 game with Yugoslavia in Podgorica, formerly Titograd, for a friendly against Montenegro in August 2009. There was uncertainty about Bellamy's future when he failed to appear after a mix-up between his club Manchester City and the FAW. Wearing specially embroidered shirts in support of Hartson, the Welsh team lost 2–1. Both West Ham's Jack Collison and Reading's Simon Church withdrew from the squad to face Russia a month later following the deaths of their respective fathers. There were also more absentees, including Koumas, who had announced his international retirement. With only 11,589 fans turning up for the 1–3 defeat, captain Bellamy again looked forward to Wales' games being moved away from the Millennium Stadium. "There are a lot of empty seats and that's been the case for a number of years now. I'm just grateful a few Russians came along," he said.

Wales reached a new low when Toshack was unable to raise a full squad for the 1–2 defeat in Helsinki in October 2009. "The retirements of Carl Fletcher, Carl Robinson, Paul Parry and Jason Koumas compounds the situation," he admitted. "Eight midfield players is a big loss for any country, let alone us. There is no question those who retired would have played a part this weekend, particularly with their experience. They see Collison, Ramsey, Ledley and Edwards coming through and think that they themselves aren't going to get many games. But when you get injuries to those players, it hits you even harder."

Ramsey scored his first Welsh goal in a welcome 2–0 win over Lichtenstein in Vaduz in October 2009. The Welsh following made up almost a third of the 1,858 crowd and chanted for Toshack to be sacked throughout the game. Under pressure, the manager mounted a stout defence of his record. "I can only repeat what I said when I came into the job. The team had gone 10 competitive games without a win, average age of 29, players finishing and staff leaving. I still believe in the future we will get the rewards out of what we're doing."

But time was running out for Toshack, and he needed his youngsters to step up. Relief came once more in the form of Aaron Ramsey, who gave the best performance from a Welsh international for several years when he inspired a 3–0 win over Scotland in the first international played at Cardiff City's new stadium in November 2009. Ramsey's display was so influential that it was immediately obvious that any future Welsh manager would need to build his side around the driving midfielder. While Wales had often been blessed with some excellent players, Ramsey was the first who could control and dictate a game from the centre of the pitch. There seemed no doubt that the burden of Welsh hopes would be placed on his shoulders for the next decade.

Secretary-General David Collins retired from the FAW in January 2010 and was replaced by former Coca-Cola marketing executive Jonathan Ford, who was given a brief of generating greater income. Ford attacked the role zealously and introduced a new badge and branding for the major Welsh competitions. He also started a controversial compulsory membership scheme for travelling Welsh fans, which some saw as a way of charging the most loyal supporters for the right to buy tickets. It was the decision to replace the famous crest that upset most supporters however, though one former player, Gary Sprake had never been fond of the royal design. "The only downside of playing for Wales," he wrote, "was that bloody badge. It looked as though it came off a dodgy, second-hand blazer. And because it was so big, when it rained my body would be covered in red dye, and it would take forever to shower it off."

2012 European Championship

Toshack rode out calls for his removal, and began planning for his fourth qualifying campaign. Wales were drawn in Group G alongside Bulgaria, Montenegro, Switzerland, and the accountant's dream, England. As always, Wales looked forward with fresh hope and unrealistic optimism. But in February 2010 disaster struck when Ramsey had his leg broken when tackled late by Stoke's Ryan Shawcross. The news affected the Welsh players badly and they struggled to shake off the gloom as they lost to Sweden in Swansea a month later. Toshack had planned to build the whole campaign around the young Arsenal player, but Wales would be without their fulcrum for a full year. Without Ramsey, Toshack's future looked ever more uncertain.

The increasingly isolated manager lost 14 players from his original selection for the May friendly in Croatia, and it was no surprise that Wales lost 0–2. Pressure was being heaped upon Toshack as the World Cup approached. A convincing home friendly win against Luxembourg at Llanelli would buy some time, and a 5–1 victory provided some relief. During the game, Robert Earnshaw became the 29th Welsh player to earn a golden cap in recognition of 50 games for his country. Earnie was one of the most loyal Welsh players during a period when many were cutting short their international careers, or cherry-picking their games. Despite regular knock-backs and selection as substitute,

Earnshaw was rarely unavailable to his adopted country. His early career scoring record deserved far greater respect and many more opportunities.

Wales' first game of the qualifying campaign was away to Montenegro, and just as everybody was becoming used to the idea that Toshack would see out another campaign, he finally, if reluctantly, resigned after defeat in Podgorica. "I thought after three matches of this group we would review everything," he said, "but we have come to the agreement that this might be better for everyone concerned." Wales deserved a point against a team who the press had expected them to beat, but as in previous campaigns' opening games against Georgia and Romania, the pre-match publicity about Montenegro's perceived weakness was unmerited. This was a physical Montenegrin side who would trouble every team in the group.

Brian Flynn was appointed caretaker while the shocked FAW took their time to find the right candidate to replace Toshack. Many supported Flynn's promotion, including most of the young players who had thrived in his under-21 side. He was given the job for two games, at home to Bulgaria and away to Switzerland, but was considered too close to Toshack to gain the position permanently. Good results in both games would have made it difficult to appoint anybody else, even though certain FAW personnel were looking for a more recognisable, big-name manager to promote the game in Wales. Meanwhile the respected broadcaster Ian Gwyn Hughes was the surprise, but popular choice as Head of Public Affairs at the FAW. His appointment would appease critics who had long complained about the association's attitude to the Welsh language.

The Welsh players had long made it known they would prefer to play home matches in a smaller ground. A long series of disappointing performances had depleted the crowd at the Millennium Stadium, and the huge arena would echo with few voices of encouragement. With this in mind, the FAW agreed to use Cardiff City Stadium for the important home game against Bulgaria in October 2010. But while the atmosphere was improved, the performance was disappointing, and a depleted side struggled to make any impact against the Bulgarians in a 0–1 defeat. It was apparent that the loss of Bellamy and Ramsey to injury would give Flynn little chance of making an impact in his two-game trial. But his young players were keen to repay the manager who had nurtured them, and an enthusiastic squad faced Switzerland at St Jakob Park in Basel. In the most exciting Welsh performance for a long time, it seemed Bale's excellent equalizer had given Wales a great chance to earn a result, but somehow the Swiss took the game 4–1, with a scoreline that hardly reflected the play.

The two defeats consigned Flynn to his old position with football development for Wales, and just before Christmas 2010, it was announced that the new national manager would be Gary Speed. Born in Mancot, Speed was the son of English parents, but his loyalties had never been split. "I was born and bred in Wales," he said. "I went to a Welsh school and I grew up learning Welsh from an early age. It was never an issue for me." Speed had been present as a supporter when Wales beat England 4–1 in 1980, and made his playing debut against Costa Rica in 1990, a day after playing for the under-21s against Poland at Merthyr. After leaving his job at Sheffield United where he had enjoyed mixed success, he was welcomed by the Welsh players. One of his first innovations was the appointment of Craig Bellamy's physiotherapist, Raymond Verheijen, a controversial Dutchman not slow to offer his opinions on the backroom staff at professional clubs. Verheijen believed passionately in the 'periodisation' system which gives players more rest and concentrates training into shorter sessions designed to protect from injury. His system would prove attractive to the Welsh players and along with the respect they held for the new manager, it was hoped that finally, Wales would be able to call on its best players consistently.

Speed's international managerial debut took place in Dublin in February 2011, and a curious public, split on his appointment, watched with interest. But the first game of the new Celtic Cup was a huge disappointment as expensive ticket prices and general apathy ensured a poor turnout in Dublin. The Welsh performance was no better as Speed's team followed the same pattern of dull football that the fans had suffered under Toshack. It was a rude introduction to international management for the young boss who watched helplessly as his threadbare side lost 0–3.

But a far more important game was on the horizon with England due to visit Cardiff at the end of March. An innovative kick-back scheme, which saw £80,000 returned to clubs who purchased tickets, was acclaimed as a great success until it was discovered that the FAW had over-sold tickets and thousands of fans would be disappointed when their applications were returned. Aaron Ramsey was the surprise choice as captain, but Welsh hopes were deflated by a pre-match injury to Bale, and two early England goals gave them a comfortable win. For his part, Speed again looked lost and in need of a senior figure to turn to on the bench.

There was no sign of progress as Wales played out the other fixtures in the Celtic Cup. A tepid defeat to Scotland was followed by a hollow victory against a shockingly poor Northern Ireland. But at least it was a win – Speed's first after three defeats. And then came another defeat, but there were some signs of progress in the 1–2 loss to a strong Australian team. For the first time, Speed's team showed glimpses of a developing system and there seemed to be light at the end of the tunnel. Wales had four games left in the European Championship qualifiers, and it was time for Speed to make his mark.

The recovery began with a 2–1 victory over Montenegro at

an excited Cardiff City Stadium. Montenegro had surprised people with their strong showing in the group, and though Wales were fortunate to win, the result greatly encouraged the long-suffering public. Sadly, but understandably, only 8,194 fans were there to see it, in an echo of the poorly attended 1974 victory against Hungary which dramatically reversed the fortunes of Mike Smith's team. Wales had nothing to lose when they went to Wembley in September 2011, and Speed's side should have come away with at least a point against England. They were the better side for parts of the game, and Earnshaw, of all people, missed an open goal which would have sealed a well-deserved draw. However, the result was rendered unimportant when tragedy struck and a Welsh supporter died after an attack by an English fan on the Wembley concourse. Michael Dye was a 44-year-old Cardiff City fan, killed by a single punch. Death and Welsh football had met once again.

Speed's popularity coupled with the high-tech training approach of Verheijen encouraged the attendance of the top Welsh players at squad meetings for the first time since the Mark Hughes era. Suddenly Welsh fortunes seemed transformed. Bellamy, Bale and Ramsey were all available after long-term injury, and the manager's system played on the talents of his three most influential players. The more incisive tactics, with a patient build up from defence, combined with explosive breaks from Bale and Bellamy on the flanks, worked like a dream. Switzerland were dispatched 2–0 at Swansea in November 2011 and Welsh supporters regained an optimism that had been missing for almost a decade. Wales were on the verge of a new era. Welsh football was on the up.

When they went to Sofia in their final game of the tournament and beat Bulgaria by a goal to nil, the whole of Welsh football could smile again. A win at home in a friendly against Norway was now expected rather than hoped for, and the 4–1 procession only confirmed suspicions that the early exposure of Toshack's young sides was finally paying off. These were good times, and other teams would not want to face Wales during qualification for Brazil 2014. Wales had finally found a manager and a group of players happy with each other and finally, finally Wales would qualify for a tournament. It would take a thunderbolt to divert us from the prize that had evaded us so cruelly for more than half a century. Surely Welsh football couldn't suffer any more misfortune and tragedy. Our time had come at last.

* * *

I stared in disbelief at the news. That simple four-word sentence on the screen made my head spin and my stomach churn. I felt the same gut-wrenching, end-of-the-world emotions I had experienced when Mikey Dye's death was relayed on that dark Wembley night in 2011. The heart-sinking feeling took me back to that sickening evening in 1993 when news filtered through the despondent post-Romania, Cardiff pubs that John Hill had been killed by a flare.

Our 42-year-old manager's apparent suicide touched the British football public in a way that hadn't been seen since the death of Bobby Moore; and never has a Welsh sportsman been so widely mourned.

The striking thing about the display of grief following Speed's death was its diversity. Not only was he being honoured at the northern clubs he represented, but there were tributes at other clubs too. Makeshift shrines sprang up spontaneously across the UK: at Bolton, Sheffield, Everton, and Newcastle; at Cardiff, Wrexham, and of course, at Elland Road, where he first blossomed.

That Sunday was awful. People appeared online to register their shock, but then disappeared. Nobody was speculating; they were just devastated. A day later, memories began to be shared. Everyone had a story to tell. Dozens of unseen photographs began to emerge of the smiling, handsome leader in a patient pose with a beaming admirer.

When football fixtures recommenced the fans took their own opportunities to pay respect. Leeds' sell-out away following planned to chant their former number 11's name from the 11th minute of their fixture at Nottingham Forest, but like Swansea, they couldn't help themselves and the vocal tributes began well before kick-off. Forest fans even applauded their opponents. Then when a tearful Craig Bellamy was substituted at Stamford Bridge, Liverpool fans chanted the name of his lost mentor, a proud Evertonian. Cardiff fans wore Welsh colours and began their chants in the 85th minute, as Speed had represented his country 85 times. The ubiquitous, unaffiliated respect for Speed was unique in the modern era.

In the following days we shared the emotions of those who counted him as a friend. Robbie Savage's tearful broadcast on the BBC's *606* programme was heartbreaking, and colleagues such as Mark Bowen, Howard Wilkinson and Gary McAllister were evidently grief-stricken. News reporter Bryn Law broke down live on Sky Sports, while *Sgorio*'s numbed tribute felt harrowing and intrusive as we bore witness to the emotional disintegration of Malcolm Allen and John Hartson.

Welsh football and fans from every club went into mourning and took comfort from each other. Speed's death undoubtedly brought us closer, for a while at least. From Ynys Môn to Gwent, from Ceredigion to Denbighshire, we've shared so much misfortune, so much hope, so much despair.

Welsh football began with a north versus south rivalry that has never really disappeared. We're a country divided by tribalism and conflict. The latter years of Welsh football have seen Cardiff fighting Swansea, the Exiles fighting the FAW, and minor disputes breaking out between clubs and personalities all over the country. But the death of a man who had served his country so passionately blurred our differences and shone a light on our similarities. It turns out that we're not so different after all. We all wept when Gary Speed died.

Bibliography
of Welsh Football

(with assistance from Martin Johnes)

Football Association of Wales General Histories

Corrigan, Peter, *100 Years of Welsh Soccer*, Cardiff, 1976.

Lerry, G G, *Association Football in Wales, 1870–1924*, Oswestry, 1924.

Lerry, G G, *The Football Association of Wales: 75th Anniversary, 1876–1951*, Wrexham, 1952.

Stennett, Ceri: *As Good As It Gets, The Centenary Book of the WSFA, 1911–2011*, Cardiff, 2011.

National Team

Risoli, Mario, *When Pelé Broke Our Hearts*, Cardiff, 1998.

Davies, Gareth M, *Soccer: The International Line-Ups & Statistics Series – Wales, 1876–1960*, Cleethorpes, 1995.

Davies, Gareth M & Garland, Ian, *Who's Who of Welsh International Soccer Players*, Wrexham, 1991.

Llewelyn, Dylan, *Awê!*, Cardiff, 2003.

Welsh Cup

Garland, Ian, *The History of the Welsh Cup, 1877–1993*, Wrexham, 1993.

Lerry, G G (writing as 'XYZ'), *The Story of the Welsh Cup*, Oswestry, 1933.

European Competition

Grandin, Terry, *Red Dragons in Europe – A Complete Record*, Westcliff-on-Sea, 1999.

Autobiographies

Barnes, Walley, *Captain of Wales*, London, 1953.

Burgess, Ron, *Football – My Life*, London, 1952.

Charles, John, *King of Soccer*, London, 1957.

Charles, John, *The Gentle Giant*, London, 1962.

Charles, Mel, *In the Shadow of a Giant*, London, 2009.

Davies, Dai, *Never Say Dai*, Mold, 1986.

Giggs, Ryan, *Giggs: The Autobiography*, London, 2005.

Ford, Trevor, *I Lead the Attack*, London, 1957.

Hughes, Mark, *Hughesy!*, Edinburgh, 1994.

Hughes, Mark, *Sparky – Barcelona, Bayern and Back*, 1989.

Jones, Cliff, *Forward with Spurs*, London, 1962.

Jones, Joey, *Oh Joey, Joey!*, London, 2005.

Kelsey, Jack, *Over the Bar*, London, 1958.

Murphy, Jimmy, *Matt, United and Me*, London, 1968.

Paul, Roy, *A Red Dragon of Wales*, London, 1956.

Ratcliffe, Kevin, *The Blues and I*, London, 1988.

Rush, Ian, *Rush*, London, 1985.

Rush, Ian, *My Italian Diary*, London, 1989.

Seed, Jimmy, *The Jimmy Seed Story*, London, 1957.

Southall, Neville, *Everton Blues: A Premier League Diary*, Edinburgh, 1997.

Toshack, John, *Tosh*, London, 1982.

Yorath, Terry, *Hard Man, Hard Knocks*, Cardiff, 2004.

Biographies

Bagshaw, John, 'Tommy Griffiths – our own international soccer star', *Inheritance*, Issue 2, Autumn 1985, p.45.

Farmer, David & Stead, Peter, *Ivor Allchurch MBE*, Swansea, 1998.

Gwyn Hughes, Ian, *Pêl-droedwyr Gorau Cymru o'r 60au Hyd Heddiw*, Llandysul, 2007.

Harding, John, *Football Wizard – The Billy Meredith Story*, Derby, 1985.

Hayes, Dean, *Wales – The Complete Who's Who of Footballers since 1946*, Stroud, 2004.

Jenkins, Geraint H, *Cewri'r Bêl Droed yng Nghymru*, Llandysul, 1977.

Lile, Brian, 'Nice One Cyril!', *The Footballer*, vol.2, no.7, 1990.

Pyke, Philip, 'The Jones Dynasty', *The Footballer*, vol. 7, no.4, 1990.

Rowlands, A, 'Roy Paul: Red Dragon of Wales', *The Footballer*, vol.2, no.7, 1990.

Stennett, Ceri, *The Soccer Dragons*, Cardiff, 1987.

Academic Works

Bale, J R, 'Geographical Diffusion and the Adoption of Professionalism in England and Wales', *Geography*, vol. 63, 1978, pp.188–197.

Evans, Alun, 'Football on the Edge: The Relationship between Welsh Football Policy-Making and the British International Championship', M.A. thesis, De Montfort University, 1996.

Frankenberg, Ronald, *Village on the Border: A Social Study of Religion, Politics and Football in a North Wales Community*, London, 1957.

Johnes, Martin, 'That Other Game: A Social History of Soccer in South Wales, *c.*1906–39', Univeristy of Wales Ph.D. thesis, 1998.

Johnes, Martin and Keenor, Fred, 'A Welsh Soccer Hero', *The Sports Historian*, 1998.

Johnes, Martin, 'Irredeemably English?', *Planet: The Welsh Internationalist*, 1998.

Lile, Brian and Farmer, David, 'The Early Development of Association Football in South Wales, 1890–1906', *The Transactions of the Honourable Society of Cymmrodorion*, 1984, pp.193–215.

Wagg Stephen, 'The Missionary Position: Football in the Societies of Britain and Ireland', in Williams, John & Wagg, Stephen (eds.), *British Football and Social Change: Getting into Europe*, Leicester, 1991.

Stead, Peter, 'Almost a Team', *New Welsh Review*, vol.4, no.3, Winter 1993–94, pp.25–28.

(The myths and realities of being a life-long Welsh soccer fan in the aftermath of Wales's elimination from the 1994 World Cup.)

Miscellaneous

Harvard, Robert and Thomas, Dennis, 'Lost Tribe or European Nation?', *Planet: The Welsh Internationalist*, 74, April/May 1989, pp.11–19.

(An examination of the feasibility of a Welsh National Football League.)

Davies, D W, *The Magalonians: 100 Years of Football in Machynlleth, 1885–1985*, 1985.

Godwin, Paul, 'Soccer at the Pithead', *FA Book for Boys*, pp.29–32.

Jenkins, Derrick, *Football in Cardiff, 1888–1939*, 1984.

Jenkins, Gwyn, *The History of the Aberystwyth & District League, 1934–1984*, Aberystwyth, 1984.

Jenkins, G H, *Dewch i Chwarae Pêl-droed*, Talybont, 1983.

Lloyd, Howard, *Chware Teg*, Llandybie, 1967.

Lloyd, Howard (gol.), *Crysau Cochion: Cymry ar y Maes Chwarae*, Llandybie, 1958.

McAllister, Laura, 'Taking Liberties: The Politics of Football', *Radical Wales*, no.21, Spring 1989, pp.14–15.

Matthews, John E, *From Pit to Pitch: A Pictorial History of Football in Rhos*, Rhosllannerchrugog, 1991.

Parry-Jones, David (ed.), *Taff's Acre: A History and Celebration of Cardiff Arms Park*, London, 1984.

Pressdee, Harry, 'Sporting Days', in Anne Eyles, *In the Shadows of the Steelworks II*, Cardiff, 1995, pp.109–115.

(Features information on local and schoolboy football in Splott, Cardiff.)

Williams, M and Daniel, H (eds.), *Swansea Schools FA 75th Anniversary*, Swansea, 1989.

Cardiff City

Anon, *Lets Talk about Cardiff City*, London, 1946.

'Citizen' (Dewi Lewis), *A Short History of Cardiff City AFC*, Cardiff, 1952.

Crooks, John, *Cardiff City Chronology, 1920–86*, Cardiff, 1986.

Crooks, John, *The Bluebirds: A Who's Who of Cardiff City Football League Players*, Pontypool, 1987.

Crooks, John, *Cardiff City Football Club: The Official History of The Bluebirds*, Harefield, 1992.

Jackson, Peter, *Cardiff City Story*, Cardiff, 1974.

Jenkins, Derrick and Stennett, Ceri, *Wembley 1927*, Cardiff, 1985.

Morgan, J H, '... Reviews Fifty Years of Sport in Cardiff', in Stewart Williams (ed.), *The Cardiff Book*, vol.1, Barry, 1973, pp.19–36.

Shepherd, Richard, *Cardiff City Football Club, 1899–1947, From Riverside to Richards*, Chalford, 1996.

Newport County

Ambrosen, Tony, *Ironsides: A Lifetime in the League: A Who's Who of Newport County*, Harefield, 1991.

Ambrosen, Tony, *Amber In The Blood: A History of Newport County*, Harefield 1993.

Ambrosen, Anthony, 'Newport Go Out', *The Footballer*, vol. 1, no.1, 1988.

Shepherd, Richard, *The History of Newport County FC, 1912/13–1972/73*, Newport, 1973.

Shepherd, Richard, *Newport County '79/80: A Season of Triumph*, Newport, 1980.

Shepherd, Richard, *Seventy Years of Newport County: A Pictorial History, 1912–82*, Newport, 1982.

Shepherd, Richard, *Newport County Football Club, 1912–1960*, Chalford, 1997.

Swansea City

Burgum, John, *Swansea City FC (Illustrated History)*, Manchester, 1988.

Farmer, David, *Swansea City 1912–82*, London, 1982.

Matthews, B E, *The Swansea City Story*, Swansea, 1976.

Matthews, B E, *The Swans: A History of Swansea City FC 1912–82*, Swansea, 1987.

Other Welsh Clubs

Anon, *Heroes All: Borough United*, published by the club, 1964.

Barrett, C and Davies, R, *100 Years of Spa Football, 1883–1983*, Llandrindod Wells, published by the club, 1983.

Garland, Ian and Gray-Thomas, Wyn, *The Canaries Sing Again: A History of Caernarfon Town FC*, Caernarfon, 1986.

Jones, Arwel, *Y Darans: A History of Llanberis FC*, published by the club, 1991.

McInnery, Jeff, *The Linnets – An Illustrated, Narrative History of Barry Town AFC, 1888–1993*.

Protheroe, G, *Aberdare Athletic, Programme Monthly*, no. 147, June 1993, pp.28–30.

Parry, Peter, Lile, Brian and Griffiths, Donald, *The Old Black and Green: Aberystwyth Town, 1884–1984*, Aberystwyth, 1987.

Slade, Arthur, 'Cardiff Corinithians AFC', *The Cardiff Spectator*, vol. 2, no. 13, April 1961.

Twydell, Dave, *More Defunct FC: Club Histories and Statistics*, Harefield, 1990. (Features chapter on Lovell's Atheltic.)

Twydell, Dave, *Rejected F.C. volume one: Histories of the Ex-Football League Clubs*, Harefield, 1992 edn. (Aberdare Athletic covered on pages 10–27.)

Twydell, Dave, *Rejected F.C. volume two: Histories of the Ex-Football League Clubs* Harefield, 1995 edn. (Merthyr Town/Tydfil covered on pages 196–229.)

Watkins, David, 'Merthyr Town A.F.C., 1908–34', in Huw Williams (ed.), *Merthyr Tydfil: Drawn from Life*, Merthyr, 1981, pp.70–89.

Watkins, David, *Magic Moments of Merthyr Tydfil A.F.C.*, published by the author, 1985.

Acknowledgements

Thanks for advice and support from Mark Ainsbury, Gwilym Boore, Tommie Collins, Matthew Gabb, Terry Grandin, Richard Grigg, the Gregarious Crew, Mervyn Ham, Ian Hamer, Nigel Harris, Lawrence Hourahane, Arwel Jones, Siôn Lewis, Dylan Llewelyn, Steve Lyell, Laura McAllister, Michael Morris, Richard Oldale, Huw Owen, Neil Roberts, Stu Ropke, Ceri Stennett, Darren Tandy, Huw Thomas, Marc Thomas, Scott Thomas, Chris Watham, Tim Williams.

A special mention for the historian Martin Johnes for his invaluable research into the history of Welsh sport, and to Gary Pritchard, both for his personal support and the use of his dynamic online database at *welshfootballonline. com*. Simon Shakeshaft is doing great work researching and preserving match-worn Welsh kits. Ken Davies was kind enough to give me information and resources from the Keith Harding Collection, and Wrexham Museum were also generous in allowing access to their Welsh Football Collection. Staff at Cardiff, Swansea and Wrexham Public Libraries, and the National Library of Wales were never less than helpful. Mel ap Ior Thomas continues to do sterling work with the Welsh Football Data Archive. Gareth M Davies and Ian Garland deserve huge credit for their pioneering work, *Welsh International Soccer Players*, without which this book could not have been written. Thanks too, to Steve Adams' eye for detail and Eirian Jones' patient proofreading. Grateful thanks to Norman Giller, Mario Risoli, Martin Johnes, Ian Garland, and Spencer Vignes for permission to include extracts from their work. And finally, grateful thanks to Lefi Gruffudd for having faith and agreeing to publish this book.

Subscribers

Llŷr ab Einion

Mark Adams

Iwan Adams-Lewis, Aberteifi

Mark Ainsbury
Home and away, 1981 to forever

Stuart Allen

Matthew Aplin
Ordered book while Wales were losing 5–1 to Serbia. Keep the faith!

Gareth Bangor
Un diwrnod mi ddaw ein hamser

Dave Battersby
Titograd in 1982 – what a trip!

Phillip Bennett-Richards

Denis Canning

Rich Clark

Paul Corkrey

Phil Daley
To Phil. Happy birthday from John and Rose

Chris Dalgleish
With love from Sian, Emma, Ewan and Jamie

Ralph Davies

Rhys Davies

Tydno Davies
To Glanmor Davies

Rob Dowling

Gareth Wyn Evans
Dal i gredu. Cymru am byth

Neville Evans, Aberystwyth Town FC

Owain & Siôn Evans, Bluebirds

Matthew Gabb

Steven Gabb

Rick Garcia

Fañch Gaume
Chief Executive, Bretagne Football Association, Brittany

Mervyn Ham

Ian Hamer

Gwion Harding
Dal i gredu

Emyr Harries

Nigel Harris

Cyril Hughes
Tad a thaid arbennig, gan deulu Garth

Guto Sion Hughes
Enillydd capiau Ysgolion, Colegau a Phrifysgolion Cymru

Hywel Hughes

Rhys Hughes
I dad arbennig iawn, cariad Brangutsi

Sara Martel Hughes
Nadolig llawen a blwyddyn newydd dda, cariad, Mam x

Richard E Huws, Aberystwyth

Telor Iwan
I Morgan a Louis, gyda chariad a chydymdeimlad!
Cadwch eich ffydd, eich tad xx

G R P James

Robbie Jenkins, East Kent Taffs

Dave Jennings

Adam Jones
Pêl-droed Cymru – mae yn y gwaed

Bethan Jones
Pen-blwydd hapus Arwel yn 60 oed

Darren Jones
Dad, Nadolig Llawen 2012!

Dylan Llewelyn Jones
I Alaw a Cian. Un dydd: cadwch y ffydd x

Elis Jones

Glyn Jones

Ifan Wyn Jones

Jeremy Jones
A sucker for punishment

Rhodri Jones

Rona Jones
Pen-blwydd hapus Herbert, oddi wrth Rona

Alan Lewis, Aberteifi
Er gwaetha pawb a phopeth "I just can't get enough!"

Karl Lindhorst
Dedication means taking almost 2 days, 2 flights and 5 hours
on the road to get to a home fixture

Mark Lloyd
One Gary Speed! RIP Speedo

Steve Lyell

Neil James Mace
Keep Cardiff blue

Zoe McKane

Alun Morris

Klaus Neuhaus

Phil Nicholson, East Kent Taffs

Chris O'Brien, Hazell Terrace

Roger O'Brien, Hazell Terrace

Alun Gwyndaf Owen
Nadolig llawen, Gwyndaf Owen

Huw Owen

Rhys Gerallt Owen, Caerffili

Gareth Ll. Parry

Mark Pitman

Steven Powell

Tom Powell

Bryn Pritchard
We'll never qualify... etc.

Gary Pritchard, Pontrhydybont

Elfyn Pugh

Daniel Richards

Jonathan Richardson
Dal i gredu

Ann Riordan

Glyn Roberts

Stu Ropke

Dave Rowe
Cymru am byth

Alan Samuel
Please, just once, qualify!

Alun Paul Shore

Darren Tandy
Affirmation of lovely misery

Huw Thomas

Marc Thomas

Russell Todd
Tîm pêl-droed Cymru – yma o hyd ac am byth

Marc Tothill

Mark & Irene Watkins

Kathryn Watts
Happy Birthday to my gorgeous husband, Mr Gareth x

Jean Williams

Walter Williams
In memory of my father, Walter Williams, Cardiff City 1942–44

Harri Wyn
Nadolig Llawen gan Mam a Dad

Richard, Debra, James & Hannah B

Red Dragons: The story of Welsh Football is just one of a whole range of publications from Y Lolfa. For a full list of books currently in print, send now for your free copy of our new full-colour catalogue. Or simply surf into our website

www.ylolfa.com

for secure on-line ordering.

TALYBONT CEREDIGION CYMRU SY24 5HE
e-mail ylolfa@ylolfa.com
website www.ylolfa.com
phone (01970) 832 304
fax 832 782